Revisiting the Falklands–Malvinas Question

Transnational and Interdisciplinary Perspectives

edited by Guillermo Mira and Fernando Pedrosa

University of London Press
Institute of Latin American Studies, School of Advanced Study,
University of London, 2021

British Library Cataloguing-in-Publication Data
A catalogue record for this book is available from the British Library

This book is published under a Creative Commons Attribution-NonCommercial-NoDerivatives 4.0 International (CC BY-NC-ND 4.0) license. More information regarding CC licenses is available at https://creativecommons.org/licenses/.

This book is also available online at http://humanities-digital-library.org.

ISBN:
978-1-908857-56-9 (paperback edition)
978-1-908857-85-9 (.epub edition)
978-1-908857-86-6 (.mobi edition)
978-1-908857-80-4 (PDF edition)

DOI: 10.14296/1220.9781908857804 (PDF edition)

Institute of Latin American Studies
School of Advanced Study
University of London
Senate House
London WC1E 7HU

Cover illustration by Marcelo Spotti.

The editors thank Catriona McAllister for her assistance in translating chapters originally written in Spanish.

Contents

	Notes on contributors	vii
	Preface	xii
	Guillermo Mira and Fernando Pedrosa	
	Introduction State, national identity and power: a historical tour in search of the causes of the Falklands–Malvinas War *Guillermo Mira and Fernando Pedrosa*	1
1.	Resisting bio-power: 'laughter', 'fraternity' and 'imagination' under dictatorship and the Malvinas–Falklands War *María José Bruña Bragado*	31
2.	Exile, the Malvinas War and human rights *Silvina Jensen*	53
3.	Attitudes towards the Falklands–Malvinas War: European and Latin American left perspectives *Fernando Pedrosa*	75
4.	The Falklands–Malvinas War and transitions to democracy in Latin America: the turning point of 1979–82 *Guillermo Mira*	97
5.	The Malvinas journey: harsh landscapes, rough writing, raw footage *Julieta Vitullo*	111
6.	Malvinas miscellanea: notes on a diary written while shooting a film in these remote islands *Edgardo Dieleke*	127
7.	Malvinas, civil society and populism: a cinematic perspective *Joanna Page*	141
8.	Flying the flag: Malvinas and questions of patriotism *Catriona McAllister*	161

9.	Leaving behind the trenches of nationalism: teaching the Malvinas in secondary schools in Río Gallegos, Santa Cruz province *Matthew C. Benwell and Alejandro Gasel*	173
10.	Chronicle of a referendum foretold: what next for the Malvinas–Falklands? *Cara Levey and Daniel Ozarow*	185
11.	The limits of negotiation *Andrew Graham-Yooll*	199
12.	It breaks two to tangle: constructing and deconstructing bridges *Bernard McGuirk*	209
	Information resources on the Falkland–Malvinas conflict *Christine Anderson and María R. Osuna Alarcón*	251
	Index	269

We dedicate this book to Andrew Graham-Yooll

Very shortly before this book was published, we learned that our friend Andrew Graham-Yooll had died. Andrew was a big part of this project: he participated in the production, writing and editing process.

Andrew was a great journalist, historian, translator and poet, but above all, a great person whom we shall always remember.

Notes on contributors

Christine Anderson is research librarian for Latin American and Caribbean studies and Commonwealth studies at Senate House Library, University of London.

María José Bruña Bragado is a full professor at the Hispanic literature department, University of Salamanca. Between 1999 and 2009 she was a lecturer, teaching assistant and postdoctoral researcher at Brown University, University of Pennsylvania, Université Paris 8 and Université de Neuchâtel. She has published *Delmira Agustini: Dandismo, género y reescritura del imaginario modernista* (Peter Lang, 2005), *Cómo leer a Delmira Agustini: algunas claves críticas* (Verbum, 2008), and co-edited the Uruguayan poetry anthology *Austero desorden: Voces de la poesía uruguaya reciente* (Verbum, 2011). She also edited *Todo de pronto es nada* (Ediciones Universidad de Salamanca, 2015) on Ida Vitale's poetry. Currently she works as an editor at RELEE (Colección Al Bies). *Cuando ellas cuentan: Narradoras hispánicas de ambas orillas* and *Peregrinaciones de una paria* by Flora Tristán are its most recent publications.

Matthew C. Benwell is a senior lecturer in human geography at Newcastle University. He was previously a Leverhulme early career fellow at Keele University working on a project exploring 'The making of the geopolitical citizen: the case of the Falklands/Malvinas'. Matthew is currently co-investigator on a HERA Joint Research Programme (Public Spaces: Culture and Integration in Europe) investigating 'The everyday experiences of young refugees and asylum seekers in public spaces'. Matthew's research interests include children and young people's engagement with geopolitics (especially in the Southern Cone), everyday nationalism and spaces of memory and commemoration.

Edgardo Dieleke is a filmmaker, editor and cultural critic. With Daniel Casabé, he directed the documentaries *The Exact Shape of the Islands* (released in 2014) and *Cracks de nácar* (released in 2013). He is a professor of film and literature at Universidad de San Andrés (Argentina) and teaches at NYU–Buenos Aires. He is the chief editor of the film books series *Las Naves*, published by Tenemos las máquinas. He has published articles in books and magazines in Argentina, the UK, Brazil and Spain. He is currently working on his first fictional film.

Alejandro Gasel is a specialist in the social sciences at FLACSO, Costa Rica. He holds a PhD in literature from Universidad Nacional de La Plata and is an associate professor at Universidad Nacional de la Patagonia Austral, Unidad Académica Río Gallegos, where he specialises in literary methodologies. He has been a doctoral and post-doctoral fellow at CONICET, visiting fellow at the Centre for Latin American and Caribbean Studies at Newcastle University and Erasmus+ programme fellow at Bergische Universität Wuppertal. He is also currently part of the Georg Forster Research Fellowship Programme for Experienced Researchers (2020–22) at the Humboldt Foundation, Germany. He is a member of the editorial team of the journal *El taco en la brea*, and has published in Chile, Brazil, Colombia, the UK and Germany.

Andrew Graham-Yooll was a multifaceted Argentine journalist of Scottish origin. In 1966 he joined *The Buenos Aires Herald*, where he became a political columnist and editorial secretary. His journalistic work investigating the crimes committed before and during the military dictatorship forced him into exile in the land of his ancestry. In London, he worked in the newsrooms of *The Daily Telegraph* and *The Guardian* and reinvented himself as a writer. *A State of Fear: Memories of Argentina's Nightmare* (Eland Books, 1986) established him as one of the most lucid witnesses to the years of terror in Argentina. In 1982, when the regime of General Leopoldo Galtieri occupied the Falklands–Malvinas, *The Guardian* sent him to cover the conflict. Threatened by the henchmen of the dictatorship, he had to escape to England, where he edited *South Magazine*, *The Third World Magazine* and, between 1989 and 1993, *Index on Censorship*. He returned indefinitely to Buenos Aires in 1994 to direct the newspaper of his youth and held the presidency of *The Buenos Aires Herald* directory until 1998. He wrote historical works, essays, poetry and travel books; he devoted himself to translation and literary criticism with the same enthusiasm and professionalism with which he embraced his journalistic life. He died during a visit to London in 2019.

Silvina Jensen was awarded her PhD in contemporary history from Universidad Autónoma de Barcelona (Spain). She is currently professor of theory and methodology of history at Universidad Nacional del Sur (Bahía Blanca, Argentina) and an independent researcher at Consejo Nacional de Investigaciones Científicas y Técnicas (CONICET, Argentina). She has taught at various universities in Argentina and has been a visiting professor in Brazil, Mexico, Chile and Spain. She is a specialist in mass political exiles in the Hispanic World from comparative and transnational perspectives. She has published numerous scholarly articles and books about the history and memory of Argentine political exile; historiography of the recent past in Argentina and Spain; exiles; political prisoners and repression in the Southern Cone in the second half of the 20th century; and exiles and transnational humanitarian networks.

Cara Levey is a lecturer in Latin American studies at University College Cork and has published widely on Southern Cone cultural memory and history and sites of memory, and second-generation memory (*History and Memory, Journal of Latin American Cultural Studies, Journal of Romance Studies, Latin American Perspectives*). She is author of the monograph *Fragile Memory: Shifting Impunity: Commemoration and Contestation in Postdictatorship Argentina and Uruguay* (2016) and co-editor of *Argentina since the 2001 Crisis: Recovering the Past, Reclaiming the Future* (Palgrave Macmillan, 2014), which was translated into Spanish and published in Argentina in 2016.

Catriona McAllister is a lecturer in Latin American cultural studies at the University of Reading. Her research focuses on Argentine literature and culture, with a particular emphasis on ideas of nationhood and relationships between history and literature. She obtained her PhD from the University of Cambridge in 2014. Her monograph on the contemporary Argentine historical novel is forthcoming with Liverpool University Press.

Bernard McGuirk, MA (Glasgow), BPhil, DPhil (Oxon), emeritus professor of romance literatures and literary theory (Nottingham), has taught throughout Europe, Latin America and the United States. His professional career began as Research Fellow at the University of Oxford and the École Normale Supérieure in Paris before appointment to the University of Nottingham. He is internationally recognized as a critical theorist, witness his recently republished monographs *Latin American Literature and Post-Structuralism* and *Falklands/Malvinas: An Unfinished Business* (both SPLASH Editions, 2018), to the latter of which he is writing a sequel entitled *It Breaks Two to Tangle: Political Cartoons of the Falklands–Malvinas War*. He has published widely on comparative literature in English and the romance languages and has devoted some two decades of research to the Malvinas–Falklands conflict and its aftermath, including the plight of veterans.

Guillermo Mira holds a PhD in history from the Complutense University of Madrid and is a full professor of Latin American history at the University of Salamanca. His research ranges from colonial mining and the formation of Latin American elites to questions of contemporary history. As a visiting fellow at the Institute of Latin American Studies and visiting professor at the Institut des Hautes Etudes en Amérique Latine (IHEAL), he contributed to the Spanish edition of the *Report on the Brazilian National Truth Commission* (Salamanca, 2017) and more recently to the collective work, *Esthétiques de la Déconstruction Mémorielle dans le Cône Sud* (Rennes, 2020). He has been a member of the Ibero-American Institute since its foundation and teaches on the European postgraduate programme LAGLOBE (Paris-Salamanca-Stockholm).

María R. Osuna Alarcón is permanent lecturer at the University of Salamanca. She has also worked at the Indias archive in Seville, Carlos III University Library in Madrid and the European Parliament Documentation Service in Luxembourg. She launched and manages the Library of the Institute of Iberoamérica at the University of Salamanca (USAL). She was a visiting professor in information studies at University College London and has been director of the master's degree in digital information systems at the faculty of translation and documentation at the University of Salamanca (2014–17). As a member of Committee 50 at AENOR (The Spanish Association for Standardization and Certification), she has been responsible for the coordination of the translation of several documents. She is an expert member of UNESCO, in the Memory of the World programme.

Daniel Ozarow is a senior lecturer at Middlesex University, London where he received his PhD. He is author of *The Mobilization and Demobilization of Middle Class Revolt: Comparative Insights from Argentina* (Routledge, 2019) and co-chair of the Argentina Research Network. He is also co-editor of *Argentina since the 2001 Crisis: Recovering the Past, Reclaiming the Future* (Palgrave Macmillan, 2014) and *De la Crisis de 2001 al Kirchnerismo: Cambios y Continuidades* (Prometeo, 2016). He has recently published in academic journals such as *Economy and Society, Sociology, Labour History* and *Latin American Research Review*. He regularly features as a political commentator on British and Argentine affairs and has appeared in print and broadcast media, including *Telesur, C5N, Al Jazeera, Radio Nacional Argentina, The Conversation, Daily Express, Telam* and *Open Democracy*.

Joanna Page is a reader in Latin American literature and visual culture at the University of Cambridge. She is the author of several books on cinema, graphic fiction, literature and visual art in Argentina, Chile, and Latin America more broadly. Her latest publications include *Science Fiction from Argentina: Technologies of the Text in a Material Multiverse* (2016), *Posthumanism and the Graphic Novel in Latin America* (with Edward King, 2017) and *Geopolitics, Culture, and the Scientific Imaginary in Latin America* (co-edited with María del Pilar Blanco, 2020).

Fernando Pedrosa, who holds a PhD in contemporary political processes from the University of Salamanca is currently a professor and researcher at the University of Buenos Aires. He specializes in studies of democratization in Latin America and Asia. He has been a visiting professor at various European and Asian universities, and is author of several books, including *The Other Left: Social Democracy in Latin America* (Capital Intelectual, 2012). He has published articles in academic journals around the world, some of which have been translated into English and German. He runs the magazine *Asia/AméricaLatina* and is also a journalist and broadcaster.

Julieta Vitullo is a bilingual writer, playwright and dramatist born and raised in Argentina. She received an MA in English and a PhD in Spanish from Rutgers University. Her writing has been published or is forthcoming in *Into the Void*, *The Normal School*, *The Fabulist*, and other journals worldwide. She is the author of the book *Islas imaginadas: La guerra de Malvinas en la literatura y el cine argentinos* (2012), and the protagonist and co-script writer of the award-winning documentary *La forma exacta de las islas* (2014). Her plays have been staged across Seattle. *Two Big Black Bags*, about an ex-combatant of the Malvinas who undertakes a magical journey across the Americas, will premiere in Seattle in 2021.

Preface

Guillermo Mira and Fernando Pedrosa

Almost forty years after the events analysed in this book, the causes and consequences of the military conflict between Argentina and the United Kingdom in 1982 still reverberate in a sea of feverish memories and oblivions. What is certain is that the conflict around the Falklands–Malvinas survives and, in the words of Bernard McGuirk (a contributor to this volume), remains unfinished business.

Every aspect of the archipelago that makes up the Falkland–Malvinas Islands (including their very name) is mired in complexity, controversy and antagonism. Despite this reality, many of those who passionately discuss the various political points that characterise the conflict between Argentina and the United Kingdom insist upon the immovable certainties behind their arguments and claims.

For this reason, among the little that can be affirmed with a degree of consensus is the irrefutable fact that the archipelago is located in the South Atlantic Ocean, that it is made up of more than one hundred islands, that they cover a total of 11,700 square kilometres, and that they are located just over 500 kilometres off the Argentine coast and 13,000 kilometres from Great Britain. Two large islands stand out from this group, and they lie just under 15 kilometres apart.

Everything else seems to be open to debate – even the Islands' geological origin, given that relatively recent scientific findings affirm that, in fact, they originate from Gondwana, which was one of the two continental blocks that existed prior to the formation of Panagea. Specifically, the islands separated from what we know today as southern Africa. The advance of glaciation caused that rupture and the islands' subsequent movement to where they are today. Therefore, at least in that sense, they have nothing to do geologically with Patagonia, as was believed for a long time.

Fortunately, the origin of this book is much simpler and easier to locate in time and space. It grew out of a work of reflection and study on recent Latin American history that we have been developing with research teams from the University of Salamanca and Buenos Aires. We have been joined by researchers from other institutions and countries, many of whom are an important part

G. Mira and F. Pedrosa, 'Preface', in G. Mira and F. Pedrosa (eds.), *Revisiting the Falklands-Malvinas Question: Transnational and Interdisciplinary Perspectives* (London: University of London Press, 2020), pp. xiii–xx. License: CC-BY-NC-ND 4.0.

of this work, as authors and for their contribution in the tasks of editing, translation and publication.

The direct antecedent of this book is a work called *Extendiendo los límites: Nuevas agendas en historia reciente* [*Extending the Limits: New Agendas in Recent History*] (Mira and Pedrosa, 2016), where we proposed the need to re-evaluate the field of recent history as one with exponential growth, but whose success produced its premature exhaustion. In that book we pointed out an issue that was little debated then, but today appears more clearly:

> Recent history will then face the test of addressing these processes no longer from the margins (as initially [happened], when the dominant academic history denied it), but from a position of power … The overarching question would be: can recent history … survive a change in the voice of the state and its agencies?

This question came to replace one aspect that had been surprisingly understudied: the role of the national state as a producer and legitimiser of visions of the past and, conversely, its role as suppressor of other voices.

The aforementioned book, which can be taken as a precedent of the one presented here, not only was not positioned within a closed or single discourse, but also offered a range of issues that sought to stretch the boundaries of recent history. This book continues that trajectory but changes the strategy: it is no longer about presenting multiple problems and approaches to stimulate new questions and make disciplinary limits more flexible; here we restrict ourselves to a single subject, but we also offer multiple approaches for new reflection.

This book is about the conflict over the Falkland–Malvinas Islands, and it is particularly focused on the War and its aftermath, analysing it from diverse perspectives, and in that process bringing together Spanish, British and Argentine specialists and researchers. It aims to put together a choral, heterogeneous and diverse work, but at the same time, a reflective one, so that it appeals to rationality and, above all, to critical thinking within a sinuous and problematic terrain. Consequently, it eschews both the mythification of bellicosity and nationalistic thinking; but neither is it a merely descriptive essay of dates and events in search of an impossible and unproductive objectivity.

This book combines approaches from history, political science, sociology and cultural studies, defined in a broad sense. The intention that moved us was to make available to the English-speaking public in general (and the British one in particular) different perspectives, which intersect and dialogue between them, away from tired and barren roads and the focus on exceptionalism that has characterised some historiographical approaches to the 1982 conflict.

Many people have accompanied us on this path. In addition to the contributors, we would like to express our gratitude to those who, over many years, have made possible a frank and stimulating dialogue between the 'two shores': Linda Newson, Maxine Molyneux, Catherine Davies, Catherine Boyle, Christine Anderson, Catriona McAllister, Bernard McGuirk, Stephen Hart,

Julio Cazzasa and Francisco Panizza, who, for many reasons and in many circumstances, have been key actors. Their reflections, advice and friendship have helped us complete the long emotional and intellectual journey that began on 2 April 1982 – amid disbelief, fear and indignation, and that has brought us this far. Special thanks to Catriona McAllister for her assistance in translating chapters originally written in Spanish.

The chapters in this book

This work begins with a text written by the compilers, Guillermo Mira and Fernando Pedrosa, who offer a series of critical reflections on academic and cultural approaches to the Falklands–Malvinas War. To carry this out, they present a composite historicisation that reveals that the War and everything that surrounded it are not only a problem of recent history, but that their roots date back to the construction of the Argentine state and nation. They propose a way to read the various productions on the subject where the organising axis is, rather than format or language, the presence of the state in search of greater legitimacy to increase its control over a conflictive and vital society.

María José Bruña presents the Falklands–Malvinas War as one of the most revealing examples of biopolitical control in recent history. For her, the War was a decision taken by two governments who knew that hundreds of young men were sent to their certain death. That is why Bruña defines it as a 'biopolitical strategy' for these governments to perpetuate themselves in power. Using Todorov's conceptualisations, the author analyses the testimony of a Falklands–Malvinas War veteran, which allows her to explore various forms of resistance by the soldiers, such as laughter, fraternity and imagination confronting the biopolitical control of power.

Silvina Jensen explores the impact of the War on Argentine exiles. They are men and women who for years – far from their country – had laboriously forged a unity of action and discourse with the sole purpose of denouncing and repudiating the military dictatorship that had usurped power in Argentina. From the margins, the author addresses a controversial issue: the popular fervour in Argentina during the decisive days that led to the War. During its course, from a visceral hostility against the United Kingdom emerged a widespread adherence to the performance of the dictatorship in the 'Reconquista' of the Islands.

Fernando Pedrosa's chapter presents the characterisation of the positions adopted by the European and Latin American political parties, many of which were members of the Socialist International (SI). Afterwards, he delves more deeply into the different visions of the Anglo-Argentine conflict, evaluating the way in which it influenced inter-party relations, the social democrats' transnational organisational strategies, and regional politics in general. This allows him to create a map of the transnational political actions taken, which is quite different from the one usually presented in the specialised literature on the subject, mainly arising from the perspective of the parties as the main characters in the political processes and on the international stage of the time. Furthermore, this approach allows us to observe the more fluid and ambiguous actions taken by the different left-wing organisations that were far from being a collective, as they were characterised by rigid and inflexible strategies.

Upon the recognition of a troubled relation between the defeat of Argentina's military dictatorship in the War and the restoration of democracy in the country, Guillermo Mira undertakes a revision of the most influential theories about transitions to democracy in Latin America, and points out their controversial aspects. Focusing on the Argentine case, he offers an explanation of why the South Atlantic War not only triggered a political earthquake that would force the Argentine military to abandon their claims to continue governing (while giving a boost to the radical transformation that Margaret Thatcher was leading in the United Kingdom), but that it also had profound repercussions at the regional and global levels.

By 2006, Julieta Vitullo – author of a subsequent chapter – was finishing her doctoral thesis, convinced that fiction had 'achieved the most complex answers to the problems and questions that the War poses' (Vitullo, 2012, p. 16). Before concluding her in-depth investigation, Vitullo decided to visit the Falklands–Malvinas. By chance, she had the opportunity of meeting two veterans who, after twenty-five years, were returning to the battlefields that had marked their lives. The researcher's improvised camera became a witness to the revived experience of those conscripts, now mature men. Following her unexpected guides, Vitullo recorded ten hours of images.

The chapters of Julieta Vitullo and Edgardo Dieleke reconstruct the winding path that led to the documentary *The Exact Shape of the Islands*, in which a literature student is involved in the plot of the very narratives she analyses, while interacting with the central actors of the tragedy. This factor allows her to develop a warm flow of empathy towards the protagonists and victims of both sides. She also develops a renewed sensitivity towards the setting where these events took place.

In this regard, the notes taken by Edgardo Dieleke, which are halfway between a travel diary and filming notes, allow us to access to the aesthetic, physical and emotional dimensions of the Falklands–Malvinas: colourful islands, with beaches, hills and ravines of melancholic beauty; the hospitality of the locals whose lives were changed by the War; the memory in the islands' music that did not get to become the film's soundtrack because its author was afraid of hurting the sensibility of the community to which it belongs.

Joanna Page's chapter delves into one of the war's thorniest questions: 'There is a sequence that is often repeated in films about the Malvinas: the archival footage of the moment at which Galtieri announces the invasion on 2 April 1982 to an overflowing Plaza de Mayo. The news is met with an ovation by the exultant thousands gathered below. How might we explain such a ringing endorsement of a bloody regime in a square that had, only three days earlier, witnessed a mass demonstration against the dictatorship?' Page presents and analyses two documentaries by Julio Cardoso. She postulates that his films provide an alternative point of view on the subject, regarding how it had been treated in the years of the transition. The author shows that Cardoso rejects the idea of the 1982 War as a fact that breaks in suddenly and nonsensically and, on the contrary, she historicises the event until it is presented as another milestone in the history of an Argentine nationalism that comes from the days of yore.

Approaching a similar question, but this time from the field of literary fiction, the chapter by Catriona McAllister also departs from the images of General Galtieri on the balcony of the Casa Rosada, cheered on by a euphoric crowd. She reflects on discourses of national identity in Argentina, focusing on the relationship between the military and patriotic celebration, both before and after the dictatorship. In order to do so, she analyses several texts by the writer Martín Kohan and focuses particularly on his novel *Ciencias morales* [School for Patriots, 2007], where he reflects on patriotic education with the 1982 conflict as a backdrop.

Returning to these questions from a pedagogical perspective, Matthew Benwell and Alejandro Gasel consider the ways in which the issue of the Falklands–Malvinas is currently being taught in secondary schools in the city of Río Gallegos, capital of the province of Santa Cruz in the deep south of the Argentine Patagonia. This work is based on interviews with high school teachers and educational officials who work at the provincial and national level in Argentina. The authors highlight the potential and relevance of the topic based on the place assigned to the Falkland–Malvinas Islands as an icon of the 'territorial nationalism' incorporated into school textbooks since the second half of the 20th century, which is based on increased state control of the national curriculum.

The chapter by Cara Levey and Daniel Ozarow weighs in on the immediate and long-term consequences of the referendum that took place in March of 2013 on whether the Falklands–Malvinas should remain a British Overseas Territory. The authors offer some ideas about what happened next, in terms of its diplomatic and political consequences. They consider that the referendum and its consequences represented a missed opportunity for the two governments to engage in a sincere dialogue, and they argue that despite the often confrontational rhetoric, Argentina and the United Kingdom share a common ground and, to some extent, a similar vision for the future of the Islanders.

In his chronology and updating of the political and diplomatic milestones that have marked the dispute over the Falklands–Malvinas, Andrew Graham-Yooll advises that new directions should be undertaken in the treatment that the dispute has received by successive authorities in Argentina and the United Kingdom. In a sometimes provocative tone, he censures the language of tension and insult against the adversary, and advises replacing it with diplomacy and moderation, in what he considers to have been a fruitless dialogue for too long.

Bernard McGuirk is a literary and cultural critic, and author of the landmark study *Falklands–Malvinas: An Unfinished Business* (2007). In his role as president of the International Consortium for the Study of Post-Conflict Societies, he has worked with people other than just politicians and diplomats in both the United Kingdom and Argentina. His text will not be easy to read for those seeking ineluctable truths, spiced as it is with critical theoretical analysis as well as an ever up-to-the-minute commentary on the peddled position-taking of the nationalists, pedants, bigots, and jingoists whose interventions abound whenever the troubled terms 'Falklands' or 'Malvinas' are raised, inevitably triggering – or being triggered by – notoriously vested interests. Iconoclasm is the keynote of McGuirk's approach to what he shows to be, sadly, the most pressing 'unfinished business' of any – if not all – the attempts at *entente cordiale*.

In the final chapter, Christine Anderson and María Osuna make available to scholars and the general public documentation about the Falklands–Malvinas War preserved in dependencies of the governments involved and other institutions that have contemporary sources on the conflict. In order to do this, the authors have followed the *Sources for History* scheme, developed by the University of Chicago (2010). Having documentary material that conserves the recent past of the region is crucial to resolving the conflict through diplomatic channels. Following the spirit in which this contribution was written, we highlight that it is a document under construction, which will need constant review and the inclusion of the sources that will be made available depending on the times of access to the repositories of the respective countries.

Introduction
State, national identity and power: a historical tour in search of the causes of the Falklands–Malvinas War

Guillermo Mira and Fernando Pedrosa

The state is a theoretical problem and an uncomfortable actor because often its voice is loudly amplified but not always clear or direct. This ambiguity in the actions and discourse of the state can cloud its presence, and filter its real interests and objectives. There, in unravelling that complex map of interests, actors, actions and strategies, lies the work of social scientists.

Most ideological traditions have issued warnings on this issue, foregrounding the problem of domination and the construction of the legitimacy that sustains the claim of state power. This is why it is striking that in most of the intellectual discussions in Argentina over recent decades, there is no explicit theoretical interest in the evident presence of the state, nor any methodological provision to warn of its attempts to impose a particular narrative.

The discourse about the past is a key arena in which the state can seek to consolidate its dominance. To do this, it has at its disposal an immense arsenal to influence discourse and identity narratives in civil society. It is where the 'fight for history' occurs, because it works as a basic tool in the construction of national identity.

In Argentina, the predominant strategies of those who have led the state – or tried to do so – are closer to the ideas of Carl Schmidt than to those of John Locke.[1] The influence of military thought, revisionism and populism have shaped a type of political and intellectual activity where the objective is not so much to question the state and its representations or identify its objectives and strategies, but rather to impose one's own discourse and triumph over the voices that oppose it.

Paradoxically, the Argentine state (the same one that initiated the war and committed the disappearances) has managed to become the object of desire not

---

1   Possibly the most appropriate term is that of 'Neoschmittianism' (Paredes Goicochea, 2018).

G. Mira and F. Pedrosa, 'Introduction. State, national identity and power: a historical tour in search of the causes of the Falklands–Malvinas War', in G. Mira and F. Pedrosa (eds.), *Revisiting the Falklands–Malvinas Question: Transnational and Interdisciplinary Perspectives* (London: University of London Press, 2020), pp. 1–29. License: CC-BY-NC-ND 4.0.

only of political and economic corporations, and workers and trade unions, but also of academics, intellectuals and specialists who have moved between giving in to the temptation of emotions and ideologies – where nationalism played a key role – or maintaining the scientific criteria in academic production.

This topic is more pressing in societies whose identities have been created by the state, and when one addresses issues that imply the legitimising role of that domination device. Even more so in Argentina, where the state occupies a predominant place both ideologically and for its ability to mobilise material resources in social life.

This is where the issue of national identity, nationalism and socially shared values becomes more important than even the material or institutional resources. That is why nationalism should not be challenged as something abstract, but rather as the use of the nation's symbols in the discourse, and in everyday concrete political practice (Guber, 2007).

Argentinity as an instrument of the state

We conceive the national identity of Argentina (the *Argentinity*, adopting García Fanlo's proposal (2010)) as an artificial phenomenon, that is, created by the state, but at the same time it is dynamic, changes over time, and incorporates new actors and imaginaries to give renewed answers to the demands and challenges that it receives from civil society.

At the same time that it is changing, it also maintains nodal issues that are reiterated diachronically, and that historically define the identity of personality. Territorial nationalism, the homeland as a unit, and militarism occupy a crucial place in this network. Argentinity is then understood as a new identity that ensures the governability of society.

> To make the Argentines governable, that is, fully adapted to the particular conditions of the capitalist order, with its social relations of power, domination and exploitation. And every time it seemed – in the 19th and 20th centuries – to achieve the goal, the social structure was modified as well as the particular forms of capitalism in reciprocal interrelation. Once again the problem reappeared ... restarting the need to invent and fabricate a 'new Argentine' and a 'new Argentina' which, this time, would be the definitive ones (García Fanlo, 2010, p. 26).

The Falklands–Malvinas War brought to its climax the possibility of appealing to nationalism to unite the population's identity, in order to divert it from its internal conflicts and corporative struggles. But that story did not start there. Iglesias (2012) locates some of the causes of the 1982 Malvinas–Falklands War in the militarism that Argentine politics adopted from 1930, since both military and Peronist governments imposed different versions of nationalism as a substitute for citizenship.

> But there are also other specific ideological elements of the Malvinas cause; among them: the idea that geography must impose its reasons over history … the principle according to which the central actors of the law are the states and not the individuals, whose destiny must be subordinated; and the idea that the main problem of Argentina is having been sacked by foreign powers … Each and every one of these ideas – evermore further from reality – are evoked directly or indirectly when it is proclaimed that 'The Malvinas are Argentine' (Iglesias, 2012, p. 12).

In the words of Guber (2000, p. 8), in the Falklands storytelling, 'the Argentines not only remember their rights but also they Argentinise the islands by Malvinising their Argentinity'. Thus, in 1982 the state managed (although briefly because of the defeat) to place society neatly in its orbit.

Below we offer a brief historicisation of this construction of Argentine national identity by focusing on the Falkland–Malvinas Islands. This answers to the fact that we consider the war and everything that surrounded it not as a problem just of recent history; on the contrary, it must be approached through contemporary Argentine history in a continuous way, from the same social and political processes that gave rise to the construction of the state and the nation in the mid 19th century.

Argentinity as a project of social governability

In Argentina, the state apparatus had proved to be very effective in tackling its multiple challenges – and challengers – during the second half of the 19th century. By that point, it had managed to build a national discourse in a sparsely inhabited and heterogeneous territory, predominantly by military action. The *Sarmientine* education (in reference to President Domingo F. Sarmiento), compulsory military service, the idea of 'to govern is to populate', and the conformation of a national army were some of the axes around which the national structuring of the state took place (García Fanlo, 2010).

Military action occupied a key role in this strategy because it was necessary to overcome provincial warlords and secure the borders against the Indians first and, after that, in the War of Paraguay. At the same time, the continuous and transcendent presence of the military in the process of emergence, independence and organisation had assured them a relevant place in the then-young country. In this narrative, glory was in the battlefields and betrayals were common between politicians and civilians.

Between the end of the 19th century and the beginning of the 20th, a huge social transformation was brewing as a result of the arrival of millions of foreign immigrants, a phenomenon that structurally remodelled Argentine society and the way in which it saw itself (Romero, 2017).[2]

---

2 'The transplant had been successful, but the transplanted subjects did not seem to favour the regeneration of the Argentine race or adapt docilely, as a work force, to the conditions of the Argentine capitalism. The immigrants were not the expected Anglo-Saxons … and, at the same

The project of a country designed for 'the Argentine desert' (Halperín Donghi, 2005a) soon became out-dated and the state had to resort to new strategies.[3] The debates and doubts about the celebrations of the centenary of independence, in 1910, showed a society full of uncertainties, concerned for the future and increasingly violent. But this had begun before the celebration.

In 1890 there were already two positions before that country in rapid transformation and the threat that loomed over the precarious 'national being'. The first of them amalgamated various ideas that coincided with a more contractualistic vision, with a positive view of the foreigners; it trusted that their contributions to the identity and to the country would be better observed over time.

The opposite position – the one that finally triumphed – posed a nationalist view that demanded the urgency of policies to homogenise the immigrant population behind a conception of essentialist and exclusionary Argentinity (Bertoni, 1992). The triumph of nationalist thought (at the same time as the nationalist ideology triumphed in Europe) had very important implications because it focused on the past – an idealised past – instead of on the possibility of articulating a common future.

At this moment of change, the use of patriotic education and its efficient 'Argentines-building machine' is found. Confidence in education, a natural idea of positivism, resulted in an institutional effort of great magnitude that sought to generate a change in the newly arrived foreigners, i.e. to *Argentinise* them, thus producing a new Argentine subject from the 'melting pot of races' (García Fanlo, 2010, p. 28).

In addition to the new gaucho ideal (which claimed the figure of Martín Fierro as a model of the 'Argentine'), other issues were reinforced as ingredients of Argentina: the struggle for independence, the military hero and father of the country, and the territory as the axis of the nation were some of the pillars that sustained this renewed nationalising ideal.

Compulsory military service also played a fundamental role in this strategy, since it established an entry point, as a rite of passage to the world of male adulthood 'through the inculcation of a warrior moral and, at the same time ... the configuration of the senses of belonging – and exclusion – to the Argentine nation'(Garaño, 2013, pp. 124, 125).

Argentina was built, then and since its inception, as a form of domination over a vibrant but heterogeneous society that had in its very formation the

---

time, they introduced in the country ideologies strange to the national being, and contrary to the capitalist social order; they were not laborious, docile and liberal masses, but revolutionary anarchists' (García Fanlo, 2010, p. 18).

3 'The 1.8 million inhabitants of 1869 became 7.8 million in 1914 ... Two out of every three inhabitants of the city were foreigners in 1895, and in 1914 ... still half of the city population was foreign' (Romero, 2017, p. 31).

challenges that characterised the popular European sectors of the time (García Fanlo, 2010).

In 1916, Hipólito Yrigoyen, the first democratic president, assumed the presidency. He had legitimised his leadership using a programme based on the idea of 'the national *cause*', construed in absolute terms. This first government that emerged from unrestricted suffrage began a process of social inclusion of new sectors – the middle classes – through the control of the state. Although it opened up new perspectives and included modern visions, it was also based on conservative ideas, especially with regard to how nationality should be integrated. 'Yrigoyen joined those who – setting a distance from the dominant cosmopolitanism – found that identity in the common Hispanic roots' (Romero, 2017, p. 55).

In the context of the crisis of liberalism in the world, and the growing hysteria aroused by the communist threat, the 'time of the sword', as a way out of the disorder, had summoned various political groups such as socialists, fundamentalist Catholics and nationalists. All of them came together in criticism of liberal democracy and formed a common space where it was difficult to distinguish between left and right.

These circumstances stimulated the appearance of the first revisionist authors, whose common position resulted in the historical recovery of the figure of Juan Manuel de Rosas.[4] However, this first group of intellectuals (which included, among others, Adolfo Saldías and Ernesto Quesada) was more linked to historiography than to politics.

On 6 September 1930, the first coup in Argentina's history took place, and ended the second government of Yrigoyen (1928–30). The military officers who assumed power were strongly influenced by the model of the German army of the time, and built an image of the armed forces that transcended the brief presidency of General José Uriburu (1930–2). In this regard, it is important to underline two main aspects. The first is the return to militarism (which had already begun in the previous period) as a positive value against democratic 'disorder'.[5] The second came with the legalisation of the *coup d'état* by the Supreme Court, which legitimised the claim of the military that the country, and the national cause, were above the law.

4   Juan Manuel de Rosas (1793–1877) was the governor of the province of Buenos Aires from 1829 to 1832 and from 1835 to 1852, before the national state could establish its rule over the territory now known as Argentina. From there he built an anti-liberal and nationalist image – that was subsequently amplified by the different revisionisms – starting with an armed confrontation with France and the United Kingdom. His adversaries made of him the model of a tyrant because he concentrated all the power in his hands, and used the para-police to attack his political rivals.

5   '[The soldiers] are the only ones who put the defense of the country and nationality above all things, including the law and military regulations … The soldiers are the only ones able to objectively define when, how and why the country is in danger, and … they can save it. The armed forces are healthy, immaculate, incorruptible, unable to do anything contrary to the national interest' (García Fanlo, 2007, p. 4).

The opposition to liberalism occurred in a framework of Hispanic vindication and strong criticism of the United States, in response to its expansionism after the war of 1898 against Spain. In this scenario, the rejection of the British occupation of the Falklands–Malvinas was common ground for groups that shared no other cause, as illustrated by books published in 1934 by the socialist leader Alfredo Palacios and the nationalists Julio and Rodolfo Irazusta.

Perhaps the most important innovation of these revisionists proved to be the connection between history and politics that, according to Halperín Donghi (2005b), was the key to their success in broad sectors of public opinion. The presence of anti-liberalism and the heterogeneity of the intellectual groups within the various political parties characterised the political debate until the mid 20th century, but mainly on the issue of what position should be taken in the Second World War.

This issue was a crucial boost for the second coup, which occurred in 1943 and rested upon the decision of the armed forces not to declare war on Germany. The country declared war only a few moments before the end of the conflict. The nationalist stream and Catholic fundamentalism marked the tone: 'authoritarian, anti-liberal and messianic, obsessed with the foundation of a new social order and avoiding the chaos of communism' (Romero, 2017, p. 137). It was from then that Juan Domingo Perón started to take his first political positions, up until his triumph in the presidential race of 1946.

With the democratic arrival of Perón to the government in 1946, changes and continuities occurred in the idea of 'the national'. Continuity is visible, in the first place, in that the military leadership was maintained, although renewed, and now embodied in the figure of the new president. Second, the intellectual presence of nationalism and Catholicism continued as agglutinating axes of the state discourse. Third, the United Kingdom, along with the United States, continued to occupy a central place in the nationalist rhetoric's criticism. Fourth, the process of social inclusion was executed, as before with Yrigoyen and the middle classes, with the control of the state and with a strong appeal to the idea of 'the national'.

There were other relevant changes too. Peronism led to a mutation in the idea of Argentinity. The first thing that should be stressed is the appeal to the *people* and the state as a single element. The image of the leader on the balcony and the people in the square as the staging of that act became iconic of 20th-century Argentine politics and, not coincidentally, was present on 2 April 1982.

The people as a key actor have two facets. First, the real one: mobilised and organised from the workers' unions and state leadership. The *people* in the square are the protagonist of the story, as a complement and sustenance of the leader on the balcony of the government house. In the second facet, the people are also a rhetorical element: the continuity of the *Yrigoyenist* idea of the nation embodied in the popular will. Thus, democracy became a mere plebiscitary action of the leader, that together with popular mobilisation, replaced the republican elements of the political regime (Romero, 2017).

The law lies below the will of a homogeneous people that, at the same time, embody the homeland. With this operation, Peronism turned the people into the axis of sovereignty and nationalism detached itself from the merely territorial. Although the Falklands–Malvinas do not occupy a central place in this story, they are integrated into the nationalist discourse because they are functional to it with the idea of usurpation.

This lack of centrality of the Falklands–Malvinas in the nationalism of the first stage of Peronism stimulated a dialogue around the Islands. Then the Argentine government put forward their only Argentine proposal outside the diplomatic claim in place since 1883. In 1953, on the occasion of the coronation of Queen Elizabeth II, the Peronist government sent a mission headed by the senate president (who later became the nation's vice-president), Alberto Tesaire, in order to offer to buy the Falkland Islands from the United Kingdom as the state had done with the railroads.

After conversations at the highest level, the Argentine proposal was rejected by Winston Churchill's government (Bosoer, 2013). The decision took into account the negative repercussions that it would bring to the then prime minister. The British argument was based on the fact that the inhabitants of the Islands were British, which shows that from that moment this issue was already a central axis of British policy towards the Islands.

In 1955 there was another coup in Argentina that ended the Peronist experiment, but that could not resolve the real and latent conflicts in the country. The years after the fall of Perón's government were unstable, confusing, lacking an agreed political path and, above all, with a growing increase in political violence. Portantiero (1973) called these years between 1955 and 1966 'a hegemonic draw'. He did so taking into account the number of governments and economic projects that took place in this period, the conflicts between groups and the constant changes in state policies.

Even the democratic governments were unable to generate long-term political agreements, as was seen with the weak radical presidents Arturo Frondizi (1958–62) and Arturo Illia (1963–6). In terms of the conflict over the Islands, these governments maintained an ambiguous nationalist republicanism that did not change the dominant trends.

Internationally there was some movement. By the mid 1960s, the United Nations General Assembly was very active in matters of decolonisation, approving Resolution 1514 of 1960 with a more global meaning, and Resolution 2065 of 1965, specifically dedicated to the Falklands–Malvinas issue. This was read by the Argentine governments (and is still considered today) as a diplomatic victory although, in short, it summoned both parties to enter into rapid negotiations.

In Argentina, the second half of the 1960s marked a resurgence of political violence in the context of a zeitgeist that fed on the strong hegemonic crisis affecting the United States (Halliday, 1986). At the same time, an explosion of social challenges of varying importance and form made its way around the world. The Vietnam War and the communist overturning of the Cuban revolution led Latin American armed forces to consolidate a repressive scheme in their links with society. In that context, the first guerrilla groups appeared in Argentina.

This coincided with a change in military doctrine, that went from being linked to national autonomy and the external enemy, to what is known as the 'national security doctrine' (Leal Buitrago, 2003). The new military objective was to guarantee security within the country's borders and, therefore, the 'anti-subversive war' became the new problematic axis pointed to by the Latin American armed forces (Portantiero, 1973). With the military in power, sovereignty was once again linked to territory and, therefore, the Falklands–Malvinas issue occupied a much more important place in public discourse. 'Malvinas' (in military governments) and 'people' (with Peronism), each one as a substitute for the other, were alternately occupying the centre of the state's nationalist discourse, stimulated by the cyclical instability of the country's political regime.

During those years, the so-called 'Operativo Cóndor' was carried out, whereby about twenty Peronist militants hijacked a plane of Aerolíneas Argentinas in flight and diverted it to the Falkland–Malvinas Islands. Once there, they raised a series of Argentine flags and took the chief of police of the Islands and the head of the English Infantry hostage before surrendering to the British authorities. The members of the group came from nationalist factions of Peronism that, over the course of the 1970s, were incorporated indistinctly to the different left and right groups into which the Peronism of the time was divided.

Radicalised groups, including armed factions within Peronism, resumed the Falklands–Malvinas issue, which they approached from the same logic of *territorialistic* nationalism, but also from anti-imperialism. In this context, a violent action to recover what historically 'belonged to us' did not seem so outrageous. This notion reached its paroxysm in 1982, when during the war against the United Kingdom, the Montoneros (an armed organisation with Peronist roots), even having been decimated by the illegal repression and exile, offered the military government a truce to go fight together with their executioners in the Islands.

As a sign of the contradictions of the state in general, and Argentina in particular, in 1971, while Argentine nationalism was 'remalvinised', Argentina and Chile agreed to the United Kingdom's being the arbitrator in the dispute over the Beagle Channel that had been dragging on since the late 19th century (Infante, 1979).

During the 1970s, Argentine society experienced, in different ways, a climate of permanent violence and confrontation. This was not only because of the state repression already present under the Peronist government (Franco, 2012), or the clashes between military, paramilitary and guerrilla groups. Violence as an instrument had been naturalised in the everyday relations of a majority of the population, which did not participate in political activism, and much less in ideological extremism (Carassai, 2013).

This contributed to the creation of conditions for the revaluation of the discourse of order (also associated with violence) proposed by the 1976 military coup (Romero, 2017). The bellicosity of the military turned to the internal level, but also to the external one. In 1978, the dictatorship led the country to the brink of war with Chile by rejecting the arbitration convened in 1971 and delivered to the parties in 1977. As already mentioned, the arbitral task had been assigned to the United Kingdom, although the final opinion was drafted by an international tribunal. The mediation of Pope John Paul II managed to prevent direct confrontation.

In the conflict with Chile, it was already observed that much of the problem on the Argentine side was the bureaucratic and complex way that the Argentine military junta made its decisions (Villar, 2014). As claimed above, the field of recent history found certain limits to progress on these roads because it turned sharply towards memory studies and generally had no major dialogues with international relations or political science (Mira and Pedrosa, 2016).

The 'war that was not' is an indispensable step towards understanding the war that did take place. And possibly at this point the works of historians on the Falklands–Malvinas require greater dialogue with other disciplines that have analysed this subject more extensively.[6]

In 1982, war itself unfolded, with the consequences we all know. The Argentine military defeat caused the regime to fall, and later the dissemination of the backroom of the organisation of the war and the issue of human rights violations became the centre of the political scene. Defeat in the war caused the conflict around the Falklands–Malvinas to rise to the level of an irreversible and permanent cause. With the arrival of a new democratic shift, new and diverse voices of civil society began to take the floor.

The post-war years

The arrival of Raúl Alfonsín of the Radical Civic Union to the presidency in 1983 was a moment of rupture with the past but also, as happens in any historical process, of continuities with what had come before. Alfonsín

6 It would be interesting to include in the research agenda the different social and political repercussions of the conflicts around the Falklands–Malvinas and the Beagle Channel. The dispute with Chile over the issue of the Beagle was not recurrent in the intellectual or political environments; neither had it had much social impact, despite the constant disputes originated in the area in which both countries were involved (Valenzuela Ugarte and García Toso, 2008).

decided to subsume the Falklands–Malvinas policies to the general strategy of diminishing military power. In that field, he had to be guided by the relations of forces that he maintained at each juncture. Alfonsín took advantage of the discrediting of territorialistic nationalism to confront it and deactivate through a referendum one of the urgent problems that kept the military in a warring state: the dispute with Chile over the Beagle Channel that had almost led both countries to war in 1978 (Miguez, 2018).

However, the task was not unambiguous, and abroad the radical government issued confusing signals. Alfonsín did not declare the cessation of hostilities in the Falklands–Malvinas, and that implied – at least theoretically, and as a warning to the British – that the conflict over the Islands could be restarted. In that context, Alfonsín did not yield to the pressure of the western powers and refused to sign the Nuclear Non-Proliferation Treaty, known as the Tlatelolco Treaty. At the same time, the Cóndor II programme continued (it had been initiated immediately after the defeat by the military government) for the development of a missile capable of reaching the Islands. The air force (like many others) did not feel defeated and raised the old military autarchy principle for possible future war events.

Alfonsín did not maintain good relations with the United States or the United Kingdom. This ended up feeding the image of distrust that already existed among the Western powers about the country as an international actor. This could not be read in any other way than under the lens of the Falklands–Malvinas War.

In 1989, the first constitutional handover under normal conditions since 1928 took place. The new president, the Peronist Carlos Menem, enacted neoliberal policies and established an alliance with the United States. The normalisation of relations with the Western powers was one of the key points in the change of government (Romero, 2017).

Menem decreed the cessation of hostilities (seven years after the surrender of the Argentine authorities in the Falklands–Malvinas) and re-established the diplomatic relationship with the United Kingdom. In this context, a 'sovereignty safeguard clause' was agreed (known as the umbrella clause), to separate issues relating to the sovereignty of others which both countries intended to move forward, such as fishing and oil extraction. For the first time, government policy was to try to improve relations between Argentines with the people who were one of the main sources of contention after 1982 (Palermo, 2007; Niebieskikwiat, 2014). In 1995, Argentina finally signed the accession to the Tlatelolco treaty and abandoned its membership in the group of non-aligned countries. For all this, it was accepted as an extra-NATO ally, which incorporated the country into a defensive alliance of a military type that also included the United Kingdom.

Nostalgic sectors of the military regime accused the governments of the transition as having a policy of 'demalvinisation' – a synonym for demilitarisation

– and that they were using it to survive (in the case of the Alfonsín government) and to consolidate their leadership (in the case of Carlos Menem). However, together with the differences maintained by the governments of Alfonsín and Menem, nationalist and territorialistic views continued to dominate public policy, especially in the field of education and culture, with the addition that the political and social elites had not yet accepted responsibility for the war.

Although there is still debate about whether it is possible to separate the military dictatorship from the Falklands–Malvinas War, that discussion made no sense for Alfonsín and Menem, since the armed forces, the dictatorship, human rights and the war were all part of an indissoluble whole, and a problem to solve if the new political regime was to be consolidated.

At the end of his term in 1999, Menem was replaced by the radical Fernando De la Rúa, who led a government characterised by weakness and lack of leadership. With regard to the Falklands–Malvinas, De la Rúa contributed little, but due to pressures from different directions (the armed forces and the veterans, among them), 2 April was re-enacted as a national holiday, when the country commemorates the capture of the Islands, quite the opposite of what Alfonsín had sought when he repealed the same holiday imposed by the military government.

The 2001 crisis marked a before and after in Argentina; the state seemed to have lost control of the situation, but the interim government of Peronist Eduardo Duhalde (2002–3) generated the necessary conditions that led to a certain institutional normalisation. His chosen successor, Néstor Kirchner (2003–7), benefited from an economic recovery that brought an unexpected and immense boom in the price of agricultural commodities. However, he had to gain his own political power, which he built by strongly appealing to a particular narrative about the recent past (Romero, 2017).

The Kirchnerist state and its historical discourse

Almost two decades after the 1982 war, a decade of thawing Anglo–Argentine relations, and the end of an economic and political crisis, the Falkland–Malvinas Islands were not on the list of priorities of Argentine society or its ruling class. However, they were still an effective instrument in the hands of the state, as a device of unification and mobilisation of society, especially at a time when it had to rebuild its political legitimacy and had the material resources to carry this out.

The *Kirchnerista* governments looked back to the 1960s and 1970s to present themselves as those who had brought about the process of social change that took place in those years (Bermúdez, 2015). That is why Néstor Kirchner's government included the Falklands–Malvinas War in its narrative about human rights violations committed in the years of the military government.

This policy continued and was accentuated by the governments of his wife, Cristina Fernández (2007–15).

Kirchnerismo inaugurated a new stage that took the old historical claim of war as heroic deed, but tried to separate it from the dictatorship.[7] To this end, it threw the full weight of the state behind the creation of spaces dedicated to speeches, images and content about the war. In addition, it found in the nationalist appeal of the bicentennial of the May Revolution of 1810 an event that once again united the right and left behind the national flag.

The Argentine state acted decisively to position this new narrative, and it did so with an important range of economic, media and institutional resources. Thus, an alliance was consolidated between important academic and cultural sectors and the generous system of state financing, which produced a boom in productions of all kinds on the subject of the memory of what happened in the years prior to 1983, and immediately after.

The new interpretation of the Falklands–Malvinas *heroic deed* suggested that, although the war had meant continuity with the repressive model of the state since 1976, at the same time there was a historical imperative that led to the separation of the issue of sovereignty from those who had initiated the war. At the same time, there was an association between the soldiers conscripted with the young victims of the repression of the dictatorship.

The historiographical operation was once again supported by familiar reference points of nationalist discourse: Argentina's indisputable sovereignty, her victimisation by imperial powers, the betrayal of the military, and appeals to what the war *could have been* in other political circumstances. Argentina repeated its history once more.

In the next section we propose to read the academic and cultural production about the Falklands–Malvinas that tries to build an identity discourse whose purpose is to consolidate and legitimise a powerful device of state domination.

The post-war period and the social sciences

There are a large number of academic and cultural productions on the war that began on 2 April 1982, bolstered by state initiatives that promoted the subject from 2003 onwards and, even more importantly, the thirtieth anniversary of the war in 2012.

This happened not only in the academic sphere, but in other areas too, such as biography, journalism, essays, military technology and of course the fictional record in its various written or audio-visual formats. This large corpus includes all kinds of approaches, methods, devices and speeches. The need to give order to them led specialists to propose different clusters that would allow for some preliminary conclusions on what was produced, and evaluate trends.

---

7   To deepen awareness of the policies on the Falklands–Malvinas at this stage, see Perochena (2016).

Federico Lorenz (2011) divides this corpus into four groups, while pointing out that they not only oppose each other, but also overlap. The first of these is the 'patriotic group', which foregrounds the national cause, the unity of the Argentine people and does not consider the characteristics of the military government that carried out the war as being important. The second is the 'victimising narrative', which is placed at the time of the democratic transition, and which is read as being part of 'the self-exculpatory vision that society sought to build on itself' (Lorenz, 2011, p. 51). The third group incorporates the speeches produced from the redefinition of the role of the combatant made by the first associations of veterans, as well as from the characterisation of the war as part of the Latin American anti-imperialist struggle. Finally, the fourth group brings together works dedicated to military history, whether technical or linked to diplomacy and the explanation and description of war chronicles.

Another of the specialists recognised in the subject, Rosana Guber (2017), reduces the corpus to three different groups. The first is based on what she calls the political and military history of the archipelago; the second concerns those who address the impact of the Falklands–Malvinas issue in relation to national culture and politics; and the third, and most recent, is based on the studies of human action on nature in the South Atlantic.

Another original classification proposal is that offered by María Elena Molina (2008), who groups the production on the Falklands–Malvinas into two sets, the triumphant version and the mournful version. She states, as Lorenz does, that these two modes do not necessarily oppose each other, but intersect. Molina then proposes the space of literature and fiction as the one that truly manages to speak, ask questions and self-criticise about the facts surrounding the 1982 war.

To raise a discussion that addresses the role of the state as a producer of social discourse, we propose to group the written production into three large and heterogeneous groups.

The statist set

The first of these is the 'statist' one, which includes the productions that fluidly accompanied the voice of the state throughout the 19th, 20th and 21st centuries. Given the abundance of existing texts in that sense, we can subdivide it into two large streams: the sovereigntist one, and that of the new epic.

The sovereigntist stream describes the works that are directly or indirectly vehicles of reaffirmation of the assumptions that historically sustained the Argentine claims. This is a heterogeneous subgroup but not necessarily militaristic or supportive of the government that produced the war. It includes traditional views, those of the technocrats, diplomats, journalists and academics that, in different ways, see the issue of sovereignty and the Argentine claim as central axes (e.g. Kohen and Rodríguez, 2015).

The new epic can be identified from the late 20th century onwards, with approaches, methods and problems linked to the social sciences, including issues going beyond mere sovereignty over the Islands. The predominant trends in this group go hand in hand with the official voice of each moment. In the 1980s, these productions were linked, for example, to the victimisation of conscripts, and since 2003, they have been directly related to the attempts to remove the military government from the scene of the war, in order to renew the identity pact of Argentinity with the Falklands–Malvinas issue.

Unlike the first subgroup, these works do not provide a detailed exploration of matters related to sovereignty. However, a strong Argentine claim is made relating to an anti-imperialist or anti-colonial discourse. Another contrast is observed with the classic revisionist studies, since these place the conflict over the Falklands–Malvinas in a timeline that extends from the 19th century onwards. For the statist studies linked to the more current visions in the social sciences, the war is included in the mainstream of recent history, and inside the issue of human rights violations and state terrorism.

The emphasis is on the protagonists, their memories, biographies and an analysis that recreates an epic story without crediting the military. Lorenz is the historian who expresses this position most fully.[8] Author of an extensive and varied body of work, Lorenz removes the assumptions of sovereigntist literature, while reinforcing (even in his role as a novelist) the Argentine government's central axes of speech since 2003, that is, communicating a connection to the political situation and the political actors of the 1970s.

The characterisation proposed by this typology is somewhat broad given the diversity of productions that are grouped together – approaches which range from military studies to work that assimilates conscripts with those disappeared under military repression. However these approaches are historicised in the long term (and not in the chronological limits of recent history), a common matrix can be identified. All occupy the space enabled, and also limited by, the state itself and society. They are 'acceptable' modes of speech, which have conditions of social audibility, in an arena where being heard is difficult. For this reason, it is important to highlight those discourses that challenge the official versions of events.

The challengers

The second group in which we propose to organise cultural production on the Falklands–Malvinas and the war is the smallest: the works that oppose the state's discourse and question the core of the nationalist narrative in all its forms and stages. This heterogeneous group includes contemporary anti-war activism from exile, such as that carried out by Néstor Perlonger and León

---

8 Although their approaches sometimes dabble in classical nationalist discourse, e.g. '10 questions to explain Malvinas to children', Supplement 12, *Diario Página 12*, 3 April 2009.

Rozitchner.[9] It also includes the work of critics such as Beatriz Sarlo and Carlos Altamirano, writing in the magazine *Punto de Vista*. There are also the works or public interventions of those who manifested their opposition as best they could from within the country, such as Juan José Sebreli or Jorge Luis Borges, who allegedly called for the Islands to be given to Bolivia 'so it has access to the sea'.

Perlongher may have been the first, at the time the war was taking place, to express lucidly that behind the military adventure was the state and a nationalist call that neither the right nor the left – he admitted bitterly – could ignore. At the same time, he belittled the disputed Islands as 'unhealthy islets' (1982) and lamented that the military had carried to the Islands the state of exception of the Continent. Perlongher, finally, decides to do what a national cause hates most: ridicule it.

> In the midst of such folly, the most elegant way out is humour: if Borges recommended giving the Islands to Bolivia, thus giving it an exit to the sea, it could also be proclaimed: all the power of Lady Di or the Vatican to the Falklands/Malvinas so that the ridiculous power that a suicidal chorus legitimises is exposed. As someone sensibly proposed, before defending the occupation of the Falklands/Malvinas, the inoccupation of Argentina by the self-styled Argentine army should be postulated (Perlongher, 1982).

By the post-war period and with elaborate arguments and a systematic study, the work of Vicente Palermo (2007) is the biggest challenge to the 'Malvinising' discourse of the Argentine state, and to the construction of its nationalist appeal linked to the territory. According to Palermo, 'Malvinas' is included in this discursive configuration, which includes a national identity linked to loss, victimhood, a 'meek and calm' nature, and a wait that ends when the patience of the 'noble Argentine people' runs out.

The war, then, would be the direct result of this territorial configuration of national identity rather than ambition or a whim. Palermo is possibly the Argentine intellectual who has most reflected on the subject, and who has done so regularly over time, discussing the most widespread assumptions about the 'Falklands/Malvinas cause', whether factual (the relationship with the Islanders) or counterfactual ('if it were not for the war the Falklands/Malvinas would be Argentine').

Rosana Guber, another recognised researcher in this field, has also challenged the nationalist discourse of the 1980s and 1990s (Guber, 2000), but at the same time, and unlike the authors of the statist group, she has carried out investigations that call into question the versions proposed by the Argentine state from 2003 onwards. In her study of air force pilots in the war, Guber challenges the notions of the 'repressive military' or 'Falklands–Malvinas hero':

---

9   See Rozitchner (2015). To reconstruct some of the debates on Perlongher's ideas, see Svetliza (2017). To delve into issues of exile and debates about war, see Silvina Jensen's chapter in this book.

> Why can't I live with complexity, accept that there was a force that did things well, that performed well above what could have been expected according to their experience and military resources? Why can't I understand that human beings are capable of both and many more in between? I don't care if what I research is simplified as laudatory or pro-military ... Because of this idea of risk, there is almost no research on the military world in Latin America ... But if one accepts that human beings and societies are complex, one can dare to understand who we are, and of what we were and are capable of. The soldier is a human being, it is good to remember. He has successes, makes mistakes, and he behaves with a logic with which I can communicate.[10]

Guber (2013) also advanced the theme of camaraderie between British and Argentine soldiers, an issue that breaks the first line of division of perpetual combat between essential enemies. But the most challenging aspect of Guber's work is her refusal to assimilate the situation on the Islands with the state terrorism that had been applied in the country since 1976:

> This idea of the extension of state terrorism is based on the emblematic figure of the conscript soldier dragged to the battlefield without training or necessary equipment and as an object of constraints ... The logistics, hunger, cold, are inherent deprivations of war. Were those failures made on purpose against the soldier as a civilian? ... When you go to war, that passage is not clear. There were abuses of authority, but there were superiors who submitted to the same conditions as their soldiers. The image of the military officer, that the only thing he knows how to do is to repress innocent people, that that is why he goes to the Falklands/Malvinas, and does the same with the civilians under the flag, is a cartoon. You cannot spend your time torturing a soldier because ... the enemy is coming.[11]

Following a similar line, the book by Fernando Iglesias (2012) is heir to the thoughts of David Held and Ulrich Beck. Iglesias is categorical: the idea that 'the Falklands/Malvinas are Argentine' is inapplicable without violating the basic principle on which Argentina was founded: the self-determination of the people. Iglesias goes so far as to question whether the national goal of recovering the Falklands–Malvinas is compatible with international law and human rights, in open reference to the situation of the thousands of people that live there. At the same time, his work may be considered one of the few questioning perspectives, deriving as it does from a sociology of globalization, which indicates the folly of nationalism and the use of the Falklands–Malvinas by the powers that be to 'deploy a huge smokescreen – a fog blanket – usable at any time' (Iglesias, 2012, p. 127).

The journalist Natasha Niebieskikwiat's book (2014) can also be included in the group of texts and interventions that challenge the state narrative. She

---

10 Interview with Rosana Guber, 13 April 2014, http://www.infonews.com.
11 Interview with Rosana Guber, 13 April 2014, http://www.infonews.com.

offered the first study of life on the Islands, which she prepared after her many trips there. The inhabitants of the Islands themselves have often been neglected in the literature, as if they were absent or irrelevant to the conflict or the future of the archipelago. Indeed, they are still referred to by the derogatory term 'Kelpers'.[12] By contrast, Niebieskikwiat's approach sees them as protagonists and incorporates them into the historical narrative, humanising them. This breaks with the idea that the Islanders exist only as a direct consequence of the British presence, and argues that the works included in the statist group, in its two variants, have maintained a stereotyped and ignorant perspective.

This group of works on Malvinas should also include the document presented in 2012 by a group of well-known intellectuals, academics and journalists, entitled *Malvinas, una visión alternativa* [*Malvinas, an alternative vision*], which engaged with debates held during the commemoration of 30 years since the 1982 confrontation.[13] It was the first time that a group of prominent citizens had called openly for a reconsideration of the degree to which society as a whole was linked to the Islands, and had raised challenging alternatives to those traditional views that were based on some kind of epic. In publishing their piece, they were entering into a discourse that had until then been occupied exclusively by the revisionists or by the official post-2003 discourses mentioned above.

The signatories carried (and still carry) a lot of weight in the social and intellectual life of Argentina. This gave the manifesto a qualitatively different dimension and impact from those of other interventions. And by examining the link between the Islanders and Argentine society, they were addressing how to begin to solve the dispute, and to change the political culture on the issue that had predominated since the 19th century. Their provocative proposal opened up the conversation to the inhabitants of the Islands, accepting their right to self-determination.

Crucially, the document underlined the repeated tendency in the different statist visions to minimise the importance of Argentina's having initiated the invasion and then, later, having misunderstood the consequences of the invasion, especially internationally. It also criticised the *Kirchnerista* government for its contradictory demand to open a negotiation that included the issue of sovereignty while announcing that Argentine sovereignty was non-negotiable.[14]

12 'The name *kelper* refers to the algae that grow on the Falklands/Malvinas coast (kelp), which are useless and annoying. For that reason, '*kelper*' connotes a devalued identity' (Ehrmantraut, 2012, p. 7).

13 Among the signatories are Beatriz Sarlo, Santiago Kovadloff, Manuel Antín, Juan José Sebreli, Marcos Aguinis, Jorge Lanata, Graciela Fernández Meijide, Fernando Iglesias, Emilio de Ípola, Pepe Eliaschev, Roberto Gargarella, Marcos Novaro, Vicente Palermo, Luis Alberto Romero, Jorge E. Torlasco, Hugo Vezzetti and Osvaldo Guariglia, among others.

14 The constitution says 'respect [the Islanders'] way of life', and that they should not be subjected to 'a sovereignty, a citizenship and a government they do not want', which was used to support

This document was heavily criticised, by right and left, and even by senior government officials of the time. It could not have been otherwise. The argument that there ought to be a reassessment of the Islanders' situation, and that they ought to be granted the right to self-determination, was put down to a 'lack of patriotism'. This period saw the peak of the debate, but it is reasonable to assume that the 40th anniversary will revive the discussion.

Audio-visual and literary discourse

In addition to written texts, cultural production in other languages and formats should be noted. Audio-visual or literary discourse represents the possibility of saying what cannot be expressed otherwise, although even in that arena the state can set limits on what can be said. These texts we consider loosely to be a third group, which might include fiction or audio-visual work that appeared after the war. It is an area that has received plenty of academic attention (e.g., López and Rodríguez, 2009; Vitullo, 2012; Varela, 2016; Molina, 2018; Fernández Ameghino, 2019) and it is not our intention to make an exhaustive review, nor delve too deeply into the content of the work.[15]

Because this type of work is produced in a variety of languages, it is not as easily grouped into a single category, as we have been proposing for the previous types. Nonetheless, it is possible to analyse some aspects of these works and then characterise them according to what kind of discourse they offer, and in what part of the debate they can be incorporated. In some cases, the relationship they maintain with the state and social conditions of audibility are key.

Post-2003, when the Néstor Kirchner government came to power, it had to renew the type of discourse that sustained its leadership claims, and this change extended to art and culture. While there were still links to the old nationalist and/or warlike paradigms,[16] cultural production relating to the Falklands–Malvinas now also confronted the traditional nationalist view from an anti-military perspective:

> Literature on the Falklands/Malvinas is relatively scarce and little-read. To some extent, this fact is explained by how sensitive Argentine society continues to be regarding this issue. If during the nineties the cause of the Falklands/Malvinas seemed almost forgotten, today it has come back with more strength. The idea of a just, but poorly managed, war is an idea still in force today (Molina, 2008, p. 1).

---

demands for the withdrawal of the United Kingdom and its military base, while all the time asserting the sovereignty of Argentina.

15 The work of Luz Souto (2018) could also be included in this list, since it proposed a categorisation of literary production based on generations of authors. It is related to one of the issues (post-memory) we tackle in our previous book (Mira and Pedrosa, 2016).

16 E.g., García Quiroga (2010).

The new state storytelling of the Falklands–Malvinas stimulated cultural and artistic production to expand enthusiastically, but conservatively, because it was engaged in dismantling a discursive paradigm that had changed little for centuries.

Writers such as Martín Kohan, Patricia Ratto, Fabiana Daversa, Patricio Pron or Federico Lorenz,[17] among others, questioned and disarticulated the official story – one that was simply anachronistic and no longer had coercive power or great social legitimacy.[18] At the same time, they legitimised the new state narrative, which was recharged with nationalist rhetoric, although in a different sense from the previously.[19]

Reiterating the statement at the beginning of this section, the corpus to be covered is very broad, and it is not our intention to make a complete study, but rather, by mediating through the selection of some examples, set trends that allow some reflection.

Uncomfortable fiction

There are works that have managed to take the war and its protagonists to places where it has been difficult for non-fiction to go. The 'deserters, rogues, imposters' appear (Souto, 2018, p. 129), as do the inhabitants of the islands and human rights abuses.

Los pichiciegos [Malvinas Requiem] by Rodolfo Fogwill; *Las islas* [The Islands] by Carlos Gamerro; the work of Rodrigo Fresán; some works by Daniel Guebel; *La construcción* [The Construction] by Carlos Godoy; and *Kelper*, by Raúl Vieytes, approach the issue from a range of different perspectives.[20] *El desertor* [The Deserter] by Marcelo Eckhardt and *Latas de cerveza en el Río de la Plata* [Beer Cans in the Rio de la Plata] by Jorge Stamadianos must also be mentioned, since they deal with a figure that is not well-drawn in the non-fiction – that of the deserter. This is important to the particular discussion in this book since as Vitullo (2006, p. 34) states, the deserter refuses to be subjected to the biopolitical control of the state and rejects its paternalistic dominance.

---

17 In the case of Lorenz (2012), his fiction completes a complex historical operation that unites the political violence of the 1970s with the Falklands–Malvinas story. Even in his 2017 novel which was not specifically dedicated to the Falklands–Malvinas issue, he takes a condescending look at the armed struggle.

18 Pron refers to his work as 'a symbolic continuation of the Falklands/Malvinas War'. This 'untimely' critic sought to desecrate a war that, by the time he was editing his novel, had already been re-sacralised in other arenas (interview with Patricio Pron, *Infobae* newspaper, 8 February 2015).

19 This includes children's literature. A book by Claudio Javier Garbolino and Antonella Garbolino Mejía (2013) was marketed as the first children's story about the Falklands–Malvinas conflict.

20 On the Pichiciegos see Bruña (2016). On the work of Gamerro, see Lardone (2012). On Guebel, see Ehrmantraut (2016). On Eckhardt, see Vitullo (2006).

Possibly the most important weapon in these works has been to strip the Falklands–Malvinas War of its solemnity and, through this simple operation, desacralise 'Argentinity', and uncover it as a farce of power. To leave the king naked. To leave the king without his heroic deed.

Cinematographic language

This dichotomy between legitimising views of the state narrative, and those that open alternative paths, is much more complex to observe in the cinema, where we find a great diversity of possibilities associated with the characteristics of cinematic language. On the other hand, not all cinematic contributions can be considered part of the fiction genre, as some works have a documentary style based on research and interviews and maintain the truth of what they postulate.[21]

A certain continuity can be seen between some key cinematic works and the official state discourse of the period. *Los chicos de la guerra* [The Boys who went to War] by Bebe Kamín (1984) is undoubtedly the most iconic representation of the narrative at the time of the transition to democracy, along with the minutes he dedicates to the Falklands–Malvinas issue in *La República perdida 2* [The Lost Republic 2], directed by Miguel Pérez (1986), and *La deuda interna* [The Internal Debt], by Miguel Pereira (1988). In this line, there are many other productions, for example *Guarisove, los olvidados* [Guarisove, the Forgotten Ones] by Bruno Stagnaro, *Hundan al Belgrano* [Sink the Belgrano] by Federico Urioste (1996), and *El visitante* [The Visitor] by Javier Olivera (1998).

But there are other films that do not coincide exactly with the predominant post-1983 discourse. Examples are: *Malvinas, historia de traiciones* [Malvinas, a Story of Betrayal] by Jorge Denti (1984), which is located in the classic revisionist discourse of anti-colonialism, and *Malvinas, Alerta Roja* [Malvinas, Red Alert] by Eduardo Alertondo, a film that premiered in 1985 with a strikingly military tone, in an era when, although some solidarity with the military persisted, the majoritarian discourse adhered to anti-military views.

The most recent official discourse was observed in the successful film *Illuminados por el fuego* [Illuminated by Fire], released in 2005, and financed by an important series of Argentine public institutions. Its director was a senior government official. Another film, *Desobediencia debida* [Due Disobedience], a documentary by Victoria Reale (2010), could be placed in the same category. Its main character is the only British prisoner of the Argentine troops, it is

---

21 There are documentaries such as *Crazy about the Flag* (2005), by Julio Cardoso, which demonstrates the breakdown of the famed Argentine national unity on the subject of the Falklands–Malvinas, although it was not what the film set out to show.

clearly located in the state discourse of the time, and was also state-funded.[22] Through the metaphor, the director discusses the law of 'due obedience' that sought to limit military responsibility in the illegal repressions (Romero, 2017).

From another perspective, *Cartas a Malvinas* [Letters to Malvinas] (2006) and *Soldado argentino solo conocido por Dios* [Argentine Soldier Known Only by God] (2016) by Rodrigo Fernández Engler, sit in opposition to official discourse but closer to traditional nationalist visions. They go against the narrative according to which the young soldiers are seen as victims of the Argentine military:

> I do not say that it did not exist, but I filmed a tribute to the Falklands–Malvinas heroes. I leave aside the political and ideological issues, the process [of national reorganisation], and Galtieri, because I ask, 'What did an 18 year-old soldier have to do with Galtieri?' Most of the soldiers felt what they were doing. I address the patriotism and companionship of that story.[23]

Other films have repeated the aforementioned strategy of stripping away solemnity from the matter, or shining a light on other behaviours and actors as a way of leaving room for critical reflection. For example, we could mention the almost avant-garde experimentation of *Teatro de Guerra* [Theatre of War], by Lola Arias, the brutal political incorrectness of *Fuckland* by José Luis Márquez, or the film that embodies the humanity of pain in Argentines and islanders alike – *La forma exacta de las islas* [The Exact Shape of the Islands] by Daniel Casabé and Edgardo Dieleke.

Those issues that have been explored in some detail in the public sphere and civil society seem to have less room to develop in fiction. For example, the human rights violations perpetrated by the dictatorship after 1976 have had few portrayals in fiction, perhaps because it has been more difficult to place the topic on the plane of the absurd, of the critical or satirical gaze.[24]

This snapshot reviews issues not explored widely until now, for example, the extent of state influence in different genres, seen in the fact that there are more works challenging the state narrative in the field of cultural production than in essays or academic works. This could be due to the fact that the state set the limits (conditions of audibility) on what could be discussed in public sphere. If this were so, culture would be an overlapping way of treating these issues, by escaping formal and informal coercions. Cultural production would be staking a claim to be the space where civil society examines issues that are occluded by

---

22 There are several studies of the British in Argentine cinema on the Falklands–Malvinas (Fernández Ameghino, 2018).

23 *La Voz* (Córdoba), 7 June 2016.

24 'Julieta Vitullo, on the other hand, affirms that "Malvinas is a malaise in the national conscience, that seems to be unable to be faced by the political discourse, but literature does"' (Souto, 2018, p. 110).

the state, and the works produced can open up conversation and reflection on what is less easy to present in all its crude reality.

Falklands–Malvinas, an experience without learning?

> Victory and defeat are circumstantial.
> The essential and atrocious is war.
>
> *Jorge Luis Borges*

A diachronic review of Argentine history based on the contention around the Falklands–Malvinas offers a variety of perspectives for a critical analysis of the future of this issue. But a systematic approach from the social sciences must resist the temptation to blame only the enemy of the day, avoid empathy with the immediate interests of the state, and place itself in the uncomfortable position of speaking truth to power. This is why we must examine the Falklands–Malvinas issue from beginning of the national narrative onwards if we are to address a broader context than that of the war. The war was the result of that process, not its genesis.

That is why our first strategy was to offer a concise historicisation exceeding the limits of the field of recent history. We did this without putting the focus on the war or dictatorship, because this would reduce 'history' merely to what happened during the 1970s and 1980s. Instead, we took the methodological decision to broaden the spectrum of analysis: to examine the war in the context of the sustained actions of the Argentine state since its consolidation as such.

This meant studying the Falklands–Malvinas as more than a mere diplomatic conflict, but rather as part of a state strategy to sustain a narrative of national identity. In various ways, and particularly during the war of 1982, the idea of a national identity for Argentina served as a useful device against a heterogeneous society that had traditionally reacted against attempts at discipline.

This mechanism worked in its territorial form (typical of military governments) or in its national and popular form, embodied in the sovereignty of a uniform people led by the state (characteristic of Peronist governments). Both tactics placed the state and the country above the law. Both versions rejected the pluralistic and heterogeneous society articulated by respect and obedience to the National Constitution. Both traditions militarised the public account and turned Argentina into a victim of external threats and looting, sometimes by foreigners (the British or the Communists), and sometimes by their 'perfidious local agents'.

The Falklands–Malvinas Islands, especially since the mid 1930s, were, for one side as well as for the other, the empirical proof of that story. A misadventure along with others, such as the defeat in the Battle of Vuelta de Obligado, the deaths of Manuel Dorrego and Facundo Quiroga, the betrayal that expelled Rosas from the government and sent him into exile, the Roca-

Runciman Agreement, the coups against popular leaders, or the handover of oil to foreign capital during the Arturo Frondizi government.

But the Falklands–Malvinas, unlike the aforementioned episodes, was the only cause that remained stable in the centre of the national narrative. The 'fact' of the 'usurpation' of the homeland taught to children in school was reinforced in adulthood by governmental, political and cultural appeals of different kinds. A large part of the problem lies within this process: how we, as Argentines, believe that we act, and how the rest of the world interprets our actions.

The traditional nationalist narrative presented Argentines as responding to the 'usurpation' in a patient, peaceful and patriotic way. In spite of ongoing political conflict, Argentines could put aside their internal differences when defending the interests of the homeland. However, if they failed in their objective of incorporating the unredeemed territory into the national soil – and in the face of humiliation upon humiliation – Argentines would lose patience. And if that happened, their reaction would be fully justified. That day arrived on 2 April 1982.

Precisely because of this, after 1982, in some quarters the war was considered a minor event that followed activity to solve the problem, and 'so much pacifism and patience'. Argentina acted as though the enemy had begun the fight. Nothing would be an obstacle to the national cause – not even international law.

However, as observed in this chapter, Argentine state policy was far from pacifist. In addition, the succession of contrasting strategies in different political cycles (and incidents such as 'Operativo Cóndor' in the 1960s) prevented Argentina from cultivating a reputation as a reliable interlocutor. These factors also undermined any attempt to solve the problem through the kind of dialogue which might offer or demand long-term commitments.

Explanations for the war range from the anecdotal ('the drunken general'); the counterfactual ('what would have happened if ...'); to those that blame international betrayal (by the United Nations or the United States); those that hold society responsible; and those that place the war in the context of a game of political survival or the poor decisions of the military government. But all we can do is unravel the historical conditions that allowed the events to occur. A critical study allows us to question and understand these conditions to try to circumvent the possibility of history repeating itself.

After the war, the tone of most reflections on the Falklands–Malvinas did not change, although the Argentine defeat ended some of the approaches conceived before 1982. In particular, it severely damaged the narrative of the national militarist epic. Meanwhile, the state concentrated on the renewal of the integrative capacity of the Falklands–Malvinas myth, and the voices engaging with the issue once again fell into line with state interests, and with the recreation of the damaged idea of Argentinity. Few chose to deviate from this. The adverse outcome of the war was key to the (re)construction of the narrative. Indeed, a victory could not have aided the process of recycling and maintaining a self-image based on the melancholic idea of defeated moral champions.

Faced with this, Vicente Palermo (a challenger to the dominant discourse), called the post-war period a lost opportunity – as was the case in post-war Europe – to renounce territorialistic nationalism and replace it with a republican patriotism that would allow the construction of a different path from the one chosen by the state since the 19th century.

Meanwhile, Federico Lorenz (in line with the renewed official discourse) preferred to believe that the discomfort of society in the post-war period was not attributable to military defeat, but to a sudden awareness of the dictatorship and its illegal repression. This intellectual operation is what enabled the state's strategy after 2003 to separate one from the other, to incorporate 'the heroic deed' into the new historical narrative without paying the price of being associated with the military that carried it out. But this manoeuvre obscures the fact society's reaction was exactly the opposite: it was defeat, more than anything else, that was intolerable. The unforgivable thing was losing the war.

This chapter argues that Palermo's 'lost opportunity' would be better located after 1990 or around 2001, rather than in the years of the Alfonsinist transition. The Falklands–Malvinas in the immediate post-war period were at the centre of the political situation, whether the Alfonsín government liked it or not. 'Malvinas' had been a synonym for war since 1982, and when Alfonsín assumed the presidency, not two years had gone by since the surrender of the Argentine troops.

By 1983, the Falklands–Malvinas were more than the centre of a state strategy to provoke nationalist feeling in society. They were a symbol of the dead, the ex-combatants, the military defending itself, the attack on democracy, the political elites that made the military a constant in the state apparatus, the stories of mistreatment and heroism, the demands of society for punishment, and the presence of nationalism in education and, of course, in popular culture. 'Malvinas' was the football game against England in the 1986 World Cup, the counter-facts at family tables and bars, and in film and literature. The war carried on in other ways, in order to achieve, even in fiction or sport, a restoration of a certain balance and national pride in the face of unexpected and dishonourable defeat.

Within the framework of the structural weakness of the Radical government led by Alfonsín, standing alone politically, and facing many challenges, it was not possible to do anything as profound as changing the course of the country's sense of self. Neither was there in the Radical party any deep conviction about what to do about the issue. Alfonsín's policies were ambiguous and subject to his bargaining power with the military establishment and opposition politics.

The political and economic conditions to produce changes were present from 1990 (especially in 1994, during the constitutional reform process). However, Menem's policy (especially in his second term) also remained ambiguous, despite efforts by his foreign minister to improve the country's image in the eyes of the islanders and the 'carnal alliance' with the United States. Once Menem consolidated his power, what prevailed were the strategies that sustained his leadership above anything else and then, a tendency to systemic corruption.

In 2003, Peronism had another opportunity. The 2001 crisis allowed Néstor Kirchner's government, mounted on economic recovery and a progressive discourse, to generate long-lasting changes in the state discourse. But he chose to repeat the existing path. What had to be avoided was not the recreation of the conditions that could reiterate the deceptive act, but the prevention of the political adversary handling the state. Even the Falklands–Malvinas War was to be justified, as if it were the 'good' people who carried it out. The important thing was to take the state, not to change its strategy. Thus, it was possible to separate the heroic deed from those who had led the war.

Despite these measures, resources and the intellectual and cultural support that the state received, its objective was difficult to achieve. It was not possible to separate the dictatorship from 'the heroic deed'. The only way is to give up the idea of the heroic deed. But without that, there is nothing left but a dictatorship acting desperately, steeped in decades of nationalist rhetoric.

Conclusions and points for further reflection

The British bombing of Buenos Aires in 1982 exists only in the imagination and in the famous songs of popular musicians. The real 'bombs' arrived in the 1990s, dropped by international terrorism, enlarging the list of deaths. Argentina was once again participating in a war, but this time following the United States' lead against Iraq.

In 1982 the Argentine government did not understand the cost of splitting from the Western world and confronting its two largest pillars. In 1990, another Argentine government did not understand the costs of getting involved in a distant war, following an automatic alignment with the same powers that it had challenged in 1982. Both contradictory moments are united by a misunderstanding of the global reality, and by an intellectual deficiency of the elites to understand the contemporary development of the world.

In the case of the Falklands–Malvinas, this misunderstanding grew out of a false and repeated image, and one which was only accepted within Argentina: the idea of a patient, continuous and peaceful claim. The islanders themselves, or 'Kelpers', as the Argentines persist in calling them, are subjects who do not count or matter. While much of the British diplomatic triumph was based on questioning the future of the islands' population, for the Argentine state, that population simply did not exist. Or, in the words of the highest authority in the country, 'they are squatters'.[25]

This was the case for the academic and cultural world, too. Even from the 1990s, when the discourse of otherness was established in the social sciences, academia preferred to build an *other* acceptable for the narrative or for the reality that the country was living in. The *other* was linked to gender issues, the native peoples and economic outsiders. These were *acceptable others*. But the islanders were, possibly, the true *other*, the other that calls into question our own identity.

The war changed everything. It brought about the end of the dictatorship; there was a public outcry over human rights violations, and an economic and social crisis that obscured the ways in which the armed forces had tried to legitimise their intervention in politics. From 1983, it was clear that the army could no longer claim to rule, impose order, or even defend the homeland. Thus the longest and most unprecedented period of democracy in the country's history was inaugurated. Everything changed with the war. Everything changed, except for the conditions that led us to it.

References

Bermúdez, N. (2015) 'La construcción kirchnerista de la memoria', *Linguagem em (Dis)curso*, 15 (2): 229–47.

Bertoni, L.A. (1992) 'Construir la nacionalidad: Héroes, estatuas y fiestas patrias (1887–1891)', *Boletín de Historia Argentina y americana*, 5: 77–111.

Bosoer, F. (2013) *Detrás de Perón: Historia y leyenda del almirante Teisaire* (Buenos Aires: Capital Intelectual).

Bruña B. and M. José (2016) *Como ranas de invierno: Reescrituras* cyberpunk *sobre Malvinas*, in G. Mira and F. Pedrosa (eds), *Estirando los límites: Nuevas agendas en Historia reciente* (Buenos Aires: EUDEBA).

Carassai, S. (2013) *Los años setenta de la gente común: La naturalización de la violencia* (Buenos Aires: Siglo Veintiuno Editores).

Ehrmantraut, P. (2012) '¿Hacia dónde viaja un argentino cuando viaja a las Islas Malvinas?', *Revista de Culturas y Literaturas Comparadas*, 1: 226–35.

— (2016) '"Impresiones de un natural nacionalista" o cómo desactivar la causa Malvinas (nada más, ni nada menos)', in G. Maier and B. Adriaensen, *Todos los mundos posibles: Una geografía de Daniel Guebel* (Buenos Aires: Beatriz Viterbo).

---

25 Interviews with LMNeuquen.com, March 13, 2013. Extracted from the LMNeuquen.com website.

Fernández Ameghino, M. (2018) 'Hambre, maltratos y estaqueos en los audiovisuales sobre la guerra de Malvinas', Ponencia presentada en el Congreso de historia oral (Asociación de Historia Oral de la República Argentina, Trelew, Argentina).

— (2019) 'Un recorrido histórico a través del cine: El caso de las islas Malvinas y el conflicto entre Argentina y Gran Bretaña', in M. Zawierzeniec (ed.), *España y América Latina – literatura, sociedad, lenguaje: más allá del mainstream* (Varsovia: Wszechnica Polska), pp. 69–84.

Franco, M. (2012) 'Pensar la violencia estatal en la Argentina del siglo XX', *Lucha Armada*, 8: 20–31.

Garaño, S. (2013) 'El debate sobre la conscripción y el activismo en derechos humanos en la post-dictadura argentina', *Observatorio Latinoamericano*, 12: 121–36.

Garbolino, C.J. and A. Garbolino Mejía (2013) *Pipino el pingüino, el monstruo y las Islas Malvinas* (Buenos Aires: Ministerio de Educación de la Nación Argentina).

García Fanlo, L. (2007) 'Emergencia de la matriz militar discursiva argentina: el discurso de Leopoldo Lugones', *Discurso y argentinidad*, 1 (1).

— (2010) *Genealogía de la argentinidad* (Gran Aldea Editores).

García Quiroga, D. (2010) *Historia de los años sin piel* (Buenos Aires: De los cuatro vientos).

Guber, R. (2000) 'La recuperación de la frontera perdida: La dimensión mítica en los derechos argentinos a las Islas Malvinas', *Revista de Investigaciones Folclóricas*, 15: 77–87.

— (2007) 'Nacionalismo y autoritarismo: algunas lecciones de la experiencia de Malvinas', *Ciclos*, 17 (16): 31/32, 239–63.

— (2013) 'Como un cierre. Igualdad, honor y amistad entre contendientes directos, después de Malvinas', *Tabula Rasa*, 19: 11–27.

— (2017) 'Las Malvinas, ¿objeto de investigación?', *Ciencia Hoy*, 157.

Halliday, F. (1986) *The Making of the Second Cold War* (London, Verso).

Halperin Donghi, T. (2005a [1980]) *Una nación para el desierto argentino* (Buenos Aires: Prometeo).

— (2005b) *El revisionismo como visión decadente de la historia argentina* (Buenos Aires, Siglo XXI.

Iglesias, F. (2012) *La cuestión Malvinas* (Buenos Aires: Aguilar).

Infante María, T. (1979) 'Controversia chileno-argentina en la región del Canal Beagle: Laudo arbitral de 18 de abril de 1977', *Revista Chilena de Derecho* 6 (5/6): 423–47.

Kohen, M. and F. Rodríguez (2015) *Las Malvinas entre el derecho y la historia: Refutación del folleto británico, 'Más allá de la historia oficial: La verdadera historia de las Falklands/Malvinas'* (Buenos Aires: Eudeba), p. 302.

Lardone, M.I. (2012) 'Las islas de Carlos Gamerro: Farsa y épica en torno a la identidad nacional', Ponencia presentada en VIII Congreso Internacional Orbis Tertius de Teoría y Crítica Literaria (Universidad Nacional de La Plata).

Leal Buitrago, F. (2003) 'La doctrina de seguridad nacional: materialización de la guerra fría en América del sur', *Revista de Estudios Sociales*, 15: 74–87.

López M. and A. Rodríguez (2009) *Un país de película: La historia argentina que el cine nos contó* (Buenos Aires: Editorial Del Nuevo Extremo).

Lorenz, F. (2011) 'El malestar de Krímov: Malvinas, los estudios sobre la guerra y la historia reciente argentina', *Estudios*, 25: 47–65.

— (2012) *Montoneros o la ballena blanca* (Buenos Aires: Tusquets).

Míguez, M.C. (2018) 'El Canal Beagle y la consulta popular en 1984: Relaciones internacionales y política interna argentina', *Si Somos Americanos*, 18(2): 78–102.

Mira, G. and F. Pedrosa (2016) *Estirando los límites: Nuevas agendas en Historia reciente* (Buenos Aires: EUDEBA).

Molina, M.E. (2008) 'Guerra de Malvinas: la literatura argentina y el desafío de la autocrítica', *Espéculo, Revista de Estudios Literarios*, 39.

Niebieskikwiat, N. (2014) 'Kelpers: Ni ingleses ni argentinos. Cómo es la nación que crece frente a nuestras costas' (Buenos Aires: Editorial Sudamericana).

Palermo, V. (2007) *Sal en las heridas: Las Malvinas en la cultura argentina contemporánea* (Buenos Aires: Editorial Sudamericana).

Paredes Goicochea, D. (2018) 'Marx y lo político: La lectura de Carl Schmitt', *Eidos*, 28: 281–304.

Perlongher, N. (1982) 'Todo el poder a Lady Dy. Militarismo y anticolonialismo en la cuestión de las Malvinas', *Persona*, 12.

Perochena, C. (2016) 'Una memoria incómoda: La guerra de Malvinas en los gobiernos kirchneristas (2003–2015)', *Anuario de Historia Regional y de las Fronteras*, 21 (2): 173–91.

Portantiero, J.C. (1973) 'Clases dominantes y crisis política en la Argentina actual', in O. Braun (ed.), *El capitalismo argentino en crisis* (Buenos Aires: Siglo Veintiuno Argentina).

Pron, P. (2014) *Nosotros caminamos en sueños* (Buenos Aires: Random House).

Romero, L.A. (2017) *Breve historia contemporánea de la Argentina 1916–2016* (Ciudad Autónoma de Buenos Aires: Fondo de Cultura Económica).

Rozitchner, L. (2015) *Malvinas: de la guerra sucia a la guerra limpia. El punto ciego de la crítica política* (Biblioteca Nacional).

Souto, L.C. (2018) 'Malvinas, las islas prometidas: Aproximaciones a la literatura de la guerra', *Revista chilena de literatura*, 98: 105–30.

Svetliza, E. (2017) 'La guerra de Malvinas y sus trincheras intelectuales: entredichos entre los editores de la revista Sitio y el escritor Néstor Perlongher', *Remate de Males*, 37 (2): 925–44.

Valenzuela Ugarte, R. and F. García Toso (2008) 'A Treinta años de la crisis del Beagle: Desarrollo de un modelo de negociación en la resolución del conflicto', *Revista Política y Estrategia*, 111: 29–70.

Vitullo, J. (2006) 'Relatos de desertores en las ficciones de la guerra de Malvinas', *Hispamérica*, 35 (104): 29–38.

— (2012) *Islas imaginadas: La Guerra de Malvinas en la literatura y el cine argentinos* (Buenos Aires: Corregidor).

Varela, M. and M. Metsman (2016) *Masas, Pueblo y Multitud en Cine y TV* (Buenos Aires: EUDEBA).

1. Resisting bio-power: 'laughter', 'fraternity' and 'imagination' under dictatorship and the Malvinas–Falklands War

María José Bruña Bragado

Moreover, while the results of men's actions are beyond the actors' control, violence harbors within itself an additional element of arbitrariness; nowhere does Fortuna, good or ill luck, play a more fateful role in human affairs than on the battlefield; and this intrusion of the utterly unexpected does not disappear when people call it a 'Random Event' and find it scientifically suspect (Arendt, 1970, p. 4).

However little sense there may be in trying to specify why I, rather than thousands of others, managed to survive the test, I believe that it was really due to Lorenzo that I am alive today; and not so much for his material aid, as for his having constantly reminded me by his presence, by his natural and plain manner of being good, that there still existed a just world outside of our own, something and someone still pure and whole, not corrupt, not savage, extraneous to hatred and terror; something difficult to define, a remote possibility of good, but for which it was worth surviving […] Thanks to Lorenzo, I managed not to forget that I myself was a man (Levi, 1959, p. 142).

Il est banal de dire que nous n'existons jamais au singulier. Nous sommes entourés d'êtres et de choses avec lesquels nous entretenons des relations. Par la vue, par le toucher, par la sympathie, par le travail en commun, nous sommes avec les autres. Toutes ces relations sont transitives. Je touche un objet, je vois l'autre, mais je ne suis pas l'autre (Lévinas, 2001, p. 21).

[It is banal to say that we never exist in the singular. We are surrounded by beings and things with which we cultivate relationships. Through sight, touch, sympathy, by work in common, we are with others. All these relations are transitive. I touch an object, I see the other, but I am not the other.][1]

---

1   All translations from the Spanish and the French are the author's own.

M. José Bruña Bragado, 'Resisting bio-power: 'laughter', 'fraternity' and 'imagination' under dictatorship and the Malvinas–Falkland Islands War', in G. Mira and F. Pedrosa (eds.), *Revisiting the Falklands–Malvinas Question: Transnational and Interdisciplinary Perspectives* (London: University of London Press, 2020), pp. 31–52. License: CC-BY-NC-ND 4.0.

Bio-power, the normalisation of violence and fortunate ethics

Los centros de poder se definen por lo que les escapa o por su impotencia, mucho más que por su zona de potencia (Deleuze and Guattari, 2006, p. 263).

[Power centres are defined much more by what escapes them or by their impotence than by their zones of power.]

[…] hoy que el capitalismo avanzado sostiene su dominación en una completa espectacularización de la historia, historizar el espectáculo nos situará en una mejor posición en la lucha contra él (Peris Blanes, 2005, p. 16).

[Currently, late capitalism sustains its dominance by completely spectacularising history; therefore, historicising spectacle would enable us to situate ourselves in a much better position to fight against it.]

Bio-power

In his 'Theses on the Philosophy of History' Walter Benjamin declares that our concept of history must be grounded in a key idea that is difficult to grasp: that we live in a perpetual 'state of exception'. Decades later, in a formulation indebted to Benjamin, Michel Foucault coined a concept that would become fundamental to thought about the frightening 20th century – so violent, just as the centuries that preceded and will follow it, as Arendt would say, since violence is intrinsic to being and to society and always makes an appearance where power staggers. This notion was further developed by philosophers such as Giorgio Agamben and Peter Sloterdijk, among others, into the concept of 'bio-politics'. In the modern era, 'bio-politics' means the absolute instrumentalisation of natural life by political power (Foucault, 1978, p. 173). 'Bio-politics' can thus be defined as the absolute political administration of life, the intervention or calculated intrusion by power-knowledge into every aspect of human life. In this regard, in the first volume of his trilogy *Homo Sacer. Il potere sovrano e la nuda vita* (1995), Agamben argues that the current paradigm of global expansion is the extreme application of 'bio-politics', namely, the concentration camp. At the centre of *Quel che resta di Auschwitz. L'archivio e il testimone. Homo sacer III* (1998) Agamben posits man not as a subject but as a living body and delivers a study of the space where this living body exists, which is simultaneously outside and within the juridical. In *Archive and Witness* (1995), the third volume of his work, he argues that the extreme situation undergone by human beings in concentration camps implies the inevitable revision of all ethical referents and parameters that are valid until the moment in which the extreme situation occurs; it also includes an interrogation of one's own moral compass. Along the lines of Agamben, both Tzvetan Todorov and Sloterdijk, distance themselves from Jürgen Habermas's utopian approach, embodied by his 'discursive ethics', while they underscore the importance of interrogating one's own moral ethics as they are understood at the moment in which the extreme situation happens. Moreover, from a philosophical point of view they posit the evident failure of post-war humanism and, from a political point of view, of contemporary neoliberal democracies.

According to Todorov, in the case of concentration camps and war conflicts, or even in instances of the genocidal wars that keep tearing up our present – for example, in Iraq or Syria – testimony, which at this juncture would replace art and imagination, can help in the task of remembering horror, speaking out against barbarity, pondering the grounds for evil. Obtaining answers would be a whole other matter; and yet testimony has proven to fail in avoiding its historical repetition:

> Good and evil are both part of our potentialities. The hope for reaching a definite state free of all evil is a vain hope, neither war, nor executions nor prison suffice. [...] The memory of the past could help us in this enterprise of taming evil, on the condition that we keep in mind that good and evil flow from the same source and that in the world's best narratives they are not nearly divided (Todorov, 2009, p. 29).

Furthermore, Jaume Peris Blanes, in his essential essay about the repressive logics of the 20th century, *La imposible voz. Memoria y representación de los campos de concentración en Chile: la posición del testigo* [*The Impossible Voice. Memory and Representation in Chile's Concentration Camps: The Witness's Position*] (2005), begins by laying out the concepts of 'state of exception', 'bio-politics', 'sovereignty' and 'concentration camp' in order to consider and to interrogate the notion of the 'ethics of the witness' as a legitimate and true strategy for resisting bio-power under military dictatorships in the Southern Cone, specifically, in Pinochet's Chile. Walter Benjamin, Paul de Man, Jacques Derrida (and, later on, also Beatriz Sarlo) would note that the holes and gaps inherent in testimonial in the first person, which is an ethical discourse from a powerless position (also noted by Todorov), constitute the sole possibility of reconstructing social memory, although in every case testimony has proven to be unable to eradicate the recurrent presence of evil in history. Thus, Levi's (1947) or Semprún's (1963) testimonies about National Socialism's concentration camps and, more recently, testimonials by Hernán Valdés (1974) or Pilar Calveiro (1998) about Chilean or Argentine concentration camps are remarkable exercises in trauma recovery through writing and enunciation; and in some instances demonstrate the impotence of being unable to utter speech, of *unsayability*.[2] In the case of Calveiro, her testimony is a theoretically illuminating exercise in contestation addressed to bio-power:

> What Calveiro makes out of her experience is original with regards to bearing witness. She affirms what the victim thinks, even when she is at the point of madness. She affirms that the victim ceases being a victim *because*

---

2   To the point that the relationship between the living and the speaking is characterised by being incomparable. The same goes for the processes of subjectivisation and de-subjectivisation, which can never coincide (Peris Blanes, 2005, p. 119).

she thinks. She renounces the autobiographical dimension *because* she wants to write and understand the experience she has undergone in much wider terms (Sarlo, 2005, p. 122).

Thus memory, as Reyes Mate (2012) affirms, is one of the most decisive categories of our time; and yet it is also amongst the most slippery, because in contrast to concepts such as 'citizenship', 'democracy', 'freedom' or 'equality' memory it is still in the making, being configured and built. A critical gaze on a totalitarian past may be, aside from healing, subversive, but we have only come to learn this.

The normalisation of violence

Traditional Christian or Enlightenment humanism does not constitute a solution to the violence intrinsic to totalitarian projects and to the western liberal democracies which allegedly oppose them and which have subjected us to living under a disquieting and permanent state of exception. Moreover, as Sloterdijk attests, it is hopeless to hold on to humanism as a civilising, 'taming', 'appeasing', 'domesticating' tool in the face of brutality and violence: 'Concentration camp and society belong to each other, as they are inexplicable one without the other. They reflect and reproduce one another' (Calveiro, 1998, p. 159).

In this regard, a reflection upon how the rhetoric of the necessity of violence was shamelessly wielded by the military dictatorships in the Southern Cone in order to impose the neoliberal model sheds light on how its excesses were carefully separated from the political and ethical domains:

> In public discourses from that era, violence is posited as a necessary element to implement the neo-liberal (modern, in military rhetoric) model, whose implementation within the parliamentary system faced enormous resistance – especially in the case of Chile. This made difficult the consolidation of market and spectacle as axes for the articulation of social realities. Because of this, we could infer that, first, modernising the State's apparatuses for repression by articulating them around management and bureaucratisation enabled the disconnection between the application of violence and political or ethical decisions, such as Bauman argues was the case in the Nazis' concentration camp system (Peris Blanes, 2005, p. 49).

Only after accepting that there is no malignant potential or 'radical evil' (Kant) as such, but rather a 'bureaucratised and official barbarism' (Adorno) as well as an intolerable, ubiquitous, trans-historical and universal 'banal evil' (Arendt) at the heart of bio-power, can and must we tell, narrate it in a complex, polyhedral way that is neither Manichean nor naïve. The 'terrorising normality', the mediocrity and banality intrinsic to evil, the 'inhuman' within the 'human' (Todorov, 2004) displayed in the Nazi concentration camps and under the Southern Cone dictatorships are difficult to assimilate. This is also the case in the Malvinas–Falkland Islands War, which is one of the most revealing examples of bio-political control in recent history:

> Acts of this kind, which seem exceptional, are perfectly ingrained in society's everyday life; this is why they are possible. They are linked to an admitted 'normalcy'. This is what is 'normal' in obedience, in absolute, final and arbitrary power, the normalcy of punishment, of disappearance (Calveiro, 2008, p. 147).[3]

In sum, to restore humanism implies confessing its impotence in the face of the violent acts of 'bio-political' power;[4] and only by understanding its complex internal dynamics shall we be able, first, to narrate the conditions and circumstances that allow the degradation of human beings. Second, through narration – in which we could have played the part of either the victim or the victimiser – we shall be empowered to find personal atonement and a certain ethical space. Only at the moment in which we are able to accept violence as an atrocious yet inevitable component of our societies shall we be able to activate resistance. Only? As we shall see, confronting the multiple tentacles of bio-power, one of which is the normalisation of horror, can only take place from consciousness and by exercising an 'ethics of testimony'.[5]

3   In the same sense, Rodolfo Fogwill affirms in his essay 'El doctor Cormillot y la gran máquina de adelgazar conciencias' [Doctor Cormillot and the great machine for thinning-out consciences], first published in *El Porteño* in February 1984: 'We were human: human just like the torturers. Because amongst the torturers there were kind, educated, order-loving, peace-loving people, people who were able to appreciate the beauty of the bodies of race horses. There were even remorseful torturers! Human! Because torturers are as human as collaborationists, and like them, they also have access to the human gifts of happiness, of the smile, sadness and regret. And yet, what kind of regret? The only valid regret is that which binds them not to carry out the same faults ever again' (Fogwill, 2008, p. 60).

4   'Let God decide according to his will, I told myself. I am going to read the Greeks', affirms Urrutia-Lacroix, the sinister and erudite main character in Roberto Bolaño's novel *Nocturno de Chile* [*Chile by Night* (2000)] at a moment of extreme historical urgency, at the moment in which bio-power will show itself with all its might in Chile. A masterly passage that mingles high culture and barbarity follows this statement: 'I also read Demosthenes and Menander and Aristotle and Plato (who is always fruitful), there were strikes and a colonel in an armoured regiment that tried to stage a coup and a cameraman died filming his own death and then Allende's naval aide was killed; and there were turmoil and bad words, Chileans cursed, painted on the walls and then almost half a million people marched in support of Allende; and then came the putsch, the uprising, the military coup, La Moneda was bombarded; and when the bombing stopped, the president killed himself and then it was all over. I stood still, with a finger on the page I was reading, and I thought: It is peaceful now' (Bolaño, 2000, pp. 97–9). Complicity between culture and horror is manifest; and this is how we can observe the failure of any humanist attempt to mould violence.

5   Calveiro recalls that the tortured drank together with the torturers in Argentine concentration camps, that they listened to soccer games side by side on the radio, and that they played cards with them after having been subjected to rape and other unimaginable abuses. This is an example of an instance of the normalisation of violence, as horror is rendered quotidian. The last part of Roberto Bolaño's novel *Chile by Night* (2000) shows this with clairvoyance when guests to María Canales' literary *soirées* discover that the cellar is, in fact, a torture site: 'I asked the following question: Why was it that one of the guests, as he got lost, came across that poor

'An ethics of fortune'

> If there is one virtue of human beings which deserves to be spoken about in a philosophical way, it is above all this: that people are not forced into political theme parks but, rather, put themselves there. Humans are self-fencing, self-shepherding creatures. Wherever they live, they create parks around themselves.[6]

In the face of everyday horror there is another indispensable notion that can be rescued from Reyes Mate's articles: the 'ethics of fortune', whose essence and projection escape all means of control, whose arbitrariness and hazardous gestures situate us, without even taking action, on one side or the other. In the extermination camps some were lucky enough not only to live but, more importantly, to catch a glimpse of humanity in atrocious conditions. As a matter of fact, this is why they lived: they lived to attest to the 'remote possibility of goodness' beyond 'fear and hatred', which Primo Levi evokes when he refers to Lorenzo in the opening quotation of this essay, a passage also mentioned by Jorge Semprún when he refers to his Muslim *Doppelgänger* whose place he will be taking, or when he discusses how an unknown young Russian man saved his life out of sheer goodness, without expecting anything in return:

> In any case, the young Russian took upon his shoulder the stone that the SS officer had given me and that was much too heavy for me to carry. Taking advantage of an unexpected moment of neglect by the sadistic sergeant, he left me his stone, which was much lighter than mine. With that gesture, I was able to complete a task that could have been fatal for me.
>
> An uncalled-for and completely gratuitous gesture. He neither knew me, nor would he ever see me again. We were equal in our absolute lack of power: anonymous, impotent countryside plebs. A gesture of pure goodness, that is, almost supernatural. Or, what is the same thing, an example of the radical freedom to do good which is inherent to human nature (Semprún, 1995, p. 61).

What interests me in that capacity to feel, to attest through the other a certain degree of what has been deemed human, pure or good in the midst of desolation, violence and horror, is to rescue 'fraternity' in death or 'fraternal death'. The latter, according to Semprún, is that solidarity within powerlessness which is erected in the form of resistance that exhales a breath full of life. He who witnesses a gratuitous gesture of pure giving, generosity, empathy and

---

man? The answer was simple: because habit relaxes precautions, as routine shades all horror' (Bolaño, 2000, p. 142).

6 'Si existe una dignidad del hombre que merezca ser articulada en palabras con conciencia filosófica, ello es debido a que los hombres no sólo son sostenidos en los parques temáticos políticos, sino que se autosostienen ellos mismos ahí dentro. Los hombres son seres que se cuidan y se protegen por sí mismos y, vivan donde vivan, generan alrededor suyo el entorno de un parque' (Sloterdijk, 2009, p. 25).

charity from his fellow prisoner is enabled to believe in humanity afterwards and to survive. By contrast, those spared from the illusion of believing in the other, lacking ethical relief, frequently succumb to bio-power. Solidarity or rather 'care' within 'everyday virtues', as Todorov put it (2004), is a powerful means of resisting and surviving in the extreme conditions of adversity in bare life:

> An extremely important aspect of life in the concentration camps is what Todorov calls 'everyday virtues'. These imply individual actions that reject the concentrational order to benefit one or more persons: always particular subjects, and not for the sake of abstract ideas. Everyday virtues were not practised in great public acts but as part of everyday life; they are imperceptible except to those who benefit from them and imply profound commitment, even to the point that sometimes the life of whoever executes them is at stake. Because they are 'imperceptible', there are fewer testimonials about them than about heroic acts (Calveiro, 1998, p. 132).

In what follows, I shall carry out a risky theoretical displacement – one I consider necessary in order to be able to observe the 'everyday virtues' that make up life in concentration camps – onto another significant example of recent bio-political rule which is frequently ignored due to the relative degree of identity dispossession and de-subjectivisation: the Malvinas–Falkland Islands War. In this conflict, as we shall see, innumerable gestures of fraternity or 'care' amongst the soldiers took place in order that they might protect themselves from total internal violence upon the body, the mind and the spirit.

Malvinas–Falklands and 'everyday virtues'

> Violence appears where power is in jeopardy, but left to its own course it ends in power's disappearance.

Argentina's defeat in the Malvinas–Falklands War on 14 June 1982 closed a long cycle of violence in that country – although it inaugurated another cycle of violence of the socio-economic kind[7] – and contributed to the demise of the dictatorship. In other words, it opened up the possibility of democracy. Thus, at a moment at which continental economic recession was imminent, the military regime, facing growing popular obliviousness, made a last, desperate attempt to keep authority through going to war, but this ended in the call for elections. During the months prior to the invasion, there was no talk of illegal repression, disappearances or human rights abuses but of inflation, dollar and interest rates and the growth in the external debt.

To wage the Malvinas–Falklands War was a conscious decision taken by two governments, the British and the Argentine, who knew that they were sending hundreds of young men to a likely death; in that regard, it was a 'biopolitical'

---

7   For a detailed conceptualisation about the role of violence in Argentine politics of the second half of the 20th century, see Mira Delli-Zotti (2009).

strategy designed to hold onto power. In the case of Argentina it failed. Power was inevitably subsumed into even more violence; and it was inevitably made to disappear by the violence itself.

What is particular to the Malvinas–Falklands conflict is that it is still in a 'grey zone' of interpretation, since, although 'la Guerra fue llevada a cabo por un gobierno dictatorial, represivo y genocida, ningún evento de la historia moderna argentina dio lugar a semejante consenso cívico-militar basado en la pertenencia nacional' (Vitullo, 2012, p. 12).[8] Furthermore, consensus was not only national but continental, as the sovereigntist cause was embraced throughout Latin America – except by Pinochet's Chile. As Verbitsky points out (2002), both military and *montonero* discourses started from opposing analyses but coincided in their conclusion that the war was legitimate, be it from the point of view of a spurious nationalism or from an anti-colonialist perspective; and always counted on decisive support from the Argentine elite. This controversial moment although stemming from diverging motivations and opposed ideological compasses, made possible unanimous support for the Malvinas–Falklands War, its ultimate invisibilisation or interested banishment and, finally, an opportunistic sovereigntist instrumentalisation in external commemorations and official homages. Even decades later, in a very different world from the world which made possible this bellicose scenario, it is still contended that it was a 'just war', supported by nationalist arguments.[9] When the time comes to adduce the 'just cause' as a consensual argument, the indissoluble link between war and dictatorial repression is subtly erased, while the thorny question of placing the war in the context of anti-imperialism or sovereigntism is avoided.

A second interesting aspect of the shameful and 'minor' character of the war when compared to the previous systematic disappearances and massive torture in concentration camps arises from the barbarity and military repression of the 'dirty war' that the conflict itself brought to light. The Malvinas–Falklands War draws a complex panorama because its fighters – those who died as well as the survivors – are subject to a double theoretical marginality; in this sense, they do not cease to be subalterns of subalternity, the latter being the victims of the Argentine military dictatorship.

8 'The war was waged by a dictatorial, repressive and criminal government, no event in the history of Argentina gave place to such civic-military consensus based on national belonging [...] In Argentina, all members of the political class, from the right to the left, supported the war and enthusiastically buttressed the armed forces' performance in defence of national sovereignty. [...] in the Falklands adventure, not only military men were burned, but also a greater part of the political leaders' credibility was consumed' (Mira Delli-Zotti, 2009, p. 6).

9 See, for example, the last section of the soldier Edgardo Esteban's testimonial *Iluminados por el fuego* [*Illuminated by Fire*] (2012, [1993]): 'I think that this war placed us even further from our dream: that the Islands be Argentinian again. We know that they belong to us, but we must understand that there are people like us with whom we must learn to share. [...] I feel that the soldiers who fought, we have, above anyone else, a right and a sentiment: that these Islands are ours' (p. 279).

This tension can be explained by the fact that, at the beginning of the 1980s, Argentine society had been rendered insensitive to human rights abuses, to notions such as 'violence', 'disappearance', or 'death' articulated around young people. It was a society that was anaesthetised and could hardly feel any more pain, although it slowly came to recognise continuity between the crimes committed by the military – the theft of new-borns, murders, kidnapping and torture – and the Falkland Islands War. However, this fact neither exculpates nor redeems Argentine society of a certain responsibility, through either action or omission.[10] The gravity of the occurrences in recent Argentine history would then provoke the omnipresence of the first subalterns and would shadow 'los chicos de la guerra' [the war kids], reducing them to 'second category subalterns' in a first moment of information saturation. Their experience was not considered a priority. Afterwards, in the final phase of the explosion of memorials, ex-combatants would remain in the testimonial back rooms due to lack of homogeneity in their discourse, by the amalgamation of partial memories, politicised and struggling amongst themselves.

These two specific paradoxes – consensus about the need for war; relegation of the victims – traverse the Malvinas–Falkland Islands War. In this context, the 'ethics of the witness' provide relief at the individual level. However, this is not enough because, as stated above, there is great confusion amongst the survivors, who, in most cases, are incapable of distancing themselves theoretically or embarking upon critical reflection and have thus succumbed to official versions and an easy nationalism. Bio-power has dispossessed them of their identity, experience, discourse and sometimes of their lives until they have been transformed from subjects into ambivalent bodies that may discern but are unable to explain the reasons for their suffering. Agamben describes the specific modality of bio-power in the 20th century in terms of forcing to survive: separating the verbal from lived experience, living from speaking beings, bio-power allows the living to survive *as the remnant* of the speaker: 'What constitutes the decisive contribution of bio-power to our times is neither life nor death, but the production of malleable and virtually infinite survival' (Agamben, 1998, p. 163).

Catharsis implies verbalising horror and speaking out extreme evil by bearing witness. It presupposes a subjective locutionary act, at least, by the remnants of that subjectivity. This act is, however, always incomplete, precarious and bordering on stammering. Different modalities, lines of flight and gazes are incorporated into the experience of the past from which the speaker can heal

---

10 In *Chile by Night*, Bolaño demands an explanation from the whole country; he asks for answers and accountability from the Church, intellectuals and civil society for Pinochet's crimes. We cannot simply cover up horror, as happens to Urrutia-Lacroix, the main character in the novel: 'Chile, Chile. How could you have changed so much? Who would?, perched on his open window, looking at the faraway glare in Santiago. What have they done to you? Have Chileans gone mad? Are you going to become something else? Are you a monster that nobody will recognise?' (p. 96).

by repulsing them, resisting bio-power. Parting from Lévinas's assertion that we do not live in the singular, 'solidarity' – mentioned above as 'fraternity' or 'care' – and a sense of humour remind us that, at a juncture of extreme violence, purity and goodness are also inherent in human beings, that evasion through aesthetics is possible. In what Todorov calls 'activities of the spirit', we are also reminded that we are something more than 'bare bodies'.[11]

Indeed, in *Facing the Extreme. Moral Life in the Concentration Camps* (1996) Todorov highlights a series of concepts with which he works and which are partly recuperated by Calveiro as social typologies built upon the reconstruction of everyday life that is present in the testimonials. He begins by classifying virtues as either 'heroic' or 'quotidian'. 'Heroic virtues' belong to the order of exception as they are produced at specific historical moments and are part of public life. 'Quotidian virtues', in turn, are imperceptible and invisibilised by their everyday occurrence in the midst of barbarity. Todorov points out three kinds of virtue which are present in the everyday lives and extreme experiences of concentration camps: 'dignity', 'care' and 'aesthetics or activities of the spirit'. We believe that holding onto subjectivity, fraternity and imagination, or to the aesthetic of bodies which are rendered transparent by evil, appears also, with overwhelming frequency, in testimonials and narratives about the war in the Falkland Islands. The three virtues were a means of resistance and survival in a bellicose conflict that shut down military dictatorship in Argentina. In what follows I shall examine how this plays out in *Iluminados por el fuego* [Illuminated by Fire], one of the best-known testimonies of the Malvinas–Falklands War.

Laughter, fraternity and imagination in *Iluminados por el fuego*

> La risa aparece en muchos de los relatos y confirma la persistencia, la tozudez de lo humano para protegerse y subsistir (Calveiro, 1998, p. 23).
>
> [Laughter appears in many of the narrations and confirms the persistence, the stubbornness of what is human in order to protect oneself so as to be able to survive. [...] Work, play and laughter were the ways in which the threatened subject defended herself.]
>
> Given the absence of the deadly wind and lying furtively under the sun, it became possible to forget, to think about something else. [...] One could tell oneself that after the roll call we had before us, just as every Sunday, a few hours of life left: a substantial portion of time that would not belong to the SS. One could close one's eyes under the sun, imagining how to fill up that available time, that weekly miracle. There was not a lot to choose from, as limits were evidently strict. [...] Although with a very narrow

---

11 Calveiro considers that suicide, hallucination that borders on madness, literal escape or deception are all legitimate mechanisms for escaping total power (1998). These options are present in several moments and repeated continuously in this book.

margin, it was possible to choose something exceptional, exclusive to
Sunday afternoons, which was real. For example, there was the possibility
of deciding to nap [...] or of exchanging signals, a few words, news from
the world, fraternal gestures, a smile, a *machorka* butt, fragments of poems
(Semprún, 2001, 16–17).

El humor era el único antídoto contra el miedo (Esteban, 2004, p. 34).

[Humour was the only antidote against fear.]

As is evident, thus far I have been interested in highlighting, from the point of view of bio-politics, the inextricability of the Argentine military dictatorship from the Malvinas–Falkland Islands War that ended it. As I have pointed out, the similarities between the procedures of extermination, silencing and the long subsequent mourning – not in vain were the military officials the same and the Malvinas–Falklands War was an exercise in state violence that remains unpunished, and the war is either the corollary or the end of the disappearances and systemic torture in Argentina. Moreover, thoughtlessness towards and the abandonment of the disappeared, survivors and their families had been neglected until recently from legal and also socio-political and ethical perspectives. This abandonment is identical to that suffered by the victims of war who lost their lives and to the ex-combatants who survived – or 'overdied', as former combatant Caso Rosendi put it in poetic and Gelmanian terms in 2009.[12] Bio-political techniques towards what Calveiro calls the 'threatened subject' are the same: 'But were we not / Were we not born in the country / Where electric shock devices / Were placed over pregnant bellies?' (Caso Rosendi, 2009, p. 39). Life was not lost in all cases in concentration camps or in the Malvinas–Falklands, but that *remnant* which stays is often an ambiguous voiceless *remnant* which borders on suicide and madness, which carries a trauma which it is almost impossible to leave behind. In that sense, survivors had the privilege of catching a glimpse of the 'human', that hidden goodness mentioned by Levi or Semprún which emerges in the midst of pain, hunger and fear – be it in the form of care, fraternity or imagination – boldly resisting, thanks to that ethical fortune, the de-humanising and de-subjectivising strategies of bio-power.[13]

For Todorov, dignity 'does not mean anything other than an individual's capacity to maintain himself as a subject with will. This simple fact keeps him at the heart of the human species' (Todorov, 1997, p. 24). The 'threatened

12 'We have come to learn this / We who have overdied / We know very well that behind silence / Comes another, atoning silence / It will always be like that' ('Después del horror' [After the Horror], in Caso Rosendi, 2009, p. 105).

13 'Everyday life, friendships forged before the imminence of death are not arbitrary, transcendental choices and the possibility of laughter, even under such conditions, the impressions left by a countryside and an inhospitable landscape, beautiful and yet transformed by war, just like when the Sea Harriers discharge their bombs from the sky, or when the remains of bleeding seagulls are mixed up with a crushed Pucará' (Mesa Gancedo, 2009, p. 12).

subject' may voluntarily choose, for example, laughter as a means to escape the most adverse conditions. Humour brings about illusion, energy and optimism – sometimes bleeding mockery of the other oppressor – in the midst of death; it enables the welding of a strengthening and protecting shield against the victimiser. Many of the survivors' testimonies gathered by Pilar Calveiro attest to this; humour is also continuously present in narratives about the Malvinas–Falklands War: 'Happily without a worry / I trotted towards the trench / The helmet was dancing / A fox-trot above my head' (Caso Rosendi, 2009, p. 49). When one reads the testimonies, it is surprising how life is always stronger than death: 'Because most of the dead in the concentration camps [...] died of exhaustion, of the sudden impossibility of overcoming an increased tiredness of living, they died from dejection, from the slow destruction of all their energy and reserves of hope' (Semprún, 2001, p. 157).

Laughter is closely tied to vitality and intelligence and is thus one of the antidotes against dejection, loss of hope, standardisation and the extermination of the subject's spirits; it is a line of flight to resist horror and violence inscribed in the body; and, finally, it helps to retain life and individuality. It is one of the will's most important resources, in order not to become de-subjectified or to die.

Besides 'dignity', within which I have highlighted laughter as one of the most efficient ways to show the will to live, Todorov mentions a second everyday virtue: 'care'. 'Care' is notably different from 'solidarity' because 'care' is not practised within a group, nor is it a communal act but rather a gesture of voluntary love or empathy towards another individual, towards a loved one, what I have designated the 'ethics of fortune'. The other is thus remembered by its remnants of goodness:

> So the secret of philosophy may not be to know oneself, nor to know where one is going; not to dream oneself, but to dream what others dream; not to believe oneself, but rather to believe in those who do believe. [...] How much more human to place one's fate, one's desire and one's will in the hands of someone else. The result? A circulation of responsibility, a declination of wills, and a continual transferring of forms (Baudrillard, 1993, pp. 164–5).

However, following Semprún, and re-echoing Lévinas, I prefer to use the term 'fraternity' as opposed to 'care' because its semantics feel more luminous, affective and balanced, in the sense that such a gesture may always be reciprocal: 'Il est banal de dire que nous n'existons jamais au singulier. Nous sommes entourés d'êtres et de choses avec lesquels nous entretenons des relations. Par la vue, par le toucher, par la sympathie, par le travail en commun, nous sommes avec les autres. Toutes ces relations sont transitives. Je touche un objet, je vois l'autre, mais je ne suis pas l'autre' (Lévinas, 2001, p. 21).

The last of Todorov's 'everyday virtues' is what he calls 'activities of the spirit' and is related to fleeing by means of the imagination, dreaming, knowledge or aesthetic experience (this is reflected accurately in the quotation from Semprún at the beginning of this section). To sum up: in order to survive bare life, the extreme experience, Todorov sketches an ethics of the I with the I, of the I with the you, and of the I with the them.

The soldier Edgardo Esteban's testimony entitled *Iluminados por el fuego. Confesiones de un soldado que combatió en Malvinas* [*Illuminated by fire. Confessions of a soldier who fought the Malvinas–Falkland Islands War*] was first published in 1993 and was filmed by Tristan Bauer in 2005. Both works contributed to making visible the neglect and forgetfulness to which the combatants in the Malvinas–Falkland Islands War had been subjected. Beyond problematic ideological, textual and epic interpretations of the text that render this subject matter extremely delicate due to concessions bestowed on historical and nationalist (especially the latter) conceptions of the Islands within such interpretations, I am interested in highlighting the function that laughter, fraternity and imagination fulfil as forms of resistance. In this regard, Esteban's testimony offers innumerable paradigmatic examples.

Laughter

Humour, that release of tension by means of laughter, joke, play or song, appears in various forms in Esteban's narrative in various instances. For the reader, it feels anticlimactic, as I find myself before a scene, in the midst of the urgency of a war conflict, in which a radio is either broken or transmits false news; and yet a ludic atmosphere predominates that relaxes, releases, relieves for an instant:

> We were absolutely almost all turned on. Each played his part and those unaware (or who perhaps did not dare to know) listened uninterruptedly or accompanied the rest with their palms or by banging jars with knives and forks in a disorderly way. We were happy and no one would hamper our happiness. […]
>
> – *Che, che*, stop! – Interrupted Sergio, who enjoyed neither singing nor listening to others sing. Cut out your Charly García; help fix this radio so we can listen to something from Buenos Aires. […]
>
> – I would like to know what is said about us prisoners in Buenos Aires. Do you understand me, you blockhead? Or do you think that Charly García's songs will save me? (Esteban, 2004, p. 121).[14]

Another humorous instance, in this case scatological, appears when Esteban describes recovering a piece of dirty underwear which another soldier had stolen from him during the war. The theft also supposes recovering dignity

---

14 In the same vein, there is Caso Rosendi's poem 'Moment': 'Lying on a great rock / We drink scotch ale / I have no idea where he got it / Soldier Villanueva / It is dusk and the only radio / In the Islands is playing *Let it be* / We drink and laugh /because while on the continent / The only thing exploding is national rock / And Charly asks that Buenos Aires not be bombarded / Here the military plays the Beatles!' (2009, p. 29).

– and identity – which are implicit in the care of the self, through hygiene. Moreover, the tone in which the anecdote is told again vindicates a certain human background, smiling in the middle of hardship, in the midst of showers that are compared to Nazi torture chambers:

> I went inside the shower, I barely washed myself and I was the first one out to get dressed. 'Hey, soldier. You are the dirtiest of all', he told me, when he noticed how fast I had finished washing up. Then he began to goof around and I did the same and started examining our mates' underwear. The best I could find was a completely soiled pair. They were shat, but healthily; there were others that were so clean that they had huge holes in them, or were unravelled. I opted for the dirty pair and I put them on. [...]
>
> We both laughed at our deed while staring at those showers that were not showers. They seemed like Nazi torture chambers (Esteban, 2004, p. 74).[15]

Indeed, even in the most tragic circumstances human beings are capable of smiling, laughing, especially in fraternity. In her essay, Calveiro recovers the voice of Geuna, a tortured woman from one of the concentration camps during the dictatorship. Geuna is absolutely astonished by her own resilience, by her own unknown, intimate capacity to oppose mechanical violence and horror with laughter. I find her words especially revealing in this regard:

> Geuna says: '[...] The human capacity to recover is absolutely astounding. Shaking with fear, waiting for a bus that may take you to your death, and yet laughing. [...] As we laughed on Christmas Day, or when the Boca Juniors won the metropolitan championship: these were instances in which life would sneak inside La Perla through a neglected crack and then transform the concentration camp into an ephemeral, precise, instantaneous party. Because life is always much more powerful than death. Laughter is one of the most efficient means of resistance man has because it reaffirms life in a situation in which men are expected to surrender themselves to death without any struggle (Calveiro, 2004, p. 116).

Of course, this capacity to recover is, up to a certain point, willed by the threatened subject and yet this attitude appears more often than we expect it or are able to admit – perhaps we feel that a certain solemnity is a more politically correct attitude in the face of evil and yet perhaps it is less effective. In that sense, canonical works about the Malvinas–Falklands such as Fogwill's *Los pichiciegos* [*The Armadillos*] (1983) or Carlos Gamerro's *Las islas* [*The Islands*] (1998) and, more recently, Federico Lorenz's *Montoneros o la ballena blanca*

---

15 Examples of scatological humour are innumerable in this testimony. Let us look at another one: 'We have not won the war, but we shat over the whole island [...] Although on second thoughts – Sergio went on – we Argentinians are such *forros* [ass holes] that we fertilised the island so that they can take advantage of it. Well, if this were the case I hope that they at least invite us to come on vacation. – 'On vacation?', I asked him. – I am never coming back even if they give me the ticket and the lodgings for free, even if they brought a British blonde for me to keep me company at night' (Esteban, 2004, p. 72).

[*Montoneros or the White Whale*] (2012) operate as meta-fictions that carry out the humorous critical 'historicisation of spectacle' of the Malvinas–Falklands War by means of pastiche, parody and laughter, which in many cases border on black humour, the absurd and delirious. The narratives constitute *montonero* counteroffensives narrated with a touch of humour: *Montoneros o la ballena blanca*; conversational joking from inside the *pichicera* [a kind of subterranean cave] – *Los pichiciegos*; fantastic science-fiction narratives grounded on historical facts –*Las islas*. These three novels, along with Rodrigo Fresán's two splendid short stories 'La soberanía nacional' [National sovereignty] and 'El aprendiz de brujo' [The witch apprentice] which are included in his *Historia argentina* [*Argentinian History*] (1992), collections of poems such as *Soldados* (2009) by Caso Rosendi and other testimonies such as Esteban's or even *Historia de los años sin piel* [*History of the Skinless Years*] (2010) by veteran García Quiroga – the analysis of which I leave for another essay – show laughter as a survival strategy. In fact, all literary genres may use humour; and they do so in order to influence the maintenance of dignity, to survive and to enable the narration of the experience afterwards.

But to return to *Iluminados por el fuego* [*Illuminated by Fire*], there is another eloquent episode when, just as the war has come to an end, soldiers enthusiastically begin a soccer game as if nothing had happened. The two teams reproduce and rewrite the conflict they have just lost with humour and agree on two ideas: on the one hand, defeat has not eliminated the nationalist impulse although it has become demystified and degraded: having been defeated only reaffirms the idea that also within a democracy we live in a permanent state of exception (Esteban, 2004, p. 70). On the other hand, the first person, that is, the soldier Esteban, humorously affirms when offered Kelpers'[16] food scraps while the others are playing soccer: 'Let's see if I could still die poisoned, just now when I have saved myself from the Gurkhas' (Esteban, 2004, p. 71).

Thus, notions and concepts that are allegedly straight, solemn and indisputable, such as 'national identity', 'life' or 'sovereignty', or the idea that it is legitimate to occupy the Islands, are questioned and deeply degraded and exaggerated through parody, albeit temporarily, This occurs in *Iluminados por el fuego* [*Illuminated by fire*] when the author, in a final twist in his text, affirms that the Islands will one day be Argentine again. When fear, cold, hunger and the pain undergone are sieved through laughter, their sense changes and they thus acquire a new dimension. Laughter is a means of resistance. In short, laughter is a demystifying tool – nuanced towards either parody or irony – which questions the establishment and emancipates. In that sense, laughter is revolutionary: 'We had not yet completely lined up when Lieutenant-Colonel Quevedo showed up, followed by the big guns; and without ceremony told us about the surrender. [...] We kept on fucking around and making our usual

---

16 'Kelper' is the name given to people from the Malvinas–Falkland Islands.

jokes as if nothing had happened, as if not wanting to acknowledge that truth, that sad truth' (Esteban, 2004, p. 58).

Fraternity

With regards to fraternity there is also much to say about *Iluminados por el fuego* [*Illuminated by Fire*]. Julieta Vitullo has written an indispensable work about fictional representations of the Malvinas–Falklands War;[17] and in a chapter in this volume[18] she mentions two figures or symbolic representations from the Malvinas–Falkland Islands War: the cowardly commander and the soldier who dies in the arms of his fellow soldier: that is, the cruel officer who abuses his subalterns and the loyal comrade who resists, embraces and accompanies the *other* in his death. The validation of that fraternity or comradeship, that humanity beyond the supposed heroism inherent in the gesture or in the idealisation with which memory adorns the gesture – such validation ends up being inevitable, in the same way arrogance, fear and cruelty are validated. The two faces of the human show themselves in extreme circumstances.

In that regard, we must consider the unity and solidarity demonstrated by the main characters in *Iluminados por el fuego* in the face of the aberrations and perverse military authorities. Second Lieutenant Gilbert humiliates them and shows an extreme degree of inhumanity, arrogance towards his subalterns. Let us remember that the officers who governed Argentina during the dictatorship were the same as those who led the Malvinas–Falklands War; and thus they translated the tactics they had used in the concentration camps and other counter-insurgent techniques to the war, but with the same soldiers: there are innumerable ex-combatant testimonies that narrate torture practices such as *estaqueamiento* and other humiliation by high-ranking officers during the war. Before bio-political control of the body and the spirit, the means to resist can be empathy, unity, fraternal friendship, beyond voluntary maintenance of one's own dignity:

> – You are piece of crap, a coward, piece of shit of a soldier and of a person. Guys like you ought to be executed. Who do you think you are to oppose my orders, you rotten soldier? You are junk and were always useless; you should have been blown away by the English. […] It was very ugly to confirm that they ignored all that and that they were capable of forcing me to risk my own life just for a few cassettes, a holster, a helmet and a recorder for them. That is when I noticed where their values were. […] They kept on insulting me in front my mates, while I ran away, humiliated. But deep inside I felt triumphant because I had dared to speak back to them as if I was their equal; it was them who had lost. They had displayed all their misery and insensibility […] even the soldiers were

17 *Islas imaginadas. La Guerra de Malvinas en la literatura y cine argentinos* [*Imagined islands. The Malvinas/Falkland Islands War in Argentinian literature and film*] (2012).

18 See J. Vitullo, 'The Malvinas journey: harsh landscapes, rough writing, raw footage', in this volume.

surprised by what was going on. Luckily, I ran into Sergio Sivoldi: he was gathering a group of soldiers who were getting ready to withdraw. There were about fifteen. – Come, come, stay here – Sergio advised. – If you are able to flee them, they will send you with us (Esteban, 2004, pp. 25–6).[19]

Another representative moment of mutual help, of that capacity to place oneself before the other and resist, takes place, like an explosion and instinctively, in the midst of battle:

> Two soldiers were bringing a fellow who had been wounded in the leg; he was bleeding and screaming in the midst of non-stop explosions. I stood there as if I were hypnotised watching them approach. I lingered hoping to be able to help them; it would be easier if done by three persons. I saw them trot clumsily over the irregular and muddy terrain. In a second, they got hit by a projectile. Instinctively, I covered my eyes with my hands and seconds later I was not able to see anything moving in the direction where I last had seen them. My blood froze and my willingness to help someone evaporated (Esteban, 2004, p. 30).

Further in the text, there is a lucid conversation amongst soldiers that reveals that need to resist with those flashes of humanity, dignity and fraternity. Sergio, outraged by the number of soldiers fallen in combat, manifests his intention to visit every home to tell parents how their sons had died. This wish or will to leave a trace of each victim is a sublime gesture of fraternity:

> – Yes, I know, while protected under a roof, soldiers keep on dying –
> Sergio insisted – And who will tell their parents that their sons died for the Fatherland? [...] Yes, you are right – Sergio answered with the same rage.
> – But if I manage to survive this whore of a war, I will be visiting all their homes and if something happens to you, you must do the same: go tell my folks what the last moments of my life were like (Esteban, 2004, p. 32).

One of the scenes in the conflict that leaves a deep impression on the soldier Esteban has to do with ethical fortune and with chance, as his life was saved because he did not occupy his post one night. The soldier who did, Vallejos, died in his place:

> I was extremely touched by his death, I was more touched by it than by the fact that I was alive, visiting him in his definite resting place. [...] In a way, Vallejos had covered him [Burgos] with his own body; and while we were walking we were talking about his destiny: he had died the night before the last night of the war. [...] Thus I told them that Vallejos would be keeping guard instead of me and Burgos said yes, that he knew because Vallejos was angry with me. It seemed that my mate's destiny would have been to remain on the Islands. But one is never sure of those things [...] (Esteban, 2004, pp. 60–69).

19 Another fragment about friendship is the following: 'Even though we were not together all the time, because we held different posts and carried out different missions, every time we got together we had a lot of fun, in spite of the bad times every one of us was undergoing. We were friends and we were relieved to realise that all four us were still alive' (Esteban, 2004, p. 33).

With Vallejos, there was no chance of fraternity, care or solidarity. On the contrary, Esteban's life is saved by a fortuitous act of fraternity – one associated with caprice or intuition – which keeps him alive but feeling guilty, traumatised:

> And yet before a mate's fresh grave, things acquired a dimension that dragged us directly to nonsense. In a way I tried to speak to Vallejos. Would he listen to me? Intimately, I tried to ask him to forgive me for being alive; to forgive me for bothering him with all these absurd things that hung around my head and that I needed to tell him. Because at that moment, everything was getting mixed up: without a doubt, I was speaking to him, while at the same time, I was speaking with death, with life, with my own life. Through his death, I was speaking with my life. With that life of mine that I barely understood, but that was the only thing that I had to be able to keep on (Esteban, 2004, p. 62).

Fear, hunger, thirst, cold, sexual desire, pain: the soldiers in the Malvinas–Falklands are reduced to bare life and only have humour and fraternity to combat these sensations,[20] but this is not always possible: 'If in order to win a war a "bullet proof" group spirit is needed, along with great reserves of energy, I was sure that we, at this point, were lacking all of that. We had reached the limits of our strength. We had given away everything we had, and there we were, tired, broken and hungry' (Esteban, 2004, p. 34).

Imagination

In *Iluminados por el fuego* [*Illuminated by Fire*] there is a moment in which we can observe how humour in resisting the hardships of war co-exists with the third line of 'everyday virtues' that Todorov mentions: 'aesthetics' or 'spiritual activities'. This becomes evident in the passage in which the soldier Esteban reads a fragment of Carlos Castañeda's *Las enseñanzas de Don Juan* [*Don Juan's Teachings*]. In a nocturnal and cathartic communal reading, his mates display two attitudes: attentive listening to what constitutes fear and how it can help to endure violence and identity dispossession during a war – personified in Sergio the soldier, a friend of the protagonist; and, second, making fun or escaping through humour – represented by the soldier Reta. Let us look at both positions as captured in this extract:

> Since I got here, I had been thinking about a written piece of paper I had in my bag. I did not want to fall asleep without having read it first and I told Sergio about it. [...]
>
> I brought it here because it is very good. Do you understand? – I tell him.
>
> – Yes, yes. Now I understand. All right, keep going – he tells me. – What was that thing about fear? Read that thing about fear, something that I can spare. [...]

---

20 'Climbing hills up and down / until reaching soldier Sañisky / He embraced him / Put between his hands / My Marlboro packet / *This is yours* – he told him – / *This is all I have* / And we committed ourselves to smoking' ('Brindis' [Toast], in Caso Rosendi, 2009, p. 103).

We all fell silent. There were other soldiers that came by to listen. I felt a bit ridiculous, but also proud. It was the first time that I was able to share with someone those typed pages that had helped me so much, when I was not yet a soldier. [...]

– What I need is a young girl. A young girl! – They screamed while others laughed and another one said: Tomorrow I'll get you a penguin to heat up your bed.

But I kept on reading. [...] 'Man feels that nothing is hidden. And this is how he has found his second enemy: Clarity! Mental clarity, so hard to obtain, disperses fear, but it is also blind.'

– That, that – Reta interrupted again – some clarity is what is lacking here because this stupid lantern is not bright enough. Don't you think, Esteban? (Esteban, 2004, pp. 108–11).

Todorov's 'spiritual activities' can be evasion or flight through literature or art, also observed clearly in Semprún, as according to Calveiro memorising Federico Gárcia Lorca's *Romancero gitano* [*The Gypsy Ballad*] poems allowed him to go beyond the camps in his mind through reading and hallucination. Therefore, imagination may be erected and it can constitute, without the aid of aesthetics, a means of holding on: memories become an inexhaustible resource with which to face annihilation and the loss of subjectivity: 'The watches were of course taken in pairs, but that night, due to a tactical issue, they left me to my own devices; so I stayed again with my cold, with my fear, but also with my memories, which never abandoned me: they could accompany me ceaselessly to any possible end' (Esteban, 2004, p. 63).[21]

These strategies, although neither always successful nor fruitful nor possible – it is not only the will that appropriate them, as we have seen – are definitely indispensable lines of flight in the face of the dimensions of absolute power: both in concentration camps during the Argentine military dictatorship and in the Malvinas–Falklands War. Thus, in all of those world narratives, pain, violence and forgetting are accompanied by humour, fraternity and dreaming. They constitute those everyday dichotomies, that of life and death; and in the last instance, they are a way of vindicating the needs of a multi-focal, polyhedral, complex, precarious and fragile memory. Together, they make up unexpected 'everyday virtues' in the remnants of beauty in the midst of the inhospitable, cruel and arbitrary embedded in human horror.

---

21 The poem by Caso Rosendi whose title corresponds to the Gaelic etymology of Malvinas–Falklands – 'Maol-Mhin' – is along these lines, as it posits beauty as a flight from death: 'It was terribly beautiful / Looking in the middle of bombardment / The softness with which they fell / The snowflakes' (Caso Rosendi, 2009, p. 47).

References

Adorno, T. (1980) [1951] *Minima moralia. Réflexions sur la vie mutilée* (Paris: Payot).

— (1951) *Minima moralia. Reflections from Damaged Life* (London: Verso).

Agamben, G. (1998) *Homo Sacer: Sovereign Power and Bare Life*, trans. by Daniel Heller-Roazen (Stanford: Stanford University Press); orig. published as *Homo sacer: Il potere sovrano et la nuda vita* (Collana: Einaudi).

— (1995) *Homo sacer. Il potere sovrano e la nuda vita* (Torino: Einaudi).

— (1998) *Quel che resta di Auschwitz. L'archivio e il testimone. Homo sacer III* (Torino: Einaudi).

Arendt, H. (1970) *On Violence* (New York: Harcourt).

— (2012) *Sobre la violencia* (Madrid: Alianza).

— (1963) *Eichmann in Jerusalem. A report on the Banality of Evil* (New York: Viking Press).

Benjamin, W. (2005) *Tesis sobre la filosofía de la historia y otros fragmentos* (México: Contrahistorias).

Benjamin, Walter, *Illuminations* [online translation by Dennis Richmond, 200]1

Bolaño, R. (2000) *Nocturno de Chile* (Barcelona: Anagrama).

Calveiro, P. (2004) [1998] *Poder y desaparición: los campos de concentración en Argentina* (Buenos Aires: Colihue).

Caso Rosendi, G. (2009) *Soldados* (Buenos Aires: Ministerio de Educación de la Nación).

Deleuze, G. and F. Guattari (2003) *A Thousand Plateaus. Capitalism and Schizophrenia*, trans. by B. Massumi (Minneapolis: The University of Minnesota Press]).

— (2006) *Mil mesetas. Capitalismo y esquizofrenia*, trans. by J. Pérez Vázquez (Valencia: Pretextos).

Drake, P. and E. Silva (eds.) (1986) *Elections and Democratization in Latin America, 1980–85* (San Diego: University of California Press).

Esteban, E. (2004) [1993] *Iluminados por el fuego. Confesiones de un soldado que combatió en Malvinas* (Buenos Aires: Biblos).

Fogwill, R. (2008) 'El doctor Cormillot y la gran máquina de adelgazar conciencias', in *Los libros de la guerra* (Buenos Aires: Mansalva), pp. 57–62.

Foucault, M. (1978) *Historia de la sexualidad*, vol. 1, *La voluntad del saber*, trans. by Ulises Guiñazú (México: Siglo XXI).

Fresán, R. (1992) 'El aprendiz de brujo', in *Historia argentina* (Buenos Aires: Planeta), pp. 11–33.

— (1992) 'La soberanía nacional', in *Historia argentina* (Buenos Aires: Planeta), pp. 83–93.

Fogwill, Rodolfo (2010 [1983]) *Los pichiciegos* (Buenos Aires: El Ateneo, 2010 edn.: Cáceres: Periférica).

Gamerro, Carlos (2007) *Las islas* (Buenos Aires: Norma).

García Quiroga, D. (2010) *Historiade los años sin piel* (Buenos Aires: De los cuatro vientos).

Kant, I. (1969) *La religión dentro de los límites de la mera razón* (Madrid: Alianza) [original version: *Die Religion innerhalb der Grenzen der bloßen Vernunft* (1793)]

Levi, P. (1959) *If This Is A Man* (New York: Orion Press).

Lévinas, E. (2001) *Le temps et l'autre* (Paris: PUF).

— (1947) *Se questo è un uomo* (Torino: Francesco de Silva).

Lévinas, E. (2002) Éthique et infini. Dialogues avec Philippe Nemo (Paris: Fayard).

Mèlich, J.C. (1998) *Totalitarismo y fecundida. La filosofía frente a Auschwitz* (Barcelona: Anthropos).

Mira Delli-Zotti, G. (2009) 'Genealogía de la violencia en la Argentina de los años 70', *Historia Actual Online*, 20: 49–59.

Peris Blanes, J. (2005) *La imposible voz. Memoria y representación de los campos de concentración en Chile: la posición del testigo* (Santiago de Chile: Cuarto Propio).

Reyes Mate, M. (2012) 'Memoria de la barbarie y construcción del futuro', *Nuestra memoria. Janusz Korczak*, año XVIII (36): 101–13.

Sarlo, S. (2005) *Tiempo pasado. Cultura de la memoria y giro subjetivo: una discusión* (Buenos Aires: Siglo XXI).

Semprún, J. (1981) [1963] *El largo viaje* (Barcelona: Seix Barral).

— (2001) *Viviré con su nombre, morirá con el mío* (Barcelona: Tusquets).

Semprún, J. and E. Wiesel (1995) *Se taire est impossible* (Paris: Arte Editions).

— (1994) *L'écriture ou la vie* (Paris: Gallimard).

Sloterdijk, Peter, 'Rules for the Human Zoo: a response to the *Letter on Humanism*', *Environment and Planning D: Society and Space* 2009: 27, pp. 12–28.

Todorov, T. (1996) *Facing the Extreme: Moral Life in the Concentration Camps* (New York: Holt).

— (1991) *Face à l'extrême* (Paris: Seuil).

— (2004) *Les abus de la mémoire* (Paris: Arléa).

Valdés, Hernán (1974) *Tejas verdes. Diario de un campo de concentración en Chile* (Barcelona: Ariel)

Verbistky, H. (2002) *Malvinas. La última batalla de la Tercera Guerra Mundial* (Buenos Aires: Editorial Sudamericana).

Vitullo, J. (2012) *Islas imaginadas. La Guerra de Malvinas en la literatura y el cine argentinos* (Buenos Aires: Corregidor).

2. Exile, the Malvinas War and human rights*

Silvina Jensen

In *Historia reciente: Perspectivas y desafíos de un campo en construcción*, Marina Franco and Florencia Levín signal one of the most pertinent challenges for researchers working on the Malvinas today: the need to develop conceptual precision (2007, p. 58). Through precision, they argue, we might free our analytical categories from both their status as value judgements and from the powerful connotations generated by the protagonists of a recent conflict-filled past, in the hope that research might avoid reproducing the political battles that these categories entail.

Uniting the Malvinas and human rights as a means of delving into the question of exile is far from an obvious enterprise, however. Prior to April 1982, or rather before 1 May of that year, the symbolic connotations of the Malvinas were recognisable to all Argentines – including those who lived in other countries as a result of the political violence between 1974 and 1983. The Islands were a geographical territory upon which were projected nationalist feelings and national values; and the Malvinas therefore also represented a 'patriotic cause', the claim to a land snatched from national sovereignty more than a century ago – a fact which stirred up, to differing degrees, the patriotic feelings of civil society and the military. The Islands were also a 'symbol' through which 'los argentinos sintetizaban diversos sentidos, a menudo opuestos, de su argentinidad' [Argentines synthesised different, and often opposing, definitions of their 'Argentineness'] (Guber, 2001).[1] After the 'recovery' of the Islands on 2 April, resulting in an international armed conflict, the Malvinas became associated with the war, a war whose origin lay in the landing on the South Georgia Islands ordered by the third military *junta* (composed of Leopoldo F. Galtieri, Isaac Anaya and Basilio Lami Dozo). Only days before the landing, the *junta* had suppressed a mass demonstration called by the CGT (General

---

* The interviews used in this article are part of the field work of the author's doctoral thesis, 'Suspendidos de la historia/Exiliados de la memoria: El caso de los argentinos desterrados en Cataluña (1976–)' (Universidad Autónoma de Barcelona, 2004). Available at http://www.tdx.cesca.es/TDX-1024105-231137 (ISBN B-6634-2005/84-689-0953-X). Interviewees' real names are not used, in order to protect their anonymity.

1 See also Lorenz (2006) and Palermo (2007).

S. Jensen, 'Exile, the Malvinas War and human rights', in G. Mira and F. Pedrosa (eds.), *Revisiting the Falklands–Malvinas Question: Transnational and Interdisciplinary Perspectives* (London: University of London Press, 2020), pp. 53–74. License: CC-BY-NC-ND 4.0.

Confederation of Labour) under the slogan 'Bread, Peace and Work': a violent repression of civil society.

These (distinct yet overlapping) layers of meaning surrounding the Malvinas, layers that became increasingly confused throughout the hostilities and were often impossible to consider together without creating contradictions, played a central role in the debates of those in exile in Mexico, Spain and France.

The notion of human rights is no more easily definable, particularly in terms of its conception in the 1970s and 1980s. It is true that, in the period of the terrorist state in Argentina, the denunciation of the dictatorship centred on ideas drawn from discourses of human rights, understood to mean the defence of life, liberty and physical integrity. It would not be misleading to claim, alongside protagonists of the diaspora such as Jorge Bernetti and Mempo Giardinelli (2003), or researchers studying the exiled communities such as Marina Franco (2008) and Pablo Yankelevich (2002), that the fight for human rights was the fundamental cause of the exile communities from Sweden to Brazil and from Mexico to Australia. However, the Argentine diaspora had to undergo a long process in order to form this identity of human rights campaigners, following the collapse of the revolutionary frameworks to which many of those in exile had subscribed. As a result, over the course of almost eight years of exile, the same questions were debated in the geographically disparate exile communities: who were human rights for? What was their scope? Was it the same to defend human rights within Argentina and in exile? Were human rights an absolute ethical value, a pipe dream or a philosophical abstraction; or were they in fact a historical category linked to class struggle and the particular configuration of the conflict between social groups throughout Argentine history?[2]

During the visit of the IACHR (Inter-American Commission of Human Rights)[3] to Argentina, the periodical *Criterio* (13 September 1979) had highlighted that the subject of human rights was 'polemical', 'ambiguous' and 'ambivalent'; during the Malvinas War, this ambiguity and polemic intensified among both the opposition in Argentina and in exile.

Carlos Gabetta (1983, p. 15) argues that the South Atlantic conflict represented an 'earthquake' that shook the foundations of the exile community, fracturing associations, multiplying disputes and shifting the main public focus of the diaspora towards the unmasking of the repressive nature of the military *junta*, whose thousands of victims had been killed, disappeared, taken as political prisoners or forced into exile. Taking this hypothesis as its starting point, this chapter seeks to problematise the relationship between the Malvinas War and human rights, attempting to explain to what extent Argentina's 'recovery' of the Islands interacted with the exiles' identity as human rights

---

2 A particularly in-depth analytical perspective can be found in the polemical debate between Luis Bruschtein and Héctor Schmucler published in *Controversia* (Mexico) from the end of 1979 to early 1980. For a detailed analysis see Jensen (2010).

3 Known in Spanish as the CIDH: Comisión Interamericana de Derechos Humanos.

campaigners, particularly in terms of the exiles' varying political backgrounds, strategies of resistance to the dictatorship and attitudes towards the war.

This chapter is divided into two parts. The first attempts to provide a brief overview of the positions that the political and humanitarian exile organisations adopted towards the 'recovery' and the war, attempting to highlight the ideas that dominated this hugely complex conflict. The second explores some of the debates surrounding the idea of human rights that took place in exile during the conflict between Argentina and the UK. My analysis examines how the Malvinas conflict can be considered to have been a humanitarian 'test' (Goligorsky, 1983) for the exiles, exploring some of the most stimulating polemics on the topic, including Mexico's Socialist Discussion Group (Grupo de Discusión Socialista) versus León Rozitchner (Venezuela); and, particularly, Eduardo Goligorsky versus Abel Posse and Hugo Chumbita (Spain). This section aims to analyse questions that the exiles had been debating since 1976, from the start of their fight against the dictatorship. These questions were raised each time the exiles considered the best means of garnering international solidarity, a difficult enterprise in the face of Argentina's immensely complex political map (confused by both the perplexing identities of the nation's political parties and the characteristics of Argentina's political history in the lead-up to the coup). They also came to the fore in attempts to define the public profile of the exile associations and when the exiles considered their own militant past as members of revolutionary movements.

In summary, this chapter aims to establish to what extent the Malvinas War forced the exiles to revisit subjects such as the use of violence for political aims, the justness of war, the meaning of sacrificing life and liberty, the definition of freedom and democracy, the viability of bringing the perpetrators of abuses to trial, the fight against impunity and the battle for memory. Each one of this vast array of questions drew attention to and/or created a crisis (or at least tension) within the exiles' relationship with human rights.

Exile associations and the Malvinas conflict

In describing the reactions of Argentines based in Madrid to the 'occupation' of the Malvinas, Rafael Flores[4] highlighted that between the unease, amazement and anger of some and the confidence of others, the dominant response was confusion (Flores, 1982, pp. 36–7). In Stockholm, an ex-militant of the PRT-ERP[5] in Bahía Blanca, Jaime Naifleish, identified 'ideas y sentimientos encontrados' [opposing ideas and feelings] among the expatriates, which both

4   Flores was a militant in the Resistencia Libertaria (Libertarian Resistance) and General Secretary of the Rubber Workers Union in Córdoba before the dictatorship. He was exiled in Madrid.
5   The PRT-ERP was a guerrilla group formed of factions from the Partido Revolucionario de los Trabajadores [Workers' Revolutionary Party] and the Ejército Revolucionario del Pueblo [People's Revolutionary Army].

resisted clear-cut definitions and exposed the complexity of differing positions where, days before, agreement had (erroneously) appeared to reign (Naifleisch, 1982).

Beyond the different national contexts,[6] among the organised exile groups – whether connected to a political party, working across these divides or with a humanitarian focus – three dominant positions towards the Argentine–British conflict emerged. There were those who declared themselves completely, and almost acritically, in favour of the 'recovery'; those who opposed it and even hoped that the UK would attack Buenos Aires; and the majority of those in exile, who avoided extremes and attempted to reconcile a continued denunciation of the dictatorship and the continued assertion of Argentina's claim over the Islands, with differing emphasis on the one or the other of these two factors of the equation.

The diversity of positions resulted from a large number of factors, including each person's political identity prior to exile; whether they belonged to organisations of the diaspora; their perspective on the dictatorship; their personal views on Britain and its imperialist stance; their acceptance or rejection of war as a means of resolving territorial disputes; the behaviour of the dominant political forces to which the exile was connected in their country of residence; their consideration of the political timing of the event, etc. This variety of factors and their idiosyncratic combinations resulted in a political map filled with nuances and ambiguities, revealing the acute tension experienced by the exiles between April and June of 1982 and leading many political and social commentators in the host countries to note how the Argentine communities had been 'shaken up', bringing former enemies into the same band. Marcel Niedergang, a columnist for *Le Monde*, claimed that the 'Malvinas cause' had placed the Argentine opposition, both in exile and at home, on the side of the military (Niedergang, 1982).[7] Meanwhile, the reporter in Buenos Aires for Barcelona's *La Vanguardia*, Lluís Foix, explained that the question of the Islands' 'recovery' had produced an unprecedented level of political unity among Argentines, to the point that opponents of the dictatorship not only proclaimed that '¡por primera vez me gustan las botas!' [I like [military] boots for the first time], but that 'queues of volunteers' were crowding outside the Ministry for Foreign Affairs asking to be recruited to defend the island territory. The philosopher Fernando Savater also described

---

6   For the differences between the exile communities in France, Mexico and Spain see Franco, 2008, pp. 289–312.

7   An Argentine poet exiled in Barcelona described an experience he had in *Casa Argentina*, where a fellow Argentine rose to his feet in a meeting and said: 'Mi hermano está condenado y me escribe desde la cárcel pidiendo que todos los argentinos se unan a la lucha contra Inglaterra. ¡Hay que ir de voluntarios! ¡El país lo necesita!' [My brother is being held captive and he writes to me from prison asking that all Argentines join the fight against Britain. We should all sign up! Our country needs us!] (Interview with L. L., Barcelona, 12 December 1996).

Argentina's situation as 'un enigma en estado puro' [a perfect enigma], leaving the uninitiated open-mouthed at the way that 'el honor patrio y su hermana doña dignidad nacional' [patriotic honour and his sister national dignity] could unite dictator and victim in 'un mismo espasmo de amor ante unos mendrugos de granito roídos por el Atlántico' [a spasm of passion over some scraps of granite battered by the Atlantic] (Acotto, 1982).

Whilst for the European left – and for some members of the Argentine exile[8] – this represented losing sight of who the enemy was, obfuscating the ability to identify those on the side of 'good' and 'evil' (Soto, 1982), for a large proportion of the diaspora the situation was significantly more complex. For them, clear, problem-free definitions were impossible, at least during the conflict itself. This was particularly due to Argentina's internal political situation, which many in the diaspora were describing as the 'crisis' or 'decline' of the military regime, seen as paving the way for democracy.

By way of illustration, my discussion below considers the positions of some of the most important exiles and exile associations in Sweden, France, Spain and Mexico, examining their descriptions of the enterprise launched by the *junta* on 2 May and the nuances, emphases, tensions and ambiguities in their public actions and declarations, first in relation to the 'recovery' and then during the war itself.

A revolutionary Marxist group in Paris defined Malvinas as 'la expresión absurda y criminal' [the absurd, criminal expression] of two States in deep crisis. They denied the war's status as an anti-colonial struggle for liberation, and described it as a conflict 'inventado por la dictadura, [...] usado por el imperialismo británico también en crisis' [invented by the dictatorship and exploited by the imperialist British, who are also in crisis] (*Divergencia*, 1982). Similarly, a socialist militant from the Casa Argentina a Catalunya labelled the Malvinas a 'curse', a 'caricature' and another 'trick' of the dictators who manipulated the Argentines' weakness for all things national(ist) in order to remain in power. But were the exiles in Paris and militants in Barcelona saying the same thing? Not really, or at least not fully. R. E. felt that there was 'nothing to defend': 'A mí, las Malvinas, la idea de defender las Malvinas, no me iba a hacer poner en peligro ni un solo brazo de un joven argentino' [Personally, the Malvinas, the idea of defending the Malvinas, was not going to make me put even one limb of a young Argentine at risk].[9] In contrast, Luis Alonso and Ángel Fanjul from the Paris Marxist group separated out Argentina's rights to

8   In his testimony, R. E. stated: 'Los catalanes no estaban acostumbrados a tanta versatilidad. Nadie podía comprender el apoyo popular a la toma del archipiélago, después del acto fantástico de la Plaza de Mayo de dos días antes y de la represión terrible ... los periodistas catalanes estaban como locos' [Catalans were not used to such versatility. Nobody could understand the popular support for the seizing of the archipelago after the unbelievable demonstration in the Plaza de Mayo two days before and the terrible repression. [...] The Catalan press were going crazy] (Interview, 20 January 1997).

9   Interview with R. E., Barcelona, 20 January 1997.

the Malvinas and the demagogic, opportunist manoeuvring of the dictatorship (*Divergencia*, 1982).

On the non-Peronist Left, a human rights activist from Barcelona also recognised the 'invented' nature of 'lo de Malvinas' [the Malvinas matter]. In her view, the military '[se lo] habían sacado de la manga para unir y sacar el patriotismo' [had pulled it out of their sleeve to bring people together and stir up their patriotism]. Her opposition to the 'cause' and the war was founded on its dual condition as a 'patriotic cause' or, more precisely, its jingoism and territorialism. As M. D. stated:

> Yo soy marxista y los pueblos no nos metemos en esas guerras, guerras territoriales. Yo no soy patriota. Estoy en contra de los patriotismos. Me parecen mezquinos, engañosos. Yo soy trabajadora. Tengo consciencia que soy de un grupo que ha trabajado toda la vida y que tiene que trabajar. La gente de mi familia eran todos laburantes. Y creo que las banderas de la Patria y de todo eso son las banderas de la burguesía. (Interview, 30 May 1996)

> [I am a Marxist and the people do not get involved in these wars, territorial wars. I am not a patriot. I am against patriotisms. I see them as small-minded, deceptive. I am a worker. I am conscious of being from a group that has worked all their lives and who have to work. My family were all labourers. I believe that the flags of patriotism and all that stuff are the flags of the bourgeoisie].

Although in M. D.'s case class identity determined her radical opposition to the Malvinas cause and the war, many members of the Argentine Communist Party in exile joined the Frente Antiimperialista Latinoamericano [Latin American Anti-Imperialist Front], positioning themselves in opposition to Britain's colonial machinations and in favour of the 'recovery' of the Malvinas archipelago. The divergences in opinion between different sectors of the Argentine Left permeated the dynamic of the Comisión de Familiares de Presos Políticos, Muertos y Detenidos-Desaparecidos [Commission of Relatives of Political Prisoners, Victims and Disappeared Detainees] in Barcelona, the organisation in which many militants had been working together since 1976.

In relation to the idea that the occupation of the Malvinas represented a 'fabrication', 'invention', 'trap' or 'manoeuvre', the Cordobese ex-union leader Rafael Flores, then based in Madrid, argued that the occupation of the Malvinas was not 'invented' by the military, despite its use as a tool to silence the popular movement that on 30 May had chanted that '¡se va acabar, se va acabar, la dictadura militar!' [the military dictatorship is going to end, it's going to end]. This was not a strategy that appeared out of the blue. The military academies taught officers that the Malvinas represented one of the longest-standing national military operations; and the Malvinas were, moreover, an essential component of the Argentine imaginary, actively taught from primary school (Flores, 1982, pp. 36–7).

At the same time, Luis Rodríguez wrote in *El Periódico de Catalunya* that the Malvinas were one of the 'grandes mitos nacionales' [great national myths] and that Galtieri was exploiting it in order to maintain the status quo.[10] Rodríguez claimed that, beyond the dispute with the UK over sovereignty and the economic potential of the Islands, the *junta*'s decision stemmed from the need to achieve 'una dinámica que unificara al país tras una empresa histórica y cuyo rédito sería capitalizado por las FFAA' [a dynamic that would unite the country behind a historic enterprise whose benefits could be capitalised upon by the armed forces]. In the same line of argument, but ascribing even less depth to the invasion, Eduardo Goligorsky condemned Malvinas as a 'slogan' used by the military to stimulate 'la irracionalidad atávica y la credulidad de un conglomerado humano que últimamente se mostraba escéptico y remiso a dejarse llevar por las narices' [the atavistic irrationality and the credulity of a population who had recently been sceptical and unwilling to fall into line] (Goligorsky, 1983, p. 239). A few days after the 'recovery', Goligorsky (a Radicalist exiled in Barcelona) was in Buenos Aires and stated that Argentina was engaged in an 'irredentist delusion' led by Galtieri (Goligorsky, 1983, p. 210).

In the diaspora, a significant number of voices denounced the military actions of 2 April as a desperate manoeuvre seeking to 'borrar el pasado con un sablazo' [erase the past with a swipe of the sword], bringing to light 'un problema eterno, pero siempre desactualizado, tema de pequeños conciliábulos nacionalistas y de almirantes retirados' [an eternal but outdated problem, a topic discussed in small, secretive nationalist gatherings or among retired admirals] (Bayer, 1982). But other readings also developed, including those of the Peronist Comisión Argentine des Droits d l'Homme (CADHU), the Trotskyist Centre Argentin d'Information et de Solidaritè (CAIS) and the Comisión de Solidarité des Parents des Prisionniers, Disparus et Túes en Argentine (COSOFAM) in France. These organisations recognised that the Argentine intervention was intimately bound up with the internal political problems experienced by the dictatorship, but they did not cease to support the Argentine people's 'sovereign rights' over the Islands ('En el exterior', 1982, p. 36).

In an announcement published in *Le Monde* (16 May 1982), the Argentine committees in France provided an argument with an important nuance: the only sovereignty over the Islands, or legitimate right to lay claim to their possession, rested with the Argentine people. The text's condemnations of the Royal Navy's 'aventura belicista' [warmongering enterprise], of the Argentine dictatorship and its opportunistic manoeuvre and of the behaviour of the European Economic Community[11] are mixed with defences of liberty,

10 Rodríguez (1982).
11 The EEC had placed economic sanctions on Argentina as a result of the invasion.

human rights, justice, popular sovereignty and territorial sovereignty over the archipelago, demonstrating the disorientation of the exile organisations ('En el exterior', 1982, p. 36).

This plurality of positions and multiple emphases was not restricted to differences between associations, but was found at times among people united under the same banner who disagreed on how to interpret the conflict. This was influential in determining the dynamic of each association, which depended on the difficult negotiations taking place within each one, both in terms of the possibility of reaching agreements and the ruptures that took place. An example can be found in the public declarations of the Swedish and French branches of the Association of Relatives of the Victims of Repression (COSOFAM). In Sweden, the Association declared itself opposed to the invasion, whilst in France it began by condemning the war led by the *junta*, but eventually focused on denouncing the warmongering attitude of Britain and the US and reiterating Argentina's sovereignty over the Islands (*Divergencia*, 2 July 1982).

For the exiles, it was extremely important to differentiate between the legitimacy of the Malvinas 'cause', dear to Argentine national sentiment, and its political, demagogic exploitation by the military.[12] In the same way, the exiles considered it essential not to confuse support for military intervention in the Malvinas (in some cases even endorsing the war) with a decline in the repudiation of the terrorist nature of the *junta* that had governed the country since 1976.[13] A member of the Confederación Socialista Argentina de Cataluña explained that 'una cosa era la reivindicación y otra cosa era que los militares se montaran sobre esa reivindicación para continuar en el poder' [the demand for sovereignty was one thing, but the military jumping on the back of this demand in order to remain in power was another] (Interview with C. R., Barcelona, 13 December 1996). The same interviewee explained that defending Argentina's sovereignty over the Islands and denouncing British imperialism were not the same as supporting whoever made the recovery of the Islands possible.[14] Beyond

12 From the headquarters of the *Associació d'Amics de les Nacions Unides* in Barcelona, Hugo Chumbita, a militant in Nilda Garré and Vicente Saadi's Intransigencia Peronista, outlined a distinction between the justice of the national demand and the temporary context of the government that had launched the military action (*Testimonio Latinoamericano*, 14 May/June 1982, pp. 11–16).

13 Andrés Cornelli, a representative of the PCA (Partido Comunista de la Argentina) who participated in the debates surrounding the Malvinas in Barcelona, emphasised the need to avoid confusing support for the recovery of the Islands with an abandonment of the fight to recover democracy.

14 The Madrid branch of the CSA made the same point through the words of Andrés López Acotto, one of its members. In a letter published in *El País* (6 April 1982) he stated: 'Independientemente de la opinión que cada uno tenga sobre el actual gobierno de la Argentina, de su origen, de su continuidad y de sus móviles – puntos sobre los cuales hemos

these positions, the Confederación Socialista Argentina even declared that any mention of the Malvinas problem should be preceded by a condemnation of the murderous activity of the military *junta*.

It was necessary to question the supposedly anti-imperialist nature of the action of 2 April,[15] given the military's history of both ceding and breaking up national territory (CSA – Cataluña Branch. Internal document, 1982).

The Argentine socialists in Mexico summarised their position in a dual demand: '¡Por la soberanía argentina en las Malvinas! ¡Por la soberanía popular en Argentina!' [For Argentine sovereignty in the Malvinas! For popular sovereignty in Argentina!]. The Argentine socialists declared that the conflict could not be read exclusively through the prism of the internal politics of the warring nations. This went against simplistic interpretations that identified support for the Malvinas cause with a pardoning of the dictatorship, arguing instead that the military dictatorship was no less a dictatorship for merely having occupied the Malvinas.[16]

Among those who recognised Argentina's rights over the Malvinas, some favoured a peaceful solution through diplomatic routes whilst others, in light of the fact that the Islands had been seized, ended up supporting the war. In the latter group, some even came to consider it a 'just war', the response to an initial violent act of colonial 'theft' by Britain (which had 'usurped' part of

---

hecho pública la nuestra, en tanto claros opositores al mismo – hay un hecho muy claro que no puede ni debe tergiversarse: Las islas Malvinas han sido, son y serán argentinas' [Irrespective of the opinion that we each hold of the current Argentine government and its origin, continuity and motives – upon which we have made public our position of opposition – there is a clear fact that cannot and should not be distorted: the Malvinas Islands have been, are and will be Argentine] (*Resumen de Actualidad Argentina*, 55, 1982).

15 An Argentine exiled in Madrid, Roberto Páez, denounced the apparent anti-imperialist nature of the military occupation of the Falklands–Malvinas as false: 'La dictadura no defendió intereses nacionales, sino eventuales negociados de sus personeros con firmas multinacionales, así como un esquema geoestratégico en el que se reservaba cierto protagonismo que no excluía la ingerencia imperialista norteamericana' [The dictatorship did not defend national interests, but possible deals between their officials and multinationals, as well as a geo-strategic vision in which their protagonism did not exclude the imperialist interference of the US] ('La ocupación y la democracia', *Resumen de la Actualidad Argentina*, 75, November 1982, pp. 24–6).

16 *Grupo de Discusión Socialista*, 'Por la soberanía argentina en las Malvinas. Por la soberanía popular en Argentina' (*Visión socialista*, 1982).

Argentina's territory in 1833),[17] an 'excessive' but 'legitimate' defence,[18] or an anti-imperialist war of national liberation similar to the cause of third-world colonies.

Although the Malvinas cause has a long political history and was a popular demand prior to the act of military occupation, it was crucial to evaluate the political circumstances of the invasion in order to denounce the *junta*'s 'opportunism';[19] to define the impact of the occupation on the 'health' of the government; and/or not to miss the opportunity of what some perceived as an imminent return to democracy which would include their own return to the country.[20] As Héctor Borrat explained, those who supported the 'recovery'

17 The Grupo de Discusión Socialista declared in 'Por la soberanía' that: 'La aventura de la *Junta* Militar se corresponde con una posición inglesa anterior, no por disimulada menos violenta. Nos referimos a la prolongada e irritante renuncia de Gran Bretaña a cumplir una resolución de las Naciones Unidas que tendía a dar solución pacífica al conflicto en torno a la soberanía de las Malvinas. Esta disputa había tenido a su vez un comienzo violento que los británicos gustan olvidar o justificar con datos históricos muy poco convincentes. En 1833, una corbeta inglesa despojó por la fuerza a los argentinos de las islas que habían heredado como resultado de su independencia del dominio español' [The military *junta*'s operation corresponds to a position previously sustained by Britain and is no less violent for being masked. We refer to Britain's prolonged, infuriating refusal to fulfil a United Nations resolution that sought to provide a peaceful solution to the conflict over the sovereignty of the Malvinas. This dispute had, in turn, begun with violence, which the British prefer to forget or justify with rather unconvincing historical facts. In 1833, a British corvette used force to strip Argentines of the Islands they had inherited as a result of their independence from Spanish control] (Rozitchner, 2005, pp. 147–8). This line of argument was common among the revolutionary militants of the 1960s and 1970s in debates over who had 'thrown the first stone' in Argentine politics.

18 This was the position of the Partido Intransigente member Eduardo Andriotti Rondanin, who participated in the round-table discussion on the Malvinas organised by the Centro de Cultura Popular in Barcelona on 28 April, a few days before fighting began (*Testimonio Latinoamericano*, 14 (May/June 1982, pp. 11–16).

19 Separating the recognition that Argentina was experiencing a dictatorship from the recognition that the military had fulfilled a long-standing national, popular desire was not easy, particularly as no-one could predict the impact that the occupation would have on the internal political situation. The Madrid-based Agrupación Eva Perón stated that: 'Con la recuperación de Malvinas, Georgias y Sandwichs del Sur para el patrimonio nacional, la Junta militar que hoy gobierno la Argentina ha producido un acontecimiento histórico cuyas consecuencias políticas, económicas y militares exceden la intencionalidad de los autores al tomar esa decisión' [With the recovery of the Malvinas, South Georgia and South Sandwich Islands, the military *junta* currently ruling Argentina has created a historical event whose political, economic and military consequences exceed the intentions of those who took this decision].

20 The disputes surrounding the causal link between the 'recovery' of the Islands, the outbreak of the Argentine–British conflict and the continuation/end of the dictatorship were very heated. In response to some Peronist groups in Catalonia who trusted in the surge which the popular mobilisation for democracy in Argentina had achieved in the context of the invasion, the Grupo de Exiliados de Barcelona denounced the opportunism of those who had come out in favour of the 'Malvinas cause' without reflecting on who had brought about the 'recovery' of the Islands. To this end, they stated: 'Los principales perjudicados inmediatos de esta aventura serán las masas trabajadoras. Haya o no haya guerra. Si hay guerra, el desangre económico y humano. Si no hay guerra, la bancarrota nacional por el bloqueo económico y el ahogo

of the archipelago assumed that, regardless of the outcome of the war, the consequence at a national level would be the restitution of democratic rule. If Argentina suffered military defeat, the *junta*'s regime would be discredited, hastening its downfall. If, however, Argentina retained sovereignty over the recovered national territory, the victory would not belong solely to the regime; and in any case the conflict would have been important in bringing about the mobilisation of parties, unions and movements (Borrat, 1982).

Debating human rights: The Malvinas invasion as a humanitarian test

It is no easy task to explain the interpellation of the question of human rights in the Argentine–British conflict over the Malvinas. The following pages will explore what it meant for the exiles to live with what Flores (1982) termed the 'desgraciada paradoja' (deplorable paradox) of the fact that the military who were perpetrating genocide were also responsible for 'recovering' the Malvinas, and to what extent this 'paradox' placed their human rights activism in crisis.

As outlined above, one of the dilemmas experienced by the exiles between April and June 1982 was how to wrestle 'ownership' of the Malvinas question from the military, whilst attempting not to distance themselves too greatly from what they perceived as an action that had galvanised popular support in Argentina. In this context, the exiles found themselves confronting a double challenge: contesting their characterisation by the military – also deeply entrenched in civil society – as 'subversives', 'traitors' and 'deceivers'; and reinforcing their status as human rights activists, even though stressing their anti-dictatorship fight risked further alienating parts of the country beyond Buenos Aires. In fact, as the philosopher Horacio González noted from his exile in São Paulo, during the war Galtieri had employed the familiar strategy of dismissing condemnations of human rights violations, but had added the spin of declaring them to be another 'cunning trick' by the British Foreign Office or war 'propaganda' from the heart of imperialism that was disseminated by 'anti-Argentine' elements abroad (González, 1982). We must not forget that there were groups in exile, such as the Movimiento contra la guerra en el Atlántico Sur in Barcelona, which did not hesitate to condemn some of the 'Malvinas heroes', including the captain Alfredo Astiz, the commander of the South Georgia detachment remembered for his participation in kidnappings and

---

financiero. Todos aquellos sectores que en nombre de una pretendida brecha democrática entran en el juego patriotero compartirán con la Junta Militar la responsabilidad de las consecuencias que lleven esa aventura' [Those who will be worst affected by this operation are the working classes, whether or not there is a war. If there is a war, through the economic drain. If there is no war, through the national bankruptcy caused by economic blockades and financial collapse. All sectors who, in the name of a 'democratic breach', enter into this jingoistic game will share with the military *junta* the consequences of this operation] (*Resumen de la Actualidad Argentina*, 55, 1982).

torture in the ESMA (Navy School of Mechanics) (Manifiesto, 31 May 1982). At the same time that this group of exiles drew attention to the perpetrators of genocide, now celebrated as Malvinas 'heroes' in Madrid, Flores (1982) expressed his dismay at this harsh reality: 'lo retorcido de nuestra suerte, la desgraciada paradoja reside en que los asesinos de nuestros hermanos – que no hermanos suyos – los más sistemáticos entregadores de la soberanía y dignidad argentina, sean los que ejecutaron la ocupación de Malvinas y Georgias del Sur' [The cruel twist of our fate, the deplorable paradox, lies in the fact that those who murdered our brothers – and even their own –, those who have most systematically dismantled Argentine sovereignty and dignity, are also the ones who executed the occupation of the Malvinas and South Georgia Islands].

It is commonly asserted that Peronist and Montonero exiles expressed the greatest enthusiasm for the recovery of the Islands and even for the war. However, as we have seen above, almost no exile committees or organisations escaped visible tensions, whether they represented a union across political divides fighting against the dictatorship, a single political party (including the non-Peronist and non-armed left) or groups focused on human rights. Although many exiles continued to emphasise the condemnation of the dictatorship and many opposed the war, there were also many who recognised that Argentina had legitimate rights over the archipelago. Even the slogan of the Madres de Plaza de Mayo[21] – a key reference point for the exiles in the anti-dictatorship fight – validated Argentine sovereignty over the Islands, albeit without losing a critical perspective.

As a result of this situation, the consensus that had been established in defining opposition to the dictatorship in terms of human rights was, if not destroyed, at least shaken, becoming a topic of concern, debate, reclamation and even revision in terms of form, content and opportunity.

The Malvinas invasion also opened a debate in exile on the use of force in the solution of border disputes and international disagreements.[22] By extension, this debate impacted on the incomplete revision of the past recourse to violence as a legitimate method of political action and means of seizing power. This revision had led the revolutionary militants of the diaspora to evaluate (and critique, repent, ask forgiveness for, re-examine or adapt) their participation in the armed struggle that culminated in the military coup of 1976 with its tragic toll of deaths and disappearances. The conflict over the Malvinas therefore re-ignited discussion over types of violence (just, reparative, in legitimate defence) and the need to contextualise past judgements and

21 'Las Malvinas son argentinas, los desaparecidos también' [The Malvinas are Argentine, and the disappeared are too]. In the same vein, the Trabajadores y Sindicalistas Argentinos en el Exilio (TYSAE) adopted the slogan: 'Las Malvinas son argentinas, los muertos, presos y desaparecidos también' [The Malvinas are Argentine, and the dead, imprisoned and disappeared are too].

22 The exiles were divided in their categorisation of the events of 2 April, debating whether to define them as an 'occupation', a 'recovery' or a 'conquest'.

present evaluations on the recourse to arms as a means of collective action. In a text written as an 'open letter' to his fellow exiles, Eduardo Goligorsky (1983, pp. 217–8) argues that the idea that the use of force is a valid means of recovering national sovereignty can be applied in unexpected ways, leading even to the paradoxical situation where violence against the British can be used to pardon the violence of Argentina's military governments since 1966. Goligorsky's contribution reflects the extent to which the Malvinas conflict reopened the debates among the diaspora community of the existence of 'one' violence or multiple violences (exercised from above or below; violence dealt or received; violence and counter-violence; violence for exploitation; and violence for defence, etc.). Goligorsky's text also demonstrates how some sectors of the diaspora demonised others when he concludes that:

> Más aún, se refuerza el desvarío de quienes desearían reanudar la experiencia homicida de la guerrilla y el terrorismo, desde esta perspectiva ni siquiera se podría descartar la conjetura de que algunos de quienes corrieron a reclamar armas y a enrolarse como voluntarios para la guerra contra los ingleses, sientan mañana la tentación de encauzar los instintos violentos por los carriles de la insurgencia (1983, pp. 217–8).
>
> [Moreover, it fuels the insanity of those who wish to resume the homicidal practices of the guerrilla and terrorism. From this perspective, we could not even exclude the possibility that some of those who rushed to take up arms and enrol as volunteers for the war against the British might tomorrow feel tempted to channel their violent instincts into insurgency.]

Once British forces arrived in the South Atlantic and hostilities began – including the sinking of the Belgrano and the death of 323 people on board – the exiles had to adopt a position on whether to support the war or raise the flag of peace as an absolute value, regardless of the cause (the *patria* or homeland; sovereignty; liberty; revolution; etc.). The diaspora communities debated whether the means (the war) could be justified by the end in ethical, political or national terms. Some political groupings considered the fight against imperialism, colonialism and in favour of national liberation an absolute value that would be sufficient to suspend the respect for the right to life.

For other exile groups, no life was negotiable.[23] Writing in Mexico, the dramatist Alberto Adellach described the human costs of the war in terms of Galtieri's penchant for whisky: 'Si cada botella contiene un litro de whisky y cada ser humano adulto seis de sangre, se puede considerar que los 74 días de la guerra en las Malvinas, le costaron al país 18.000 litros de sangre joven y valiosa y 100 litros de whisky importado. Buen promedio, sin duda. Muy buen promedio' [If each bottle contains a litre of whisky and each adult human contains six litres of blood, we can consider that the 74 days of war in the

---

23 The Madrid-based Mesa de la Izquierda described the Malvinas war as 'un crimen más de la dictadura' [another crime of the dictatorship]. However, the group still insisted that it was also 'un crimen más del imperialismo' [another crime of imperialism] (*Divergencia*, 2, July 1982).

Malvinas cost the country 18,000 litres of young [...] blood and 100 litres of imported whisky. An impressive average, without a doubt. Very impressive] (1982). In Barcelona, Goligorsky described Malvinas as 'otra guerra sucia' [another dirty war] (1983, pp. 242–3). Far from a 'loca aventura militar' [crazy military operation], he believed that the Malvinas conflict had produced 'un tendal de muertos, mutilados y desaparecidos, argentinos y británicos, auténticos, de carne y hueso, con nombre y apellido' [a string of deaths, injuries and disappearances on both the Argentine and British sides, of real people, human beings of flesh and blood, with a name]. The Radical journalist accused some of his exiled compatriots of being as inhuman as Galtieri, who had dismissed the Malvinas tragedy with the assertion that the war in the South Atlantic had caused fewer deaths than were caused by road traffic accidents in Argentina.

In his important debate with other members of the diaspora in the Centro de Cultura Popular and the Agrupación Peronista in Barcelona, Goligorsky criticised his fellow exiled compatriots for their 'insensibility' towards the deaths that had taken place in the occupation of the Islands. Jaime Naifleish also made a similar observation from his exile in Stockholm, highlighting the 'macabre' nature of the Malvinas operation launched by the 'macabre' dictatorship and denouncing the casualties suffered by Argentina. It was now 'las madres de los asesinados en las islas' [the mothers of those killed on the Islands] who were grieving for 'esos otros hijos, que no eran los de las Madres de Plaza de Mayo' [those other children, who did not belong to the Mothers of the Plaza de Mayo] (Naifleisch, 1982). Naifleish criticised the lack of attention given to these victims, who 'fueran devueltos sin vida o mutilados desde los páramos australes' [were returned dead or badly injured from the Southern plains]. The journalist exiled in Barcelona, Goligorsky, denounced the supposed 'guerra limpia y patriótica' [clean, patriotic war] which continued to ravage the nation's young. With the wounds of the 'dirty war' still open, the military were 'enviando al matadero a la camada inmediata posterior, como si se hubiera planificado el exterminio sistemático de una generación' [sending the next-youngest group to the slaughterhouse, as though they planned systematically to exterminate a whole generation] (Goligorsky, 1983, p. 210).

Goligorsky criticised Chumbita and the Peronist militants for rewriting the Cuban revolutionary slogan 'Patria o muerte' [Homeland or Death] as 'Soberanía o muerte' [Sovereignty or Death] (Goligorsky, 1982a).[24]

24 'Pero lo que termina por descalabrar los frágiles cimientos que sustentaban la credibilidad de la adhesión sincera a la causa de los derechos humanos, es la vehemencia acrítica con que muchos miembros de la diáspora argentina han reaccionado ante un operativo militar que, como el de las Malvinas, lleva implícitas acciones de guerra, con su secuela de muerte y mutilación para ambos bandos. Aún quienes han denunciado las especulaciones utilitarias y nada patrióticas por las cuales el Gobierno argentino inició esta peligrosa maniobra de distracción, han optado por la dialéctica de las armas, anteponiéndola a la de las ideas y las negociaciones, y han abjurado de su compromiso con la intangibilidad de la vida humana por miedo a

He also accused the Mexican *Grupo de Discusión Socialista*[25] of abandoning their self-critique of the past temptation to engage in violence in the name of 'grand ideas' such as 'sovereignty', the 'pueblo' [people] or the 'patria' [homeland]. In his view, the authors of the pamphlet *Por la soberanía argentina* were repeating 'su manía de convocar a la lucha popular cada vez que en una hecatombe realimentaban sus ilusiones de pescar en río revuelto' [their habit of calling for popular struggle after every incidence of mass bloodshed in the hope of bolstering support for their cause] (Goligorsky, 1983, p. 214).

However, the situation did not merely present a simple choice between good and evil in order to pass (or fail) a humanitarian test. In describing his response to the sinking of the Belgrano, film-maker David Blaustein explains how he was able to mourn his compatriots who had been killed 'porque de repente se me juntaron las imágenes de los pibes del Belgrano, hundiéndose, con la figura de Augusto Conte (su amigo y compañero de militancia, secuestrado mientras hacía el servicio militar)' [because suddenly the images of the kids sinking in the Belgrano fused in my mind with the figure of Augusto Conte (his friend and fellow militant, kidnapped whilst undertaking military service)] (Lorenz, 2006, p. 45), highlighting the dramatic nature of the dilemma posed by the Malvinas War for the exiles.

The Malvinas conflict invoked the fight for human rights in exile in a third way. Early on, the members of the diaspora had organised themselves in their host countries to demand the release of political prisoners, clarification of the situation of the disappeared detainees and the recovery of the freedom of expression, of association and of work (etc.). In the period prior to 2 April,

---

perder el tren de una movilización popular. Reincidiendo en viejos tics, han exhumado la consigna "Soberanía o muerte", como si no hubieran tenido suficientes testimonios de que la segunda de las dos alternativas debe ser erradicada, no sólo cuando se está en el bando de los perdedores sino, sobre todo, cuando se puede estar en el de los victoriosos. Y aunque el territorio reivindicado descanse en un mar de petróleo' [But what finally destabilises the fragile foundations that underpinned the credibility of the sincere support for the human rights cause is the acritical vehemence with which many members of the Argentine diaspora have greeted a military operation which, like that of the Malvinas, includes actions of war, with its trail of death and mutilation by both sides. Even those who have denounced the utilitarian, unpatriotic reasons behind the Argentine government's launch of this dangerous strategy of distraction have opted for the dialectic of arms, putting it before that of ideas and negotiations, and have turned their back on their commitment to the preservation of human life for fear of missing out on a popular mobilisation. Falling back into old habits, they have exhumed the slogan 'Sovereignty or Death', as though they had not seen sufficient proof that the second of those two alternatives should be eradicated, and not only when we are on the losing side but, above all, when we might be on the victorious one. Even if the claimed territory is floating in a sea of oil] (Goligorsky, 1982a).

25 Among those who signed the document 'Por la soberanía argentina en las Malvinas: por la soberanía popular en la Argentina' (10 May 1982) were José Aricó, Sergio Bufano, Ricardo Nudelman, Jorge Tula, Emilio de Ípola, Néstor García Canclini, Juan Carlos Portantiero and others (Rozitchner, 2005, pp. 139–53).

references to a probable forthcoming 'Nuremberg' for the perpetrators had become common.

Days before the 'recovery' of the Islands, the lawyer Gustavo Roca highlighted the impossibility of an exit/retreat/'trick' by the military, despite the frequency of this occurrence in the many military governments of Argentina's recent history. Even if the *junta* were able to provide the military with a significant boost – which the Madrid-based CADHU campaigner imagined to be an Argentine intervention in Central America alongside the US army under the Reagan administration – Roca argued that sooner or later 'se improndrá el justo castigo a los responsables del genocidio de nuestro pueblo y de la depredación de nuestro país' [a just punishment will be imposed on those responsible for the genocide of our people and the plundering of our country] ('A seis años vista', *Resumen de la Actualidad Argentina*, 62, 1982, pp. 34–5).

In this analysis prior to Malvinas, Gustavo Roca trusted in the increasing isolation of the *junta* and the economic, social and political crisis experienced by the regime to bring about its downfall. However, when opinions on the enemy began to change, the fear of impunity became palpable and became a topic of debate in exile.

The Mexican Grupo de Discusión Socialista stressed that asserting Argentina's 'indisputable sovereignty' over the Malvinas 'no implica [...] echar un manto de olvido sobre su política desde 1976 hasta el presente' [does not mean [...] casting a veil of oblivion over the *junta*'s actions from 1976 to the present] (Rozitchner, 2005, p. 149). Writing in Venezuela, León Rozitchner launched a criticism of the group, claiming that they had abandoned political 'ethics' by casting Britain as the principal enemy rather than the dictatorship, thereby 'estabilizando una alianza de objetivos comunes con los genocidas' [coming to share the same objectives as the perpetrators of genocide] (Rozitchner, 1996, p. 143). In response, the Grupo Socialista claimed that the only legitimate position was to support the 'cause' of the war because that was the stance of political, union and human rights organisations and therefore of the people (Rozitchner, 2005, pp. 152–3).

As can be seen from the complex picture described above, the exiles had radically different views about the impact which the war could have on the regime's future, with some envisaging the possibility that the military would be tried for their participation in systematic human rights violations. The editors of *Testimonio Latinoamericano* and the Agrupación Peronista de Barcelona entered into a polemic with Eduardo Goligorsky on this point.[26] In the view of

26 From a different political position, Osvaldo Bayer refused to interpret the behaviour of the Argentine people in terms of the demonstrations on 30 March and along the same lines as the European media. In his view, these perspectives had missed the most important element: 'que en la manifestación realizada con motivo de la llegada de Haig a Buenos Aires, el ministro de Reagan, fue estruendosamente silbado por la multitud. El propio dictador Galtieri fue abucheado y silbado al automencionarse "Presidente de la Nación" e "intérprete del pueblo argentino"' [In the demonstration held to protest Haig's arrival in Buenos Aires, Reagan's

Álvaro Abós and Hugo Chumbita, the courageous, hard-fought reconstruction of the political and social opposition which had come forward to demand 'Bread, Peace and Work' and democracy on 30 March had not been dismantled by the events of 2 April. By contrast, those in the military who were aware of the danger posed by this unrest sought to substitute the looming 'Argentinazo' with a 'Malvinazo', which, although instigated by the *junta*, could lead to the destruction of the regime despite support for military victory on the battlefield (*Testimonio Latinoamericano*, 12/13, April 1982, pp. 13–14, 24–5).

If the outcome were victory for Argentina, the periodical imagined two possible scenarios: 1) Galtieri taking advantage of the boost in support to launch an electoral campaign, seeking to become a pseudo-Perón; and 2) a more probable retreat by the regime, which, through 'el gesto histórico de rescatar las islas' [the historic feat of recovering the Islands] would manage to diminish their record of crimes and corruption (*Testimonio Latinoamericano*, 12/13 April 1982, pp. 3–5, 13–14 and 24–5). The periodical's editors claimed that 'la exaltación nacionalista no es un sentimiento fácilmente manipulable' [nationalist passion is not a feeling easy to manipulate] (*Testimonio Latinoamericano*, 12/13, April 1982, pp. 3–5). In contrast to those who decried the passionate nature of the Argentine people, particularly some politicians and union leaders who were little more than the regime's puppets, Abós and Chumbita protested that the people's willingness to support this cause did not mean they had forgotten what the regime was and what it represented. Moreover, they argued that this people, who, despite responding to the military's call, were able to distinguish between support for a cause and approval of those behind the action would obtain important political capital which would force the regime to step down (*Testimonio Latinoamericano*, 12/13, April 1982, pp. 13–14 and 24–5).

When the outcome was confirmed as defeat, *Testimonio Latinoamericano* declared that although the military had sought to bring to fruition 'una causa que le era ajena' [a cause that did not belong to them], the *junta*'s status as a reactionary, anti-popular regime had rendered success unlikely. If Argentina's citizens had supported the invasion it was because they knew that democracy could not exist without full sovereignty, which could not be achieved without the Malvinas. The periodical argued that when it became clear that the talk of national dignity and sovereignty was little more than empty words in the mouth of dictators, these same citizens returned to the Plaza de Mayo on the night of 14 June to demand that Galtieri step down. For the editors of *Testimonio*, this meant that the people had not shown inconsistency. In any

---

minister [the Secretary of State] was loudly booed by the crowd. The dictator Galtieri was also booed when he referred to himself as the 'President of the Nation' and 'spokesperson for the Argentine people'] (Bayer, 1982).

case, as a Peronist film-maker exiled in Paris observed, the Argentines had by no means given *carte blanche* to the military.[27]

The Malvinas, so deeply rooted in the Argentine collective imaginary, taught as part of the notion of *patria*, or homeland, from primary school onwards, became for many exiles the means of measuring the democratic and humanitarian commitment of their fellow Argentines both at home and in the diaspora. From his exile in Spain, Eduardo Goligorsky engaged in debate not only with the Mexican *Grupo de Discusión Socialista* and with Peronist groups in Barcelona (*Testimonio, Agrupación Peronista, Centro de Cultura Popular*), but also with a man employed in the civil service under the dictatorship, the writer and diplomat Abel Posse, who was working for the Argentine Embassy in Paris.

Posse and Goligorsky exchanged several articles in the pages of *La Vanguardia* in May 1982. The civil servant working for the military government declared that the exiles could not continue to interpret all the regime's acts through the framework of anti-dictatorship resistance because the Malvinas invasion was part of an anti-imperialist war that had nothing to do with the 'defensa humanista' [humanist defence] of the dictatorship's victims. Posse compared certain sectors of the diaspora with the liberal, left-wing politicians who in 1946 had turned their back on the people, allying themselves with their right-wing enemies. This sector of the left, Posse argued, was 'bobo, indisciplinado y opinativo' [stupid, undisciplined and opinionated] and their insistence on bringing Astiz to trial echoed the mistake of accusing Perón and Evita of being Nazis, attempting to 'conformar un nuevo tribunal de Nüremberg con falsas denuncias de torturas y desapariciones' [establish a new Nuremberg Trial with false claims of torture and disappearances].

Posse denounced the 'stupidity' of this left as unique in Latin America and the wider world, noting that while Cuba, China and the USSR supported Argentina in the war, what he termed the 'izquierda justina'[28] was positioning itself to become 'el undécimo miembro del Mercado Común Europeo y

27 The 'liberal, left-wing' component of the diaspora had reservations about this argument. When the war ended, Eduardo Goligorsky stated: 'Quienes la apoyaron para no perder el tren de una movilización popular, ¿harán su autocrítica? ¿Adoptarán, finalmente, algún principio ético universal que los disuada a alistarse, personalmente o de manera vicaria, en todas las conflagraciones que desangran a su país y al mundo? ¿Se sentirán, por esta vez, más o menos responsables ante las madres de los nuevos muertos y desaparecidos y mutilados como los apologistas de la represión lo son ante las Madres de Plaza de Mayo?' [Will those who supported the war to avoid missing out on a popular mobilisation engage in self-critique? Will they eventually adopt an ethical, universal principle that will dissuade them from enlisting themselves (directly or indirectly) in all the conflicts that ravage their country and the world? This time will they feel some degree of responsibility when faced with the mothers of those who have now been killed, injured or disappeared, as the apologists of repression do when faced with the Mothers of the Plaza de Mayo?] (1982b).

28 By comparing Justine, the masochist character created by the Marquis de Sade, with this branch of the Argentine left, Posse argued that 'su profesión es poner en evidencia el mal de los otros en vez de imponer su bondad' [their profession is to highlight the evil in others rather than impose their own goodness].

hasta anda queriendo quedar bien con los ingleses' [the 11th member of the European Common Market and even hopes to curry favour with the British] (Posse, 1982).

For his part, Goligorsky argued that the war was a mistake and lamented the shameful spectacle of the Argentine people applauding the *junta*'s decisions. His criticism was directed at all the exiles, however, and their inability to maintain unity in their fight against the dictatorship.[29] Goligorsky contended that the war had revealed the focus on democracy, the rejection of Manichean binaries and the critique of irrational frameworks to be nothing more than empty words, tactical positions or false guises. For that reason, he called on the exiles to engage in self-critique in order to reconsider the place given to 'la reforma pacífica y el cambio gradual, compatibles con un sistema de elecciones democráticas con respeto por las minorías y de alternancias en el poder' [peaceful reform and gradual change, compatible with a democratic electoral system that respects minorities and allows changes of government] (Goligorsky, 1982a). The journalist argued that supporting Galtieri's decision cast the strength of the exiles' commitment to democracy and human rights into doubt. The Malvinas brought the rebirth of slogans, such as 'Soberanía o muerte' [Sovereignty or Death], that had played a significant role in the armed militancy of the 1970s, demonstrating the fragility of the expatriates' new focus on life over heroic death. For Goligorsky, a truly humanist conviction must acknowledge that the respect for human rights is not restricted to occasions when we find ourselves on the losing side, 'sino, sobre todo, cuando se puede estar en el de los victoriosos. Y aunque el territorio reivindicado descanse sobre un mar de petróleo' [but, above all, when we might be on the victorious one. Even if the claimed territory is floating in a sea of oil] (1982a).

Goligorsky also rejected the strategy of claiming Argentine democratic or humanist 'peculiarities'[30] in order to disguise lapses in allegiance to values that were absolute, universal and constant. When the 'irridentists' supported the Malvinas War, he argued, they not only forgot the dictatorship's crimes, but also revealed the fragility of their humanist convictions and the continuation of the ideas that had, in the past, been used to justify violence 'from below' and now seemed to suggest that there were certain situations in which someone's

29 From Stockholm, Jaime Naifleish criticised 'la dispersión del exilio con sus equívocas unidades antidictatoriales' [the dispersion of the exiles with their confused anti-dictatorship groupings]. After the end of the war, the PRT member insisted that the political future could not be based on 'el ilusionismo, el "porlomenismo" del mal menor' [wishful thinking or 'being content' with the lesser of two evils] and that progress had to be made towards true dialogue (1982).

30 In response to the editors of *Testimonio*, who talked of 'peculiarities' (for example in the Peronist conception of democracy as taking place in the *plaza* rather than in parliament), Goligorsky declared: 'Los latinoamericanos han de ser, según esta doctrina, "originales": Sin habeas corpus, sin libertad para elegir a sus gobernantes, sin poder ver ni oír ni leer lo que se les antoje' [Latin Americans will, according to this doctrine, be 'original': without *habeas corpus*, without the freedom to choose their government, without liberty to see, hear or read what they wish] (1983, p. 95).

humanity could be 'violada legítimamente' [legitimately violated] (Goligorsky, 1983, p. 216). For someone who considered the crimes of terrorism to be as reprehensible as those of a repressive regime, it was not strange to find that fellow Argentines who had been persecuted by the dictatorship were now in agreement with a diplomat in one of the regime's most notorious embassies.

For Goligorsky, the Malvinas were 'un *test* sobre las virtudes del libre examen y del debate racional, contrapuestas a los vicios de la retórica apocalíptica, de los estereotipos maximalistas, de las implicaciones dogmáticas y de los desafíos tribales' [a *test* of the virtues of *liberum examen* and rational debate in opposition to the vices of apocalyptic rhetoric, maximalist stereotypes, dogmatic entanglement and the challenges of tribalism] (Goligorsky, 1983, p. 227). Framing the war in this way was neither a casual observation nor the personal view of one man who had learned 'la naturaleza sacrosanta de la vida humana, propia y ajena' [the sacred nature of human life, both one's own and that of others] after so much death (Goligorsky, 1983, p. 227). Goligorsky's position exposed an unresolved debate in the diaspora, exacerbated by the Malvinas conflict, which centred on the complex transformation of the former revolutionary militants into human rights activists in exile – a transformation that could be either profound and definitive, or tactical and opportunist. It is this same complexity that today demands that researchers undertake a careful and detailed purging of the meanings attached to the definition of human rights in this troubled recent past.

References

Adellach, A. (1982) 'Cartas a Madrid', *Resumen de la Actualidad Argentina*, 70, pp. 39–40.

Bayer, O. (1982) 'La aventura de las Malvinas', *Resumen de la Actualidad Argentina*, 65: 29.

Borrat, H. (1982) 'Las coincidencias forzosas', *Testimonio Latinoamericano*, 14 (May/June): 8–10.

Confederación Socialista Argentina. Delegación Cataluña (1982), internal document.

Chumbita, H. (1982) 'Malvinas, el dilema de Europa', *Testimonio Latinoamericano*, 14 (May/June):11–16.

Los Derechos Humanos (editorial) (1979), *Criterio* (13 Sept.): 18–19.

Mensaje de los marxistas revolucionarios argentinos organizados en la IV Internacional de Argentina, España y Francia. Leído en el meeting del Internationalist Marxist Group de Londres (1982), *Divergencia*, 2 (July).

Grupos de Trabajo contra la Dictadura, por la Libertad y la Democracia en Argentina (1982) 'Comunicado', *Resumen de la Actualidad Argentina*, 69 (28 June): 36.

Flores, R. (1982) 'Exiliados y Malvinas', *Resumen de la Actualidad Argentina*, 68 (25 Jan.): 36–7.

Franco, M. (2008) *El exilio: Argentinos en Francia durante la dictadura* (Buenos Aires: Siglo XXI).

Franco, M. and F. Levín (2007) *Historia reciente: Perspectivas y desafíos de un campo en construcción* (Buenos Aires: Paidós).

Gabetta, C. (1983) *Todos somos subversivos* (Buenos Aires: Bruguera).

Goligorsky, E. (1982a) 'El derramamiento de sangre y los arrebatos emocionales', *La Vanguardia*, 11 May.

— (1982b) 'Ahorrar sangre de gaucho', *Testimonio Latinoamericano*, 15–16 (July–Oct.): 6.

— (1983) *Carta abierta de un expatriado a sus compatriotas* (Buenos Aires: Sudamericana).

González, H. (1982) 'La paradoja kelper', *Testimonio Latinoamericano*, 15–16 (July–Oct.): 3–5.

Grupo de Discusión Socialista (1982) 'Por la soberanía argentina en las Malvinas. Por la soberanía popular en Argentina', *Visión socialista* (México), 10 May.

Guber, R. (2001) *¿Por qué Malvinas? De la causa nacional a la guerra absurda* (Buenos Aires: Fondo de Cultura Económica).

Jensen, S. (2010) *Los exiliados. La lucha por los derechos humanos durante la dictadura* (Buenos Aires: Sudamericana).

Lopez Acotto, A. (1982) Letter, *El País* (6 April), rpt. in *Resumen de Actualidad Argentina*, 55.

Lorenz, F. (2006) *Las guerras por Malvinas* (Buenos Aires: Edhasa).

Naifleish, J. (1982), 'La primera guerra de Malvinas', *Comunidad*, 31/32, (Sept./Oct.): 12.

Niedergang, M. (1982) 'Puntos de vista. La mirada europea', *Testimonio Latinoamericano*, 14 (May/June): 5.

Páez, P. (1982) 'La ocupación y la democracia', *Resumen de la Actualidad Argentina*, 75 (8 Nov.): 24–6.

Palermo, V. (2007) *Sal en las heridas. Las Malvinas en la cultura argentina contemporánea* (Buenos Aires: Sudamericana).

Posse, A. (1982) 'La guerra y la izquierda justina', *La Vanguardia*, 11 May.

Resumen de Actualidad Argentina (1982) 55.

Resumen de Actualidad Argentina (1982) 62.

Resumen de Actualidad Argentina (1982) 68.

Rodríguez, L. (1982) 'Argentina, a la hora de las Malvinas', *El Periódico de Catalunya*, 9/10 Apr.

Rozitchner, L. (1996) *Las desventuras del sujeto político. Ensayos y errores* (Buenos Aires: El Cielo por Asalto).

— (2005) *Malvinas: de la guerra sucia a la guerra limpia. El punto ciego de la crítica política* (Buenos Aires: Losada).

Savater, F., 'La mirada europea', *Testimonio Latinoamericano*, 14 (May/June): 5–6.

Soto, E. (1982) 'La sangre no lava la sangre', *Testimonio Latinoamericano*, 14 (May/June): 25.

Yankelevich, P. (2002) (ed.) *México, país refugio. La experiencia de los exilios en el siglo XX* (Mexico City: Plaza y Valdés).

3. Attitudes towards the Falklands–Malvinas War: European and Latin American left perspectives

Fernando Pedrosa

This chapter takes a different approach to the issue of the Malvinas–Falklands War, which saw Argentina and England confront each other in 1982. The war has been studied mainly from the military point of view or according to the impact it had on the countries engaged in the conflict. However, the consequences of the military conflict between two western-block countries were broader and have not been properly tackled. The following pages will consider, first, the characterisation of the positions adopted by European and Latin-American political parties, many of which were members of the Socialist International (SI).[1] Then this chapter will delve more deeply into different visions of the Anglo-Argentine conflict, evaluating the way in which it influenced inter-party relations, the social democrats' transnational organisational strategies and regional policy in general. This will allow a mapping of the transnational political actions taken which is quite different from that usually presented in the specialised literature on the subject, above all because of the inclusion of the parties as main characters in the political processes of the time on the international stage. Furthermore, this approach will allow us to observe more fluid and ambiguous actions taken by the different left-wing organisations that were far from being a collective characterised by rigid or inflexible strategies.

The Malvinas war

On 2 April 1982, the infantry forces of the Argentine Navy landed on the biggest of the Islands, expelling the British authorities and sending them to Uruguay. A day after that, England would break off diplomatic relations and decide on the dispatch of troops. Shortly after that, the United Nations Security Council passed Resolution 502, which demanded Argentina's withdrawal from

1 This research was conducted between 2007 and 2008 in the archives of Socialist International located in the Internationaal Instituut voor Sociale Geschiedenis (IISG) in Amsterdam (The Netherlands).

F. Pedrosa, 'Attitudes towards the Falklands–Malvinas war: European and Latin American left perspectives', in G. Mira and F. Pedrosa (eds.), *Revisiting the Falklands–Malvinas Question: Transnational and Interdisciplinary Perspectives* (London: University of London Press, 2020), pp. 75–96. License: CC-BY-NC-ND 4.0.

the Islands and the immediate start of negotiations. This resolution, considered a diplomatic defeat for Argentina, was at the core of every discussion and negotiation that aimed to avoid, and later stop, the war. A week after the conflict started, the US secretary of state, Alexander Haig, arrived in London to begin a mediation agreed upon by both parties. However, this US intervention would prove to be fruitless due to the participants' intransigence. In addition, there was the dispute within the US government itself with regard to the role it should play in the conflict. This US ambiguity enabled the Argentine military to maintain the illusion of US abstention from the conflict. On 30 April 1982, Haig's mediation was declared officially over. Consequently, President Reagan made US support for England official. At the same time, he backed the European position of imposing economic sanctions on Argentina. After other failed mediation proposals introduced by Fernando Belaunde Terry, then President of Peru, and the UN Secretary General, Javier Pérez de Cuéllar, the conflict moved forward to a military solution (Pérez de Cuéllar, 1997). On 14 June 1982, the war ended with the return of the Islands to British control thanks to military victory by their troops.

Democratic processes of the third wave in Latin America

The conflict between Argentina and England took place in a changing global environment. Shortly before the war a time characterised by a significant easing of tension between the US and the Soviets had come to an end. An important part of this period – known as the *détente* – occurred during US president Jimmy Carter's administration (1977–81) (Halliday, 1983). The *détente* had allowed other political and social actors who sought, by means of transnational actions to avoid becoming trapped in the Cold War polarisation, to have a higher profile. It is no coincidence that several revolutions occurred within that period: Nicaragua, Iran and Grenada, as well as the radicalisation of the official parties in Jamaica, the Dominican Republic and Guyana. Thus the Permanent Conference of Political Parties of Latin America and the Caribbean (COPPPAL) was created, as well as the revitalisation of the Non-Aligned Movement and the signing of the Treaty for the Panama Canal by Omar Torrijos and Carter (Pastor, 1984). That is how, seizing the opportunity created by the lack of tension, these non-aligned actors increased their activity in favour of their own projects and interests over those of the so-called 'super powers'. The leaders and political parties became key instruments in the process that had transnational organisations as the main actors (for example, SI, the Christian Democrat International and Liberal International, among others (Grabendorff, 2001)).

Gradually, international tension started to mount again, even under the Carter administration. The Soviet invasion of Afghanistan (1979) and the hostage situation at the US Embassy in Iran (1979–81) triggered a change during this period. However, it was not before the Republican Ronald

Reagan came to office (1981–89) that the conditions that prevailed during the détente changed drastically for Latin America (Carleton and Stohl, 1985). Paradoxically, the increase in geo-political conflict also coincided with many democratic openings in Latin America (Sikkink, 2004). The transition from dictatorships to democratic governments in southern Europe in 1974 (Spain, Greece, Portugal) commenced a process of regime change that ended with the establishment of democracies in a great number of Latin American countries (Huntington, 1994). This enabled new opportunities to arise for the transnational actors to continue their political activity beyond the limits imposed by this 'second cold war' (Pedrosa, 2012; Scott and Walters, 2000).

In this sense, the South Atlantic conflict was a key moment in the process of democratisation in the region since the English victory hastened the downfall of Argentina's military government. The rapid return to a democratic system was important for speeding up the same process in neighbouring countries that were still ruled by dictatorships of different kinds. On the winning side, Margaret Thatcher consolidated her political power, since the war would have an impact on the electoral process in 1983 (Clarke, Mishler and Whiteley, 1990). Thatcher's image became relevant worldwide. Together with Ronald Reagan and Pope John Paul II, she became part of the trinity that some years later would put an end to the global communist project.

The recent history and third-wave democratisation

During the last decades, the interest in third-wave democratisation processes in Latin America has decreased considerably. Social scientists have been drawn to other investigative agendas and new open problems in the changing Latin American democratisation processes. However, parallel to this, historians have turned their attention to the subject, particularly in a disciplinary field calling itself 'recent history' (Mira and Pedrosa, 2016). Works on this subject – numerous, eclectic and of differing quality – have not continued a dialogue with the former literature on the subject (López, Figueroa and Rajland, 2010), or, more importantly, with what was published in the fields of political science and international relations. The latest literature has focused on politics viewed through the prism of democracy (Lesgart, 2002).

Academic developments relating to democratisation in Latin America started in the 1980s. These agendas, novel for the time, were put into practice by a group of political scientists who, besides pursuing their own academic goals, wished to use their work to influence and improve the quality of the democracies that were being established (Guilhot and Schmitter, 2000). These experts engaged with democracy, with the idea that it provided national political leaders – the political elite – with a good chance to build a system capable of channelling the conflicts of each society harmoniously. They recommended that a minimum version of democracy be introduced which, because of its 'minimalism', would generate better consensus and avoid the appearance of new dictatorships (O'Donnell, Schmitter and Whitehead, 1994).

'Recent history' proposed itself as a radical break with these academic traditions; interest in democratic regimes, institutions and political elites received diminished attention. Besides, this new approach no longer showed much interest in the already extant democracies (Oberti and Pittaluga, 2004/5). Thus, issues were highlighted which related to the traumatic events that characterised the period, such as genocides, dictatorships, social crisis, political violence, state terrorism and the different ways society found to offer resistance. To this end, it supported itself, sometimes exaggeratedly, with memory and the testimonies of the main actors as privileged sources for investigation (Sarlo, 2003). Thus, interest in the role played by human rights organisations, trade unions, armed groups and intellectuals, and the biographical works of the victims of state repression, was strengthened. At the same time, the left-wing universe reduced itself to those who kept radical and anti-system stances. This occurred to the detriment of other left-wing democratic projects that, like those of social democrats, were overlooked by specialised literature.[2]

Nevertheless, in this alleged theoretical and discursive cut, the works framed in recent history kept some of the characteristics of the preceding literature and of that from which they sought to differentiate themselves. This could be seen, for example, in the privileging of national methodologies of historical processes (Lvovich et al., 2011). At the same time, academics in recent history ignored the actions of politicians and their organisations in the study of democratisation processes (Soto, 2004). If regime change towards democracy was no longer a subject for investigation, nor could political parties be.

An earlier version of this discussion was made when historians applied the idea of 'transnational politics' (Keohane and Nye, 1971) to debates, making reference to world interactions in which at least one of the participants was non-state in nature, such as political parties or their international party organisations. The systematic application of this concept gave way to a prolific literature that began to extend to the Latin American case. It was acknowledged that processes of democratisation had been strong globally and that, in many cases, transnational actors had been important in their development. Studying transnational activity enables us, in a less forced fashion, to describe political actions of domestic actors outside their countries at the same time as acknowledging their national interests (Keck and Sikkink, 2000). However, this transnational academic approach failed to integrate the political parties and the networks of which they were part, prioritising the role of organisations dedicated to human rights, women, indigenous communities or the environment (Markarian, 2004). The transnational activity of the European social democrat parties and SI in particular, were crucial in the third-wave

---

2   Some exceptions are Mujal León (1989) and Pedrosa (2012).

democratisation processes in Latin America (Mujal León, 1989). However, it is only recently that academic studies have started to account for this (Pedrosa, 2012). To analyse their action within the processes of democratisation might incorporate another perspective that contributes new information and, at the same time, stimulates dialogue between the many social disciplines.

Malvinas: the political background of Socialist International

The conflict between two western-block allies not only surprised the US and Great Britain, it also blindsided SI. However, the political echoes of the dispute had already appeared on the SI agenda in 1976, when there was an increase in tension between the governments of Isabel Perón and the Labour prime minister James Callaghan (Trías, 1977). An English government mission to the Islands territory had been the trigger and resulted in the mutual withdrawal of their ambassadors.

During the SI meeting held in 1977 in Madrid, the Argentine socialist leader Víctor García Costa intended to incorporate the topic of the Malvinas into the discussion. The issue had not been discussed in the meeting held in London the previous year, even though it had been formally scheduled. However, it was not discussed on the second occasion either due to 'time issues'. The conflict surrounding the Malvinas was something social democrats intended to avoid, since it challenged two long-time SI members. The British Labour Party (BLP) was a classic exponent of the social democratic family. At the same time, Argentine socialism had been the first of its kind within Latin America and a historical partner to European social democracy against Marxism since the times of the Second International.

Argentina's mission to Madrid succeeded in having the issue accepted for the next SI meeting, to be held in Rome. For this, it was important that the Dominican leader José F. Peña Gómez had rallied to Argentina's position. Peña Gómez had growing influence within the organisation at the time. At the end of the meeting, the BLP delegation asked for a bilateral interview with Argentina's socialists.[3] Participants in the meeting were Ian Mikardo (Deputy and International Secretary for the BLP), Víctor García Costa (Argentina People's Socialist Party [PSP]) and Carlos Parra (Chile Radical Party) as the interpreter. Later, Parra's position was severely criticised by García Costa on the grounds of alleged favouritism shown towards the English.[4]

In spite of their belonging to the same 'political family', it was a very tense meeting. Deputy Mikardo started it by stating his alienation because socialists cared more for the Malvinas issue than they did for human rights. The BLP was the most critical of Argentina's ruling dictatorship and upheld

---

3   Letter from Víctor García Costa to Bernt Carlsson, 1 Aug. 1977 (Bernt Carlsson papers, boxes 9–21, IISG).
4   Personal interview with Víctor García Costa (Buenos Aires, July 6, 2012).

that argument until the end of the conflict. García Costa replied cryptically, 'Sovereignty does not admit exclusionary considerations'.[5] As the meeting went on, some common positions appeared and Mikardo was authorised publically to announce that the Labour Party's position was different from that of Callaghan's Labour government. At the same time, he asked the Argentines to submit a document that showed commitment to a common position in order to avoid 'a discussion which was not easy to become engaged with'.[6] The leader of the Argentine PSP agreed to the request and, soon enough, sent a document entitled 'The SI requests the Labour Party's attention to the most urgent acknowledgment of Argentina's sovereignty over the Malvinas Islands and its immediate restitution'.[7] The title itself left no place for reaching an agreement, not even a common position between both parties. That is why Labour made no attempt to answer it.

In the following meeting, held in Rome, SI once again avoided taking a position. Thus, the parties passed a resolution that supported UN Resolution 2065 from 1965, aimed at reaching a negotiated way out of the conflict over Malvinas sovereignty. However, SI added a significant point to the text: Argentina's government could not exercise sovereignty since the National Congress had sole legal authority on the matter and the Congress had been dissolved after the military coup.

The war and the parties of Socialist International

The conflict took place in a region that was not very important to the SI, which was more involved in Central America and the Caribbean where the Cold War had one of its main scenarios. However, the war had a direct impact on the SI: once the hostilities began in April 1982, the Latin American leaders of the SI manifested, publicly, against the European Social Democratic leaders. The motives for the conflict were the positions taken towards the Central American conflict, especially those in Nicaragua and El Salvador. Latin American parties such as Democratic Action from Venezuela (commonly abbreviated as AD), the National Liberation Party from Costa Rica (PLN) and the Dominican Revolutionary Party (PRD) were openly opposed to the approach to Cuba of the Sandinista National Liberation Front (FSLN) and the Farabundo Martí National Liberation Front (FMLN). The Europeans, on the other hand, were more sympathetic to those revolutionary movements. The exception was Felipe González from the Spanish Socialist Workers' Party (PSOE), who aligned himself with the Latin Americans (Blázquez Vilaplana, 2006).

5   Bernt Carlsson papers, boxes 9–21, IISG.
6   Bernt Carlsson papers, boxes 9–21, IISG.
7   Bernt Carlsson papers, boxes 9–21, IISG (the original Spanish: 'La IS solicita al Partido Laborista su atención al más urgente reconocimiento de la soberanía argentina en las Islas Malvinas y su inmediata restitución').

Towards 1982, the situation in the Argentine and English parties affiliated to SI was quite different from that of the mid 1970s. Argentina's socialism was divided into several factions competing for SI recognition. All of them were minuscule and in continuous conflict among themselves. The official party, the PSP, remained suspended on the verge of expulsion. Thus, there was no Argentine representation within SI at the time the war broke out. The British Labour Party was in no better position. It was distanced from the new SI leadership and in the middle of an internal crisis that had led it into division and out of government. The crisis had resulted in the creation of the Social Democrat Party (26 March 1981) in which were grouped many of the historical leaders of Labour's moderate wing (Crewe and King, 1996). The left-wingers were left to the traditional Labour Party (Freeman, 1984). With the Malvinas invasion in mind, the British Labour Party's first statement addressing the international scenario left no doubt as to the political characterisation it was making. It was based on the anti-democratic attack launched by Argentina's government and on its actions. Finally, it contemplated the Kelpers' right to live under the sovereignty of whomever they chose and the necessity to protect them.[8]

On 22 April 1982, in a telegram addressed to SI and the British Labour Party, Argentina answered, claiming that siding with the British government would mean committing treason against SI's fundamental principles.[9] At the same time, it would mean an attack on Latin America as a whole. The message made it clear that the pacifists' efforts were not enough in themselves, but should contain the express recognition of Argentina's sovereignty. The other political parties in the country unanimously supported government action (Romero, 2012). The Labour position was to cling to the UN's position. In this way, they found an intermediate position that allowed them to avoid direct confrontation with their own government at a time of war. Thus, they claimed Thatcher should obey Resolution 502 and call a ceasefire; and they claimed that Argentina should abandon the Islands immediately, as the resolution itself

8   '[T]he Labour Party condemns without qualification the actions of the Argentinean military fascist government in taking over the Falkland Islands by force. [...] It supports the efforts being made to resolve the situation by diplomatic means and, in particular, welcomes the resolution of the UN Security Council calling for Argentina's withdrawal from the Falklands Islands, and urges that every action should be taken to make this resolution effective' (BLP statement, 4 Apr. 1982, signed by Jenny Little (Secretary of International Relations), IISG, Socialist International Archives, Falklands–Malvinas Commission, 1982, Box 979, IISG).

9   '[The] support and colonialist political defense of the British Conservative Party in the Malvinas war ... constitute a total and flagrant violation of the idea that gave rise to the SI. Consequently, the armed aggression towards Argentina will also be an attack against the Latin American countries. That is why an unforgivable responsibility will also fall on the British Labour Party and the SI, if they do not urgently intervene towards a peaceful solution, with express recognition or the sovereignty of Argentina' (telegram to the SI and PLB signed by Nestor Martinez Eraso, Secretary of International Relations-PSP, 22 Apr. 1982, Socialist International Archives, Falklands–Malvinas Commission, 1982, Box 979, IISG).

demanded. In turn, they rejected the British government's use of its veto and supported the UN Secretary General's mediating efforts.[10] In the uncertain climate and confusion to which the war had led, SI seemed not to take any position other than to issue an appeal to end the conflict and to state their respect for UN. However, things would not be that easy. Without consulting SI authorities, the Socialist International Committee for Latin America and the Caribbean (SICLAC) issued a statement that placed the Malvinas issue at the centre of the social democrats' agenda.

SICLAC and the war

The SICLAC was an internal organism of SI that grouped together the region's parties and their main leaders. This organism was led by the Dominican José F. Peña Gómez, who had already supported Argentina's position for some years. The communication issued by SICLAC had the immediate effect of introducing the problem within SI. This was reinforced by the existence of conflicts between Latin American and European Parties on the Central American conflict. The war exacerbated the internal SI problem and placed SICLAC in the eye of the climate storm.

SICLAC's communication (enclosed in a letter from Peña Gómez to Bernt Carlsson)[11] had been a direct reaction to the European Economic Community's decision – with the support of social democrat governments – to apply sanctions to Argentina. The document adopted several positions implying support for Argentina's claim. At the same time, no mention was made of its government's non-democratic characteristics:

> SICLAC ... expresses complete solidarity with our brothers the Argentine people ... and their rejection of war as a means to put an end to the controversies among the states. [...] considers that the UN should exercise its mediating function and cease the conflict that has regrettably already started since the British fleet took the Georgias'. The Malvinas are Argentine. [...] We hereby ask European affiliated parties and the SI presidium to mediate with European governments so that their mediating efforts be united and adopt a considerate attitude towards the Latin American people who are unable to understand or accept the drastic and precipitate actions adopted by the EEC.[12]

10 BLP statement on the Falklands signed by Michael Foot and Tony Benn, 28 Apr. 1982 (IISG, Socialist International Archives, Falklands–Malvinas Commission, 1982, Box 979).

11 'We held several phone calls with Carlos A. Pérez and the other members of the Committee and we came to the position stated in the annex statement. This document has not been signed by our English-speaking fellows Michael Manley (Jamaica) and O'Brien Trotman (Barbados) for we could not reach a satisfactory agreement' (SICLAC Circular 3/82, Santo Domingo, 28 Apr. 1982, signed by José Francisco Peña Gómez, Socialist International Archives, Falklands–Malvinas Commission, 1982, box 979, IISG).

12 SICLAC Circular 3/82, Socialist International Archives, Falklands–Malvinas Commission, 1982, box 979, IISG.

In addition to taking a stand for Argentina, the SICLAC communication used the name of 'SI'. This fact generated broader repercussions and forced the SI authorities to include the issue in the organisation's agenda. Besides this, the communication was widely distributed by the secretary general Bernt Carlsson himself, who harboured an old resentment towards the Labour movement. SICLAC's statement not only embittered the climate within SI, but also seriously complicated the situation of the British Labour Party, which was in the middle of a serious electoral dispute. The nationalist climate grew as the war progressed until it became one of the main issues of the British electoral campaign.

Labour's response to SICLAC's statement came swiftly and was widely disseminated. Labour's secretary general, Ron Hayward, telephoned Carlsson to ask him whether the statement had been issued by SI's office. The affirmative answer deepened the existing tensions with Carlsson and ended in his resigning his post in 1983. In a telephone call to the SI secretary general's office, a leading British Labour MP, Gwyneth Dunwoody[13] questioned Latin America's position in harsh terms, threatening to withdraw the British Labour Party from SI.[14] The BLP issued a highly diplomatic, but robust statement through the national executive committee (NEC). It started by sharing the concern expressed by SICLAC in its own recent statement about the Malvinas crisis but went on to demolish the points made by SICLAC one by one. The NEC agreed that the Argentine military government was behaving anti-democratically, however, and this criticism became central to their argumentation:

> The NEC has emphasised in its statement on the crisis that the British Labour Movement has no quarrel with the Argentinian people, who are the victims of a vicious, blood-stained dictatorship whose record on human rights is a disgrace to the continent of America and the rest of the free world. Like the CALCIS, the NEC wishes to express its solidarity with the Argentinian people whose interests – in terms of political freedom, civil rights and social justice – have most emphatically not been served by the decision of the Galtieri *junta* to abandon negotiation and send armed forces to invade the Falklands against the will of the local community and against international law … The NEC does not share the Committee's view that the 'war activity' was initiated by the British fleet through its invasion of South Georgia. It calls the attention of the Committee to the fact that

---

13 Gwyneth Dunwoody was a prominent Labour MP and daughter of the first secretary general of the SI and former secretary general of the BLP, Morgan Phillips.

14 'With reference to our talk, I write to you to confirm that the statement of April 27, 1982, by the Socialist International Committee for the Latin America and the Caribbean, was sent to the member parties of the Socialist International for information in the form of a press release. Concerning the allegations made by Ms Gwyneth Dunwoody in her phone call to our Secretary today that the "SI member parties in Latin America are fascist in character" and her threat that the British Labour Party is going to leave the SI, I prefer to consider these comments are her private views only' (confidential letter from Bernt Carlsson to Ron Hayward, 6 May 1982 (Bernt Carlsson papers, boxes 9–21, IISG)).

the first act of war took place when the military *junta* of Argentina, whose domestic policies have so often been justly condemned by the SI in the past, dispatched forces to overrun the Islands and to subjugate the local population. We share the Committee's view that war must not be used 'as a means to put an end to any dispute between states'. In the past, however, such a view has not been shared by fascist dictators. The NEC has made it publicly clear that it deplores the mood of chauvinism whipped up by right-wing factions in both Argentina and Great Britain. Nationalism – even when expressed in the form of 'continental solidarity' – is a sterile creed, one rejected by all true international socialists, wherever they come from … The Committee's statement refers to the support already received in this dispute by Argentina from other Latin America states. The NEC notes that supporters of the *junta*'s position include many sworn enemies of democratic socialism, as understood by the SI, and governments which, unlike the British labour movement, have been subdued in their condemnation of deep-rooted characteristics of life in Argentina under the military *junta*. (BLP statement signed by Ron Hayward (secretary general) and submitted to Bernt Carlsson; copied to Jenny Little and J. E. Mortimer, 24 May 1982.)[15]

The war in the political parties' transnational scenario

Latin American political parties also began to take a position on the war. Support for Argentina came from the entire political forum, even from those parties which tended to reject its government. In this regard, the conflict was exploited to suit each actor's interests. For example, Argentina received support from countries in conflict with the US; and these nations – mainly those closer to the Soviet bloc, such as the Communist Party of Cuba and the members of the Non-Aligned Movement – thus used the situation to settle the account of their own realities. On the other side, English-speaking Caribbean parties with a strong English influence supported Britan. Manley and Trotman's case was notorious within SI.

Numerous Latin American leaders, such as the Uruguayan socialist leader José Cardozo, made public statements in favour of Argentina. However, these were the first ones explicitly to refer to the democracy issue: 'Latin America awaits some reflection about SI, far from European emotiveness with regard to old wounded hegemonies, based on the Argentine people's right to achieve not only the recovery of that territorial space, but also the sovereignty of its internal dignity based on social justice and essential democratic freedoms'.[16] An article published in *Barricada*, a Nicaraguan Sandinista newspaper, denounced US solidarity with British naval aggression, a stance which showed the Inter-

15 SI Archives, Falklands–Malvinas Commission, 1982, box 979, IISG.
16 10 May 1982, San José, Costa Rica (on the occasion of the inauguration of Luis A. Monge as 39th president of Costa Rica), (SI Archives, Falklands–Malvinas Commission, 1982, box 979, IISG).

American Treaty of Reciprocal Assistance, a kind of NATO of the Americas, to be a farce. The Sandinista National Liberation Front argued that the attack on Argentina was an attack on Latin America's people and urged Great Britain to embrace UN and international law. While criticising the US repeatedly, at the same time they cryptically stated that Nicaragua was 'on friendly terms with Great Britain'.[17]

However, within European countries, although not unanimously, the position was favourable to Great Britain. The big picture seemed more varied than the one which Latin Americans appeared to recognise: in Italy because of their historical relationship with Argentina; in Ireland because of their historical differences with Great Britain; and also in Spain, related to the Gibraltar situation. Argentina reaped support especially from the PSOE[18] and the Communist Party of Spain.[19] European support for Argentina even came from the most radical British left wing[20] and from international trade union organisations.[21] The SI youth branch issued a statement as well, which was very favourable to Argentina's position, although it contained strong criticism of their government and maintained Labour's position.[22] The German Social

17 *Barricada*, official organ of the FSLN, 10 May 1982 (SI Archives, Falklands–Malvinas Commission, 1982, box 979, IISG).
18 'Be aware of the relevance the Gibraltar issue has in Spain ... and that in Spain neither the right nor the left wing is fond of English people. Curious, isn't it? This is surely for historical reasons, which are centuries-old. In other words, between England and Argentina we are always on Argentina's side. But besides that, a colonial fact much like that of Gibraltar makes public opinion side with Argentina and so does the left wing. Besides, there was little time to think of what would have happened if the military in Argentina had won .... We experienced it knowing there was a contradiction as well, didn't we? Of course we had no doubts about it, not least because of Thatcher being there, for whom we hold a visceral dislike' (personal interview with high-ranking leader of the PSOE, Luis Yáñez-Barnuevo, a regular attender at SI meetings, Brussels February 2007).
19 'Reaffirming the acknowledgement of Argentina's sovereignty [The Spanish Communist Party] pronounced in favour of ending hostilities by means of a cease fire ... Spanish national conscience is affected by the uncertainty raised by the fact that a country that wages a war miles away, in order to keep a colonial territory, might feel willing to take the ongoing negotiations with Spain to a conclusion and thus Gibraltar be returned to Spanish sovereignty' (PCE statement on the Falklands, signed by the Secretariat of the Central Committee of the PCE, 5 May 1982, IISG (SI Archives, Falklands–Malvinas Commission, 1982, Box 979)).
20 'We are not pacifists, we detest the Galtieri dictatorship, we dismiss the notion that the Argentinian seizure of the Falklands is progressive on anti-colonialist grounds. Nevertheless we believe that, in a war between Britain and Argentina, the defeat of British imperialism is the lesser evil. The main enemy is at home' (Hallas, 1982, p. 366).
21 'Act to stop British imperialism's colonial war adventure in South Atlantic' (Press communiqué, *World Federation of Trade Unions*, Praga, 27 Apr. 1982. SI Archives, Falklands–Malvinas Commission, 1982, box 979, IISG).
22 '1- Ask for pacific solution to the Anglo-Argentine conflict within the international institutions; 2- Acknowledge Argentina's claim; 3- Demand withdrawal of troops from the South Atlantic; 4- Condemn US government's Foreign Policy; 5- Urge European Economic Community governments to lift the ban imposed on Argentina; 6- Demand Argentina put an end to the repression directed by the police against the people, to legalize the political parties,

Democrat Party tried to keep a difficult balance between the need to keep SI together under Willy Brandt's leadership and their allegiance to German socialist Chancellor Helmut Schmidt, who was in charge of supporting the pro-British policies. Meanwhile, the socialist French president Francois Mitterrand gave his firm support to Britain from the start: in NATO, in the UN Security Council as well as in his voting on sanctions in the European Community. Active French participation on Britain's side was due to a number of different reasons. At the time, their bonds to Latin America were weaker than those of the Germans, Swedes and Spanish. Besides, France had been a marginal participant in the process led by Brandt in order to renew SI. At the same time, French socialism firmly opposed the military government in Argentina. That could be seen in the influence of the determined activism by exiles that found its high point in the boycott of the football World Cup in 1978. However, the French government never stopped providing Argentina with arms.

There was a perception that the US and Europe had 'betrayed' Latin America and that Latin America found itself alone in facing developed countries' governments and political parties around the continent, even those not related to social democracy or the left.[23] As the war progressed and the US's position moved closer to Britain's, its position in Latin America became more complicated and its influence seemed to re-enter a moment of crisis.[24] Other international and transnational organisations gave their support to Argentina, such as the Non-Aligned Movement and the Permanent Conference of Political Parties of Latin America and the Caribbean (COPPPAL). The Non-Aligned Movement gave a strong endorsement of Argentina's position. Its president at the time, who was no other than Fidel Castro, notoriously welcomed the Argentine chancellor Nicanor Costa Méndez to the plenary of the organisation held in Havana. The same thing happened in the following meeting held in New Delhi. The COPPPAL resoundingly supported Argentina. At the same

---

and to organize free elections. Finally, the solidarity with Argentine people on its fight towards a free, plural, just and egalitarian society; 7- Recognize BLP position on its opposition to Thatcher's Malvinas 'Policy' (Bulletin no. 43, International Union of Socialist Youth (IUSY), June 1982 (SI Archives, Falklands–Malvinas Commission, 1982, box 979, IISG).

23 'Thus, on 5/27/1982, Venezuelan Chancellor, José Alberto Zambrano, criticised the American support for London and requested within the XX American Chancellors' Consultation Meeting the creation of an inter-American armed force to join Argentina in its war against Great Britain' ('Las relaciones con Venezuela', available at: http://www.argentina-rree.com/14/14-054.htm (accessed 10 June 2019)).

24 'The Ecuadorian president, Osvaldo Hurtado, thanked [Leopoldo] Calvo-Sotelo for the "support that has already been given in the recent crisis in the Malvinas through Spanish diplomatic back-up in the Latin American cause". ... Calvo-Sotelo could prove in ... Ecuador, as he would be able to do in ... Colombia and Peru, the disenchantment suffered by the Latin American world in regard to US support of British policy on the Malvinas issue, which had opened a breach of unpredictable consequences between these countries and their neighbour from the North' (Diario, *El País* (Spain), 7 Aug. 1982). Available at: https://elpais.com/diario/1982/08/07/espana/397519203_850215.html (accessed 10 June 2019).

time it harshly criticised the US and British positions. Only at the end of the statement did it say anything that could be understood as a request to the Argentine government to become more democratic.[25]

In the absence of an Argentine leader within SI, it was Carlos Andrés Pérez who took the main action in favour of the South American country. Given the influence of the Venezuelan leader both inside and outside SI, his position would certainly increase the pressure exerted on the transnational social democrat organisation's leadership to put the issue on the agenda at the next formal meeting of the decision-making body. Pérez consolidated his extended international leadership (Gamus, 1990) to prove the strength of his influence in Latin America but also vis-à-vis his European partners, with whom, due to the differences with Nicaragua and El Salvador, he was not on the best of terms at the time. The Venezuelan ex-president immediately understood that the Malvinas War was the final blow for the North–South project with which Willy Brandt had seduced the national leaders of the then so-called Third World.[26]

The prevailing logic of east versus west in the Cold War had prioritised the superpowers while relegating the other countries to secondary roles. On the other hand, the imposition of 'North–South' logic would include developing countries as main actors on the geo-political agenda (Quilligan, 2002). Thus, they were incorporated into the centre stage of international politics with their own needs and not as mere locations where foreign conflicts took place. The conflict in the Malvinas decreed the end of this intention, which could

25 'Argentina is assisted by right and reason in its claim, as has been acknowledged … by the progressive thinking of our time. … We reaffirm our solidarity with the just claims of all peoples and nations of Latin America and the Caribbean whose countries have suffered violation or abuse in their rights through … colonial domination. … We demand that, together with an immediate ceasefire, recognition be made of the rights of that people's claim to sovereignty. … Finally, we express our recognition of the value and patriotism of the Argentine people in their unequal fight aimed at having their sovereignty respected. We hope that as a result of their sacrifice they be granted, henceforth, full exercise of their individual and social freedoms as well as a growing democratic participation in national public life', signed by Ricardo Valero (Secretary of International Affairs, Institutional Revolutionary Party, Mexico), and sent on behalf of Pedro Ojeda Paullada (President of COPPPAL), 13 June 1982 (SI Archives, Falklands–Malvinas Commission, 1982, box 979, IISG).

26 In a speech delivered in Algeria during a meeting on the north–south project, Pérez showed his pessimistic view on the future of such projects: 'Thus it has been proved in the conflict between Britain and Argentina with impressive firmness. We do not hesitate to qualify it as a north–south conflict. […] Beyond the argument used about Argentina's decision to resort to force in order to recover sovereignty … there is the violent and colonialist reaction of Great Britain and the EEC, as well as the US, in turning their backs on a nation of the hemispheric community … Europe did not even consider the reaction that this aggressive and precipitate conduct would cause in our people, or the unexpected consequences of the punitive measures taken by the EEC with hurry, ignorance and violation of the UN declaration about the economic duties and rights of the states' ('North–South economic cooperation and the Falklands War', a speech by Carlos Andrés Pérez (former president of Venezuela), Algeria, 22 May 1982, SI Archives, Falklands–Malvinas Commission, 1982, box 979, IISG).

only be sustained during periods of *détente* in Carter's era. As Carlos Andrés Pérez cogently pointed out, the war would have political consequences in the region, for it would alter relations between countries from Latin America, the USA and Europe.[27] The situation in Latin America was complex because of insurmountable differences on Central America, the economic crisis that started to bite (that same year the so-called 'debt crisis' was unleashed) and the political alienation that Latin American countries suffered from the polarisation of the geo-political map. The Malvinas War challenged Latin American politicians to address their influence in the world.

The war within Socialist International

The next I meeting was scheduled for 26 and 27 May in Helsinki. The topic of the Malvinas was not originally included on the agenda for the meeting, which was to be devoted to the Middle East, Central America and disarmament. The meeting had large press coverage but, in order to avoid public repercussions of their internal problems, an unprecedented measure was taken: to ban public and press presence. The Malvinas issue 'came in through the back door', generating broad discussion and dominating the meeting's development. Its inclusion on the agenda was suggested by Carlos Andrés Pérez, supported by most of the Latin American delegates, and emphasised the terms included in the SICLAC's communication.

The answer to this was under the charge of the British delegate Alex Kitson, who, besides condemning the use of force, proposed to take into consideration the Islanders' right to self-determination, to condemn Argentina's dictatorship and to highlight Great Britain's anti-colonial tradition in Africa and India.[28] However, it was the French delegate's intervention that generated a strong reaction among the Latin Americans and finally caused the meeting to be adjourned.

A participant in that meeting reported in an interview conducted for this investigation that 'There was a moment of disruption; besides, I remember that, for France, Lionel Jospin was very hard on the Latin-Americans – very hard! Just imagine how he was if Brandt asked, "Please, let us stop for 15 minutes"'.[29] In a further letter delivered by the Argentine socialists, the French position was answered with strong criticism:

27 'Contadora group, more than a decision seeking to mediate in the Central American conflict, is a decision that comes after the Malvinas War seeking to find a solution to our differences and problems by ourselves' (Diario *El País* (Spain), 18 Aug. 1986).

28 The magazine of the IS, *Socialist Affairs*, described the meeting, at which the existence of different positions are observed. However, *Socialist Affairs* makes no mention of the depth of the divide between Latin America and Europe (*Socialist Affairs*, 1982, no, 4, pp. 131, 143).

29 Personal interview with Elena Flores, former PSOE delegate to Socialist International (Madrid, March 2010).

> We have received your report ... in principle; the information is incorrect: the aggressor was Great Britain, which attacked the Islands (in) 1833 ... In 1976 and 1977 we warned SI about the subject. [...] Saying that Argentina is the aggressor is as absurd as it would have been to say that the Nazis, occupants of France, had maintained that the allied invasion to liberate it from its usurper was an aggression. Such an attitude places the comrade secretary nearer to the wrong position held during the Algeria and Indochina conflicts than to the anti-colonialist and anti-imperialist position that should be the ideological basis of socialist thought. ... Yours sincerely in SOCIALISM.[30]

The discussion was postponed until the following day, as requested by the British delegation. However, according to information from a personal interview with one of the delegates, the climate of division was such that Brandt himself had to call the meeting off and ask a PSOE delegate to find a solution to the conflict:

> One of the hardest Councils I have attended was held in Helsinki, where the break between Europe and Latin America was brutal ... From the European side, it could be seen that it was a military dictatorship, a dictatorship absolutely, and that there were no reasons listened to [as to] whether the Malvinas were a decolonisation issue or not: he [Gen. Galtieri] was simply a dictator, which was nothing but the truth, catching the wave and doing all these things. And, naturally, there were the Latin Americans, who only saw Argentina's sovereignty over the Malvinas. So, at some point, there was a discussion going on about a statement and, since the fracture was so brutal and no agreement would be reached, Brandt called off the meeting. He took some minutes and called me in because I was already trying to bridge our differences. He called me in and said: 'Are you able to release a statement that will satisfy both sides?' I reply: 'It will be an absolute hybrid statement, but I will try'. Thus it took me 15 to 20 minutes to write a statement and that was what prevented the break from occurring at the time.[31]

Finally, a group coordinated by Thorvald Stoltenberg (International Committee of the Norwegian Labour Party) was formed; they wrote a resolution that contained some of the generic points agreed on by all parties. The points included rejection of the use of force (without clarifying which side had initially used it) and support of the UN Secretary General's efforts at mediation.

Given the magnitude of the internal conflict caused by the war, SI decided to create a Falklands–Malvinas commission that included everyone interested in the issue to avoid repercussions from the conflict striking the whole organisation. The commission had eight members: three from Latin American political parties, three from European ones, plus Labour and an Argentine

---

30 PSP (National Committee) document, Buenos Aires, 31 May 1982, signed by Víctor García Costa (secretary general) and Nestor Martinez Eraso (secretary of international relations) (SI Archives, Falklands–Malvinas Commission, 1982, box 979, IISG).

31 Personal interview with Elena Flores, former PSOE delegate to SI (Madrid, March 2010).

representative. It aimed at supervising the conflict and keeping the SI leadership informed.[32] Its coordination was under the charge of the Norwegian Labour Party and its first meeting was to be held on 21 July 1982 in Paris. However, the war developed faster than the SI commission and, according to the forecasts, would end before the commission could be brought together. The high level of internal conflict and Latin America's claims forced the meeting to be brought forward. Due to the turmoil of the moment, it was not held in Helsinki, as would have been most natural (since the delegates were already there), but in Portugal,[33] with the aim of making progress in organisational matters before the subsequent gathering in Paris.

The meeting was chaotic. It enjoyed the presence of those who were able to travel and endured the criticism of those who were not.[34] Given important absences, the commission abstained from beginning political discussions and limited itself strictly to exchanging points of view about the commission's future work programme. Everything developed too slowly. According to those present, the commission was right to include debates on the ongoing conflict but should have focused mainly on exploring ways to avoid endangering future relations between SI members. There were some informal conversations about Argentina's representation within the commission, since SI had no Argentine member party. It was agreed that the Argentine representative should be accepted by every socialist party and groups in Argentina and inform all these groups and parties on the matter.[35]

From June 1982, Argentina's position on the military was unsustainable.[36] All that remained to be seen was the time when the final assault by the British troops would come. A decision had to be taken on whether to continue with the commission and its activities or not. In one of his personal notes, Brandt

32 Resolution on Falklands Islands–Malvinas (*Socialist Affairs*, 1982, no. 4, p. 142).

33 'Impossible to understand why the meeting was to be held in Lisbon on 29 May when everybody was assembled in Helsinki on 27 May' (Bernt Carlsson's notes on a meeting with Leonard Larsen, Ivar Leveraas, Reiulf Steen and Thorvald Stoltenberg, 14 June 1982 (Bernt Carlsson papers, boxes 9–21, IISG)).

34 'I express our deepest disappointment at the unacceptable procedure for convening the meeting of the eight-member committee of the SI for the Falklands–Malvinas, which has prevented us from participating in this first meeting due to an absolute lack of time. The cable sent on 28 May was delivered on Saturday 29 at the party's general address and handed over to my office on Monday 31' (Margherita Boniver, International Secretariat, Italian Socialist Party, to Bernt Carlsson, 3 June 1982, copied to the Norwegian Labour Party (Bernt Carlsson papers, boxes 9–21, IISG)).

35 Statement by the Norwegian Labour Party, Oslo, 4 June 1982, signed by Reiulf Steen (SI Archives, Falklands–Malvinas Commission, 1982, box 979, IISG).

36 'According to Karl L. Hübener, with whom I met this morning, the US and the British government had come to an agreement through which the British will delay the final assault on Port Stanley until after President Reagan's visit to England and the end of the North Atlantic Treaty Organization (NATO) Summit in Bonn' (Bernt Carlsson's notes, Socialist International Falklands–Malvinas commission, report from the meeting on 9 June 1982 (Bernt Carlsson papers, boxes 9–21, IISG)).

Carlsson showed that he was aware of the challenge posed by SI: 'The moment of truth has come for SI. The South Atlantic conflict has opened up a gap between most European and Latin American parties. [...] The commission we created for the Malvinas crisis will probably not do much to solve the conflict. However, what we can actually do, at least, is to avoid the conflict from extending itself within SI'.[37]

On 23 June the commission's first official meeting was finally held in Paris.[38] At that time, since the war was already over, significant changes were introduced to the meeting's objectives. However, the political conflict among the parties in SI continued. In the following meeting of the Falklands–Malvinas commission, Argentina's SPP raised its own political situation within SI, while Labour sent a second-line delegation. The few agreements reached were on the basis of the repetition of commonplace arguments. Latin American representatives were among the most eager to continue this discussion in order to re-position themselves and increase their influence, which the war had been shown in its true proportions. The contents agreed in the text already openly included references to Argentina's political situation and to the democratic process. Latin American parties began to emphasise this subject, leaving aside the demands for sovereignty that had characterised the time prior to the surrender of Argentina's troops.

One of the few agreements reached at this meeting was to hold another meeting, this time in Caracas, on 20 and 21 July. By then, gathering the SI Falklands–Malvinas commission together once again seemed of no relevance, to the extent that it was held without the presence of the British Labour Party. The British claimed that they had no funding for the trip. This circumstance was exploited by those present to settle an agreement without the British present and thus to improve SI relations with the Latin American parties.[39] Taking advantage of the BLP's absence and a certain European lack of interest in continuing with the subject, the Latin Americans reached a consensus with the German social democrats, some Nordic parties and the SI secretary general on a final statement by the commission. It demanded that negotiations be quickly reactivated and, in the meantime, that the Malvinas be under UN administration. It did not acknowledge Britain's presence in the Islands. The most remarkable detail of the document was that it decisively moved forward in Argentina's democratisation, a fact that, until then, had only been supported

---

37 Bernt Carlsson's notes, Socialist International Falklands–Malvinas commission report from the meeting on 9 June 1982 (Bernt Carlsson papers, boxes 9–21, IISG).

38 The meeting was attended by representatives from Argentina, Great Britain, Italy, Germany, Barbados, Norway, Venezuela and Chile (Bernt Carlsson's notes on the Socialist International Falklands–Malvinas commission, report from the meeting on 9 June 1982 (Bernt Carlsson papers, boxes 9–21, IISG)).

39 Notes on the conversation between Leonard Larsen and Bernt Carlsson (9 Aug. 1982, Bernt Carlsson papers, boxes 9–21, IISG).

by European parties. The end of the conflict and the British victory left no place for the insistence on a ceasefire or for Argentina's claims to sovereignty.

After the war and General Galtieri's resignation as president of Argentina, Latin American parties changed the focus of their claims tying the conflict's final resolution to the immediate restoration of democracy.[40] They insisted there was now no reason to delay elections.[41] To exert pressure in this regard, the commission also called for an international campaign[42]. The statement also upon the SI authorities to embrace the conclusions without waiting for November's SI general meeting.[43] The document (agreed unanimously) was an attempt by Latin American countries to demonstrate a political triumph, something they had been unable to do elsewhere. At the same time, it showed the SI leadership's intention to give its Latin American partners the kind of compensation that had been missing during the development of the conflict.[44]

Labour stated their rejection of the document and issued another statement.[45] Repeating their previous criticism of the need to condemn the actions of the

40 'That the SI declares itself fully in favour of the early restoration of the process of democratisation in the republic of Argentina … We consider this objective of paramount importance. We feel strongly that this demand by the people of Argentina should be met by the military without delay. It would have the advantage of contributing considerably to the creation of a favourable atmosphere for the definitive solution to the controversy in the South Atlantic' (report by the SI working group on the Falklands–Malvinas, Caracas, 7 July 1982 (SI Archives, Falklands–Malvinas Commission, 1982, box 979, IISG)).

41 The document also expressed support for 'Multipartidaria,' which grouped together the different Argentine parties that had sent a delegation to the meeting, even though none of them was an SI member.

42 'It is for these reasons that we consider the postponement of the electoral process until 1984 to be an unnecessary delay which could well have unforeseen and adverse consequences for the future development of peace and democracy in the Argentine Republic. In view of the foregoing, the Commission proposes that the Socialist International and its member parties conduct an international campaign, in particular directed to the military government with the view to pressuring it to honour its commitment given by President General Reynaldo Bignone for the restoration of the democratic process through free and fair elections' (report of the SI working group on the Falklands–Malvinas, Caracas, 7 July 1982 (SI Archives, Falklands–Malvinas Commission, 1982, Box 979, IISG)).

43 'To request the president and the general secretary of the Socialist International after consulting with its member parties to implement the conclusions proposed above without waiting for the bureau meeting in November. This proposal arises from the dynamic and fluid nature of the circumstances surrounding this delicate matter' (report of the SI working group on the Falklands–Malvinas, Caracas, 7 July 1982 (SI Archives, Falklands–Malvinas Commission, 1982, box 979, IISG)).

44 Report of the Socialist International working group on the Falklands–Malvinas, Caracas, 21 July 1982 (SI Archives, Falklands–Malvinas Commission, 1982, box 979, IISG).

45 '1- The statement makes no specific condemnation of the act of aggression from the Galtieri junta which precipitated the conflict. This is regrettable and must be rectified. The Labour Party feels it very important that the community of socialist parties loses no opportunity to express its extreme disapproval of all attempts to use violence to resolve international disputes … 2- The Labour Party associates itself fully with the view that the restoration of democracy in Argentina is of "paramount importance" … 4- At this juncture, after deep

Argentine military *junta*, they noted that this matter was not made explicit in the commission's document. The BLP argued that calling for negotiations in the short run was not realistic since the wounds were still open and Argentina's political future was unclear. Finally, they asked for their points of view to be included in the SI Falklands–Malvinas commission's final statement. The SI secretary general proposed adding such a statement to the commission's official statement as a minority view, but the BLP rejected the proposal. British Labour Party leaders wished to incorporate their own arguments into the final statement, which is why they asked for another meeting of the commission.[46] Somewhat belatedly, the BLP realised that the final statement was a political defeat and that it would be exposed to the whole community of social democrat parties. Carlsson answered, once again, that it was impossible to accomplish the British demand and, as a possible solution to this (in consensus with Brandt), he suggested calling a meeting in 1983 to see if positions could become more flexible.[47] This never took place, partly because the conflict was already in the past and also because Carlos Andrés Pérez rejected such a possibility.[48]

For SI the Malvinas chapter was closed. Even if the result of the conflict and political process did not enjoy great respect from the Latin American parties, within SI at least, they succeeded in having some kind of compensation. This was shown in the delivery of a final report in the meeting held in Basle in November 1982. The SI leadership was more concerned about healing the wounds than about the arguments that gave rise to the conflict, even though

---

passions have been aroused on both sides of the Atlantic and after the trauma through which the Falkland Islanders have been forced to live, it is however unrealistic to call for direct negotiations between Britain and Argentina at this stage. Furthermore, the political situation inside Argentina is in state of flux, it is impossible to predict how long this government will last when elections will finally take place, etc etc. ... we do not consider it appropriate for at least the immediate future to endorse the policy of direct negotiations' (BLP statement signed by J.E. Mortimer (general secretary) and sent to Bernt Carlsson on 2 Sept. 1982 (SI Archives. Falklands–Malvinas Commission, 1982, box 979, IISG)).

46 'Dear *Cofrade*: Thank you for your letter of 8 October 1982 enclosing the report of the Falklands/Malvinas Commission. I am afraid that it is unacceptable to the Labour Party that the report be circulated in the form you suggest. We obviously wish to see the points we raise considered and we would hope incorporated in the statement. We would not support the report as it now stands. I would like to suggest that either there is a further meeting of the commission prior to the Basle meeting or that if the report goes to the Bureau as it now is, adequate time is given for debate and so that we can submit amendments' (letter from J.E. Mortimer (general secretary, labour party) to Bernt Carlsson, 20 Oct. 1982 (SI Archives, Falklands–Malvinas Commission, 1982, box 979, IISG)).

47 Letter from Bernt Carlsson to J.E. Mortimer, London, 28 Oct. 1982 (SI Archives, Falklands–Malvinas Commission, 1982, box 979, IISG).

48 'With regards to another Commission meeting ... I disagree, since this Commission put an end to its meetings in Caracas on 21 July 1982, as stated in the agreement of the same date that was submitted to your consideration and of the president's, Willy Brandt, as duly clarified in the Basle meeting in late November' (letter from Bernt Carlsson to J.E. Mortimer, London, 28 Oct. 1982 (SI Archives, Falklands–Malvinas Commission, 1982, box 979, IISG)).

the relations between some Latin American and European parties seemed a one-way street.

Conclusion

The South Atlantic War was irrefutable proof that the path taken by the US under Ronald Reagan's leadership would not be modified. The main conflict was with the USSR, and every effort was to be directed there, even though it implied abandoning old allies, such as the Argentine military. On the non-aligned and transnational actors' stage, the war was also a warning in that sense. The phase of *détente* was over. The growing polarisation left no space for different projects from those led by the world powers. This fact decisively affected the transnational relations that had been articulated among several left-wing groups of SI and, in particular, under the leadership of the German Willy Brandt. The differences between the SI parties were not merely tacit and showed a certain lack of concern from the Latin Americans towards the problem of democracy and their structural bonds to nationalism. The proximity of electoral processes in Venezuela, Costa Rica and the Dominican Republic restricted the SI-affiliated parties' margins for manoeuvre even more, since their electorate expressed concern about the communist expansion in Central America. To sum up, there was pressure on SI members to prioritise their primary interests as national organisations over collective construction. This eroded the transnational project that the SI had successfully embodied since 1976. Within that framework, to enlarge the focus on the Malvinas War – traditionally reduced to its military aspects – may show the broad framework of relations and political transnational activities of the parties as well as the existing difficulties in consolidating a left-wing democratic space worldwide.

A comprehensive approach to the history of democratisation requires us to deepen our understanding of the interactions in transnational party networks, as well as the current debates about left-wing politics in the region. It must build a full picture of the actors' universe on the left, its programmatic traditions and the history of its heterogenic strategies and alliances.

References

Barricada (official organ of the FSLN), 10 May 1982.

Blázquez Vilaplana, B. (2006) *La proyección de un líder político: Felipe González y Nicaragua 1978–1996* (Seville: Centro de Estudios Andaluces).

Carleton, D. and M. Stohl (1985) 'The foreign policy of human rights: rhetoric and reality from Jimmy Carter to Ronald Reagan', *Human Rights Quarterly*, 7 (2): 205–29.

Clarke, H.D., W. Mishler and P. Whiteley (1990) 'Recapturing the Falklands: models of Conservative popularity, 1979–83', *British Journal of Political Science*, 1 (20): 63–81.

Crewe, I. and A. King (1996) [1995]) *SDP: The Birth, Life, and Death of the Social Democratic Party* (Oxford: Oxford University Press).

Freeman, A. (1984) 'El laborismo británico: el dilema de las alianzas', *Nueva Sociedad*, 72: 68–77.

Gamus, R. (1990) *Una fugaz convergencia. CAP y la IS en Centroamerica* (Caracas: Consejo de desarrollo científico y humanístico, Universidad Central de Venezuela).

Grabendorff, W. (2001) 'International support for democracy in contemporary Latin America: the role of the party internationals', pp. 201–26 in L. Whitehead (ed.), *The International Dimensions of Democratization: Europe and the Americas* (Oxford: Oxford University Press).

Guilhot, N. and P. Schmitter (2000) 'De la transition à la consolidation: une lecture rétrospective des democratization studies', *Revue Française de Science Politique*, 50 (4/5): 615–31.

Hallas, D. (1998) [1982] 'Socialism and war', in L. German and R. Hoveman (eds.), *A Socialist Review* (London: Bookmarks), pp. 366–73.

Halliday, F. (1983) *The Making of the Second Cold War* (London: Verso).

Huntington, S.P. (1994) *La tercera ola. La democratización a finales del siglo XX* (Barcelona: Paidós) (Spanish translation of S. P. Huntington (1991) *The Third Wave: Democratization in the Late Twentieth Century* (Norman, OK: Oklahoma University Press)).

Keck, M.E. and K. Sikkink (2000) *Activistas sin fronteras* (Mexico City: Siglo XXI) (Spanish translation of M.E. Keck and K. Sikkink (1998) *Activists Beyond Borders: Advocacy Networks in International Politics* (Ithaca, NY: Cornell University Press)).

Keohane, R.O. and J.E. Nye (1971) 'Transnational relations and world politics: an introduction', in R.O. Keohane and J.E. Nye (eds), *Transnational Relations and World Politics* (Cambridge, MA: Harvard University Press), pp. 329–49.

Lesgart, C. (2002) 'Usos de la transición a la democracia. Ensayo, ciencia y política en la década del ochenta', *Estudios Sociales*, 22/23: 163–85.

López, M., C. Figueroa and B. Rajland (eds) (2010) *Temas y procesos de la historia reciente de América Latina* (Santiago de Chile: ARCIS/CLACSO).

Lvovich, D., E. Bohoslavsky, M. Franco and M. Iglesias (eds) (2011) *Problemas de historia reciente del Cono Sur*, 2 vols (Buenos Aires: Prometeo Libros).

Markarian, V. (2004) 'De la lógica revolucionaria a las razones humanitarias: la izquierda uruguaya en el exilio y las redes transnacionales de derechos humanos (1972–1976)', *Cuadernos del CLAEH*, 89 (2): 85–108.

Martz, J.D. (ed.) (1988) *United States Policy in Latin American: A Quarter Century of Crisis and Challenge, 1961–1986* (Lincoln, NE: University of Nebraska Press).

Mira, G. and F. Pedrosa (eds.) (2016) *Extendiendo los límites: Nuevas agendas en historia reciente* (Buenos Aires: Eudeba-Ediciones Universidad Salamanca).

Mujal León, E. (1989) *European Socialism and the Conflict in Central America* (Washington, DC: Center for Strategic and International Studies).

Oberti, A. and R. Pittaluga (2004/2005) 'Temas para una agenda de debate en torno al pasado reciente', *Políticas de la memoria*, 5: 9–14 (Buenos Aires: CEDINCI).

O'Donnell, G., P. Schmitter and L. Whitehead (eds) (1994) *Transiciones desde un gobierno autoritario* (Barcelona: Paidós).

Pastor, R. (1984) 'Continuity and change in US foreign policy: Carter and Reagan on El Salvador', *Journal of Policy Analysis and Management*, 3 (2): 175–90.

Pedrosa, F. (2012) *La otra izquierda. La Internacional Socialista en América Latina* (Buenos Aires: Capital Intelectual).

Pérez de Cuéllar, J. (1997) *Peregrinaje por la paz* (Lima: Aguilar).

Romero, L.A. (2012) *Breve historia contemporánea de la Argentina* (Buenos Aires: Fondo de Cultura Económica).

Quilligan, J. (2002) *The Brandt Equation: 21st Century Blueprint for the New Global Economy* (Philadelphia, PA: Brandt 21 Forum).

Sarlo, B. (2003) *Tiempo presente: notas sobre el cambio de una cultura* (Buenos Aires: Siglo XXI).

Sikkink, K. (2004) *Mixed Signals: US Human Rights Policy and Latin America* (Ithaca, NY: Cornell University Press).

Soto Gamboa, Á. (2004) 'Historia del presente: estado de la cuestión y conceptualización', *Historia Actual Online*, 3: 101–16, available at https://dialnet.unirioja.es/descarga/articulo/829443.pdf (accessed 16 Aug. 2018).

Scott, J.M. and K.J. Walters (2000) 'Supporting the wave: western political foundations and the promotion of a global democratic society', *Global Society*, 14 (2): 237–57.

Trías, V. (1977) 'El Atlántico Sur: Encrucijada del Futuro Latinoamericano', *Nueva Sociedad*, 33: 129–39.

4. The Falklands–Malvinas War and transitions to democracy in Latin America: the turning point of 1979–82

Guillermo Mira

The commemoration of the 30th anniversary of the Falklands–Malvinas War (April–June 1982) saw the intensification of the polemic surrounding the circumstances and consequences of the war, particularly in Argentina: the conflict's intimate connection with the military dictatorship, the place in history of the young conscripts summoned to defend the *patria* and of their military leaders and the link between defeat in this conflict and the recovery of democracy in 1983 were all subject to renewed discussion. Conducted against the backdrop of Argentina's vociferous assertion of claims to sovereignty and Britain's pointed silence on the matter, the then current positions of the British and Argentine governments were subject to intense debate and revealed deep divisions, no longer between the opposing nations but within Argentina itself.[1] The content of this debate paves the way for a reconsideration of the transition to democracy in both Argentina and surrounding countries. This article establishes a dialogue between history and political science, disputing the homogeneity of the concept of the 'third wave' of democracy to describe the dissolution of authoritarian regimes in Latin America; and instead proposes a distinction between the recuperation of democracy prior to and following the period between 1979 and 1982, divided precisely by the outbreak of war. Moreover, the revision of the Argentine case offers the opportunity to reconsider substantial questions relating to the transition which, despite having lost their previously central position and urgency over time (and in light of the triumph of the pro-democratic 'ethos'), remain to a large degree unanswered and still represent an underlying influence

---

1   Both the British and Argentine media echoed and participated in this debate, although it appears that the debates garnered greater public interest in Argentina. See, for example: Lorenz, 2011a, 2011b, 2011c, 2012a; Veiga, 2011; Palermo, 2012a, 2012b, 2012c; Tokatlian, 2012; Romero, 2012a, 2012b; Menem, 2012; Storani, 2012; P. O'Donnell, 2012; Jenkins, 2012a, 2012b; Carlin, 2012; Milmo, 2012; Herren, 2012; Goñi, 2012.

G. Mira, 'The Falklands–Malvinas War and transitions to democracy in Latin America: the turning point of 1979–82', in G. Mira and F. Pedrosa (eds.), *Revisiting the Falklands–Malvinas Question: Transnational and Interdisciplinary Perspectives* (London: University of London Press, 2020), pp. 97–110. License: CC-BY-NC-ND 4.0.

on the configuration of these democracies in the present day. These substantial questions can be summarised in three areas of enquiry:
- The reasons behind the return of democracy in Latin America in the 1980s;
- The effect of the international context and external influences on political change within Argentina and other Latin American countries in this period;
- The relationship between the type of transition and the subsequent development of the emerging democracy in each case; and the potential long-term impact of this transition on the present-day form of democracy.

In 1986, David Rock and Suzanne Avellano analysed the return to democracy in Argentina as follows:

> It is difficult to depict the Argentine elections of 1983 as part of a broader transition from authoritarian towards democratic systems throughout Latin America. The election has no simple connection to the current political transition in Latin America which, as an outgrowth of the debt crisis, calls to mind the domino-like spate of political changes that occurred between 1930 and 1933 and from 1944 to 1946. Argentina's return to constitutional government in late 1983 was its fourth such transition in the previous twenty-five years, the most recent expression of a long-established cycle of alternating military regimes and civilian representative governments. In general, simplified terms, these shifts from one form of government to the other have occurred as a result of economic breakdowns arising from balance-of-payments crises. True to the pattern, the latest transition in Argentina reflects the failure of the economic program of the late 1970s, which led to the economic collapse of 1981 and the country's subsequent foreign debt crisis. In 1982 as the crisis loomed, the military regime made a final, desperate effort to consolidate its dwindling authority by occupying the Malvinas/Falkland Islands. The failure of this adventure left the regime with no option but to abdicate and schedule elections (Rock and Avellano, 1986, p. 189).

More than thirty years have passed since this text was written, leading us to ask what we have learned in the intervening years. We can assess whether Rock and Avellano's judgement is accepted by the majority of scholars today and explore what can be said about the link between the Argentine transition and the 'third wave of democracy' from the viewpoint of the present. We can ask whether the time that has passed allows us to produce an interpretation that is more informed, better documented and more impartial; or whether, instead, the debates over memory and the wide range of versions circulating in the public sphere render reconstruction a more complex enterprise and obscure our understanding of this nebulous past. Finally, we can interrogate the influence of intellectual and academic output on the dismantling of the authoritarian regimes and the establishment of the present-day democracies.

Causes

In order to account for the recuperation of democracy across much of Latin America between the end of the 1970s and the start of the 1990s, at least three possible explanatory paradigms have been advanced:

1. The theory of agency or 'interaction' outlined in *Transitions from Authoritarian Rule*, a work complied by Guillermo O'Donnell, Philippe C. Schmitter and Laurence Whitehead, the second part of which is dedicated exclusively to the study of Latin America (O'Donnell, Schmitter and Whitehead, 1986, pp. 15–329). The influence of this work on our conceptualisation of democratic transition has been both extraordinary and long lasting; and yet, despite the detailed country-by-country analysis it contains, its editors do not seek primarily to explain the causes of transition, but rather to explore its outcomes (as the text's subtitle attests). The editors centre their theoretical framework on what was happening at the time of writing and what could happen in the future, leaving aside consideration of the past. This is not due to lack of knowledge on the subject but to the fact that the study seemingly does not aim to establish causal connections between past and present, seeking instead to record and account for the political change taking place at the time. Broadly speaking, the interpretative framework of this seminal work does not emphasise the 'why' but the 'how'. The international context and other external factors are not ignored (in fact Whitehead dedicates a chapter to the topic) (Whitehead, 1986, pp. 3–46), but they are relegated to a secondary plane. The actors allocated most importance are the internal political agents, particularly the elites, who are considered as the driving force behind regime change. It is this perspective that informs the 'theory of agency' which shapes the work's interpretation, including its focus on outcomes and the uncertainty surrounding the results of this process of 'institutional engineering' (Diamond, Linz and Seymour, 1989).[2]

2. The second interpretative paradigm stems from Huntington's concept of the 'third wave' (Huntington, 1991). In essence, this perspective does not contradict the suppositions of the previous 'interactionist' interpretation, but grounds them in the historical process. Employing the concept of 'wave' in order to explain how democracies come into being, this theory offers a vision over the long term (with three waves – three historical moments – considered in strict chronological terms). This vision introduces international factors (which, for Huntington, are crucial to understanding the withdrawal of the authoritarian regimes); and its

---

[2] See also: Pastor, 1989; Karl, 1990; Mainwaring, O'Donnell and Valenzuela, 1992; Haggard and Kaufman, 1995; Linz and Stepan, 1996; Whitehead, 1996; Agüero and Stark, 1998; Garretón, 2003; Mainwaring and Pérez Liñán, 2003; Domínguez and Shifter, 2003.

focus in some way 'universalises' the interactionist theory, endowing it with worldwide implications. From its opening pages, *The Third Wave* displays a clear ideological stamp: written in the midst of the collapse of communism, it proclaims the superiority of the 'liberal democracy' embodied by the United States.

3. The third option stems from an emerging area of study undertaken by historians which is slowly beginning to erode some of the conclusions so solidly established by the preceding theories. In a revision of Latin America's political traditions, Alan Knight recognises the fundamental role played by the national elites in the last wave of democratisation, although he nuances this statement by highlighting that these same elites and the wealthy were initially in favour of the dictatorships (in order to contain the left-wing 'threat') and only supported the return of democracy in the light of changing circumstances. Knight also provides a warning about the type of democracy that was implemented:

> Before we get too self-congratulatory, however, we should recall that democratization processes have typically been 'padlocked'. [...] Indeed, in recent years the 'padlocks' have tended to get thicker and more unpickable. That is to say, recent military withdrawals from rule have been accompanied by policies designed to remove the original reasons for military intervention (radicalism, Marxism, 'economic populism', militant unionism, peasant mobilization, threats to the army as an institution). Indeed, it has even been suggested that recent scholarship on democratization [...] both embodies and endorses this 'padlocking' process. According to Paul Cammack (2000, p. 405), 'O'Donnell and Schmitter [...] make perfectly clear (as do Linz and Stepan) that they choose to stress elite strategy over structure because democracy will only work if the capacity of the left and working-class forces to shape it is limited'; hence, Cammack concludes, their 'neutral contribution to political science' is, in fact, 'a highly ideological intervention in contemporary politics' (Knight, 2001, p. 176 and footnote 60).

In line with these assertions, Knight highlights that 'bottom-up' public pressure was a negligible factor in the recent Latin American processes of democratisation. His analysis also stresses the inconsistencies in the behaviour of influential international actors:

> The US – the primary external actor – welcomed the Brazilian and Chilean coups; but later exerted pressure for a return to democracy. US thinking in this sense roughly paralleled that of domestic elites: authoritarian rule was preferable to supposed chaos or communism; but a moderate padlocked democracy was preferable to either, in terms of both normative values and practical politics (Knight, 2001, p. 178).

More recently, Paul Drake has described the wave of 'neoliberal democracies' established across Latin America as a democratic 'tsunami' (Drake, 2009, pp.

201–43). Yet Drake recognises the difficulty of explaining why these neoliberal regimes were able to establish themselves so firmly despite the mediocrity of their results. His interpretation provides a different configuration of the local and international factors highlighted by the theories outlined above. Whilst accepting that national actors played a crucial role, Drake emphasises the absence of drastic changes (whether cultural, economic or institutional) at the heart of Latin American societies which would explain this sudden democratic turn. In order to resolve this enigma, Drake underlines two significant considerations:

> The biggest change in thinking about democracy was the emphasis on its intrinsic value as a set of institutions and procedures rather than outcomes. Many Latin Americans moved away from popular democracy toward protected democracy, or at least closer to the U.S view of democracy as essentially a way to organize governance (Drake, 2009, p. 215).

As this judgement suggests, the brutal human rights violations, the errors in the management of the economy and other examples of misconduct by the military had rendered a more moderate idea of democracy acceptable, providing it put an end to the period of dictatorship. Second, and perhaps most importantly:

> Under the aegis of economic and political neoliberalism, protected democracies prevailed over popular democracies in terms of mass mobilization and benefits (…) At least up to the 2000s, it seemed that so long as civilian and military élites agreed that protected democracies were desirable, almost regardless of other variables, those democracies could persevere, despite their shortcomings (Drake, 2009, pp. 214–5).[3]

But it is to international factors that Drake attributes the greatest importance, organising these under four subheadings: economics, imperialism, ideology and the domino effect. Drake's insistence on both the impact of the economic crisis of the 1980s and the movements of powerful international actors (the United States, the Vatican, the European Economic Community and the USSR) echoes the argument put forward by Huntington. However, Drake's perspective departs from that of the US political scientist in one crucial point: his narrative of the influence of the United States recognises a far more complex political landscape:

> In this latest period, the Unites Sates played a contradictory role. Until the late 1980s, the Cold War kept the United States sympathetic to anti-communist dictators and leery of less vigilant democrats. After supporting military dictatorships in the 1960s and early 1970s, most infamously in Brazil and Chile, Washington championed human rights and democracy under President Jimmy Carter in the late 1970s. The Colossus of the North tried to take some credit for the surge of democratization in the

---

3 Note that Drake's idea of 'protected democracy' contains an echo of Knight's 'padlocked' democracy.

1980s and 1990s [...] However, in most cases, Washington essentially played a reactive role (Drake, 2009, pp. 211–2).

In response to this range of interpretations, the section below explores the impact of international factors, including the ambiguous actions of the United States, on the evolution of the Falklands–Malvinas War and its effects on both Argentine politics and the international context.

The influence of external factors: lessons from the Argentine case

The circumstances of the Falklands–Malvinas War display substantial differences from other types of military intervention or conflict that set in motion processes of transition, such as in Greece and Portugal (to take examples from the third wave, but the cases of Germany and Japan could be included if we adopt a broader focus). In Argentina, the full spectrum of the political classes, from left to right, supported the war and gave their enthusiastic approval to the armed forces' action in defence of national sovereignty. Strictly speaking, the Falklands debacle not only tarnished the military, but also damaged the credibility of the nation's political leadership as a whole.[4]

To return to the apparently self-evident but problematic connection between 'defeat in the Falklands' and the 'recovery of democracy', it is essential to note that the end of the war did not bring about the fall of the dictatorship but instead produced a political earthquake that opened a deep crater: crucially, the way in which that vacuum would be filled was unresolved. Yet it must also be recognised that if the war had occurred three or four years previously, it would have taken place within a very different international context. Before discussing these changes, it is worth making two observations about the meaning of the term 'international context' within the perspective outlined in this article:

1. The understanding of this term here departs from the vision that purports a clear separation between 'internal factors' and 'external or international factors' (a separation implicit in both the 'interactionist' and third-wave theories), adopting instead a focus akin to that proposed by Fernando Pedrosa in his study of Socialist International in Latin America (Pedrosa, 2009). Instead of two clearly delineated categories, Pedrosa outlines a history of interactions between transnational actors, reflecting a patchwork of reciprocal, although unequal, influences.
2. References to the 'international context' here allude to at least three dimensions: the geo-political situation, the international economic

4 On the evolution of the Falklands–Malvinas War and its political and cultural repercussions at a national and international level, see: Gambini, 1982; Laffin, 1982; *The Sunday Times*, 1982; Hastings and Jenkins, 1983; Verbitsky, 1985; Rozitchner, 1985; Adams, 1986; Burns Marañón, 1992; Blaustein and Zubieta, 1998; Guber, 2001; Balza, 2003; Novaro and Palermo, 2003; Freedman, 2005; McGuirk, 2007; García Quiroga and Seear, 2009; Yofre, 2011; Lorenz, 2012.

conditions and status of the financial markets (in the capitalist world) and the 'spirit of the age', meaning both the principles, ideologies and political imaginaries governing international relations and the margins of action that are affected by material and symbolic factors.

Following on from the first of these points, this article contends that the events of the period 1979–82 profoundly altered, in a very short space of time, several key aspects of the international context. The promotion of democracy and human rights by the Carter administration (from 1977), the election of Pope John Paul II and his crusade against communism, beginning with his native Poland (1978), the Nicaraguan Revolution (1979), the Iranian Revolution (1979), the election of Margaret Thatcher in the United Kingdom (1979), the Soviet invasion of Afghanistan (1979), the electoral victory of Ronald Reagan in the United States (1980), the *coup d'état* in Poland (1980), the Falklands–Malvinas conflict (April–June 1982) and the Mexican debt crisis (August 1982) were defining episodes in the fabric of the period.[5]

The impact of this explosion of events in the space of four short years shaped profound differences between the transitions that took place before and after the date that concludes the period (1982). From this starting point, this article questions the homogeneity of Huntington's third wave: despite the powerful nature of this metaphor, the wave did not break at the same time or in the same way on different shores. Within Latin America, the transitions to democracy in the Dominican Republic, Ecuador, Peru and even Bolivia (perhaps the most ambiguous case: a 'transition within a transition') were not driven by the same forces or subject to the same conditions as the return to democracy in Argentina, Uruguay, Brazil, Chile or Paraguay. The Central American countries can be considered a separate group, but one more closely allied with the post-1982 transitions than those that took place prior to this date.[6]

In short, if we consider external influences as dynamic processes in constant interaction with other (internal) factors, rather than as fixed circumstances to be taken into account, the dynamic of the democratic wave is substantially altered. This article proposes the events of the period of 1979–82 as a dividing line between two types of transition. Until 1979 the Soviet threat to the capitalist system remained a potent force; and, moreover, the crisis of free-market capitalism in 1973 had boosted the attractiveness and plausibility of an alternative to a system that Marxist theorists considered condemned to founder. In this context, it seemed logical to imagine and fight for a version of the socialist model. In other words, the left (whether armed or not) was still synonymous with the idea of revolution (as demonstrated in the cases of Nicaragua and El Salvador). However, in the period following the conclusion

---

5 Useful sources on these events include Carothers, 1991 and Lowenthal, 1991.
6 For a more detailed discussion of the relationship between historical circumstances and regional factors in the implementation of Latin American democracies, see Mira Delli-Zotti, 2010.

of the Falklands–Malvinas War (June 1982) and the outbreak of the debt crisis immediately afterwards (August of the same year), the image of the Soviet Union as an imminent threat had faded; Thatcher and Reagan's 'conservative revolution' presented itself as an effective and audacious means of both reinvigorating capitalism and defeating communism; and the explosion in the level of external debt across Latin America was interpreted as sounding the death knell of the developmentalist model of import substitution, considered to be in urgent need of replacement. As far as revolutionary utopianism was concerned, in the wake of the brutal repression of these ideals in the 1970s the flourishing of democracy that spread from country to country removed this as a realistic political option.

The typology of transitions: the transitional matrix and its conditioning factors

Despite the overwhelming consensus that Argentina's transition to democracy was caused by the collapse of the military dictatorship, brought about in turn by defeat in the Falklands, this affirmation appears to rest less on a detailed examination of the facts and more on the limited range of options offered by the typology of transitions developed by political science. Perhaps the most sophisticated classification is that presented by Share and Mainwaring (Share and Mainwaring, 1986), who distinguish between three different situations: transition through 'regime defeat', through 'transaction' or through 'extrication'. In the first case described by these authors, transition is brought about by an external military defeat or a severe internal crisis that shatters the regime (such as in Germany and Italy after the Second World War, Greece and Portugal in the 1970s, or Argentina after its defeat by the British). Under this type of transition, the regime loses all negotiating capacity, unlike in the other two cases. In a 'transition through extrication' the weakening of the authoritarian government forces it to liberalise the regime and move towards democracy, retaining some capacity to influence the transition process (such as in Uruguay and Bolivia). Finally, in the 'transition through transaction' the elites of the authoritarian regime retain enough power to guide the change towards a 'tutelary democracy', such as in Brazil or Chile. Although Share and Mainwaring place Argentina in the first of these three categories, it is worth reconsidering whether the Argentine transition can truly be considered an example of 'regime defeat'. In a sense, the Argentine case can be placed partially in all three categories outlined above and at the same time in none. An expert on the topic – a specialist in political communications – provides a careful explanation of this hybrid character:

> The Argentine transition oscillates between a total rupture with the military regime and a certain continuity, in the sense that there was no abrupt breach with the regime [...] Seen from this perspective, the

Argentine transition is a hybrid one, where although there was no legal continuation of the military regime, neither was there an abrupt breach with it. In fact, in the Armed Forces and the Civil Service, structural changes occurred only at the upper echelons of both organisations (Catterberg, 1989, pp. 19–20).

To characterise the Argentine transition as an example of 'regime defeat' or collapse is, therefore, far from satisfactory. In the first place, the concrete effects of the war on the dictatorship and the country were irrelevant: It did not affect the infrastructure of any government in Latin America and the military immediately replaced the weaponry destroyed in the war, bankrolled by the public purse. Second, once the *mariscales de la derrota* (those responsible for defeat) had been identified, the army took control of the situation and continued to govern alone. The pressure to hand over power to civilians was neither immediate nor intense, which explains the time lapse of 505 days between the end of the war and the holding of elections.

The fact that the military did not remain longer in government was due to the *junta*'s inability to manage the economic situation, but they sought to prolong their time in power as far as possible in order to leave things 'tied up nice and tight' (Burns Marañón, 1992, pp. 155–70).[7] In short, this represented an attempt to establish protection against future accusations of accountability, particularly regarding the 'dirty war' against subversion (as it was termed by the *junta*), but also in terms of 'los ilícitos' (economic and financial operations of dubious legality that were undertaken, supported or approved by the military). Lastly, it is inadequate to refer to the 'collapse of the dictatorship' not only in light of the parsimony with which the army managed the transitional post-Malvinas period, but also in terms of the role of the armed forces as the principal destabilising factor under the first democratic government. It would be more accurate, therefore, to speak of the military as having withdrawn to the barracks, which would bear a closer resemblance to Share and Mainwaring's concept of 'transition through extrication'. This categorisation opens a series of further questions, including whether it was an orderly or chaotic withdrawal, what guarantees about the future political governance of the country were demanded by the armed forces and whether those guarantees were fulfilled.

The military sought to protect all the actions of the 'proceso' (particularly those relating to the fight against 'subversion') from judicial scrutiny, passing the Law of National Pacification in 1983, a clear self-amnesty. The acceptance of this law would demand some degree of agreement with the 'democratic forces'. All transitions in the Southern Cone occurred through negotiation between the military governments and the civil elites who would take their

---

7   Ch. 8: 'Una transición renuente'. See also: Yofre, 2011, Ch. 7 (pp. 489–536): 'Bignone, el último presidente de facto. El destape'. Significantly, the title of the documentary produced for television by Tranquilo Producciones on the 25th anniversary of the 1983 elections (Buenos Aires, 2008), was *505 días. La Transición argentina* [*The Argentine Transition*].

place (in the mould of 'transition through transaction'). All, that is, except the case of Argentina. The 'Malvinas effect' removed the possibility of a 'transición pactada', or 'negotiated transition', as the political parties refused to negotiate the return to constitutional order with a military dictatorship that had been completely discredited and widely condemned after defeat in the war. However, it is necessary to reflect upon the internal implications of this external setback. The armed forces immediately set about hiding, minimising and twisting the reasons behind the war and its failure, with a not inconsiderable degree of success. Why was an immediate public investigation about what happened in Malvinas not launched? Why was the Rattenbach Report not officially distributed until thirty years after the war's conclusion? Why were the Malvinas trials brought to a halt? The military had much to hide, and therefore much to negotiate (Lorenz, 2012b, pp. 177–98).[8] The democratic parties, in turn, dissolved the coalition known as the 'Multipartidaria', realising that it now made little sense to negotiate with the discredited military as a block, and instead embarked upon their electoral campaigns as individual parties.

Despite all the factors discussed above, negotiation did take place, covered up to protect the party which had agreed to it in order to avoid the condemnation of many supporters and members of the party who had been severely affected by repression under the dictatorship. In the Argentine return to democracy, an agreement (*pacto*) – impunity in exchange for governability – was sought between the outgoing military *junta* and the political force best placed to achieve an electoral win: the Justicialist Party (Partido Justicialista). Despite the secrecy, during the transition the leader of the Radical Party (Partido Radical) denounced the agreement between unions and the military, although no proof was offered. The defeat of Ítalo Luder, the Justicialist presidential candidate in the October elections that year, prevented the realisation of the agreement and contributed to the sidelining of the accusations aired during the political campaign.[9] Today, witnesses to the agreement corroborate its existence, which adds a crucial element to our revision of the transition and its results.

Conclusion

This chapter has explored the surprising turn to democracy in Latin America three decades ago and, in the case of Argentina, has provided a closer examination of the nature of this change. We can conclude that it was not a transition through collapse, as is commonly argued, or through extrication. Instead, we could say that the Argentine case was subject to attempts to control or condition the transition through negotiation (such as in Chile and Brazil), but these plans failed when the party that should have won the elections lost them

---

8   Ch. 7: 'Guerreros de dos guerras. Los militares y Malvinas'; *505 días. La transición argentina* (2008), DVD 2: 'La derrota en Malvinas'.

9   *505 días. La transición argentina* (2008), DVD 3: 'Comienza la campaña'.

instead. This fact renders the Argentine transition ultimately unclassifiable and unique: neither regime defeat, nor transaction nor extrication. Moreover, the chapter has reconsidered the Falklands–Malvinas War through an international lens: the war not only affected the future of the Argentine dictatorship, but also formed part of a series of events that would change the conditions for the processes of change underway in other Latin American countries, which until now have been considered primarily in terms of a single, homogenous wave.

Important areas of consideration present themselves for future study. In the case of Argentina, the results of the uncontrolled, open transition generate worrying questions which are yet to be answered:

1. What happened between 1984 and 1989 to create the conditions for Carlos Menem, at the head of the Justicialist Party, to dedicate his first electoral term to institutionalising – with popular support – the same economic policy and model of society pursued by the widely condemned military dictatorship?
2. What were the outcomes of the democratic transition in the short term?
3. Is a political analysis sufficient to determine what type of transition took place?

References

Adams, V. (1986) *The Media and the Falklands War* (London: Macmillan).

Agüero, F. and J. Stark (eds.) (1998) *Fault Lines of Democracy in Post-Transition Latin America* (Miami, FL: North-South Center Press).

Balza, M.A. (2003) *Malvinas. Gesta e incompetencia* (Buenos Aires: Atlántida).

Blaustein, E. and M. Zubieta (1998) *Decíamos ayer. La prensa argentina bajo el Proceso* (Buenos Aires: Colihue).

Burns Marañón, J. (1992) *La tierra que perdió sus héroes. La guerra de Malvinas y la transición democrática en Argentina* (Buenos Aires: FCE).

Carlin, J. (2012) 'Thatcher, libertadora argentina', *El País*, 1 April, https://elpais.com/internacional/2012/03/30/actualidad/1333127708_772000.html

Carothers, T. (1991) *In the Name of Democracy. U.S. Policy Toward Latin America in the Reagan Years* (Berkeley: University of California Press).

Catterberg, E. (1989) *Los argentinos frente a la política. Cultura política y opinión pública en la transición argentina a la democracia* (Buenos Aires: Planeta).

Diamond, L., J.J. Linz and S.M. Lipset (eds.) (1989) *Democracy in Developing Countries: Latin America* (Boulder: Rienner).

Domínguez, J.I. and M. Shifter (eds.) (2003) *Constructing Democratic Governance in Latin America* (Baltimore, MD: Johns Hopkins University Press).

Drake, P. (2009) *Between Tyranny and Anarchy. A History of Democracy in Latin America, 1800–2006* (Stanford, CT: Stanford University Press).

Freedman, L. (2005) *The Official History of the Falklands Campaign* (London: Routledge).

Gambini, H. (1982) *Crónica documental de las Malvinas* (Buenos Aires: Redacción-Sánchez Teruelo).

García Quiroga, D.F. and M. Seear (eds.) (2009) *Hors de Combat. The Falklands–Malvinas Conflict in Retrospect* (Nottingham: CCCP).

Garretón, M.A. (2003) *Incomplete Democracy: Political Democratization in Chile and Latin America* (Chapel Hill, NC: University of North Carolina Press).

Goñi, U. (2012) 'Argentinian president attacks UK refusal to negotiate on Falklands', *The Guardian*, 2 April.

Guber, R. (2001) *¿Por qué Malvinas? De la causa nacional a la guerra absurda* (Buenos Aires: Fondo de Cultura Económico).

Haggard, S. and R.R. Kaufman (1995) *The Political Economy of Democratic Transitions* (Princeton, NJ: Princeton University Press).

Hastings, M. and S. Jenkins (1983) *The Battle for the Falklands* (London: Michael Joseph).

Herren, G. (2012) 'Argentina renunció a la fuerza militar disuasiva para recuperar Malvinas y el espacio austral; Gran Bretaña y Estados Unidos, no', *Argenpress*, 2 April.

Huntington, S. (1991) *The Third Wave. Democratization in the Late Twentieth Century* (Norman, OK: Oklahoma University Press).

Jenkins, S. (2012a) 'Margaret Thatcher's biggest debt was to Argentina's navy', *The Guardian*, 22 March, https://www.theguardian.com/commentisfree/2012/mar/22/margaret-thatcher-argentina-falklands.

— (2012b) 'Falklands war 30 years on and how it turned Thatcher into a world celebrity', *The Guardian*, 1 April, https://www.theguardian.com/uk/2012/apr/01/falklands-war-thatcher-30-years.

Karl, T.L. (1990) 'Dilemmas of democratization in Latin America', *Comparative Politics*, 23 (1): 1–22.

Knight, A. (2001) 'Democratic and revolutionary traditions in Latin America', *Bulletin of Latin American Research*, 20 (2): 147–86.

Laffin, J. (1982) *Fight for the Falklands!* (London: Sphere).

Linz, J.J. and A. Stepan (1996) *Problems of Democratic Transition and Consolidation: Southern Europe, South America, and Post-Communist Europe* (Baltimore, MD and London: Johns Hopkins University Press).

Lorenz, F. (2011a) 'Se habla de Malvinas al estilo Billiken', *Página/12*, 19 June.

— (2011b) 'Malvinas todavía necesita Memoria, Verdad y Justicia', *Clarín*, 28 Sept.

— (2011c) 'Malvinas, el revisionismo y el rubor de Laura', *Página/12*, 9 Dec.

— (2012a) 'Simplificaciones Malvineras', *Página/12*, 5 March.

— (2012b) *Las guerras por Malvinas 1982–2012* (Buenos Aires: Edhasa).

Lowenthal, A. (1991) *Exporting Democracy. The United States and Latin America* (Baltimore, MD and London: Johns Hopkins University Press).

McGuirk, B. (2007) *Falklands–Malvinas. An Unfinished Business* (Seattle, WA: New Ventures).

Mainwaring, S., G. O'Donnell and J.S. Valenzuela (eds.) (1992) *Issues in Democratic Consolidation: the New South American Democracies in Comparative Perspective* (Notre Dame: University of Notre Dame Press).

Mainwaring, S. and A. Pérez Liñán (2003) 'Level of Development and Democracy: Latin American Exceptionalism, 1945–1996', *Comparative Political Studies*, 36 (9): 1031–67.

Menem, E. (2012) 'Las Malvinas son nuestras', *La Nación*, 17 February.

— (2012b) 'Una visión alternativa sobre la causa de Malvinas', *La Nación*, 23 Feb.

Milmo, D. (2012) 'UK struggle to strike Falklands oil', *The Guardian*, 2 April.

Mira Delli-Zotti, G. (2010) 'Transiciones a la democracia y democratización en América Latina: un análisis desde la Historia del Presente', in E. Rey Tristan (ed.), *XIV Encuentro de Latinoamericanistas Españoles* (Santiago de Compostela: Universidad de Santiago de Compostela), pp. 1456–75.

Novaro, M. and V. Palermo (2003) *La dictadura militar 1976–1983: del golpe de Estado a la restauración democrática* (Buenos Aires: Paidós).

O'Donnell, G.A., P. Schmitter and L. Whitehead (eds.) (1986) *Transitions from Authoritarian Rule. Prospects for Democracy*, vol. 1 (Baltimore, MD and London: Johns Hopkins University Press).

O'Donnell, P. (2012) 'Agentes de la Colonia', *Página/12*, 23 Feb.

Palermo, V. (2012a) 'La estrategia de la ambigüedad', *La Nación*, 30 Jan.

— (2012b) 'Malvinas, un laberinto político', *La Nación*, 16 Feb.

— (2012c) 'Cuánto de cortina de humo tiene Malvinas', *Clarín*, 7 April.

Pastor, R. A. (1989) *Democracy in the Americas: Stopping the Pendulum* (New York: Holmes and Meier).

Pedrosa, F. (2009) 'Los límites del voluntarismo. La Internacional Socialista y las transiciones a la democracia en América Latina', unpublished PhD dissertation, University of Salamanca.

Rock, D. and S. Avellano (1986) 'The Argentine elections of 1983: significance and repercussions', in P. W. Drake and E. Silva (eds.), *Elections and Democratization in Latin America, 1980–85* (San Diego, CA: University of California), p. 189.

Romero, L.A. (2012a) 'Dos miradas sobre un conflicto que sigue perturbando a los argentinos ¿Son realmente nuestras las Malvinas?', *La Nación*, 14 Feb.

— (2012b) 'Conmemorar Malvinas, sí; pero hacerlo el 14 de junio', *La Nación*, 22 March.

Rozitchner, L. (1985) *Las Malvinas: de la 'guerra sucia' a la 'guerra limpia'* (Buenos Aires: CEAL).

Share, D. and S. Mainwaring (1986) 'Transiciones vía transacción: la democratización en Brasil y en España', *Revista de Estudios Políticos*, 49: 87–135.

Storani, F. (2012) 'Improvisar menos con las Malvinas', *Página/12*, 23 Feb.

The Sunday Times (1982) *The Falklands War* (London: Sphere).

Tokatlian, G. (2012) 'El valor de una capacidad disuasiva', *La Nación*, 2 Feb.

Tranquilo Producciones (2008) *505 días. La transición argentina*, 5 DVDs (Buenos Aires).

Veiga, G. (2011) 'El héroe que resultó desertor', *Página/12*, 10 July.

Verbitsky, H. (1985) *La última batalla de la Tercera Guerra Mundial* (Buenos Aires: Legasa).

Whitehead, L. (1986) 'International aspects of democratization', in G. A. O'Donnell, P. Schmitter and L. Whitehead (eds.), *Transitions from Authoritarian Rule. Prospects for Democracy*, vol. 3 (Baltimore, MD and London: Johns Hopkins University Press), pp. 3–46.

— (ed.) (1996) *The International Dimension of Democratization: Europe and the Americas* (Oxford: Oxford University Press).

Yofre, J.B. (2011) *1982. Los documentos secretos de la guerra de Malvinas/Falklands y el derrumbe del Proceso* (Buenos Aires: Sudamericana).

5. The Malvinas journey: harsh landscapes, rough writing, raw footage

Julieta Vitullo

There is little room for first-person writing in the realm of doctoral dissertations in American academia. As if subjective experience obstructed the flow of intellectual reflections, the two sides of the brain of an academic are not supposed to mix. The same is true in scientific discourse, but in the world of science, it is all about the experiment. Even in the driest and most objective language of a scientist, even if the passive voice disguises the presence of an agent, the 'I' is integral to the text: I performed this experiment and came up with this. Studies in the humanities, despite the name and the object they examine, tend to erase any traces of the subject who writes. Reading and writing are solitary and silent acts. When cultural and literary critics refer to a personal experience that led them to come across a certain book or to approach a corpus of works, they do so timidly and almost apologetically, in a footnote, a foreword or an epilogue.

I was not the exception when in 2006 I went to the Falkland Islands (or Malvinas, for us Argentines) with the intention of writing a travel journal that would give closure to my doctoral research. Justifying a request for money was only the beginning of the problem. Field studies are not uncommon in the humanities, but the request was slightly unorthodox: was there room for a first-person narrative in a piece of scholarly research? Why did I need to travel to the Islands if all I was studying were the imaginary representations of them, the fictional narratives produced around the Malvinas–Falklands War of 1982? From then on, I found myself in a sort of limbo, one foot in the library, the other on the Islands. The timeline was the five years spanning the 25th and 30th anniversaries of the war, that is, between the conclusion in 2007 of my doctoral dissertation, later published as the book *Islas imaginadas: La guerra de Malvinas en la literatura y el cine argentinos* [*Imaginary Islands: The Malvinas War in Argentine Fiction and Film*] (2012), and the release of *La forma exacta de las islas* [*The Exact Shape of the Islands*] in 2012, a documentary that I co-wrote with the directors of the film, Edgardo Dieleke and Daniel Casabé.

J. Vitullo, 'The Malvinas journey: harsh landscapes, rough writing, raw footage', in G. Mira and F. Pedrosa (eds.), *Revisiting the Falklands–Malvinas Question: Transnational and Interdisciplinary Perspectives* (London: University of London Press, 2020), pp. 111–25. License: CC-BY-NC-ND 4.0.

This chapter looks at what the journey has been like for me, a researcher into the cultural discourses produced around the war who became the protagonist in one of those discourses. I discuss what the process of making the film was like and how my previous connection to the topic evolved into something else as a result of new experiences and new paths of expression. Without going into details that readers can find out by watching the film, I explain how I positioned myself in regards to the analysis of the relationship between collective and individual trauma after having suffered a loss that was inextricably linked to my experiences in the Malvinas. I also look at how certain representations of the landscape displace the idea of sovereign territory in the narratives of Malvinas and, at the same time, become a vehicle for representing individual and personal trauma.

The limits of genre

The documentary film *The Exact Shape of the Islands* came out of the experiences of two trips I took to the Islands in 2006 and 2010. The first time, as I explained in the research statement I wrote to justify the need for travel funds, I went because I wanted to see with my own eyes that place overshadowed by loss which I had read so much about, a place that had been written about mostly from the imagination. My plan was to be a *flâneur* in the barren land and, in the idle time I would have, to write an epilogue for my thesis, a first-person text conceived as either a chronicle, a journal or a travelogue. Once I was there, the plan for my trip changed because I met Carlos Enriori and Dacio Agretti, two Argentine ex-combatants who were returning to the Islands for the first time after 25 years. I took the excursions I had planned, but did not just look at things and keep a journal: I watched Carlos and Dacio and, through the camera lens, I watched what they were watching. The eight hours of rough material I recorded became a sort of voyeuristic insight into their experience. That and the notes I took when I was alone made up a portion of what I brought back from the Malvinas.

Upon my return from the Islands, I used my notes and recollections to write an 'Epilogue' that I described as 'a journey of the researcher towards her object of study'.[1] I explained that the 'Epilogue' represented a shift or displacement from the fictional to the physical: I confronted the space that had been built from imagination with a personal and somewhat intimate chronicle written from the actual space of the Islands. I used the first person to describe my wanderings around Stanley and what locals refer to as 'the camp' (the countryside). The initial idea of the trip, I said, was to:

> contrast the representation of a space that was constructed based on scholarly and reference materials, based on testimonial accounts from those who were on the islands under the exceptional conditions imposed by the

---

1 Vitullo, 2007a, p. 12. Translations are the author's own.

war and based on the recent fictional narratives of those who received both those materials, with an *in situ* narrative, one that would enable me to see in what way the reconstruction of an unknown space had been operating in literature (Vitullo, 2007a, p. 12).

The result reflected in the 'Epilogue', as I continued to describe it, was 'a journey to the origin', one in which those unknown islands revealed themselves as a space of nostalgia and longing for something that was missing (Vitullo, 2007a, p. 12).

I brought back more than just the initial thoughts for my 'Epilogue' and eight hours of raw footage but, in terms of my research, I was not sure what I was supposed to do with what I had gathered. I articulated some partial thoughts that did not do justice to the rest of my work, my role as a witness to the testimonies that the two ex-combatants offered, my experience as a traveller on the Islands or my own personal story. The personal ramifications of my life experience on the Islands were too intimate to fit into even a first-person narrative.

An article based on that initial version of the 'Epilogue' was published in the cultural magazine *Ñ* for a special edition on the 25th anniversary of the war.[2] The fact that the editor cut the first paragraph of the submitted text, in which I made specific mention to those ramifications, is evidence of the problematic status of the first-person within certain channels of circulation, even non-scholarly ones. That text, which the editor described as a travel account and entitled 'La nostalgia del falso terruño' [Nostalgia for a False Homeland], was a chronicle with autobiographical undertones. What could have had an interesting impact was not the specific personal information that was provided in the text, but the fact that such information was being introduced along with other pieces in the special edition of a weekly magazine, an edition that dealt with the public, rather than the private, dimensions of the war. 'La nostalgia del falso terruño' was the chronicle of a researcher who travelled to those islands to study the fictions produced around the war. The medium in which the text was published was a special edition on the Malvinas which included a dozen articles in different genres, from interviews to reviews, and dealt with many subjects, including politics, aesthetics, history, cinematography and literature. My text presented a personal twist which introduced a link between the private and the public in the context of a key chapter in Argentina's historical narrative, bringing an uncomfortably intimate component into the discussion of a national, eminently public and often solemn commemoration. The drastic cutting of the first paragraph erased that connection but, incidentally, the mention of the personal that came in later in the text was left unclear and disconnected. That paragraph, which did make it to my dissertation, read:

---

2 See Vitullo (2007b).

> I am going to the Malvinas to see if being there helps me uncover the veil (the 'misty quilt') of the national cause that we Argentines have been constructing for over a century. I am going to the Malvinas so I can say, happier than a little girl with a new toy, that I met the king penguins, younger siblings of the emperors in *March of the Penguins*. I am going to the Malvinas so that I can brag about drinking beer with the Kelpers. I am going to the Malvinas to bump into two Argentine ex-combatants who have very good reasons to go back to the Malvinas. I am going to the Malvinas to contrast the scholarly versions and the testimonies from those who were there in 1982 with my own critical insight, *in situ*, and also to see how this unknown space was constructed in recent fictional representations. I am going to the Malvinas to conceive a son (Vitullo, 2007a, p. 172).

A modified version of that opening paragraph made its appearance as a voice-over in *The Exact Shape of the Islands*. In that case, the paragraph was modified not because the lines between genres had to be kept straight, as in the edited version published in *Ñ*, but for plot purposes, to avoid giving away the full story at the beginning of the film:

> I am finally on the Malvinas. I'm coming to the Malvinas to finish my dissertation. I'm coming to the Malvinas to contrast the school versions of the war and to contrast the testimonial versions of those who fought it in 1982. I'm coming to see how this space was imagined in Argentine literature and film. I'm coming to the Malvinas to meet the Kelpers. I'm coming to the Malvinas and I meet Carlos and Dacio, who have very good reasons to return (*The Exact Shape of the Islands*).

By the time I had to give closure to my dissertation and defend it, life had gone on and some of the things I had said in the initial version of the 'Epilogue' and in the *Ñ* chronicle were no longer valid. If there had existed a gap between the actual space of the Islands and the image associated with the fictional and non-fictional accounts I had read, there was now a second gap between the Islands of that trip and the personal landscape that was starting to be reshaped in my head as memories populated with new and unexpected meanings.

In the end, it was the documentary format and the intervention of a third-person narration which enabled reflection on the ways in which that landscape had been reshaped once and again through the pages of books, right before my eyes, through the lens of my camera and from the memory exercises that took place in between trips. If the need to *go* had driven the 'Epilogue', the urge to *return* would eventually lead me back to the Islands and become a thread in the narrative fabric of the documentary. That urge, which had also been a theme of the fictional accounts and testimonies I had studied, was later present in the raw footage I collected by filming Carlos and Dacio and would finally be a part of my own story within the film.

The status of the first person, the autobiographical, the limits of genre, the relationship between the private and the public are, precisely, some of issues with which *The Exact Shape of the Islands* deals. The gaps mentioned above adopt a different form in the film: they are layers which the film juxtaposes by using the materials I captured in 2006; those recorded in 2010; third-person voice-overs from the film directors; different entries from my diaries recorded by an actress; quotations from 19th-century accounts by Charles Darwin; or more recent insights from Rodolfo Fogwill and Carlos Gamerro.

Still, within the context of my academic research, a first-person reflection about my experiences on the Islands in 2006 remained partially undercut by the very fact that the Islands had become not just a place to witness and record the testimonies of others but a stage in my own personal story of loss. The time that elapsed between the first trip and the publication of *Islas imaginadas* did not provide enough distance for the present reflection to come into being. Only after completing the film, watching it several times, showing it at different festivals and going through the exercise of reflecting on the last six years[3] of this Malvinas journey does it seem possible to express what I have had such a hard time writing down and what directors Dieleke and Casabé struggled for a whole week of shooting on the Islands to have me say in front of the camera, only to hear me say it on the very last day: that during my first trip to the Islands I conceived a baby, Eliseo, who died shortly after he was born.

The object, the subject, the witness

Researching the literature and films produced after the war in 1982 between Great Britain and Argentina over sovereignty of the Falkland Islands has required different kinds of journeys and discoveries. The first is common to what most researchers must undergo when they initially come up with an object of study. Something in the sphere of personal memories, personal experiences, place of origin, a picture kept or seen, a book stored on a shelf, a word spoken to us leads us to that object.

In my case, I was about to turn six when the war happened in 1982 and I was in first grade. I remember the chants against Margaret Thatcher that our teacher forced us to sing; I remember tears from my mother when the ARA General Belgrano Cruiser was sunk by the British Royal Navy. More than anything, I remember the feeling of fear and shameful pride every time I sang the national anthem and the 'Malvinas March'. That the feeling of pride was tainted by shame speaks to the fact that the Malvinas represent a sort of 'blind spot' in Argentine history: as I explained in *Islas imaginadas*, the war is an alienated event extirpated from the time frame implied in the term 'dictatorship' but also estranged from 'democracy'; it was supported by the majority of Argentine society while the regime that was launching it was about to collapse; its victims do not have a corpus of legitimised narratives and testimonials like the one which the disappeared and the survivors of the

3   This piece was written in 2011.

concentration camps have in the *Nunca más*, the Report of the Argentine National Commission of the Disappeared; finally, it is a war that for almost two decades was more or less neglected by academics. At my age, my shame derived from the fact that my parents had told me that I had to chant against the military, not against the British. They were the 'bad guys', so instead of jumping while chanting 'If you don't jump you're English', I needed to jump and shout, 'If you don't jump you're from the military'.

The memories that gave rise to the selection of the Malvinas as a research topic, shared almost identically by too many Argentines, worked their way through in three different ways throughout this intellectual journey. First, they inspired me to choose a topic for my doctoral dissertation. The personal connection was deep enough on an emotional level to motivate passion, interest and enough devotion to spend the next few years dealing with the topic at hand. This goes to reinforce the point that pretending that, formally, research can be devoid of subjective interventions is an illusion, one that can only lead to an unproductive split.

This recognition explains not just the fact that because of my own personal experience I could relate to the emotional roots of the national cause for the Malvinas with its patriotic fervour and symbols, but also that nationalism, emotional in nature, permeates the idiosyncrasy of entire generations. As I discussed in my book, the idea of the 'just cause' was hegemonic within the testimonial, political, historical and journalistic discourses that followed Argentina's defeat in the war and was rooted in a territorial type of nationalism. Whether those accounts were expressed in triumphal registers or mourning undertones, they all subscribed to the idea that the war had its origins in a just cause. According to the triumphal version, the war of 1982 could be told as an epic story, a people's heroic deed. The testimonies of the soldiers, the letters written by their relatives, their friends or just the common citizen, the official speeches, the media – all of these manifestations illustrated that triumphal version. Imposed by the defeat, the second version, with its mourning undertones, did not differ much from the triumphal one. Even though it tried to question the celebratory nature of the first account, it participated in the same logic of the National Narrative. The elementary national discourse upon which both versions were based was not necessarily ideological. It was, rather, founded on a type of 'diffuse' nationalism, one that, according to Benedict Anderson's well-known idea, is a 'hegemonic cultural construct'. It is important to emphasise that without the national narrative and the epic discourses, there would not be texts from authors such as Rodolfo Fogwill, Carlos Gamerro, Osvaldo Lamborghini, Rodrigo Fresán or Martín Kohan. Ranging from allegory to parody, those texts dismantle the national narrative of heroism, epic and lament, leaving behind only their fragments. Without the nationalistic and territorial discourses, without the literature that was built upon them, *The Exact Shape of the Islands* would not exist either.

Second, those memories came up as material for interpretation within the fictions I was studying. It is precisely the patriotic feeling, the mix of nervousness, pride and shame associated with it, that is at stake for some of the characters in the testimonies and fictions of the war. Testimonial accounts by ex-combatants reference the rapture triggered by the sounds of those patriotic songs. Fictional narratives use the patriotic matrix as an opportunity to mock and undo the national discourse.

Third, and most importantly, those memories ended up turning into points within the plot of *The Exact Shape of the Islands*. In one instance in the film, the return of one of the ex-combatants to the Islands 25 years later, someone else voices part of my story. Carlos refers to me in the third person while he talks to his friend Dacio, looks at the camera that I am holding and addresses me, partially to verify some of the facts: I was six when the war happened; I had carried that inside me since that time; then the moment came for me to decide on a research topic and I chose the narratives surrounding the Malvinas. In another instance, the actress who speaks for me reads from one of the entries in the diary I wrote during my first trip to the Islands in December of 2006: my mother was getting me ready to go to school and we heard on the radio the news about the sinking of the light cruiser Belgrano.

Those individual memories, in which the public and the private overlap, traverse the entirety of this Malvinas journey from the initial research stages to the completion of the documentary. However, what enabled me to become a subject in one of the narratives which now belonged to the same type of object I had chosen for my research – that is, the corpus of narratives I had been set to write about seven years previously – was bearing witness to somebody else's personal memories.

At first, that role as witness was fortuitous. In the initial version of my 'Epilogue' I explained that I had met Carlos and Dacio in the street and recognised them as Argentine by the *mate* they were drinking as they walked by me. This and other anecdotes regarding our interactions, and the story around how they managed to travel to the Islands 25 years after the war, took up an important part of that 15-page chronicle. Interestingly enough, I made no mention of the fact that I had filmed them, that a good number of our interactions had happened through the camera lens, or that many of my impressions of the Islands came out of the dialogues I had had with them. In that narrative, I am neither a witness nor a participant: I am something in between, an excited and curious observer who interjects and gets involved and shows a relative lack of self-awareness. The life events associated with that trip were too intimate and overwhelming to make their way into the narrative of a doctoral dissertation. Still, bits and pieces made it in, intrusively but timidly.

When the time came for me to rewrite the 'Epilogue' to include it in my book, I decided to leave out completely the encounter with the two ex-combatants because that part of the Malvinas journey exceeded the limits of an

'Epilogue' and had now become *The Exact Shape of the Islands*. As if the person who travelled to the Malvinas in 2006 had been there completely on her own and had finally had time to think, the first-person voice in this final version is reflective and collected, in sharp contrast with the verbose and tangential tendencies of the voice in the initial version.

As soon as I had returned from my first trip to the Islands, I watched the eight mini-DV tapes I had recorded. As I moved through the tapes, I could see a shift in my role behind the camera: from a fortuitous event, my encounter with the ex-combatants was becoming increasingly purposeful. In the first tape, the camera is always pointing at Carlos and Dacio and trying to capture everything they say, with little or no attention to the space around them. I had no idea at first whether the opportunity to film them was going to come up again, so I had to get as much material as I could. Certain segments of this first tape happen almost in real time, with very few cuts. The two friends are tracing back the steps they had taken 25 years earlier when they had arrived at the old Stanley airport and walked eight kilometres to the town. They are walking in the opposite direction, we all are and this reverse movement is also a movement towards the past. The landscape only matters insofar as it can be checked against what Carlos and Dacio can remember of it and can ascertain the passing of time. What we see is not what I see. It is not even what they see when they are being filmed. Instead, what we see is their way of experiencing the difference between what they see now and what they remember from having been there 25 years previously. Of course, when one watches some of these initial scenes at the beginning of *The Exact Shape of the Islands* the narrative frame switches and the audience experience a different kind of shift in time and perspective.

As time goes by and the connection between me as witness and them as my subjects develops, things start moving in different directions. On the one hand, one can see that I started to stage things, asking them to introduce themselves, requesting that they walk in certain places, or inviting them to address specific questions. On the other hand, as the relationship deepens, it is easier to catch them 'off guard', that is, to get spontaneous thoughts and reactions that do not fit the parameters of what they are used to saying. As they are both active militants in organisations of ex-combatants, their ideas about the war and its aftermath are clear and articulate. Dacio's discourse is seamless, reasoned and eloquent; as the hours go by, it becomes clear that his sayings are supported by two decades of elaborating and formulating the same thoughts repeatedly. Carlos's discourse is less absolute, more hesitant, more spontaneous, more complex and flawed and yet, more forthright. In neither case do I need to ask them to talk. However, any illusion of the documentarian as mere observer is unsustainable: their presence changes the nature of my trip and mine affects theirs. At some point, they start giving me feedback on the movie that I am making, a film that does not exist and never will. Not as such.

Figure 5.1. Dacio Agretti and Carlos Enriori at a beach near Stanley, 2006. Photo by Julieta Vitullo.

Territory, space, landscape

The first time around, the baggage I had brought to the Islands was made up of the childhood memories discussed above and of all my readings and my research. Even though the focus of my work was on the fictions that managed to elude the nationalistic mandates, once I was on the Islands there was no distance, no parody, no humour, no literary device that could be interposed between me and the landscape in front of me: a barren, desolate land; the hills where the battles had taken place and war objects had been left behind as in an improvised outdoor museum; a small town overflowing with war monuments and memorials; the Argentine cemetery with half its tombstones labelled 'Soldado argentino sólo conocido por Dios' [Argentine soldier known only to God]. As I explained in the first version of my 'Epilogue', war cemeteries attempt to emphasise the homogeneity of the war experience by laying out a uniform landscape that equalises all soldiers as brothers-in-arms. The Argentine cemetery at Darwin takes that to extremes by accentuating the anonymity of so many of the graves, emphasising the abandonment suffered by the citizens by a state that neglects them and deserts them. As I also explained, only fiction could be an effective diversion from such sadness, a 'refuge'. I could distract myself from the scene in front of me by thinking that the days to come would bring me to the places where the fictional characters I had studied had set foot. This pointed at a contradiction that I would only be able to understand later: if before my trip fiction had been the most valid form of discourse to articulate the real – that is, the war – fiction was now a diversion or a refuge from that reality.

Two particular tombstones in Darwin stood out for me now: those belonging to Private Ramón Orlando Palavecino and Lieutenant Luis Carlos Martella. Private Palavecino had been hit by the expansive wave of a bomb dropped close by while he was coming down the mountain to gather some projectiles. He had died in Carlos's arms. The second man, described by Carlos as a coward who abused his authority and did nothing but pray as the bombs dropped, died during the Battle of Two Sisters, fought from 11 to 12 June 1982, two days before the Argentine surrender. Both names were in the glossary that I handed to directors Dieleke and Casabé as we entered the first stage of our five-year film project. After having read the history of the war while I was doing my research, these stories Carlos told me made the war less anonymous and more personal. I was now participating in the search for these meaningful landmarks and bearing witness to stories I had only read about within the context of a testimonial genre about which I had had many reservations. Those testimonies I had read before were questionable because they bought into the national narrative and were framed within the idea of the just cause. A well-known example of one of these narratives, which I analyse in my book, is the film *Iluminados por el fuego* [*Illuminated by Fire*], as comfortable and politically correct as a film about the war can be. The testimonies I was now witnessing switched my perspective, at least for the duration of my trip. After all, there was something to be said about the epic matrix that the fictional narratives mocked and dismantled. I knew perfectly well how much abuse the conscripted soldiers had suffered at the hands of their superiors. But the undertones were not pitiful anymore. I was now being drawn into the epic tones of a story in which the conscripted soldiers, loyal and brave, were at odds with cowardly and abusive officers. More than this, I was letting myself be seduced by it. Even more: what was at play was a life drive coming to odds with a death drive.

As I was starting to discover and would later elaborate further, by meeting the two ex-combatants I had found a new set of characters. I could witness and record their present adventures, hear their past stories and give a specific direction to wanderings that would have otherwise been pathless. The appeal for me was in the individuality of the experiences I had in front of me, in the fact that they were real and that, despite my previous distance and scepticism towards anything that had an epic flavour to it, they were an example of bravery, courage and camaraderie. My trip turned into an adventure and my movements became deliberate. I was participating in their search for the traces of what had been there 25 years before. I was looking for their trenches, searching for a place to plant a cross that would signal the death of Private Palavecino. There is perhaps one and only one moment of reflection in the material which made it into *The Exact Shape of the Islands*. Carlos found the place where his friend had died and turned it into a memorial. He has told me the story of his friend's death and poured out 25 years of painful memories in front of the camera. I stop to film him and, for the first time, I move the camera away from the character to pan through the landscape. The slow and silent panning is interrupted by Carlos's request that we find our way back to town. In the film, what follows is a pivotal moment for the development of the plot and the characters.

Nevertheless, generally speaking, a look at the raw material from that trip shows that there was little room for reflection during that week. Contrary to the solitary and introspective activity I had imagined when I had pictured myself strolling around without a clear direction, observing, reflecting and transferring my thoughts into a journal, I could only relate to that space by moving through it, going from landmark to landmark, from memory to memory, following the footprints of a previous journey. When I returned to the Islands four years later with the clear purpose of finishing the film whose seeds had been planted on the first trip, I brought a different kind of baggage with me. This time it was all about my own personal experiences four years previously. This time I was searching for my own footprints and memories. Once again, the Malvinas were a space to be walked around in search of an older footprint.

Again, the journey was conceived as a search. However, now I was not the one who controlled the way in which the search was conducted and recorded. As *The Exact Shape of the Islands* proposes in one of the opening scenes, I may decide whenever I am ready to talk and be the one who sets the stage and the tone of my reflections in front of the camera, but the film can also manipulate that, interrupting, intervening and controlling. That entire week of shooting was characterised by a productive tension between what the directors wanted me to say and what I was ready or willing to share, their request to visit certain places and my refusal to go there again, the questions they wanted to ask and the ones I wanted to answer. That they were close friends who had been present for the four years this journey had taken complicated things even more but was, in the end, what made it all possible. How else could two male directors have approached a story that is deeply feminine and have done justice to it if the relationship had not been grounded in trust? The tension continued as we watched the raw footage of that second trip and worked on a timeline and a series of voice-overs. I refused to accept the scene in which one of the directors interrupts a thought I am starting to articulate in my very first appearance in front of the camera, six minutes into the documentary. However, the scene was left as it was, the first example of a device often utilised in the film in which the directors intervene into my speech, contributing to the creation of a puzzle of contradicting and complementing voices.

Simon Schama reminds us that national identity 'would lose much of its ferocious enchantment without the mystique of a particular landscape tradition: its topography mapped, elaborated, and enriched as a homeland' (Schama, 1996, p. 15). The general impression according to the Argentine nationalist imaginary has always been that the Malvinas represent a sort of missing homeland. However, the Malvinas are a territory alienated from most people's experience which, due to the oft-repeated but erroneous slogan 'The Malvinas are Argentine', has been ingrained in the collective national conscience generation after generation. The pro-war discourse that circulated largely through most of Argentine society during the weeks of the conflict did nothing but echo a formalised textbook account that, decade after decade, had promoted the idea of the unredeemed territory. The popularly accepted ideas perpetuated by this literature were not based on a formal survey of this land, but on journals by 18th- and 19th-century travellers such as Louise-Antoine de Bougainville and Charles Darwin whose journeys contributed to the mystique of the Malvinas–Falklands landscape. If, prior to 1982, the Falklands constituted a mythical space that any Argentine schooled under successive authoritarian or military regimes had to be ready to defend with his own blood, after the war the Islands gained materiality. Whatever remnant of immateriality remained in the image of this landscape, nation and nature were now merged through the blood spilled onto the soil of the Islands.

Those perspectives, the mythical and the material, exist under a nostalgic imperative, one by which I felt captured upon my first arrival on the Islands. According to Svetlana Boym (2001), the great wars and the great nationalisms of the 20th century bear a nostalgic longing for a never-owned homeland. During that first trip to the Islands, there was no way to escape that feeling of nostalgic longing. Clearly, the Islands were not pure nature: they were a landscape, that is, an artefact constructed by humans and loaded with meanings that did not have a natural correlation to it.

In these islands, overbearing forms of harshness and barrenness co-exist with exuberant forms of life. The king penguins that I found on my two trips to the Malvinas had a way of overemphasising that contrast. Forever subject to national claims, the Falkland Islands force us to pose a question. This question, under the perfectly calculated forms of the exploitation of natural resources that has always been at the core of capitalism, should certainly apply to every piece of land on Earth: who should be in charge?

The unfortunate words of the Argentine commander-in-chief who, on 2 April 1982, greeted the nation with the news that the Malvinas had been recovered – 'The Malvinas are a feeling. We do not care about the oil or the strategic position of the Islands' – resonate today in the current state of affairs between Argentina and Great Britain. Of course, everyone cares about the oil. But the potential consequences of an ecological disaster caused by oil exploitation would render all questions of national claims rather useless.

The wide variety of the narratives about the Malvinas–Falklands War offers an interesting example of how the tragedies of history can return repeatedly through cultural artefacts. Often the causes and consequences of war have a way of being forgotten. In the case of the war that gave rise to my research, fiction provides us with plenty of reminders, interrupting the narrative of the

Figure 5.2. The warrah wolf in a postcard sent from Stanley, 2010. Photo by Matthew Smith.

media and the social to become knowledge, a specific knowledge about the war, with its own characters and rules.

In his *Voyage of the Beagle* (1839), Darwin documented his two visits to the Falklands in 1833 and 1834. Among other lessons learnt in what he described as these 'miserable islands' he found a species of fox-like wolf called the warrah, the only native land mammal of the Islands, and later remarked: 'As far as I am aware, there is no other instance in any part of the world of so small a mass of broken land, distant from a continent, possessing so large an aboriginal quadruped peculiar to itself' (Darwin, 2011, p. 194). Darwin predicted that this gentle animal would not survive human settlement. In effect, the species became extinct in 1876, when the last warrah was killed on West Falkland. Perhaps the image of the gentle warrah looking at us from a remote place and time is more productive, as a nostalgic turn, than the one which incites us, in loud nationalistic tones, to long for a home that we never owned.

It took me two trips and some life-changing experiences to distance my own perception of this place from that nostalgic outlook and find in that image of the warrah a productive metaphor for trauma, for loss, for longing, for warning against the exploitation of nature by humans. My individual experiences, the weight of the personal memories associated with that place, paved the way for a new topographic outlook. The nostalgic turns of these islands started to show a more personal face, different from those ruling the dilemmas of nationalism.

Are all the inhabitants of these islands not marooned, after all? 'Dreaming of islands', Gilles Deleuze says in his article 'The deserted island', 'whether with joy or in fear, it doesn't matter – is dreaming of pulling away, of being already separate, far from any continent, of being lost and alone – or it is dreaming of starting from scratch, recreating, beginning anew' (Deleuze, 2004, p. 10). The scene of me looking at the sea on a sunny day on the beach outside Stanley was in fact based on one of my many dreams about the Islands. I had dreamt about the Malvinas before and in between trips. I still dream about the Malvinas. The exact shape of each dream is different and indefinable, but the underlying story is always the same: these islands continue to be an enigmatic place in which to start anew.

A local man of Dutch origin who had left his country 20 years previously and went on board ship as a cook, only to fall in love with a Falkland Islander and never to return to Holland, told me during my second trip, 'I'm a castaway'. One of the voice-overs introduced towards the end of the film is an entry from my 2009 journal in which I describe one of my recurrent dreams: 'Sometimes I'm in a shipwreck and I get to the coast by raft. Once, the sailing boat I was in sank in a whirlpool and I never made it. And the dream ended there'.

Had I not been turned into a castaway as well for all those years, marooned between my home and those islands, dreaming of sunny days in the Malvinas, white sands and a turquoise sea, sailing treacherous waters never to reach land?

Figure 5.4. Julieta at a beach near Stanley during the filming of La forma exacta de las islas in 2010. Photo by Leo Hermo.

References

Boym, S. (2001) *The Future of Nostalgia* (New York: Basic Books).

Darwin, C. (2011) [1839] *Journal of Researches Into the Natural History and Geology of the Countries Visited during the Voyage of H. M. S. Beagle round the World under the Command of Capt. Fitz Roy, R. N.* (Cambridge: Cambridge University Press).

Deleuze, G. (2004) 'The deserted island', in *Desert Islands and Other Texts (1953–1974)* (Los Angeles and New York: Semiotext), 9–14.

The Exact Shape of the Islands (2012) dir. by D. Casabé and E. Dieleke (Ajimolido Films).

Schama, S. (1996) *Landscape and Memory* (New York: Vintage).

Vitullo, J. (2007a) 'Ficciones de una guerra. La guerra de Malvinas en la literatura y el cine argentinos', PhD dissertation, Rutgers University–New Brunswick.

— (2007b) 'La nostalgia del falso terruño', *Ñ Revista de cultura*, 183: 28–29.

— (2012) *Islas imaginadas. La guerra de Malvinas en la literatura y el cine argentinos* (Buenos Aires: Corregidor).

6. Malvinas miscellanea: notes on a diary written while shooting a film in these remote islands

Edgardo Dieleke

I was born in 1980 and I have no recollections of the Malvinas War in 1982 or the last Argentine dictatorship. I was never lured by the nationalistic discourses or by the sovereignty claims, though I understand their tactics. Maybe it has to do with my generation, born at the end of the dictatorship. Maybe it has to do with the fact that when I started to make a film on the Malvinas I was living in the United States during George W. Bush's war on terror. My fascination with the Malvinas was a little simpler and perhaps childish: what are these islands like? Who lives in such an isolated place? I became aware of the origins of this fascination only later; once I had finished the documentary I shot there, in 2010. Even if the film is related to the war of 1982, I learned that what took me there was beyond these reasons.

As a child and teenager, I used to read stories of travellers and pirates in the 'Robin Hood' collection (a series of books by classic authors targeted at young readers and famous for their yellow covers). I used to read the books by Emilio Salgari, Jules Verne and Robert Louis Stevenson: stories about treasure islands and buccaneers in the Caribbean. There were also books on battles and wars but they were distant and exotic to me. Perhaps I was actually longing for that when I became interested in the Malvinas; maybe I was just longing for a sort of return to the exotic stories of my childhood. Back then, as a child, I used to collect maps, postcards and stamps of places I had never visited. When I returned from the Malvinas these were the only tangible things I brought with me.

One of the main concerns in the film was how to capture the Islands outside of the war. In Argentina, the word Malvinas equals the war. I knew our film was going to address this but I wanted to be able to show the Islands as well, actually to know what the Islands and their people are like. When approaching how to do this I realised that the Argentines do not have an insular tradition. Even the sea is strange to us. Domingo Faustino Sarmiento wrote that the *pampa* (or the 'desert', as he called it) was in a way our ocean and our cities were

E. Dieleke, 'Malvinas miscellanea: notes on a diary written while shooting a film in these remote islands', in G. Mira and F. Pedrosa (eds.), *Revisiting the Falklands–Malvinas Question: Transnational and Interdisciplinary Perspectives* (London: University of London Press, 2020), pp. 127–39. License: CC-BY-NC-ND 4.0.

the islands (or our oases). In fact, he wrote this without knowing the *pampas* all that much. He described and invented a tradition by reading accounts by French and English travellers. But I am neither a rural person nor a man from the 19th century.

Even though my gaze might be, like Sarmiento's, corrupted by foreign books and films, islands remain something of an oddity, alien to 'our' tradition (I recently learned that in other latitudes there is a relatively new academic field: 'Island Studies'). But like everything that is strange to us, I think that the Malvinas provoked me and stirred the possibilities of imagination. The Islands I knew might then carry an altered perception, a perception by which a barren landscape, the arrival of a new settler, or the visit of a ship might turn into an extraordinary event. A peasant from the Malvinas who might resemble Benny Hill for a British person of the metropolis could also be the son of a legendary runaway, a maroon or an outcast.

Let us now stick to the facts. It was a documentary that made me travel to the Islands in November 2010. I had started this project in 2007 with my close friends Julieta Vitullo (also a contributor to this volume) and Daniel Casabé (with whom I also directed another film). Initially, Julieta was going to be the main character in our documentary. It all started with her trip to the Malvinas in 2006, where she went to finish a dissertation and where she shot some amazing and very spontaneous material: her encounter with two Argentine ex-combatants. Many things happened between the project and the film, but we ended up shooting on the Islands three years after the beginning of the project. We were a crew formed of the producer Alejandro Israel, the cinematographer Leonardo Hermo and Lalo Guerra as the sound technician. After an almost impossible editing process and after a thousand films were set aside, we finished the film by the end of 2012. The way I see it now, our documentary is no longer just a film about the war or about Julieta's experience, but instead a film about the Islands. I also think this was reflected in the very process of choosing a title: we finally settled for *The Exact Shape of the Islands*. It might be unnecessary to say this, but our Islands are far from being precise. I will leave it up to the film itself to explain what our intentions were or what is to be found behind the title. All that is true should hold a mystery or a secret, so let us stop right here. Let me explain, if you will allow me, what I intend to propose in these pages.

During the week I spent in the Malvinas, there were many things we shot that did not make it into the actual film, characters and stories that exceeded our focus but remained in my diary, in my notes or just in my memory. In addition, there were things and people we did include in the film that somehow, probably due to the very nature of the film-image, were reduced to only one or two features. Words sometimes allow for more nuances. Here, then, I will attempt the following exercise: to recover the spirit of that diary and to expand it. What you will read below is a partial recollection of my Islands. The Malvinas became for me the ideal source for infinite stories (and maybe this explains how difficult it was to finish the film). When making a documentary, one tries somehow to step outside oneself. In the process I learned that this is true for both fiction and documentary, even more so when the film is located on an island. The people and places you will get to know below are 'people of this world' but they are more isolated, they are set aside, they live in a more autonomous place, a more fictional one. When making a film you start slightly to 'fictionalise' in the moment you set aside and select certain features and attributes of your subjects. More to my point: remote islands could be places for new beginnings where many go in need of fashioning a new identity, to be somehow better. Moreover, do we not all want to think this is possible?

The Malvinas in colours

We already knew these islands in Argentina. The problem was that we had seen them too much, to the point that few people were interested in them (many people asked me why I had decided to spend so much time on a film on the Malvinas War). However, the Islands we have seen are made of a collage of TV footage from the war and magazine covers showing pictures of 18-year-old conscripted soldiers. The other images are those of films attempting to re-enact the war and its aftermath (there are very few things I hate more than fictional re-enactments: on this see the amazing documentary *The Act of Killing* by Joshua Oppenheimer). In all these visual memories, the Malvinas have a dark green tone or the black-and-white memory of newspapers. The word Malvinas also provokes in many a sort of automatic embarrassment and sad feeling. Others give no reaction at all: few things are less empathetic to the contemporary sensibility than the Malvinas anthem or the feelings it would seek to inspire. Everything changes once you see the Islands from the plane.

Before we travelled to the Malvinas, many Argentine friends would ask me the same questions. Were we authorised to go? How would we get there? Once I finished asserting that there were no obstacles, no one showed any real intention of visiting. It is possible to go there, but it is still more expensive than a plane ticket to Brazil or Peru. There are two ways to get there from Buenos Aires, but for our reduced budget, we had only one. Luckily, it was also the shortest one. Every week there is a flight by LAN Airlines that leaves from Punta Arenas to the Malvinas, but Punta Arenas is in the south of Chile (meaning travel to Santiago de Chile first and from there to Punta Arenas). Instead, our option, operated by LAN only once a month, was a flight from Rio Gallegos in Santa Cruz. Coming from Buenos Aires, we had our stop in Rio Gallegos, where we waited for several hours before boarding the plane. We spent some hours chatting in a café in the airport where we spotted a group of ex-combatants who were making their traditional pilgrimage to the battlefields. We shared some *mates* and exchanged our travel plans but we decided not to record them during our week on the Islands. Julieta had already done that on her previous trip and it formed the basis for our film. Hers was the most truthful account of ex-combatants that I have seen. In any case, this group of friends we met in the airport surprised us on board the plane.

They were sitting at the back of the aircraft and we would peek at them now and then. Suddenly, we saw them trying to speak English with a man in a military uniform. After we approached them with Leo (the cinematographer) and helped them with the translation, the Argentine ex-combatant became excited and started hugging his former enemy. The man had a friendly face and a chest filled with medals from Iraq, Afghanistan, Kosovo, Cyprus and the Malvinas. The scene had the clichés of many TV documentaries except in this case taken to excess. The Argentine ex-combatant kissed his brother-in-arms with exaggeration, even attempting a kiss on the mouth (in Argentina we say 'piquito', a small kiss on the mouth). Later in the week we found out that the 'Argies' offered the 'Brits' a lamb roasted on a cross, following the tradition of the gauchos. When we were finally returning to our seats, the captain made the announcement. We were beginning the descent into Mount Pleasant Airport. Oddly enough, the Chilean airline only mentioned the name of the airport, always avoiding all mention of the names Malvinas or Falkland.

Finally, we saw the Islands in colour. We saw light green hills and white sands; we saw a turquoise sea and a virgin landscape. I thought I could also be in the Caribbean or the Cyclades. Once in the capital town of Port Stanley, the island kept revealing its colours: vivid reds, bright yellows and navy blue roofs. I even saw red and orange flowers. The summer was approaching and the washed out greens and greys of April, May and June were somehow way behind, on TV and in old magazines. The military regime had had the idea of retaking the Islands just before the beginning of winter. I could not seem to find an argument to support such an idea.

Two very different towns

Mount Pleasant is an airport, but more than an airport, it is a military base. When you descend from the plane you can see the other kind of planes in the distance, jeeps, hangars and a group of not-so-welcoming blondish soldiers guarded by their German Shepherds (where were their terriers and bulldogs?). Mount Pleasant (oh, such a peaceful name!) is 50 kilometres away from the capital, Port Stanley. They both have around two thousand people but Mount Pleasant has a cinema and a cricket field and is populated only by military people. This large compound is a sort of void zone: why so many soldiers in such an isolated spot? What are they hiding?

On our last night we met three members of the British Special Forces (those in charge of counter-terrorism), right outside one of the pubs in Stanley. It was 11 p.m. and the pub had just closed. They were desperate: they wanted to get drunk and they could not. They had come from Afghanistan and when they realised we were 'Argies' they stressed that no one really cares about the Malvinas or Argentina for that matter. 'You're just pawns', one of them told us. I did not say it, but I remember thinking that I did not mind keeping it that way. When I saw those men I could not help but imagine them screaming angrily at night, with their faces painted black, attacking the positions of 18-year-old conscripts. I think I started to grasp how difficult it actually is to understand the fear and the pain of others. Having been through a war, having witnessed the death of others, having survived that, I started to think, makes you an Island-type of person. You set aside a traumatic experience; you separate that fear from your continental part or you invent a new island. There is also the possibility of thinking that there is a community of people in pain who always return to their own metaphoric island. I believe that we all share a larger or smaller personal island. The thing is that the islands of the ex-combatants resemble the Malvinas: they are as remote and barren as it gets.

There is only one weekly flight to the Islands and so you are forced to stay an entire week. The visitors who make it here are divided into two large groups: war tourism and eco-tourism. That is to say, on one side the soldiers, their families and film-makers who travel here to visit the cemeteries and battlefields. On the other side, bird-watchers and penguin enthusiasts: the Malvinas have royal penguins, the Emperor type can be spotted on their beaches. Of course, we spent an entire afternoon with them (before reading Sandokan I used to collect a series of pictures of animals with scientific descriptions called 'Safari Club'). The isolation that defines the Malvinas is not just geographical. It is intensified by politics. The Argentine government, with the support of its regional allies, maintains a blockade. Everything comes from Europe. In 2010, the price of two tomatoes was around seven dollars. In any case, the connections with the mainland persist ('mainland' is the word they use to refer to Argentina, the unnamable). Anyway, geographical proximity still beats any form of nationalism. The first islander with whom I spoke was in the airport, working on the luggage carousel. He was in his sixties, planning his retirement. His daughter was majoring in tourism in a private university in Córdoba. England was too far and too expensive for his salary.

After passing through customs, we board a sort of van and head for Stanley. The road consists of 50 kilometres of undulating hills with not even a bush. Once in the town we check in at Celia Stewart's. She owns a small and beautiful house that she runs as a bed and breakfast: too many sausages, baked beans and eggs for our regular diet but perfect for an intense shooting week. Celia seemed very reserved, but Stanley is a very small town. As the days went on, Celia started to leave us messages that were passed onto her by different people who found out who we were. They wanted to be in the documentary. We started to meet some of them as long as our shooting plan allowed us.

Oil in the African islands

There is a small, neat office located in Stanley that guides the possible investor on oil matters and the curious tourist. On the main street, right across from the post office and the red phone booth, you will find the Department of Mineral Resources. It seems that the bottom of the ocean around the Malvinas has oil. The problem, so far, is that it is very expensive to extract oil from such depths. However, according to this department that task is not impossible. We decided to find out about this and shot an interview with a person working there. A very agreeable blonde woman received us; she was in her fifties. Later we discovered she was a schoolteacher. A fellow teacher, I thought. Maybe that is why I liked her. Despite this, her information was suspicious. I know almost nothing about geology but at that office (as well as in the local museum) they presented a pretty absurd theory on the formation of the Islands. According to some researchers the Malvinas were part of Gondwana, thus linked to what today is South Africa. It is a convenient theory to avoid any Argentine claim to sovereignty. According to a different group of researchers, in the event of an oil spill Argentine shores would be safe. This is extremely difficult to believe, though in any case I liked the teacher. She was living in England when the war started and in that moment she decided to return home and work as a teacher. How many Argentine teachers are willing to fight Sarmiento's battle in such an isolated town?

Brief notes on 'war tourism'

We needed a proper vehicle to be able to visit the battleground and the positions where the main characters of our film had fought. We had hired a guide, Tony, who is a native of the Islands and who runs a small tourism company. We went with him and his friends on almost all the excursions: Mount Two Sisters, Goose Green, as well as the Argentine cemetery. I liked Tony: he was affable and he really knew his work. He had done a similar job with larger film and TV crews from all over the world. I could not find out much about his life other than the fact that he was married to a Brazilian woman and that they often travelled to Buenos Aires.

Our first important excursion with Tony was to Mount Two Sisters. Most of the material that Julieta had shot on her first trip had been recorded there. Our film combines what we shot on this return visit with the original material from Julieta's recordings in 2006, made with a home-video camera. This Mount is an important space in both recordings and I had a sense of odd familiarity when I was there on Two Sisters. It felt like a return because we were literally following and returning over her footsteps. We somehow knew those steps because of the number of times we had seen Julieta's footage. When we were editing her material, Daniel Casabé and I ended up repeating and becoming awkwardly familiar with all the possible tones in the voices of the subjects of the film. Finally being on the Mount was an exciting moment and at the same time felt like a repeated experience. Despite this sensation, right when I thought I was recognising my steps we got lost. Luckily, Tony was there with us.

After walking for many hours on Two Sisters, we could still see the effects of the war. We had seen several crosses honouring Argentine soldiers, pieces of a mortar and other weaponry. We also saw several holes in the ground caused by the bombings. In any case, I was expecting that and I have seen those images before. What caught my attention was the overwhelming presence of shoes and cheap boots. They were scattered around the Argentine trenches (actually known as fox's lair). This footwear was relatively new; it was impossible that it had belonged to the soldiers. Later, I also saw that many remaining objects of the war kept appearing, something particularly odd on such a windy mount. I became suspicious and cynical. Was all that planted for visitors to be able to experience the war at least partially, even after so many years?

The 'Flying Dutchman'

I remember the legend of the Flying Dutchman, the story of a ghost ship that has haunted sailors since the 17th century. It is a Dutch ship that can never make port and is condemned to sail the oceans forever. It announces tragedies to those who encounter it at sea. It was a popular legend but also an apt metaphor: that of a wanderer, the one who never finds rest. In Stanley we met an extraordinary man, a Dutchman, living far away from his native Utrecht. We interviewed Rob Yssel towards the end of the week. He was a fatalist. He understood fate almost like a character from a Borges short story. The day he set foot on the Malvinas was the day he encountered his destiny, the day he became who he was.

Rob had lived many lives. He had lived in cities like Amsterdam before coming to these shores. He had an indefinite age, a look that revealed the excesses of his youth combined with melancholy. He had lost Jane, his lifelong partner (his 'other half' were his words), in a car accident in the Argentine Patagonia less than a year before. He had arrived on the Islands in 1984, when he was a cook working in a merchant ship. We may venture to suggest that he was tired of many noisy and crowded ports. The day he landed on the Malvinas he met Jane and he became a sort of stranded man, in his own words. When we met him he was in pain, anguished by his loss and surrounded by Jane's possessions. She had been the archivist of the Falklands and her books were still open in the study, on the sofa, even in the kitchen. Her presence was almost asphyxiating; I could not imagine that constant mourning process, remembering every second his 'other half'. I peered into one of the rooms and I could see her tombstone lying on the floor. I think he was not ready to inscribe anything on it, as if that piece of stone would force him to stop mourning, would make him focus on the unloving task of forgetting her.

The Malvinas have many characters like Rob (maybe, again, this is just my projection). Many men and women living there had made difficult choices; they have learned the power of acceptance. Many have endured hostile winds and have chosen isolation. We recorded an interview that lasted almost two hours and then we continued talking in Stanley's only restaurant, the Malvina House Hotel. That night all of us felt the need to drink a little more wine than we should have. It was getting too late for us but Rob prevented us from leaving: we were his new friends on an island with too many repeating faces. We had to say goodnight around 2 a.m., only three or four hours of sleep ahead of us. He said goodbye with a pessimistic prediction: 'If they find oil in the islands, it is the end. But if not, it's also the end'.

The children of the war

Today we shot different scenes in the town. We also did an interview not knowing if it was going to fit in the editing room (this particular interview we finally had to discard, unlike Rob's, though it was also a powerful interview). The man in question in this case was John, who found out about our plans and left a message for our producer, Alejandro Israel. Before the interview, we knew that he had been ten years old and thus had a unique recollection of the war. We had also noticed in him a sort of distant and suspicious look. We finally set up a conversation between him and Julieta, first recording them walking in the streets of Stanley and then sitting on the bench in a square. The dialogue started with ordinary topics. He told us how life in the camp had been (camp is a word they use there to refer to the countryside, borrowed from the Spanish *campo*). From the beginning, he wanted the British history of the islands to go on record. As in the Argentine version, and as in many nationalist discourses, it has many cracks and holes, papered over with anachronistic emphases (small lives at the time become heroic ones, thanks to retrospective analysis). John defended the argument of 'the one who saw them first'. According to the British, the first to set foot on the islands was Captain John Davis, who was stranded in the islands in 1592. However, and very politely, Julieta contrasted this with conflicting views. Thus, she mentioned that the first map in which the islands appear is from 1522, based on a Portuguese expedition; also, that there are claims that the Yaghan people – should we say nation? – had arrived before the Europeans.

In any case, the first settlement was actually French. John was not much concerned with historical (or geographical) accuracy. Nationalism is somehow a form of belief. John was at the time particularly angry at the Argentine government and its policy on the Falklands. At the beginning, we looked suspicious to him, just for being Argentines. He needed to say to us how badly the Argentine military had treated them, them being the islanders and the Argentine troops. We did not like his extreme nationalism, but soon enough we understood he was speaking from a distant place.

When the war began, when the Argentine troops were preparing their positions – according to John – a group of children and some women were locked in a big barn near the rural town of Darwin. This barn was his experience of the war. He spent almost two months locked in there. This barn, John continued, was close to Goose Green, the site of an important battle. He could hear the planes; he got used to the explosions. He insisted he was poorly fed and ill-treated. He also said that the young soldiers were hungry as well. There was something he had had to go through during those days which was still there, that he could not tell us. Though I could not know exactly what it was, I understood he would not be able to name it; most of him remained in the barn. As he spoke he started mumbling, getting more and more annoyed. He kept repeating, randomly that the Argentine government should stop 'bullying' the islanders. He took this personally: the exact phrase he would repeat was: 'Don't bully me. Don't bully me'.

Then, after we thought the message was maybe too clear, he described the end of the war. Once the Argentine troops had lost the battle of Goose Green he could leave the barn. Once he was out, he had to see corpses on the ground, mutilated soldiers, young men screaming and crying. After that, there was a long silence and we continued to shoot only to ease the transition, but that was all he had to say. He added, though, that we should not change his testimony. He was tired of Argentine journalists changing their versions. We partially betrayed him, his scene did not fit into our film, but this is one of the reasons for this text.

New settlers

A half-hour pause in the shooting. We had finished some still shots of the town and in that break we went with Daniel to take a walk. Then we witnessed an ordinary sample of what this island is. We started to see some movement in the facilities of the fire fighters. It was like a performance. There were four of them. Two of them looked like astronauts; we had never seen a suit like that before. The costumes were extremely colourful: pink, violet, something like that. These two fire fighters walked like astronauts, practising, getting acquainted with the suit. Their colleagues were teasing them. We approached them and talked a little. One of them was from Chile and lived there permanently. He told us they even had a helicopter at their disposal.

Later that day we went to the supermarket. It was like any other chain supermarket. A sort of non-place but a more expensive one. It also had a coffee shop, one of the few in town, a sort of meeting place to chat and read the latest royal gossip. The hot topic was the wedding of Prince William. The fiction of the royal family seemed more powerful there. The supermarket also had a clothing shop. Most of the employees there were dark-skinned, and their ethnicity was not familiar to me, not from when I lived in New York or in my four months in London in 2000. They were from Saint Helena, another remote island in the South Atlantic, another absurd colony. These relocated islanders were the descendants of African and Indian slaves (who, in their turn, had also been relocated there). As in the Malvinas, Saint Helena had no native population. The difference was that at present the Malvinas offered better options for employment: Stanley has one of the highest GDP per person (and too many subsidies for very few people). Inside the supermarket, in the coffee store, we interviewed a young mother (she was in her twenties). She was blonde, with pinkish skin, a bit overweight. All her needs were met in Stanley, though she seemed bored. I could imagine her living a completely different life in a big city.

How to behave in cemeteries

Today we visited the Argentine cemetery in Darwin, a name that was given on account of the closest settlement (actually a group of houses only, several barns; John was probably held in one of these). The name was given after the visit of Charles Darwin in 1833, right after the British re-occupation (was science behind all this mess?). Brief digression: Darwin described during his visit a species called the 'warrah', a mixture of the fox and the wolf. The name was an English version of the Guarani word 'aguará', a wolf from the northeastern region of Argentina. Darwin noticed that the warrah was too sociable, not afraid of men, and thus predicted with success its extinction. I like the warrah as a metaphor for the Islands' status as well as a symbol of the rewriting of national traditions. Its name was perhaps given by the implanted gauchos (who in their turn were a prior iteration of the St. Helenans: gauchos and Charrua Indians were among the first forced settlers). On an infinite turn, these gauchos also ran 'cuadreras' (horse races from the *pampas*), still popular today in summer celebrations in the Malvinas. This was not a brief digression after all.

Let us return now to the deceased in the name of God and the Nation. The Argentine cemetery at Darwin was certainly one of the most important locations for our film. However, we ended up using very few images shot there. What I registered in my notes after this visit was something that the camera was not able to capture. Indeed, the cemetery in itself is overwhelming. On a deserted and barren hill you see 237 white crosses. We experienced there something difficult to convey.

We were there for more than two hours. We first took some wide-angle shots, then some close shots of the graves and the Virgin, then a sort of scene with Julieta that was a complete failure. This scene was a sort of conversation,

Julieta speaking about the war and myself and Daniel doing a lousy job with our questions. We started to feel a sense of unease; Julieta started to answer in a bad tone and I became angry at her, somehow frustrated. We started blaming each other. The scene had no truth, no emotion, there was nothing going on. In the meantime, Leo, operating the camera, instinctively moved away from the dialogue; there was nothing to shoot there. It was a disaster. We were there in what was supposed to be one of the more significant places for our film and we blew it.

Then our producer called for a break. We resumed after a while but we were too tired, too frustrated. I remember that Tony, our guide, had told us that the constant wind made everything more difficult. Later that night we all talked about what had happened in the cemetery. We all were somehow angry, though we were supposed to be in control. We had been walking in circles over 237 dead men. Half of them were still unidentified. They only had a carving on the tombstone that said 'Argentine soldier known only to God'. I have never seen ghosts or talked to the dead but I guess that being in such a barren and windy place is pretty close to that feeling. I understood later that this feeling has nothing to do with the fact of being in a cemetery but with the kind of cemetery it was.

On the other hand, Stanley has the most beautiful cemetery I have ever seen (I like Recoleta Cemetery at Buenos Aires as well). This is a simple cemetery, no luxury or excessive décor. What it does have in excess is the wind. We went there on a sunny day, on our very first day. It is slightly elevated and you access the place using a staircase that has a military monument to honour the 43 Islanders killed in the world wars. Once you enter the cemetery, you can see ten to 15 rows of graves and crosses with a view facing the bay. In the distance you can see the Mounts, even the Two Sisters. The graves reveal the origins and antiquity of the settlers: Butler 1885; Clarke 1851; Faulkner 1860; Lellman 1889; Pauloni, no date. While we were shooting there (we did include these images), we could see three kids shouting and jumping in the yard of a neighbouring house. They shared the same view of the bay.

Short scene: how to behave in a pub

The Globe is the name of one of the most popular pubs in Stanley. Then there are Deano's, the Victory Bar and Rose Bar, run down by the wind and the sea. Many things may happen in a pub. Of these three pubs, the Globe, starting with its name, attempts to be a sort of imperial pub. It looks like a bar from the 19th century. It is filled with all the possible variations of the British colours. It also looks like a theme-bar, like a Hard Rock Café type of bar, though in this case the 'theme' is nationalism. There were very few customers, not more than five or six, and they clearly knew who we were. It was three or four o'clock in the afternoon and we were celebrating the end of our shooting. We had our beers and we made a toast. We had no idea what was going to happen in the editing room but we were happy. Right after that, the barman or someone in charge decided to play a video for us. We started to hear *God Save the Queen* followed by some images of the war. I need to say that overall everyone on the Islands was very kind to us, except for that little provocation. Oddly enough (or may be not), the man behind the bar was not English.

A friendly farewell with Kelper music

After the scene in the pub we shot some additional scenes, some still shots in town taking advantage of the good light. We had few hours left on the Islands. I remember during all that week my friend Daniel insisting on visiting the lighthouse at Cape Pembroke, near Stanley. Finally, the opportunity presented itself in a very friendly manner.

Rod is Celia Stewart's neighbour; he lives right across from her bed and breakfast and takes care of her wonderful winter garden. We hardly got to know him until this last day. He offered us a ride to the lighthouse in his Land Rover. Daniel, Alejandro (the producer), Leo and I were fortunate that the rest of the crew were too tired to go (or was it like this after some negotiation?). Rod gave us the most amazing farewell possible. The sunset was beginning when we arrived and we shot some beautiful takes of the shores and the Mounts in the distance. Unfortunately, Rod did not fit into our film and we did not know how to thank him for all his generosity.

On the half-hour ride to the lighthouse, we learned that Rob had come to the Islands two years after the war. He was working for the government and made a life here. He and his late wife would teach dance lessons and were happy with the simple life of Stanley. I admired this possibility of living in such a place. I did live for some years in a small town but ended up moving. Not only had Rod encountered a happy life here but he had also decided to stay. He had relatives in England (I think a daughter and a son) but he could not imagine himself living anywhere else, even after many years as a widower. After talking for a time and telling us a bit about his life, he decided to play a cassette. He did not say what it was. We could not believe our ears.

At first, we heard the sound of a guitar in the style of country music. The singer had a British accent though it sounded Irish or even like American country music. It was joyful music though the lyrics had some of the rural anguish you find in many folk genres. When I started to understand some of the places mentioned I was amazed. It was Kelper music. The singer was referring to Mount Two Sisters or even his life in the camp as well as his difficulties with a beloved woman. We were seeing an amazing sunset accompanied by Kelper music. All of us immediately wanted to use that music in our film. We could not think of a better way to start capturing the Islands in a different manner than using this strange music.

The first thing we did once we were back in town was to record this Kelper album by Rock Berntsen called *White Grass Memories*. The week in the Malvinas could not have had a better ending. Before returning to the bed and breakfast, Rod bought us some beers in a pub. It was a warm night and there was a full moon. I think we were all very happy that night. After many attempts, I finally managed to get in touch with Rock Berntsen, the Kelper musician. This was several months after we had been to the Islands. I told him that we desperately wanted to include some of his songs in the film. I explained to him that our film was also about the possibility of a dialogue and the idea that there is more to show about these islands than their sovereignty. However, he decided not to play along, to keep the music only for the locals. This made me sad. However, I am glad I heard the songs and that now, some years later, they remain part of a diffuse memory of that trip.

7. Malvinas, civil society and populism: a cinematic perspective*

Joanna Page

Argentine films on the Malvinas War often turn the story of an international conflict into one about human rights. They position themselves within a much larger archive of images depicting the brutality of Argentina's most recent military dictatorship, the regime that ordered the invasion of the Islands in 1982. Since the return to democracy, the imperative to uncover and denounce the military's crimes towards civilians – whether committed on the Islands or on the continent – has forestalled other ways of remembering the war that do not focus on the reckless adventurism and violence of the armed forces. Films on the Malvinas draw heavily on the themes and discourses of films about the dictatorship, not least in their polarised representation of civil society as innocent victim or (more rarely) guilty accomplice of the regime.

This essay discusses two recent documentaries by Julio Cardoso that provide an alternative, if no less schematic, perspective. Where post-dictatorship films – especially those made by children of the disappeared – express rupture and disillusionment with regard to the ideology of left-wing militants in the 1970s and particularly their belief in a popular revolution, Cardoso's films *Locos de la bandera* (2005) and *Malvinas: Viajes del bicentenario* (2010) trace continuities and look for a common denominator. Far from representing civil society as victim or accomplice, these films transform it into the *pueblo*, the bedrock of Argentine society, bearer of popular and nationalist values and staunch in its defence of freedom against the nation's elite and its imperial invaders. A strategic appeal to discourses of the 1960s and 1970s enables Cardoso to construct a revisionist reading of the nation's history in which the Malvinas

---

* This essay was written in 2012 as a reflection on debates surrounding the 30th anniversary of the Malvinas War. For this reason, it does not include a discussion of films produced since that date, and refers to the political context of the Kirchner government in place at the time in Argentina. A Spanish version of this essay was published as 'Malvinas, sociedad civil y populismo' in María Angélica Semilla Durán, comp., *Relatos de Malvinas: Paradojas en la representación e imaginario nacional* (Villa María, Córdoba, Argentina: Eduvim, 2016), pp. 301–31.

J. Page, 'Malvinas, civil society and populism: a cinematic perspective', in G. Mira and F. Pedrosa (eds.), *Revisiting the Falklands–Malvinas Question: Transnational and Interdisciplinary Perspectives* (London: University of London Press, 2020), pp. 141–60. License: CC-BY-NC-ND 4.0.

War is extricated from the context of the dictatorship's crimes against its own citizens and treated as one more battle in the long and ongoing struggle of the *pueblo* against oppression. This version of history is just as politically determined as the other. However, by revealing blind spots in what have now become hegemonic representations of the war, these films do make a contribution to the important task of bringing greater diversification to post-war memory.

Cinema and *desmalvinización*

Many consider that a process of 'desmalvinización' (demalvinisation) held sway after Argentina's defeat in the war over the Malvinas in 1982. The term has been used to refer to the official silence imposed upon the returning soldiers and the state's reluctance to provide compensation, as well as to a more insidious kind of social invisibility with which the war was cloaked as a humiliating misadventure conducted by a brutal regime from which society wished to distance itself. Vicente Palermo argues, however, that while the Malvinas *war* was treated in this manner, this has allowed the Malvinas *cause*, the claim to sovereignty, to flourish unquestioned, as – in the often-repeated phrase, possibly coined by García Márquez – 'una causa justa en manos bastardas' [a just cause in the hands of bastards] (Palermo, 2007, p. 352). While blame for the war could be laid squarely at the door of the dictatorship, the wider cause, and the specific version of nationalism underpinning it, have remained impervious to critical interrogation (p. 283).

Cinema since the return to democracy in 1983 has certainly colluded in reducing the Malvinas War to just another arena for the dictatorship's brutality. Many films of the early post-dictatorship period in particular were primarily concerned with bringing to light the extent of the human rights abuses perpetrated by the armed forces. The political urgency of this task led in many cases to a wholesale demonising of military officers who had subjected terrified and demoralised conscripts to torture and abuse on the Islands just as they had persecuted dissidents and civilians at home. From the very beginning, however, it was clear that the denunciation of military violence in the context of the Malvinas War provoked more complex responses from those who had fought in the war. The portrayal of the conscripts in *Los chicos de la guerra* (Bebe Kamín, 1984) as victims of their military superiors – frightened, inexpert adolescents press-ganged into an absurd battle – provoked angry responses from many ex-combatants. The soldiers' own personal convictions about the purpose of the war entirely disappear in the film's representation of a conflict that seems only to take place between conscripts and officers. As Rosana Guber states, 'Los británicos sólo proveen el escenario donde se despliega el drama argentino' [The British only provide the stage on which the Argentine drama unfolds] (Guber, 2004, p. 88).

This sidelining of the nature of the war as a territorial dispute with Great Britain is repeated two decades later in Tristán Bauer's *Iluminados por el fuego* (2005). What have now become stereotypical images of the war are paraded enthusiastically past us. The conscripts are again depicted as terrified, demoralised and too caught up in the business of survival to be able to conjure up any patriotic sentiments; their sufferings – hunger, frostbite, exhaustion – are exacerbated by a lack of proper equipment and clothing, as well as the brutal treatment by their officers. While much truth is to be found in these allegations, *Iluminados por el fuego* (like *Los chicos de la guerra*) simply repackages the war as a set of divisions within Argentina to which Britain appears to play the role of mere accessory. Full blame is placed on the dictatorship: as Esteban, the ex-combatant protagonist reflects, 'la improvisación, el sadismo y la traición de los que habían torturado a su propio pueblo nos habían llevado a la derrota' [improvisation, sadism and the treachery of those who tortured their own people had led us to defeat]. The war continues today, but only in the sense that in the film's present (the financial crisis of 2001–2002) citizens face the need to fight for their survival again, betrayed once again by the state, this time through its failure to provide social and economic protection. This rather crude analogy is underlined by Gastón Pauls, the actor who plays Esteban, speaking about the film: 'También habla de la guerra cotidiana en el hoy, de una guerra que continúa. Una guerra que todavía tienen los ex combatientes y una guerra que tienen los cartoneros, los pibes que están limpiando los vidrios en la esquina' [The film is also about the everyday war of here and now, a war that is still going on. A war that the ex-combatants are still involved in, as are the rubbish-pickers and the kids washing car windscreens on the street corner] (Ranzani, 2005).

The lyrics of León Gieco's song 'La memoria', which plays in full at the end of the film while we see Esteban paying homage to the dead in Darwin Cemetery, place the war within a much broader (and over-generalised) history of violence and exploitation in Latin America. Both Gieco and Bauer ignore the wider significance of the Malvinas claim within the national imaginary, reducing the war to a cruel and expensive mistake from which the nation should move on as best it can. The discourse of closure in *Iluminados por el fuego* – Esteban returns to the Islands to 'cerrar la historia' [bring the story to a close] and exorcise the ghosts of the past – ironically announces the film's own role in closing off a number of potentially productive points of conflict or tension in memory of the Malvinas. *Iluminados por el fuego* provides a clear example of the way in which reducing the war to an irresponsible adventure on the part of the dictatorship effectively erases the ongoing Malvinas cause, the historical claim to sovereignty over the Islands that has not yet been resolved. I turn now to another film, also released in 2005, which also appropriates discourses of memory developed in the post-dictatorship context. However, it does so precisely to mark a clear divergence from these and to reintroduce the

Malvinas as a national cause that cannot be reduced to the war fought by the military regime in 1982.

Locos de la bandera and the transmission of political thought

> La *causa Malvinas* es única, porque no sólo es extremadamente significativa para todos, sino también y principalmente, porque tiene el poder temible de hacernos creer que posee casi los mismos significados para todos (Palermo, 2007, p. 22).
>
> [The Malvinas cause is unique, not only because it is extremely significant for everyone, but also, and chiefly, because it possesses the fearsome power of making us believe that it signifies almost the same for everyone.]

Julio Cardoso's *Locos de la bandera* adopts the perspective of the son of a soldier killed in action, now grown to be the same age as his father when he died. As I shall show, the film establishes a clear dialogue with productions since 2000 which have been directed by the children of militants disappeared under the military regime, including *Papá Iván* (María Inés Roqué, 2000), *Historias cotidianas* (Andrés Habegger, 2000), *Los rubios* (Albertina Carri, 2003), *HIJOS, el alma en dos* (Carmen Guarini and Marcelo Céspedes, 2005) and *M* (Nicolás Prividera, 2007). One of the key differences between *Locos de la bandera* and these other films, however, is to be found in the way that it imagines and performs inter-generational transmission. If the films made by children of the disappeared bear witness to a deep rupture in the transmission of political thought between the older generation and the younger, Cardoso's film demonstrates a much greater continuity between them. While *Locos de la bandera* is successful in resituating the war within the broader historical framework of the Malvinas cause, it goes to the other extreme by obscuring its embedding within the context of the dictatorship. The film makes a contribution to contemporary debates about the relationship between the Malvinas and a resurgent nationalism by considering what form patriotism might take in democracy; however, it reinforces many of the long-standing tenets of Argentine nationalism which, for Palermo and others, have remained unquestioned as a consequence of the excision of the war from the cause itself.

Locos de la bandera was made in collaboration with the Comisión de Familiares de Caídos en Malvinas e Islas del Atlántico Sur [Commission of Relatives of the War Dead in the Malvinas and Islands of the South Atlantic]. As one might expect, therefore, the film centres on the experience of mourning the death of a son, father, husband or brother in the war, and on the importance of acts of commemoration. But it moves beyond registering the legacies of loss, defeat and silencing to mount a searching investigation of the meaning of the war for the present. Neither its propositional form, nor its emotional weight, nor its political seriousness would seem to invite comparison with the playful *Los rubios*, released two years earlier, a film that has been criticised for casting both the violence of the dictatorship and 1970s militant activism in a frivolous or over-subjective light (Kohan, 2004; Sarlo, 2005, pp. 146–51). However, there are surprising points of convergence between the two films. Tracing these will throw into relief the very different approach taken in *Locos de la bandera* to the task of memory.

Both films explore the second-generation perspective of someone who was a small child during the dictatorship but is now of a similar age to the parents who were disappeared (in Carri's case) or the father who died in combat (in the case of *Locos de la bandera*). Both hover between testimony and fictional performance: Carri employs an actress to play her part in many of the scenes; and an actor is also used in *Locos de la bandera*, in this case a composite figure given the generic name 'Juan' to signify that he stands for many children in a similar position: his story is made up of the testimonies and experiences of a generation. Echoing some of the distancing devices used in *Los rubios*, Juan is present on screen but always silent: we hear his questions and reflections only in the form of a voice-over. Both films contain fictional reconstructions of the past, but ones in which the mimetic illusion is deliberately destroyed: in *Los rubios*, the abduction of Carri's parents is performed by Playmobil figures filmed in stop-motion animation and the film includes shots of the director telling her protagonist how to play her role; in *Locos de la bandera*, the verisimilitude of the re-enacted war scenes (performed by actors and shot in Río Gallegos) is undermined by the chronologically impossible intrusion of Juan into these shots.

Both films adopt a highly reflexive approach, insisting on the mediated quality of memory. In a voice-over at the beginning of the film, ex-combatants in *Locos* explain that their memories take the form of brief images, not 'recuerdos propios' [memories of their own] or 'un recuerdo completo' [a complete memory] but 'pequeñas imágenes sueltas [...]. Puedo contar anécdotas pero no son mías, yo sé que no son mías' [brief, disconnected images [...]. I can tell anecdotes but they're not mine, I know they're not mine]. In *Los rubios*, Carri – through Analía – acknowledges in a very similar way that she is unable to distinguish between her own personal memories and those of her sisters: 'Lo único que tengo es mi recuerdo difuso, contaminado por todas estas versiones' [The only thing I have is vague memories, contaminated by all these versions]. The films also establish a similar mise-en-scène for the child's detective work. Like Carri's actress, Juan writes in a notebook surrounded by documents, photos and other objects from the past. Recorded testimonies play in the background while the camera focuses on the protagonist in the present who, like us, is listening, watching and trying to fit everything together.

For different reasons, these films do not share the denunciatory stance adopted by some of the other children of disappeared militants, evident in productions such as *HIJOS, el alma en dos*. Carri's film is not a manifesto against the crimes of the past and the impunity of the present, but a more personal exploration of the impact of loss and absence. Cardoso explicitly warns us against the dangers of dividing society too neatly into 'goodies' and 'baddies'. As images of murky water and foggy landscapes fill the screen, Juan reminds us: 'Hay quienes necesitan inventarse un pasado transparente, donde sólo haya buenos y malos' [There are those who need to invent a transparent past for themselves, inhabited only by the good and the evil]. He goes on to observe sagely: 'Por lo general, los que recuerdan así se anotan siempre del lado de los buenos' [In general, those who remember in that way always chalk themselves up on the side of the good].

It is evident, too, that *Locos* positions itself in dialogue with many films about the dictatorship in its strategic appeal to the lexicon of human rights discourses. One mother interviewed, whose son's body was not recovered, speaks of the difficulty of mourning without a body and claims that her son 'es un desaparecido' [is one of the 'disappeared']. On one of the official visits family members have been able to make to the Argentine cemetery in the Malvinas, one of the mothers tries to comfort another who does not know which of the many unidentified crosses marks the spot where her son was buried. Consciously or unconsciously, in telling her that '*todos* son nuestros hijos' [they are all our children], she echoes one of the key declarations of the Madres de la Plaza de Mayo. These appropriations are fully part of the film's project to construct the Malvinas as an axis for possible national reintegration.

However, despite the number of discourses it shares with post-dictatorship cinema, *Locos de la bandera* insists that the soldiers who went to the Islands were not mere victims of an abusive regime fighting to retain credibility: instead, they went as protagonists of a military venture, serving a popular, national cause, namely the claim to sovereignty over the Islands. This shift belongs to a diversification of discourses that, for Federico Lorenz, became evident on the 20th anniversary of the war in 2002, when '[l]os hombres que habían combatido se transformaron en modelos a imitar' [the men who had fought became models to imitate] (Lorenz, 2012, p. 374). The early 2000s saw a similar shift in the representation of 1970s militants, restoring agency to figures previously depicted merely as victims of state terror (Jelin, 2007, p. 337). Films made by the children of disappeared militants, such as *Papá Iván*, *M* and *Historias cotidianas* (Andrés Habegger, 2000) have focused precisely on their parents' choice to remain involved in militancy in the face of very likely capture and death. In the same way, *Locos de la bandera* does not present the soldiers who went to Malvinas as victims, but as patriots who willingly risked their lives for the sake of a national cause.

Here, however, is where an important divide opens up between *Locos de la bandera* and films made by children of the disappeared. Carri, Roqué, Habegger and Prividera struggle but largely fail to understand and accept why their parents sacrificed so much and left them with an unrecoverable loss. In *Los rubios*, Analía recites: 'Me cuesta entender la elección de mamá. ¿Por qué no se fue del país? me pregunto una y otra vez' [I find it hard to understand my mother's decision. Why did she not leave the country? I ask myself again and again]. In *Historias cotidianas*, Habegger struggles to understand the choices his father made, doubting that he would be able to give up his own life for such a reason. Roqué in *Papá Iván* explains that she made the film with the aim of trying to understand why her father did what he did, but she does not fully reach that point and admits that 'prefería tener un padre vivo antes que un héroe muerto' [I would rather have had a living father than a dead hero]. In contrast, the sons and other relatives of the Malvinas combatants in Cardoso's film not only understand their sacrifice but have fully adopted the cause for which they died. Carri reflects in *Los rubios* that she lives in 'un país lleno de fisuras' [a country full of rifts] and one of these rifts is clearly the discontinuity between the ideological orientation of her generation and that of her parents. *Locos de la bandera* posits instead the possibility of generational continuity. Leandro de la Colina, the son of a pilot killed in the war, speaks earnestly about the example his father has given him of a life sacrificed for others and feels a 'traspaso', a kind of transferral, from him. Juan, who remembers at the start of the film that his father 'no pensaba en la guerra. Pensaba en lo que la Argentina pudiera llegar a ser si estuviera completa' [didn't think about the war. He thought about what Argentina could become if it were complete], ends up taking exactly the same attitude to the material he has collected: he discovers that 'no me importa la guerra ahora' [the war doesn't matter to me now] but that instead – repeating precisely the words of his father – 'pensaba en lo que la Argentina podría llegar a ser si estuviera completa' [I thought about what Argentina could become if it were complete].

Although both *Locos* and *Los rubios* make use of imaginative reconstructions and are structured around an investigation, these devices are put to very different ends. If in *Los rubios* the inclusion of fiction announces the impossibility of any resolution to the film's search for identity, in *Locos* its use does not undermine the quest for knowledge but facilitates it. The insertion of Juan as an observing presence in fictional reconstructions of the past is certainly a self-consciously artificial and anachronistic device and appears to replay Carri's emphasis on the mediated nature of memory. In mocked-up archival footage cast in appropriately bleached tones, Juan surveys the intense activity of volunteers packing boxes of food and other supplies to send off to the war and watches sailors rush past him in the burning passageways of the Belgrano. His presence on screen clearly announces the footage to be simulated, as does the conspicuous use of filters and lenses to produce sepia tones or a grainy archive effect. Anachronistically, he appears to be of the same age in these scenes from 1982 as he is in the film's present in 2006. However, the purpose of such reconstructions in *Locos de la bandera* is not to suggest the elusiveness of the past but the reverse: to dramatise the transfer of knowledge and experience from one generation to the next.

These reconstructions, in which Juan seems to share the same time and space as the combatants at war, recall some of the techniques used in the photography and visual art produced by children of the disappeared, in which montage is often used to simulate an encounter between the child and the absent parents.[1] Paradigmatic of this approach are the photo collages created by Lucila Quieto, suggesting likenesses between a parent and child who would never otherwise be able to share the same space.[2] Another example would be *Conversación con Antonio*,[3] in which Gabriela Bettini photographs herself in a stance that suggests that she is conversing with her father, whose portrait hangs on the wall beside her.[4] As Jordana Blejmar argues, this juxtaposition of temporalities 'breaks with the linearity of history and invites us to read the past not only for what it was but for what it should have been' (Blejmar, 2012, p. 114). These patently impossible encounters are also, in the words of Ana Amado, an attempt to 'recuperar lazos entre lo que es y lo que fue' [recover ties between what is and what was] (Amado, 2004, p. 49).

A similar desire motivates the interpellation of Juan in *Locos* into scenes from the past, but here it is fully realised. The final reconstruction on the battlefield marks the culmination of his search, providing a moment of complete recognition and identification. With the help of an insert shot at the crucial point, when Juan looks down at one of the fallen soldiers, he sees himself lying there in uniform. Is he projecting himself into that experience, or is he imagining his father lying there, who would have been of the same age as Juan is now? Either way, the encounter with the past is complete, marking a difference from the photo montages of Quieto and Bettini, which always bear witness to absence and rupture. The fictional reconstructions of *Locos de la bandera* therefore perform a function that is entirely opposed to their role in *Los rubios* and in many other films and visual artworks by children of the disappeared. If, in Carri's film, fiction and fantasy are used to demonstrate the impossibility of accessing the past, in Cardoso's, fiction performs an encounter with that past and demonstrates the unbroken continuity between one generation and the next.

A divergence is also evident in the two films' treatment of objects of memory. When he visits the Malvinas, Juan finds there 'una forma de mirar. Es una mirada que está siempre en contacto con su tierra' [a way of looking. It's a look that is always in contact with the land]. *Locos de la bandera* constructs a vision that is intimately bound up with a physical relationship with earth

---

1 The question of intergenerational transmission in photography, film and other art works by children of the disappeared is extensively explored in Blejmar (2012).
2 Some of these collages are published by the Fondo Nacional de las Artes in a catalogue to accompany an exhibition held in 2007 with the title *Arqueologías*.
3 From *Recuerdos inventados* (2003).
4 See http://www.gabrielabettini.com/RECUERDOS-INVENTADOS (accessed 16 October 2018).

and material objects. In Carri's film, photographs and other objects testifying to the past are emptied of meaning and eventually discarded in favour of the blond wigs donned by the whole film crew, but these – while they echo the childlike playfulness of the film or express new forms of companionship – remain signifiers of false memories, reminding us of the neighbours' mistake in remembering the Carri family as blond. In Cardoso's film, objects are successful carriers of the past into the present and the future; and they also serve to link an individual past with that of the nation. Juan touches everything he comes across on the Islands: remnants of clothing and rusting machinery. One by one, he handles all medals, photos and rosaries kept by the family members of soldiers who died in the war and runs his fingers through sand recovered from the sea bed beneath the Belgrano. All the family members who have visited the Malvinas since the war have brought back handfuls of earth or stones. One woman keeps hers in a flowerpot, while others have displayed theirs in little shrines in a corner of their homes. Carri reflects in *Los rubios* that 'cualquier intento que haga para acercarme a la verdad voy a estar alejándome' [any attempt I make to get closer to the truth takes me further away from it]. For Juan, in contrast, the past *is* there; it can be touched; it can be understood.

The film's emphasis on the material is entirely consonant with a claim that is first and foremost one about land, about physical territory. The marble monument to the fallen erected in the cemetery is not just significant as a permanent reminder of the loss of life, but (as Leandro de la Colina clearly states) part of an ongoing sovereignty claim. It is not simply an object of memorialisation but the physical presence of Argentina on the Islands. *That* part, at least, is not in dispute, says Leandro. The transfer of stones, earth and other objects from the mainland to the Islands and back again is a performative action in *Locos de la bandera* which demonstrates not just the historical intermingling of these areas of land but an ongoing campaign for their future integration.

If, for Carri, her country is 'lleno de fisuras' [full of rifts], for Cardoso, it is 'lleno de escombros' [full of rubble]. Both films depict the nation as divided and littered with ghosts from the past that have not been properly put to rest, but for Cardoso that rubble is formed of stones from which memories and a sense of national identity *can* be rebuilt. As Juan reflects: 'Escribo desde un país lleno de escombros. Miro el pedregal, y escucho decir que aquí no hay nada más que piedras falsas. Los recuerdos son como las piedras. Están ahí. Esperan a que vos decidas cómo usarlas. Y acá yo veo piedras. Piedras que según cómo las mires, podrían sostener tu casa' [I write from a country that is full of rubble. I look at the rocky ground and I hear people say that there is nothing but imitation stones here. Memories are like stones. They are there. They wait for you to decide how to use them. And here I see stones. Stones on which, depending on how you see them, you could build your house].

Underlying both *Los rubios* and *Locos de la bandera* is a call to remember the past differently, or at least to allow space for different memories. But Cardoso's film explicitly acknowledges the relationship between how we remember the past and what we build for the future. If it is true, as Juan freely acknowledges, that among those who fought the war were 'cobardes, traidores, oportunistas, vendidos, incompetentes' [cowards, traitors, opportunists, colluders, incompetents] it is also true that 'uno se parece a los recuerdos que elige conservar. Y yo quisiera ser mejor. Por eso miro y busco' [you take on the appearance of the memories you choose to preserve. And I want to be better. So I look and search]. The way we remember the past in *Locos* is not simply about being faithful to that past; it is also about finding ways to become something different, and better, in the future. For that reason alone we should remember not just the stories of abuse or incompetence, but also those of courage, solidarity and sacrifice. This is the vision that is lacking in many of the films made by children of the disappeared, who find little or nothing to emulate in either the sacrifices made by their parents or the complicity and apathy of society at large.

Of course, by rejecting portrayals of the combatants as victims, the film is certainly guilty at times of recasting them as glorious heroes. Some nuances of representation do emerge, however, for example in the depiction of officers both as brutal disciplinarians and as courageous protectors of the men in their charge; and these moments contribute to the work of adding what Lorenz has called 'densidad histórica' [historical density] to memory of the war (Lorenz, 2012a, p. 328). In one of the fictional reconstructions we see an official sentence a conscript to an 'estaqueamiento', a form of military 'discipline' in which a soldier is left stretched out between stakes in the ground and which has been roundly condemned in many texts as an example of the kind of human rights abuses often performed by military officers during the Malvinas War. However, the episode – replayed in so many films on the Malvinas – gains complexity here as we understand that it is the third time that the soldier in question has deserted his post and left his companions in danger and one of these has been badly wounded (mortally, we suspect) as a result. Although there is no whitewashing here of the brutal or improvised nature of the conduct of the war, much is found to praise in the dedication and professionalism of a good number of those involved in fighting it and taking many difficult decisions along the way, including officers, many of whom were not torturers but showed great heroism in protecting the conscripts under their command.

In the context of the 30th anniversary of the war, Lorenz identified the need for new approaches to memory that might take us beyond what he calls 'la falsa dicotomía entre patriotismo y democracia' [the false dichotomy between patriotism and democracy] (Lorenz (2012b), p. 58). 'La democracia va acompañada de la patria' [Democracy goes hand-in-hand with the homeland], says one mother in *Locos de la bandera*. In certain respects, *Locos de la bandera* opens up a way of thinking about the relationship between patriotism and democratic citizenship that would have been unthinkable in the early post-dictatorship period. Luis Alberto Romero, for example, has signalled the extent to which the inculcation of a hatred of the regime, a weight of feeling that guaranteed the solid embrace of democracy, came, and continues to come, at the expense of a genuine historical understanding of the period (Romero, 2002, p. 118). The fact that 'condenar parece ser más importante que comprender' [to condemn seems to be more important than to understand] ironically threatens the basis of democracy itself, as such a Manichean approach has led to a new form of intolerance of those who do not fully participate in what has, at points, become an unthinking denunciation of the regime and everything it is seen to stand for, even erupting in acts of violence.[5]

The greatest lesson the war can teach us, the film seems to suggest, has little to do with either irresponsible war-mongering or epic heroism and much more to do with models of citizenship based on self-sacrifice and mutual support in times of crisis. One ex-combatant considers that '[d]e todas las enseñanzas que me dejó Malvinas, la primera y fundamental es que uno consigue objetivos, en grupo, buscando el bien común' [of all the lessons that the Malvinas has taught me, the first and most fundamental is that one achieves one's aims by working as a group, seeking the common good]. Picking his way through the war-strewn battlefields of the past, Juan realises that the comradeship and the sense of striving towards a common goal which many ex-combatants remember would be of great value in the here and now: 'Pienso en lo que podría ser el lugar donde vivimos si nosotros pudiéramos mirarnos con ojos tan atentos como los que se miraban acá, entre compañeros' [I think about what the place we live in could become if we could regard each other as attentively as they did here, as comrades]. Far from viewing it as a particularly nefarious episode in the military regime's campaign of national terror and fragmentation, *Locos de la bandera* elevates the Malvinas cause as a collective project around which a sense of nationhood can be rebuilt.

In an essay on 'desmalvinización', Cardoso observes: 'El asunto que nos ocupa es cómo se construye un punto de vista común […] en este verdadero campo de batalla por el significado de las cosas en el que se ha convertido la postguerra' [The issue that concerns us is how to construct a common viewpoint […] in this veritable battlefield for the meaning of things that the post-war period has become] (Cardoso, 2011). The quotation neatly articulates the tension at the heart of *Locos de la bandera*. A discursive openness akin to that of *Los rubios* is suggested by the film's imaginative reconstructions, its use of a questioning

---

5   In this respect, Romero argues: 'Una cosa es mostrarle a los vecinos de un barrio que una persona de apariencia normal es fehacientemente un torturador; otra muy distinta es su linchamiento' [It is one thing to demonstrate to those living in a particular neighbourhood that an apparently normal person is irrefutably a torturer; it is another thing entirely to lynch him] (2002, p. 117).

child's perspective and its insistent return to the word 'eligir' [to choose]. But Cardoso's phrase here, 'cómo se construye un punto de vista común' [how to construct a common viewpoint] is telling. How *does* one construct a common viewpoint without closing around a single view of the past or the future?

In fact, of course, the film does close around a particular version of nationalism, based on the notion of territorial integrity. It is evident in the reverence shown towards earth, sand and stones carried symbolically between the nation's provinces and between the Argentine mainland and the Islands, acts of intermingling which seem to prophesy the eventual reintegration of the lands. Territorial integrity is one of the key tenets of Argentine nationalism identified by Palermo, powerfully expressed in the Malvinas cause (Palermo, 2007, pp. 209–10). The film's insistence on the value of shared goals points us to Palermo's analysis of the importance of the idea of unanimity in Argentine nationalism, again exemplified in discourses on the Malvinas: '*Malvinas indica el camino: si los argentinos estuviésemos en todo unidos como lo estamos en Malvinas, entonces a la Argentina le iría bien*' [The Malvinas show us the path: if we Argentines were as united in everything as we were on the Malvinas, then everything would go well for Argentina] (p. 18). Despite its apparent openness of form and discourse, and its appeal to the values of democratic citizenship, then, the film locates the collective project it proposes within a narrow and exclusionary version of nationalism.

Civil society and populism in Malvinas: *Viajes del bicentenario*

> Otro aniversario, uno más de ese episodio con fragor a gesta y entorno de cartón pintado como escenografía berreta de película de cuarta.[6]
>
> [Another anniversary, another, of that event with its clamour of heroic feats and its painted cardboard backdrop, like the cheap set design of a third-rate film.]

There is a sequence that is often repeated in films about the Malvinas: the archival footage of the moment at which Galtieri announces the invasion on 2 April 1982 to an overflowing Plaza de Mayo. The news is met with an ovation by the exultant thousands gathered below. How might we explain such a ringing endorsement of a bloody regime in a square that had, only three days earlier, witnessed a mass demonstration against the dictatorship? In Palermo's words, attempts to account for the widespread support for the war has only resulted in 'pseudo-explanations', such as a collective delirium, which effectively sidestep the question of collective responsibility (Palermo, 2007, p. 299). Viewed in the post-dictatorship context and with the hindsight of defeat, this sequence from the archives becomes charged with a kind of shame, reflected in its compulsive

---

6   Oscar Luna, ex-soldier and psychologist (Luna, 1999).

repetition in so many films. These are phantasmal images, with all the grainy tones and exaggerated melodrama of a cheap and badly directed film, an apt metaphor for Oscar Luna (see above) for the war as whole.

The 'theory of the two demons', recently revisited by Pilar Calveiro (among others), refers to the tendency, especially in the first years of the post-dictatorship period, to depict civil society as an innocent victim caught up in a battle fought between left-wing militants and the authoritarian state (Calveiro, 2008, pp. 137, 148). Both Palermo and Lorenz observe a change in perspective towards the dictatorship and the 1970s that has made it possible to raise the question of society's complicity in that battle and thereby to begin to construct a more nuanced understanding of the period. Both maintain, however, that while memory of the dictatorship has begun to open up in this way, '[n]ada semejante ocurrió en el caso de Malvinas' [nothing like that has taken place in the case of the Malvinas] (Palermo, 2007, p. 299).

This key difference between the politics of memory of the dictatorship on the one hand and the Malvinas war on the other is patently visible in cinema. In the first films of the post-dictatorship period, such as *La historia oficial* (Luis Puenzo, 1985), the predominant vision is one of a society that knew nothing about what was going on. In later films, particularly those documentaries directed from 2000 onwards by children of the disappeared, society is instead charged with both complicity and complacency. Among the most acerbic critiques of civilian society under dictatorship is delivered by *M*. The director, Prividera, strongly suspects that one of his mother's companions is at least partly responsible for her disappearance by collaborating with the armed forces to pass them lists of those actively involved with the Montoneros. With a cold fury he denounces the present failures of the state and of society as a whole to reconstruct what happened to the disappeared and to keep their memory alive. Monuments are overgrown by bushes, or in need of restoration; the quest for information about his mother sends him bouncing from one agency to another, with no centralised data bank in existence 'en un país donde nadie se hace cargo de nada' [in a country in which no one takes responsibility for anything]. From the civilian informants who propped up the regime to those who still respond with fear or indifference to the task of remembering the dictatorship's victims, we are all – in Prividera's film – responsible for their disappearance.

Los rubios also constructs a devastating vision of the fear and indifference which supported the regime during the dictatorship and are still rife today. When interviewed, one neighbour lets slip that it was she who had collaborated with the military in the kidnapping of Carri's parents, an event that left the neighbourhood – she declares, with some satisfaction – much quieter and safer. The Carris had moved to the area in accordance with the Montonero policy of 'proletarización' through which militants were supposed to acquire the habits and perspectives of the working classes, idealised as the fount of virtues such as simplicity, sacrifice, solidarity and altruism. This image of the *pueblo* for which

Carri's parents and so many other militants were prepared to sacrifice their lives is radically undermined in *Los rubios*.

A parallel shift towards a questioning of the role of civil society has not taken place in films about the Malvinas. They consistently offer, instead, a depiction of a deceived, helpless society, such as that represented in *La deuda interna* (Miguel Pereira, 1988), in which the war becomes yet another form of exploitation of the masses by the elite, highlighting a much broader problem of inequality and social division. Compared with films such as *La deuda interna*, *Los chicos de la guerra* or *Iluminados por el fuego*, Cardoso's productions have received a much more limited distribution. However, I suggest that they merit close attention, particularly with regard to the explanations they proffer concerning the massive support of the war and the alternative vision they provide of civil society, here transformed into the *pueblo*, bearers of a popular nationalism that transcends the events and the context of the war. The difference is remarkable: if in *M* civil society is thrust into the dock, in Cardoso's film it is promoted to the role of hero.

If post-dictatorship cinema registers rupture and disillusionment with the militant ideology of the 1970s, and above all with the idea of a united, revolutionary *pueblo*, Cardoso's films find continuities. Here we see, revived, precisely that image of the *pueblo* that is destroyed in the films by Carri and Prividera. In *Locos de la bandera*, the oft-repeated scene of jubilation in the Plaza de Mayo is inserted into a broader narrative about the masses' support for the war, linking that scene to others showing the donations of clothes, food and other goods that surpassed the regime's capacity to distribute them. As the mother of a soldier who died in the war claims: 'No se puede decir, fue todo un manejo de la dictadura' [You can't say it was all driven by the dictatorship]. For Juan, it is clear that taking responsibility for that support is the duty of all: 'A quién no le gustaría tener una historia tan simple como el título de un diario. Pero no hay esas historias. La verdadera tragedia del olvido empieza cuando uno pretende tener una historia pero la quiere contar como si no hubiera sido parte de ella' [Who wouldn't like to have a history that is as simple as a newspaper heading? But that kind of history doesn't exist. The real tragedy of forgetting begins when someone claims to have a history, but wants to recount it as if they weren't part of it].

It is a wise observation, although of course it is much easier to assume responsibility if the history recounted is one of glory and not of defeat or genocidal acts. As Juan continues: 'El 2 de abril de 1982 no sólo recuperábamos Malvinas. También empezábamos a recuperar la libertad. La misma gente que dos días antes salió para decirle basta a la dictadura estuvo con todo el país diciéndole basta al imperio. No hay nada de raro en esto. La gente reconocía su bandera mucho mejor que su gobierno' [On 2 April 1982 we did not only recover the Malvinas. We also began to recover our freedom. The same people who two days earlier had taken to the streets to say 'enough' to the dictatorship were there with the rest of the country, saying 'enough' to imperialism. There is nothing strange about that. The people were identifying with their national flag much more than their government].

This repositioning of Malvinas as a popular, national cause that transcends the war becomes the main thrust of Cardoso's *Malvinas: Viajes del bicentenario*. The film narrates the battle of the Comisión de los Familiares de Caídos en Malvinas e Islas del Atlántico Sur to erect a monument in the Argentine military cemetery on the Malvinas. The monument was successfully completed in 2004 and inaugurated five years later. Between the first film and the second, Cardoso took up the directorship of the Observatorio Malvinas, based at the University of Lanús, an institute founded in 2009 with the aim of developing pedagogical materials on the Malvinas for schools and teacher-training. This new emphasis is evident in the much more didactic approach of *Viajes del bicentenario*. The young narrator of *Locos de la bandera*, who questions what he sees and reflects on the difficult task of memory, is replaced in *Viajes del bicentenario* with an anonymous, diligent, and mute primary school pupil.

The film opens in Perdriel, an iconic location chosen for reasons that are made clear in the first sequence. Famous as the site of a battle against English troops in the first British invasion of the Río de la Plata in 1806, in 1834 Pedriel also became the birthplace of José Hernández, author of the celebrated epic poem *Martín Fierro* (1872), identified in the film as 'la obra más importante de la autoafirmación cultural' [our most important work of cultural self-affirmation]. That the same site should have witnessed two events of such national importance is not presented as a coincidence in the film. As if expressing an entirely obvious connection, one of the presenters recites: 'José Hernández, Malvinas […] la autoafirmación a través de la lucha, la autoafirmación a través de la cultura' [José Hernández, Malvinas […] self-affirmation through battle, self-affirmation through culture]. 'No hay casualidades' [There are no coincidences], they agree, reverently, as if Hernández and the Malvinas were two irrevocably entwined threads of some divinely authored narrative rather than two events deliberately juxtaposed to produce a specific reading of Argentine history, inscribing them both in a popular, nationalist and anti-imperialist genealogy.

As well as interviews with relatives of the war dead, the documentary is packed with commentaries from historians allied with the Instituto Nacional de Revisionismo Histórico, created by presidential decree in 2011, including Pacho O'Donnell (the Institute's Director), Ana Jaramillo and others whose work has received approval as advancing the aims of the Institute, such as Francisco Pestanha. Its aim is clearly to install the Malvinas within a popular nationalist agenda and thereby to advance both the Malvinas cause and that of historical revisionism. The Malvinas War is presented as just one more landmark in a long history of conflict between Argentina and Great Britain that – Cardoso's interviewees claim – has played a vital role in Argentina's self-definition as a nation.

The film even provides us with a recommended reading list to accompany its revisionist approach. The books shown higgledy-piggledy on a table, as if piled randomly, have on closer inspection been carefully placed, both to advertise the works of those involved in making the documentary and to canonise a revisionist curriculum for the nation's schools. Here we see, for example, Raúl Scalabrini Ortiz's classic of revisionist history *Bases para la reconstrucción nacional*, as well as the complete works of Rodolfo Kusch, whose philosophical reflections were very much informed by indigenous thought and popular wisdom. These are jumbled up with maps of the Malvinas and works by Pestanha and Jaramillo. Prominent in this jumble of texts is an essay originally published by Jose Hernández in 1869 with the title 'Islas Malvinas: Una cuestión urgente'. In it he defends the depth of feeling provoked by the loss of the Islands, an assault on the territorial integrity of the nation which has caused grave upset, 'como si se arrebatara un pedazo de nuestra carne' [as if part of our own flesh had been wrenched from us]. The powerful image of a mutilated Argentina returns to shape the nationalist sentiment of Cardoso's film.

If, for Palermo, the Malvinas cause unites all the most powerful doctrines of Argentine nationalism, the same could certainly be said for *Viajes del bicentenario*. As well as the axioms of the territorial integrity of the nation (now mutilated), we also find the nation as the victim of ransacking by imperial powers and its own elite classes, together with the doctrine of unity, without which the country will not be able to reclaim its glorious destiny (Palermo, 2007, p. 106). This doctrine presupposes a form of regeneration that will put right the 'descarrilamiento' [derailment] that the country has experienced, casting it from its destiny of greatness (Palermo, 2007, pp. 104–5). In *Viajes del bicentenario* this regeneration is articulated in terms of the 'patria grande' [the great country, meaning the integrated Latin American continent], a discourse formed in the continent's liberators' dreams of political unity that went on to be highly influential in the armed struggle of the 1970s. There is mention in the film of the strategy of 'sudamericanizar' [South-Americanising] in relation to the Malvinas cause, with reference to the current policy of Argentina of seeking the support of other Latin American countries for their claim to sovereignty. However, the use of this term also links the Malvinas cause to the anti-colonialist discourse of the 1960s and 1970s. It is suggested, for example, that Argentines are 'ciudadanos del sur de la patria grande' [citizens of the south of the great country]. Along these same lines, the monument to the war dead in Malvinas becomes 'un homenaje a la libertad de todos los pueblos americanos' [a homage to the freedom of all [Latin] American peoples]; in Darwin Cemetery, the relatives have erected 'una bandera espiritual y cultural americana y argentina' [a spiritual and cultural flag that is both Argentine and [Latin] American]; the construction of the monument is even described as 'América recuperándose a si misma' [[Latin] America recovering itself]. This version of the past, and of the cause that stretches into the future, clearly erases the dictatorship from the Malvinas War. It is as if the *pueblo* itself had taken up arms to confront its old imperialist masters.

The locating of the Malvinas within a longer history of popular, anti-imperialist struggles is not new. From 1982 onwards many veterans have appealed to this same history when speaking about their comrades' sacrifice (Lorenz, 2012a, pp. 228–9). These voices could not properly be heard in the period immediately following the war. As Lorenz observes, at this point 'el rechazo social a la violencia no dejaba margen ni para la reivindicación bélica ni para la revolucionaria, ambas asociadas tanto al estado represor como a las organizaciones guerrilleras, los "dos demonios" funcionales a la necesidad autoexculpatoria y refundacional de la democracia [society's rejection of violence left no room for the justification of war or even revolution, both associated with the repressive state or the guerrilla organisations, the 'two demons' that facilitated the self-exculpation needed for the re-founding of democracy] (p. 373). That the war should now be seen as an arena of glory and sacrifice, and that Malvinas should be re-established as the keystone of popular nationalism, bears witness to the powerful confluence and mutual promotion of three recent trends: a revival of popular nationalism, the active appeal to 1970s discourses on the part of Kirchnerism and the resurgence of historical revisionism (sanctioned by the state).

In disconnecting the Malvinas cause from the war started by the military in 1982, one might consider that *Viajes del bicentenario* takes a step towards thinking about the forms that patriotism may take under democracy. When the mother of a soldier killed in the war says 'no hay democracia sin patria' [there is no democracy without the motherland], she opens up at least the possibility of thinking about patriotism in a way that is not defined by the violent repression of the military regime. The only possible path that the film contemplates, however, is that of populism. For O'Donnell, speaking in the film, 'siempre han sido los sectores populares los que verdaderamente supieron definirle al enemigo y enfrentárselo' [it has always been the popular classes who really knew how to identify and confront the enemy], whether in the English invasions of 1806, the Battle of Vuelta de Obligado of 1845, or the more recent war of 1982. O'Donnell maintains that, 'indudablemente han sido los sectores populares, los que siempre tienen más conciencia, ¿no es cierto?, del concepto de patria' [it has undoubtedly been the popular classes who have always been more conscious, isn't that right, of the meaning of the motherland]. Suddenly, the conflict over Malvinas becomes not a war declared by a military regime in which the *pueblo* plays the role of innocent bystander or guilty accomplice, but an expression of the enduring importance of the Malvinas cause in the popular imagination.

In its eagerness to re-invent the Malvinas as a discourse of national unity, the film emphasises the fact that the project of erecting the monument was brought to completion with the support of all sectors of Argentine society. Among the many references in the film to beginnings and ends, openings and closings, one family member urges us to 'pensar que somos hermanos. Yo creo que ése es el capítulo que se abre' [think of ourselves as brothers and sisters. I believe that this is the chapter that is beginning]. However, this discourse of apparent inclusivity and integration hides its real character as a principle of exclusion. By anchoring Malvinas so firmly in patriotism, a syllogism is set in motion: one cannot be patriotic if one does not support the claim for sovereignty.

This popular nationalism is clearly embedded in a Catholic matrix. In fact, *Viajes del bicentenario* is constructed not so much as a documentary-as-educational-tool as a documentary-as-religious-act. A close relationship is established in the film between national unity and the Catholic faith. This can be seen, for example, in those sequences that show the statue of the Virgin on its journey through every province of the country before arriving to preside over the inauguration of the new monument to the war dead on the Malvinas. The documentary dedicates a sequence of considerable length to the mass that is held as part of that ceremony. We see relatives presenting offerings to the Virgin in the name of the fallen; and we watch while they place rosaries, photos, prayer cards and other objects of religious and sentimental value in a glass box displayed in the cemetery. Indeed, the whole film takes on the form of a religious act of worship in which we witness rituals of great symbolic significance, we participate in moments of reflection accompanied by music, we learn to venerate holy objects and we follow the faithful in their search for spiritual comfort. If how to remember the war and how to recover the Islands are topics for debate, religious faith invites no such conflict or divergence in opinion. The documentary constructs its spectators, and by extension civil society as a whole, as members of the flock. We are given two missions: to keep a candle burning in the name of the dead; and to unite under the banner of restoring Argentina's sovereignty over the Islands.

To historicise, perhaps

Cardoso's documentaries on the Malvinas construct an idea of the *pueblo* and of civil society that is, in comparison to the documentaries produced by children of the disappeared, significantly closer to that of the 1970s. It is certainly true that the continuity they imagine is rather deceptive: phrases such as 'la patria grande' and 'el pueblo' are taken up again here as if nothing had happened during the period that separates us from the 1970s. One might well ask to what extent the appeal to these discourses is a genuine attempt to historicise and not to invoke, in an ahistorical manner, terms that now float free from their temporal anchoring in a very different context.

At the same time, to represent the war as one more episode in a long-held claim to sovereignty (dating back to 1833) and an even longer struggle against imperialism is to attempt to understand it, not as a sudden and senseless event that came out of the blue, but as an event that can be historicised. Here we may appreciate a convergence with recent shifts in post-dictatorship memory, which has begun to treat the violence of the military regime not as an inexplicable event that arose from nothing but as a continuation and an intensification of characteristics already present in society, as suggested by Luis Alberto Romero and Hugo Vezzetti among others (Vezzetti, 2002, p. 47; Romero, 2002, p. 120). In a similar manner, *Viajes del bicentenario* attempts to explain what for other films has remained an isolated and inexplicable event: society's support for a war conducted by the military regime. Instead of sweeping that support under the carpet or attributing it to a case of collective hysteria or delusion, Cardoso turns it into a key episode in the history of popular nationalism in Argentina.

If the valiant, wise and glorious *pueblo* can arise again as it does in Cardoso's films, blameless and the repository of the nation's hopes, it is because – unlike civil society in films about the dictatorship – it has not spent time in the defendants' dock; and because Cardoso completely severs the noble Malvinas cause from the atrocious regime that started the war of 1982. Cardoso's documentaries provide disquieting visions of an uncritical nationalism that appears to be gaining force in the present, but in many ways they do not err in their reading of the past and particularly of its nationalist and populist legacy for the present. If nothing else, these films open up alternative ways of remembering the war that are not confined to post-dictatorship denunciations of human rights abuses. As Calveiro reminds us: 'La repetición puntual de un mismo relato, sin variación, a lo largo de los años, puede representar no el triunfo de la memoria sino su derrota' [The exact repetition of a single story, without variation, over the years may not represent memory's triumph but its defeat] (Calveiro, 2005, p. 8).

References

Amado, A. (2004) 'Órdenes de la memoria y desórdenes de la ficción›, in N. Domínguez and A. Amado (eds), *Lazos de familia: Herencias, cuerpos, ficciones* (Buenos Aires: Paidós), pp. 43–82.

Bettini, G. (2003) *Recuerdos inventados*, available at http://www.gabrielabettini.com/RECUERDOS-INVENTADOS (accessed 16 Oct. 2018).

Blejmar, J. (2012) 'The truth of autofiction: second-generation memory in post-dictatorship Argentine culture', PhD dissertation, University of Cambridge.

Calveiro, P. (2005) *Política y/o violencia: Una aproximación a la guerrilla de los años 70* (Buenos Aires: Norma).

— (2008) *Poder y desaparición* (Buenos Aires: Colihue).

Cardoso, J. (2011) 'La postguerra como campo de batalla', in *No me olvides*, available at: http://nomeolvidesorg.com.ar/wpress/?p=613 (accessed 16 Aug. 2018).

Guber, R. (2004) *De chicos a veteranos: Memorias argentinas de la guerra de Malvinas* (Buenos Aires: Antropofagia).

Jelin, E. (2002) 'La conflictiva y nunca acabada mirada sobre el pasado', in M. Franco and F. Levín (eds), *Historia reciente: perspectivas y desafíos para un campo en construcción* (Buenos Aires: Paidós), pp. 307–40.

Kohan, M. (2004) 'La apariencia celebrada', *Punto de vista*, 27 (78): 24–30.

Lorenz, F. (2012a) *Las guerras por Malvinas (1982–2012)* (Buenos Aires: Edhasa).

— (2012b) 'Malvinas invita a pensar un patriotismo en democracia', *Perfil* (7 May), pp. 58–9.

Luna, O. (1999) 'Veterano, pasajero del tiempo', *Página/12* (1 April), available at https://www.pagina12.com.ar/1999/99-04/99-04-02/psico01.htm (accessed 16 Oct. 2018).

Palermo, V. (2007) *Sal en las heridas: Las Malvinas en la cultura argentina contemporánea* (Buenos Aires: Sudamericana).

Quieto, L. (2007) *Arqueologías* (Buenos Aires: Fondo Nacional de las Artes).

Ranzani, O. (2005) '"La guerra acá no se contó"', *Página/12* (8 Sept.), available at https://www.pagina12.com.ar/diario/suplementos/espectaculos/5-370-2005-09-08.html (accessed 16 Oct. 2018).

Romero, L. A. (2002) 'Recuerdos del Proceso, imágenes de la democracia: Luces y sombras en las políticas de la memoria' (La Plata: Facultad de Humanidades y Ciencias de la Educación, Universidad Nacional de La Plata), pp. 113–22, available at http://sedici.unlp.edu.ar/handle/10915/32617 (accessed 16 Oct. 2018).

Sarlo, B. (2005) *Tiempo pasado: Cultura de la memoria y giro subjetivo. Una discusión* (Buenos Aires: Siglo XXI).

Vezzetti, H. (2002) *Pasado y presente: guerra, dictadura y sociedad en la Argentina* (Buenos Aires: Siglo XXI).

8. Flying the flag: Malvinas and questions of patriotism

Catriona McAllister

Galtieri stands on the balcony of the Casa Rosada, flanked by officials and smiling, his hands open in a gesture of victorious welcome. Below, flag-waving, cheering crowds greet him with deafening chants of 'Argentina'. The crowd is euphoric, coming together in celebration to affirm a shared truth: 'Las Malvinas son argentinas'.[1] Yet by the time the *junta* launched military action in the South Atlantic, denunciations of the regime's human rights were widespread;[2] and it has become a truism to state that the invasion of the Islands was a last-ditch attempt to shore up the dictatorship's crumbling power. The scenes on 2 April 1982, the military government and the people standing as one, attest to the power of the Malvinas cause in the Argentine national imaginary. The strength of this 'guiding fiction' was such that it led to widespread public support for a war waged by a repressive military regime: an uncomfortable fact to reconcile with the post-dictatorship discourses of memory and justice.

This chapter will therefore reflect on elements of the complex symbolic territory surrounding the Malvinas in discourses of national identity, focusing on the relationship between the military and patriotic celebration both before the dictatorship and beyond. These questions receive critical treatment in Martín Kohan's novel *Ciencias morales* (2007), which provides a meditation on patriotic education set against the backdrop of the conflict in 1982. By offering a reading of this text, I shall highlight a literary treatment of the Malvinas question that embraces an understated, allusive narrative mode to dissect the patriotic heart of the Malvinas 'cause'.

---

1   Argentine television coverage of this event is available online. See TV Pública Argentina (1982).
2   See, for example, Jensen's article in this volume.

C. McAllister, 'Flying the flag: questions of patriotism and the Malvinas conflict', in G. Mira and F. Pedrosa (eds.), *Revisiting the Falklands–Malvinas Question: Transnational and Interdisciplinary Perspectives* (London: University of London Press, 2020), pp. 161–71. License: CC-BY-NC-ND 4.0.

The military, civil society and the nation

At the time of the invasion of 1982, the armed forces were able to call upon existing ideas of what constituted the Argentine nation (and their own place within that 'imagined community') to mobilise patriotic allegiance. The deeply-rooted assertion that the Malvinas belonged to Argentina, communicated above all through the education system (Lorenz, 2006, p. 17), was transformed into action. But beyond the specificity of this powerful cause, the armed forces could also invoke their own right (or duty) to protect the fabric of the nation. As Luis Alberto Romero (2004, p. 23) highlights, 'la asociación de la nación y de su destino con la institución militar' emerged as a powerful idea at the start of the 20th century, generating the narrative that 'el Ejército "nació con la patria", es el sostén último de sus valores y el responsable final de su grandeza'. By launching a military intervention that aimed to defend Argentina's borders, the *junta* reasserted their claim to a well-rehearsed role: that of the saviours of the nation and protectors of the *patria* (a claim evoked in every military coup in Argentina's history (Goebel, 2011)).

However, following defeat in the Malvinas and the collapse of the military regime, some of these previous patriotic certainties were cast into doubt. Federico Lorenz (2006, p. 17) highlights the profound questioning of the role of the armed forces in the first years after the return to democracy, including 'su relación como protectores de la ciudadanía y de los sagrados valores de la Patria'. In this light, the flag-waving scenes of 2 April became a jarring moment of alliance between the military and civil society, an expression of a historically accepted relationship that no longer held validity. In the post-dictatorial context, the 1982 conflict was quickly re-cast as a policy of the regime and associated with its human-rights abuses, rather than being perceived as a conflict in the name of civil society (Guber, 2004, p. 147).

Despite this discursive shift, the uncomfortable fact of the public support for the invasion remained; and Vicente Palermo notes the significant challenge this presented to the powerful emerging narrative that positioned society exclusively as a victim of the military regime (2007, p. 282). Lorenz argues that as a result of this ambiguity the war 'fue considerada como un síntoma de una sociedad que había militarizado sus formas de relacionarse, y que debía ser reeducada' (2006, p. 192) and cites Alain Rouquié's verdict that the Malvinas (and the public support the conflict received) revealed a 'militarización muy profunda de la vida política y a la vez una politización de los militares que no es fácil de eliminar' (Rouquié, 1983, cited in Lorenz, 2006, p. 191).[3] In 1982 patriotism had triumphed over politics, leaving crucial questions for the post-dictatorial process of soul-searching.

Rouquié's observations that the boundaries surrounding the military's role had become unacceptably (and dangerously) blurred do not relate only to the

3   Rouquié, A. *Humor*, vol 101, March 1983, p. 45.

most obviously political arenas. The flag-waving scenes of 2 April 1982 reveal an easy slippage between the military and nation that was carefully cultivated by the regime, a manipulation of the symbolic that Diana Taylor has described as a 'theatre of operations' whereby 'nation-ness was resemanticized' in line with the values of the regime (1997, p. 95).[4] In the words of Rosana Guber, the dictatorship 'se arrogó la exclusiva y absoluta representación de la Nación' (2004, p. 229). Similarly, Alejandro Grimson, Mirta Amati and Kaori Kodama argue that the military's use of the state's performative patriotic symbols had altered their potential meaning, creating a problematic association between markers of the national and the dictatorship: 'La dictadura militar produce efectos decisivos sobre la idea de nación. En la medida en que sustentaban su accionar en una retórica patriótica, consiguieron apoderarse de un conjunto de símbolos – como la bandera y la escarapela, el himno y otras canciones patrias' (2007, p. 431). At the point of the return to democracy, the state was therefore faced with the task of re-appropriating the nation's system of symbolic production. Lorenz underlines the political urgency of this dilemma for the newly instated democratic regime:

> ¿Cómo disputar a las Fuerzas Armadas o a la derecha reaccionaria elementos como los de 'soberanía' o 'patria'? El camino elegido fue el de intentar quitarle el monopolio de símbolos [nacionales] a la institución militar, reinstalándolos en el altar republicano, lo que a la vez significaba subordinar simbólicamente a las Fuerzas Armadas al poder político civil (2006, pp. 189–90).

Redefining the concept of *patria* without its previously essential military component therefore represented an indispensable political task that was partly enacted through changes in the rituals of national celebration. The military's role in the *ritos patrios* was minimised, for example, including the notable absence of a military parade in the celebrations of 25 May for the decade from 1989 to 1999 (Grimson, Amati and Kodama, 2007, p. 435; p. 447). Where once the armed forces seemed a natural part of patriotic celebration, their symbolic role was now uncertain.

Markers of the military were also present in other domains of public life as Argentina returned to democratic rule, including the national history taught in schools. For much of the 20th century, this relied heavily on tales of military glory, particularly surrounding the wars of independence that had led to the formation of Argentina as a territorial reality (Romero, 2004). Martín Kohan

---

4   Lorenz provides an important reminder that the public support for Malvinas cannot be simplistically reduced to a single, shared nationalist response but instead encompassed different understandings of the Malvinas cause and the war (2006, pp. 41–2; see also Jensen, 2017). However, Taylor's (1997) analysis highlights the difficulty of reflecting any such nuance in the performance of support for the war. If the *junta* was successfully wielding the power of national symbolism, the separation between support for the regime, support for the war and national pride could not easily be communicated through the familiar framework of patriotic performance.

has referred to this as the 'culto militarista del sistema escolar argentino' (2005, p. 14), while Rouquié asserts that 'la mayoría de los ciudadanos argentinos no está lejos de pensar que su país es una creación de sus generales. En efecto, es lo que enseña la "historia-batalla" de las escuelas, no sin fundamento' (1981, p. 73). In the years following the return to democracy, this school narrative underwent significant revision (Romero, 2004); and Lorenz links this shift directly to the impact of the dictatorship, stating that 'una de las consecuencias culturales profundas de la dictadura militar ha sido la destrucción del relato histórico nacional – total, abarcador, complaciente – como el que millares de argentinos se habituaron a recibir, compartir y transmitir en las escuelas' (2009, p. 32). A historical narrative that had remained relatively unchanged for almost one hundred years could no longer survive intact in a nation reeling from the military's abuse of power.

The public response to the invasion of the Malvinas in 1982 therefore lies at a complex intersection of ideas of patriotism, the unique position occupied by the Islands in Argentina's national imaginary and the military's self-proclaimed right to act as the 'saviours' of the *patria*. Martín Kohan's work (as both an author and an academic) offers a sustained engagement with these questions, particularly in relation to the patriotic symbolic apparatus in Argentina and the ways in which national identity narratives are produced and sustained. The implications of building a nation's history around a military epic is a theme that recurs throughout his writing, perhaps most significantly in *Narrar a San Martín* (2005), an essay charting the process that transformed a general in the wars of independence into the *padre de la patria*. Similarly to Lorenz (2006, p. 16), in this work Kohan argues that with defeat in the Malvinas 'hay todo un mundo de certezas que colapsa' in relation to nationalist discourse (2005, p. 30). Kohan's thesis, however, is that the figure of San Martín is not part of this collapse, leaving a military figure safely installed in the rituals of patriotic celebration. Despite the climate of change surrounding traditional historical narratives in the midst of a deep moment of national reflection and self-scrutiny, *Narrar a San Martín* asserts that military glory was not fully purged from the commemoration of the nation's past.

A critique of the public positioning of military endeavours is also the subject of Kohan's more recent essay, *El país de la guerra* (2014), which narrates a history of the presence of war in Argentina's cultural and political landscape. In quoting Alberdi's assertion that war is 'una manera de interpretar el mundo [...] una manera entera de organizar la sociedad' (2014, pp. 27–8), Kohan synthesises a principle that can be seen as underlying much of his fiction. Several of his novels question what it means to base a nation's *ritos patrios* around a celebration of war and military heroism, particularly following dictatorship and the disaster of the Malvinas.

Kohan's literary work therefore explores key questions surrounding the relationship between military and civil life in post-dictatorship Argentina, examining the complex connections between patriotic performance, markers of national identity and the military. In *Ciencias morales*, Kohan explicitly sets these identity discourses against the apparent moment of their collapse: the conflict of 1982. By focusing on the symbolic structures of patriotic celebration, the routines and rituals through which the nation is performed, the text asks whether the process of the decoupling of military and civil life perceived as such an urgent and fundamental task in the return to democracy has indeed taken place; and whether the re-appropriation of the symbolic domain by the democratic state has succeeded.

Ciencias morales and patriotic education

Although Argentina's post-dictatorship government recognised the need to alter the symbolic charge of markers of the national, this did not necessarily lead to a complete and permanent overhaul of Argentina's patriotic liturgy. By the end of the 1990s, markers of the national that had seemed 'contaminated' by the military regime (including the national anthem) were creeping back into usage and in 1999 a military parade was reinstated in the celebrations of 25 May (Grimson, Amati and Kodama, 2007, pp. 446–7). *Ciencias morales* (2007) was therefore published after the immediate reaction against patriotic displays (particularly those with an explicit connection to the armed forces) appeared to have passed, replaced by a certain degree of 'patriotic normality'. This gradual slide back into familiar representations of the nation provides important context for Kohan's exploration of the crisis point of 1982. By returning the reader to a point when the national and the military were still explicitly fused together, the novel tests the limits of the ideal of a civil *patria* apparently beyond the reach of its military institutions, exploring whether these deep political and symbolic connections can be unravelled.

The novel's action is played out in one of Argentina's best-known educational institutions: the Colegio Nacional de Buenos Aires (famed for schooling generations of Argentina's elite). The Colegio is positioned as a metonymic representation of the country and its past, described at one point as a 'selecto resumen' of the nation (p. 10). Its connection to nation-building is emphasised throughout: the presence of Bartolomé Mitre, the school's founder and the historian who constructed the national narrative surrounding independence, looms large; and we are reminded that Manuel Belgrano, a key independence hero and creator of the Argentine flag, studied at the school. The text references the school's efforts to 'pacify' relations between boys from the north of the country and Buenos Aires, tasking the Colegio with the same project of national consolidation as the country's 19th-century statesmen. This emphasis on the deliberate, conscious shaping of a nation by political elites reaffirms the Republic's status as a political construction rather than 'natural' entity, an 'imagined community' (Anderson, 2006) that must be continually maintained to preserve its existence.

The need constantly to produce and reproduce the nation underpins the rhythm of daily life in the text. Argentina's educational system has been explicitly charged with building patriotic pride and allegiance since its earliest days (Bertoni, 2001, p. 47) and the novel's Colegio bears out this performative mission. Static symbols and active performance merge in a patchwork of national commemoration: the daily ritual of raising and lowering the Argentine flag; the singing of the national anthem in the celebrations for 25 May; the rehearsals for the parade in honour of Belgrano (whose bust also adorns the school). These routines can be perceived as acts of 'banal nationalism' as described by Billig (1995): 'habits' with an ideological function to reproduce the nation-state. Billig's concept foregrounds the daily practices through which we are reminded of our nationality, seeing these as rehearsals for crisis points that require our allegiance. In Kohan's school setting, the next generation are learning the patriotic 'habits' that will allow them to 'remember' their national identity.

Crucially, Billig's thesis identifies an ultimate purpose to these rituals and symbols that continually recall the nation: the ability to mobilise support for warfare. He differentiates between the 'waved' and the 'unwaved' flag, with the desire to wave the flag in a moment of crisis only made possible through the 'unimaginative repetition' (p. 10) of ideological habits that reproduce the nation. In *Ciencias morales* it is the unwaved flags that take centre stage. The unquestioning daily performance of rituals invoking the nation, supported by annual events and commemorations, are there in place of the dramatic moment of overt public support for armed conflict seen in 1982. The text's insistence on these habits and routines therefore underscores their crucial function in creating a powerful imaginative construct that can be called upon in an hour of need and specifically to generate support for an act of war. We do not see the crowds filling the streets on 2 April; instead, the text shows us the careful reproduction of the nation that makes that moment possible.

The text explicitly references this ultimate purpose, portraying its acceptance as a rite of passage on the journey to 'becoming Argentine'. As the Colegio's pupils prepare for the commemorative act honouring Belgrano, the narrator imagines the scene that awaits the school children in this public demonstration of their commitment to nationhood:

> El acto patrio tendrá su punto culminante con el juramento a la bandera. ¿Hay acaso un homenaje mejor para Manuel Belgrano, su creador? Los chicos argentinos de las nuevas generaciones, y de su mismo colegio, jurarán que van a dar la vida por ella. Las madres lloran de emoción casi siempre en este momento del acto, mientras los padres gatillan fotos a repetición… (p. 205).

Through this description, the flag is transformed from a benign marker of belonging into an ideological tool. It demands not only support for acts of war in its name, but the promise that citizens will be prepared to lay down their lives in its defence. This seemingly innocuous patriotic ritual therefore serves to make sense of the unthinkable: the call for the 'ultimate sacrifice' in the name of the nation (Billig, 1995, p. 11). Crucially, the young citizens' pledge is made in front of parents who bear witness to this promise, consenting to lay their children on the sacrificial altar of the *patria*. Every aspect of the participants' behaviour is ritualised, including the gendered behaviour of the parents who willingly express their pride. This is a carefully constructed performance with a clear ideological purpose at its heart: to teach the next generation their patriotic duty.

This idea of an ultimate sacrifice in the name of the *patria* is not an abstract, distant possibility in the novel, but a real and imminent threat. The constant, brooding shadow of the Falklands–Malvinas conflict is primarily communicated through the private drama of a family who have been called upon to honour their pledge to the nation by sacrificing a son. The main character we follow, María Teresa, works at the Colegio and has a brother in the army, possibly completing national service. Her home life is dominated by the postcards he sends and her mother's increasingly delicate nervous state as his division moves ever nearer to the South Atlantic conflict zone. As the family face the reality of their patriotic contract, 'banal' reminders of nationhood pepper their day-to-day lives: the image of the Argentine flag on the telephone as the mother waits anxiously for her enlisted son to call her back (p. 155); or the flags waved at the solidarity concert featured on the news (p. 73). Through interweaving the banal and this gut-wrenching threat of grief, the text strips away the familiarity of ritual and exposes the reality of a promise to give one's life for the nation.

By revealing the 'ultimate purpose' of patriotic duty as a commitment to support and even contribute to military action, the novel troubles any notion of patriotism as a purely civic engagement. This uncomfortable association is further highlighted in the school's nation-flagging routines, which display an omnipresent military inflection. The pupils rehearse marching for the parade in honour of Belgrano, requiring them to obey associated commands: 'quier, deré, quier, deré, fir-més, descan-só' (p. 191). The daily ceremony of raising and lowering the national flag is reminiscent of military parades and is accompanied by the patriotic song 'Aurora', which (as the novel reminds us) references an 'águila guerrera' (p. 75). Kohan dissects this lyric's fusion of national origin and war in *El país de la guerra* (2014, pp. 13–17), imbuing this reference in *Ciencias morales* with increased significance. The education the novel's pupils receive is also streaked with militaristic patriotism: we witness an art lesson in which the teacher shows paintings of battle scenes from the War of the Triple Alliance (a conflict in which Argentina was on the winning side, as the narrator reminds us in an ironic aside).⁵ Presented with this complex fusion of education, patriotism and military routine, we are left to wonder what aspects of nationhood, if any, are purely civic events.

This troubling fusion is given greater political urgency in the text through the unspoken but ever-present shadow of the *proceso*. The school functions almost as a miniature police state, patrolled by a team of *preceptores* who enforce cast-iron discipline regulating every aspect of the pupils' behaviour. The text is punctuated by descriptions of the suffocating discipline that governs school life: the incessant daily routine of lining up; the 'toma de distancia' ensuring the pupils are precisely spaced in their lines; the silent filing in and out of classrooms. This echoes the political reality of the way the regime made its presence felt during the *proceso*: as Taylor reminds us, the *junta* issued strict national guidelines regarding pupil dress and behaviour as part of the policing of citizens' daily lives (p. 105). This echo is even more distinctly felt through the character of señor Biasutto, the *jefe de preceptores* (the head of discipline) in charge of orchestrating this regime of control within the Colegio. We learn that Biasutto joined the school in 1975, the year that the real-life Colegio gained a new rector: Eduardo Aníbal Rómulo Maniglia, who continued in post when the *junta* came to power, imposing extreme discipline and vigilance to eliminate 'subversion' (Pertot, 2008). The military hallmarks of the pupils' performance of national identity therefore take on an added significance through this context. They are performances not just of 'being Argentine', but of how the patriotic ideal was constructed under dictatorial rule.⁶

Significantly, Kohan chooses to deny his protagonist any internal resistance to the politically charged network of symbols and power in which she participates. María Teresa is one of the school's *preceptoras* and is therefore charged with upholding its strict disciplinary code, a role she performs with rigorous attention (and blind allegiance). This unthinking acceptance extends to her participation in rituals of national commemoration, most notably the act to mark 25 May (the day in 1810 considered the start of Argentina's bid for independence from Spain). The novel's understated description focuses on the drizzle and María Teresa's futile attempts to clear her glasses; her attention is only returned to the content of the ceremony by a shout of '¡viva la patria!' (p. 97). However, the apparent innocence of the annual celebration is abruptly shattered by a rare direct reference to political reality: as the pupils file into place, a journalist attempts to ask them their thoughts on the Falklands–Malvinas War.⁷ This functions as a potent reminder of the celebration's

---

5   This teaching of military glory is a clear reference to (and criticism of) what Rouquié describes as the 'historia-batalla' of the Argentine school system: see discussion above.

6   For analysis of the *junta*'s imposition of their own patriotic ideal, see Taylor (1997).

7   Significantly, this question is posed in French rather than Spanish, marking it as an outside intervention and preserving the non-naming of the conflict in the language of the text (the journalist simply refers to it as 'la guerre').

underlying political implication. Grimson, Amati and Kodama highlight that in the celebration of 25 May in 1982 'se remonta la acción bélica presente y la defensa de la patria hasta la gesta de 1810, se recurre a la asociación de la guerra de Malvinas con la de Mayo' (2007, p. 437). By allowing the Falklands–Malvinas conflict to intrude into the routine performance of nationhood, the text destroys the ritual's apolitical appearance, emphasising instead its potential to serve as a legitimising tool. As a result, it reveals the symbolic apparatus of patriotism as a powerful force waiting to be mobilised, in this case by a repressive regime.

The depiction of patriotic ritual in Kohan's novel therefore evokes the *junta*'s exploitation of the framework of national allegiance and critiques the characters' passive acceptance of the naturalness of their own participation in these acts. Set against this political reality, the novel's depiction of acts of banal nationalism takes on a much more powerful (and sinister) meaning. They become unconscious performances of allegiance to this project of 'national reorganisation', an unthinking transfer of habits that obscures its potentially profound implications. Kohan's text denaturalises these habits, foregrounding their military component and exposing the political consequences of blindly lending support to the national flag without regard for who is wielding its power. The novel insists that patriotism, including the Malvinas cause, does not exist 'beyond' politics and dismantles the apparent innocence of this form of national pride. It therefore demands a deeper consideration of the elements that make up a country's patriotic liturgy, asking whether the traditional (military) components of performing Argentine national identity hold validity in a 21st-century society, particularly one with a recent experience of military dictatorship.

Conclusion

And so to return to that balcony scene of 2 April, absent from Kohan's novel but resonating as a question and a provocation throughout its pages. In place of flag-waving crowds, *Ciencias morales* charts the process by which young Argentines are schooled in the practices of performing their national identity. It portrays these rituals as both a manifestation of the military government's grasp on civil society during the dictatorship and a seemingly natural part of day-to-day citizenship: a jarring combination of meanings that meet in the figure of the Malvinas.

The novel consciously engages with the broader social and political context outlined at the start of this chapter: the attempts to wrest control of the imaginative construct of the nation from the military, creating a clearer separation between the two. Its critique is therefore not restricted to the Falklands–Malvinas War (and the public support for the conflict), or to the relationship between the dictatorship and civil society, which can both be considered finite historical events. Instead, it confronts an aspect of public life which is (as in every nation) ongoing: the performance of national belonging and the education of the next generation as citizens.

By exploring the Malvinas through the prism of patriotism, the novel seems to steer away from asking what is unique about this national cause and instead focuses on its underpinning structures. This transforms the investigation from a historical one to a questioning that directly invokes the present: although the militarised routines present in the novel are tinged with the shadow of the *proceso*, the raising and lowering of the flag accompanied by the singing of 'Aurora' are still a routine familiar to thousands of Argentine schoolchildren today (as Kohan highlights in *El país de la guerra*, p. 14). This can be seen as a more challenging, unsettling provocation. It offers no comforting reassurance that the lessons of the past have been learned, or that the structures that enabled the military government to repress civil society have been dismantled. Rather than offering a clear resolution, it leaves a potent question mark over the role of familiar practices and national symbols. Having revealed the intimate fusion of national commemoration and the military, it refuses to offer any indication that this underlying relationship has been successfully unravelled, leaving the concept of civil nationhood in a seemingly precarious position. *Ciencias morales* can be seen to offer its own explanation for the public support for the Malvinas, rooted in this learned association between the military and *patria*. But it also issues a warning: that unless we change these structures, there is no guarantee that we have shut the door to the past.

References

Anderson, B. (2006) *Imagined Communities: Reflections on the Origin and Spread of Nationalism* (London: Verso).

Bertoni, L.A. (2001) *Patriotas, cosmopolitas y nacionalistas: la construcción de la nacionalidad argentina a fines del siglo XIX* (Buenos Aires: Fondo de cultura económica).

Billig, M. (1995) *Banal nationalism* (London: Sage).

Goebel, M. (2011) *Argentina's Partisan Past: Nationalism and the Politics of History* (Liverpool: Liverpool University Press).

Grimson, A., M. Amati and K. Kodama (2007) 'La nación escenificada por el Estado: una comparación de rituales patrios', in A. Grimson, M. Amati and J. Nun (eds.), *Pasiones nacionales: política y cultura en Brasil y Argentina* (Buenos Aires: Edhasa), pp. 413–502.

Guber, R. (2004) *Por qué Malvinas?: de la causa nacional a la guerra absurda* (Buenos Aires: Fondo de Cultura Económica).

Jensen, S. (2020) 'Exile, the Malvinas War and human rights', in G. Mira Delli-Zotti and F. Pedroso (eds.), *Revisiting the Falklands–Malvinas Question: Transnational and Interdisciplinary Perspectives* (London: University of London Press), pp. 53–74.

Kohan, M. (2005) *Narrar a San Martín* (Buenos Aires: Hidalgo).

— (2007) *Ciencias morales* (Barcelona: Anagrama).

— (2014) *El país de la guerra* (Buenos Aires: Eterna Cadencia).

Lorenz, F. (2006) *Las guerras por Malvinas* (Buenos Aires: Edhasa).

— (2009) '¿Sueñan las ovejas con bicentenarios?', *El Monitor*, 23: 32–34, available at: http://www.me.gov.ar/monitor/nro0/pdf/monitor23.pdf (accessed 15 May 2016).

Palermo, V. (2007) *Sal en las heridas: las Malvinas en la cultura argentina contemporánea* (Buenos Aires: Sudamericana).

Pertot, W. (2008) 'La patota del Nacional', *Página/12*, available at: http://www.pagina12.com.ar/diario/elpais/1-112385-2008-09-28.html (accessed 29 July 2016).

Romero, L.A. (2004) *La Argentina en la escuela: la idea de nación en los textos escolares* (Buenos Aires: Siglo XXI).

Rouquié, A. (1981) *Poder militar y sociedad política en la Argentina* (Buenos Aires: Emece).

Taylor, D. (1997) *Spectacles of Gender and Nationalism in Argentina's 'Dirty War'* (Durham, NC and London: Duke University Press).

TV Pública Argentina (1982) *Archivo histórico: Noticiero '60 minutos' – 2 de abril de 1982 – Guerra de Malvinas*, available at: https://www.youtube.com/watch?v=QzcgExhuCIQ (accessed 26 June 2016).

9. Leaving behind the trenches of nationalism: teaching the Malvinas in secondary schools in Río Gallegos, Santa Cruz province*

Matthew C. Benwell and Alejandro Gasel

The Malvinas have long featured as an 'authentic national cause' (Palermo, 2012, p. 18) in Argentina's political architecture and as a consequence the territories have been present in the nation's educational curricula and textbooks for just over a century, albeit to varying degrees (Escudé, 1987). The intensity of references to 'territorial nationalism' and the Malvinas in geographical textbooks fluctuated prior to the 1940s, becoming more sustained from 1945 onwards due to changes in the prevailing political and cultural environment in Argentina and the turn to greater state control of the national curriculum (Escudé, 1987, p. 120). While the Malvinas have remained a significant issue in Argentine domestic and foreign policy, particularly from the middle of the 20th century up to the present-day, the more recent arrival of the Kirchners (Néstor and Cristina Fernández) in the Casa Rosada from 2003 has seen a notable increase in attention placed on the issue by their respective administrations (Dodds and Benwell, 2010; Pinkerton and Benwell, 2014). Once again, these political developments have repercussions that can be traced through to the key themes prioritised by the Argentine Ministry of Education and the associated upsurge in the production of textbooks, documentaries, cartoons, posters and other educational resources about the Malvinas for use in classrooms throughout Argentina (Benwell, 2014). (For example, another identified educational theme encompasses memory, human rights and the last military dictatorship in Argentina, 1976–83.) Education, then, and more particularly curricula and classroom resources become a useful barometer for understanding more about the wider political concerns of the government of

---

* Matthew Benwell would like to acknowledge the support of the Leverhulme Trust and its Early Career Fellowship scheme, which made this research possible. Both authors are indebted to the respondents for generously giving up their time and agreeing to be interviewed. Finally, we extend our thanks to Guillermo Mira for his patience and unwavering support as editor.

M.C. Benwell and A. Gasel, 'Leaving behind the trenches of nationalism: teaching the Malvinas in secondary schools in Río Gallegos, Santa Cruz province', in G. Mira and F. Pedrosa (eds.), *Revisiting the Falklands–Malvinas Question: Transnational and Interdisciplinary Perspectives* (London: University of London Press, 2020), pp. 173–84. License: CC-BY-NC-ND 4.0.

the day (Bhattacharya, 2009; Escudé, 1987; Pykett, 2009; Ram, 2000; vom Hau, 2009).

Teaching resources and the form of nationalism they evoke in relation to the Malvinas have received critical analysis from Escudé (1987, 1988) in particular, although his work focuses on geography textbooks from the 20th century predominantly. Escudé's research critiques what he defines as a 'pathological territorial nationalism', which is projected in Argentine classrooms through maps and textbooks, suggesting that ideas about 'imaginary' national territories like the Malvinas only serve to instil frustration and dogma in young Argentine citizens (Escudé, 1987, p. 141). Recently, more general commentaries on Argentine nationalism have criticised the overwhelming emphasis placed on the Malvinas by the Kirchner administrations, both as a foreign policy objective and their positioning as a core aspect of national identity (e.g. Iglesias, 2012; Palermo, 2007, 2012). The perspectives of secondary-school history teachers drawn upon in this chapter suggest that they, too, have their own critiques of, and resistances to, national political discourses in relation to the Malvinas. This chapter acknowledges the instructive work of Escudé, which tells us much about the ways in which successive governments have presented the Malvinas question to young citizens in Argentine classrooms. Notwithstanding the value of such insights, we go beyond the content analysis of educational curricula and teaching resources by thinking more carefully about how teaching staff actively interpret and utilise (or alternatively ignore) discourses on the Malvinas that emanate from the Argentine Ministry of Education (Bhattacharya, 2009; vom Hau, 2009). Therefore, the research presented here starts to think critically about what happens in the space between the national and the local in relation to how the Malvinas are taught in Argentine classrooms. The interview extracts show that there is considerable scope for history teachers to develop their own interpretations of the Malvinas question in the classroom, although the context of heightened political tensions over the territories and the implicit pressures that prevail in Argentine society regarding this sensitive and impassioned issue must also be acknowledged. For example, some of the teachers interviewed looked for alternative ways to examine the Malvinas with young people in the classroom to those proposed nationally, drawing on local histories of connection and co-operation between Santa Cruz and the Islands. We suggest that such teaching approaches which emphasise shared histories (Pierini and Beecher, 2012) may provide opportunities for a more conciliatory and critical framing of an issue that has seen precious little room for mutual understanding since the turn of the century.

The substantive focus of the research was to examine how young people attending secondary schools in Río Gallegos were being taught about the Malvinas. Interviews were conducted with members of staff responsible for teaching history in seven secondary schools in the city, four of which were state schools and the three private. Educational officials were interviewed at the provincial (Santa Cruz) and national level; the latter representatives coordinated the publication of educational resources related to memory and the Malvinas for schools throughout Argentina. Finally, the minister of education for the nation, Alberto Sileoni, was interviewed. The chapter begins by briefly providing some regional context, emphasising some of the histories of social, political, economic and cultural connection in the region. These links were significant and require introduction precisely because many teachers were intent on presenting them to their students in the classroom.

Moving beyond the 'official' story: the possibilities offered by Río Gallegos

> When I ask my students I realise that the historical human links between the Malvinas and Santa Cruz are not very well known. So, I think the thing that is absent is a strengthening of this, the bonds between Santa Cruz and the Malvinas before the war […] but the national government continues to insist on focusing on the war and nothing more (History teacher, private and state secondary schools, Río Gallegos, 15 March 2013, translated from Spanish by the authors).

These words from a teacher in Río Gallegos hint at the possibility of a Malvinas narrative which considers the historical connections between the southern regions of Argentina and the Islands, emphasising a shared common past between the territories stretching far beyond 1982 (Pierini and Beecher, 2012). Rather than beginning with partisan, or as some have critiqued, pathological (Escudé, 1988) and overtly nationalistic (Iglesias, 2012; Palermo, 2007) perspectives on the Malvinas question, this teacher offers an alternative point of departure. This invites us to explore whether these accounts offer the possibility of a fresh reading of the sovereignty dispute in Argentina's classrooms. Can these shared histories and connections reach beyond the southern region from which they originate to influence how the Malvinas issue is considered throughout the nation? We pose such questions in this chapter without necessarily providing all the answers but use the inspiration of teachers in Río Gallegos to illustrate the possibilities offered by their interpretations. Before turning to these developments within educational settings we consider the origins of those discourses which emphasise connection and commonality between Patagonia and the Malvinas.

In particular, the historical influence of British communities in Santa Cruz and Río Gallegos through the *Club Británico de Río Gallegos* has been usefully explored by Pierini and Beecher (2011; 2012). Their research explores the familial, commercial and cultural links between the province, the UK and the Malvinas from the 1880s, brought to an abrupt and traumatic end (most especially for those communities with British lineage) with the outbreak of the Malvinas War in April 1982. Coronato (2011) similarly sheds further light on these links, focusing on economic interests through sheep farming in Patagonia and the Falkland Islands specifically. Babería's (1995) doctoral research refers to the peripheries of the South American continent (comprising the southern regions of Chile, the Malvinas and the Argentine provinces of Santa Cruz and Tierra del Fuego) as a self-sufficient or autarkic region, supported by the production and exportation of wool and meat to European markets from the 1880s onwards. Indeed, Lagmanovich (2005) contends that Patagonia remained, for a long time prior to these commercial interests, a 'mysterious' territory which had yet to be significantly explored. Sovereignty south of Carmen de Patagones (Buenos Aires Province) was, for successive administrations in Buenos Aires, more theoretical than real. The gradual work of explorers, missionaries, captains, merchants and scientists expanded knowledge, enabling the subsequent settlement and economic development of the region. Towards the end of the 19th century the autarkic region identified by Barbería shared economic and commercial interests largely controlled by a handful of wealthy landowners, establishing its centre in Punta Arenas (Chile). These landowners (many of English origin) possessed vast areas of land and had autonomous communication systems, banks and hospitals, maintaining only distant relations with the capital cities of Buenos Aires and Santiago respectively. This 'self-sufficient' region declined in importance between 1914 and 1920 due, in part, to the opening of the Panama Canal, which diminished the importance of the Strait of Magellan for shipping between the Atlantic and Pacific Oceans. Clearly, Barbería's research into regional autonomy and connection stems from the analysis of politico-economic processes predominantly; and its broader impact on cultural imaginations across Patagonia demands further academic analysis. However, this body of work does begin to point to some of the reasons underpinning the level of regional identification evident in the southern peripheries of the continent. The legacies of these connections are still very apparent today and our interviews and conversations with adults in Río Gallegos frequently cited nostalgic accounts of these common histories. Some fondly remembered the days of (educational, commercial and so on) connection with the Malvinas (i.e. before 1982); whilst others talked enthusiastically about family histories and heritages stretching further back in time which were bound up with migrations between the Argentine mainland, the Malvinas and the UK, for instance (Pierini and Beecher, 2011, 2012).

The Malvinas War in 1982 is understandably seen as the moment at which relations between the Argentine mainland and the Islands were severed irreparably. Notwithstanding these ruptures, it is revealing to look at the ways in which the local Santa Cruz press reported on events occurring on their doorstep. These evoke a different kind of relationship to the unfolding situation when compared to other areas of Argentina, most especially Buenos Aires. A day after the landing of Argentine troops on the Islands, *La Opinión Austral* (the provincial newspaper for Santa Cruz, *LAO*), shifted all its attention towards the Malvinas. Its editorial on 3 April 1982 declared, 'An End to the Malvinas Captivity' and stated: 'Our province, and particularly Río Gallegos, motivated by its geographical proximity to the archipelago as well as *historical bonds* by means of commercial activity and exchange from coast to coast, was perhaps *more deeply sensitive* towards the events that have happened' (*LOA*, 1982, authors' emphasis and translation). This was an account that drew heavily on the histories connecting the province and the Malvinas in ways which are, of course, not necessarily geo-politically innocent. Subsequent editorials in the newspaper were more cautious and reflected growing tensions regarding the proximity of the conflict area, 480 kilometres east of the town. The growing militarisation of the town and the preparations for war (the Argentine Red Cross started to give talks preparing civilians for war) meant that people in Santa Cruz had a very different view of what was taking place when compared to the perception of events in central areas of the country. The triumphalist discourse read in the newspapers of Buenos Aires and cities situated further north differed markedly from these local views of events. These local histories of the war and beyond, then, are suggestive of the unique relations the province of Santa Cruz has had with the Malvinas, in large part due to their geographical proximity. They are histories which many teaching staff drew upon in their classes related to the question in secondary schools in Río Gallegos.

Interpreting the Malvinas in Argentine secondary schools

Decisions about what common themes will be taught in educational institutions throughout Argentina are determined by the Argentine ministry of education, yet provincial education ministries/councils, schools and teachers have considerable scope in defining how they will interrogate the chosen issues. For instance, Article 92 of the *Ley Nacional de Educación* (2006) identifies the 'recovery of the Malvinas' as a common issue which must be present on the Argentine national curriculum. This is consistent with Argentina's Constitution (1994), which states that the recovery of territories in the southwest Atlantic, including the Malvinas, is a permanent and inalienable objective of the Argentine people. These legal doctrines have seen an increase in the production of educational resources by the Argentine ministry of education for use in primary- and secondary-school classrooms. These textbooks (e.g. *Pensar Malvinas* (Flachsland et al., 2010); *Malvinas: educación y memoria* (Ministerio de Educación de la Nación Argentina, 2012)), cartoons, documentaries and other multimedia resources typically come with suggestions for activities or discussions that might be initiated by the teacher. However, the Argentine minister of education, Alberto Sileoni, was realistic about how these teaching resources and the Malvinas aspect of the curriculum might be utilised and interpreted differently throughout provinces and schools in the nation:

> We try to make sure the message [relating to the Malvinas], the importance it is given and the way it is taught are as similar as possible. In a federal nation-state there are particularities. I have the conviction that in all the provinces the issue is treated with the maximum importance, with the maximum dedication. […] It might be that a specific teacher puts more emphasis and more passion into the issue than others and for others it might be less important and one notices this when it is taught. […] At least our obligation from here [the Argentine ministry of education] is to make sure that things are taught with truth, with scientific and historical rigour (Alberto Sileoni, minister of education for Argentina, Buenos Aires, 26 March 2013).

Indeed, there was substantial variation in how secondary school history teachers in Río Gallegos used the Malvinas materials they received from the Argentine ministry of education. The majority used them sparingly alongside their own classroom activities and resources while others chose to ignore them completely. One teacher at a state secondary school in Río Gallegos pointed out: 'The Malvinas resources that I showed you [textbooks from the Argentine ministry], I didn't work with them. The 24 March [the day of remembrance for truth and justice in Argentina], yes. I worked with those quite a lot. We did entire courses with those resources'. For this teacher the Malvinas were not an issue which she considered significant, especially when compared with debates concerning human rights and memory associated with the last military dictatorship in Argentina (although most teachers and, indeed, the Argentine ministry of education saw the Malvinas and the military dictatorship as inextricably linked and often examined the topics together). These personal preferences influenced the time she allocated to each topic and meant that the Malvinas were given cursory attention in her classes. The teacher continued: 'One teaches with one's personal style. I can't talk to the students about the sovereignty question. Yes, I have to make a speech but I'm not going to say the Malvinas are Argentine, which is the national discourse, because I don't feel it. I relate it more to the last step taken by the dictatorship in order to try and survive' (History teacher, state secondary school, Río Gallegos, 7 March 2013).

This quotation draws attention to the fact that teaching staff did not have *carte blanche* to define every topic that they covered in the classroom. There were certain formal requirements as a result of the *Ley Nacional de Educación*, as well as informal societal expectations relating to how the Malvinas would be discussed in school (i.e. by reaffirming Argentina's legitimate claim to sovereignty over the Islands and repudiating British presence in the territories). These were particularly acute in a city like Río Gallegos, which hosts several military installations, as many young people attending the schools had family members in the military and the teachers interviewed were very aware of these sensitivities. In the extract above, the teacher alludes to having to make a speech related to the Malvinas, albeit one with which she struggled to identify.

Hence, while all teachers were required to refer to the Malvinas in some way, some implicitly attempted to diminish their importance by devoting a minimal amount of time to the subject or by avoiding nationalist declarations and songs related to the Islands. Another teacher from a private secondary school reflected on the implications of exploring other sides to the sovereignty dispute in the classroom, beyond those expounded by the Argentine state:

> I think that it's still difficult [to examine British/Islander perspectives in the sovereignty dispute] but this doesn't mean that teachers can't do it. There is complete freedom, 'complete' between inverted commas, because I imagine that if a state supervisor heard you with an opinion of this nature I don't think it would be very well received (History teacher, private secondary school, Río Gallegos, 7 March 2013).

It is impossible to analyse the ways in which teachers are able to tackle the Malvinas as a subject in Argentine classrooms without wider consideration of contemporary geo-political tensions. This research, undertaken in early 2013, coincided with a marked heating up of diplomatic exchanges between the UK, Argentina and the Falkland Islands. Although there were no explicit consequences in schools as a result of these geo-political events, teachers were very conscious of the increased sensitivity attached to the issue and this informed their perceptions of the 'freedom' they had in the classroom to explore it from diverse angles. Several teachers referred to the inevitable perception by others that they would be 'betraying *la patria*' [the homeland] if they decided to take any line of argument that deviated from, or challenged, that of the Argentine state.

Notwithstanding these pressures, there was evidence that some schools and teachers were exploring the Malvinas from different perspectives and injecting their own personality in terms of how they tackled the issue. While staff responsible for the production of materials on the Malvinas at the ministry of education were very keen to point out that the issue encompassed far more than the conflict in 1982, some of the teachers interviewed in Río Gallegos expressed frustration with how much this dominated state discourses. This history teacher who had taught in state and private schools in Río Gallegos talked instead about how she preferred to examine the Malvinas in the classroom:

> So when we look at the Malvinas, there is a topic that's called 'migrations' that looks at the *malvineros* that came to live in the Malvinas. We look at foreign relations, obviously the politics of the Malvinas from the colonial era. […] So, the economic models, the exploitation of oil and gas in the Malvinas. So we explore the Malvinas from other angles, not the war, because when I send the programme to the students I say specifically that we are not going to deal with the conflict at all. It's the Malvinas viewed from other angles (History teacher, private and state secondary schools, 15 March 2013).

This particular teacher had amassed many years of teaching experience and perhaps felt more confident defining independently how she would look at the Malvinas than would a relatively junior member of the teaching staff. There was a sense from her that critical and nuanced debates about the Malvinas question were more likely to be had by discussing topics such as the exploitation of natural resources, colonial and post-colonial politics as well as regional migrations. For this reason she also resisted the common practice (particularly in Río Gallegos but also in other parts of Argentina) of inviting ex-combatants into the classroom to talk about their experiences in 1982 because, she claimed, they presented 'a view that is very partial, very subjective and not very critical of the war'. At a private school in Río Gallegos there was similar concern with the lack of critical debate that could be enabled by referring to Argentine teaching resources alone. As a result the history teacher looked at multiple perspectives when exploring historical arguments regarding the sovereignty question: 'What was the position of the Argentine government, of the British government and what happened to the people that lived in the Malvinas? What did they think? And the students were able to work on this with a little more empathy, trying to get away from their stance a little and putting themselves in different places' (History teacher, private secondary school, 7 March 2013). It should be noted that the acknowledgement and exploration of different arguments in relation to sovereignty over the Malvinas were specific to this private school in Río Gallegos (other schools involved in the research only explored Argentine sovereignty claims) and there were lengthy discussions within the institution before this project was approved, given its political sensitivities.

More commonplace in the teaching of history in these secondary schools was an emphasis on looking at what significance the Malvinas held for the local region of Santa Cruz and the city of Río Gallegos. The turn to thinking about the Malvinas through the local has been explicitly encouraged by the Argentine ministry of education and is most clearly reflected in their poster/booklet teaching resource for secondary schools entitled *Malvinas: una causa presente en cada rincón de la patria* [*Malvinas: a cause present in every corner of the homeland*]. It depicts the ways in which references to the Malvinas are present in the everyday landscapes (e.g. schools, ice cream parlours, stadia and monuments) of cities and provinces throughout Argentina, including regions in the far north of the nation (Benwell and Dodds, 2011; Billig, 1995; Edensor, 2002). This tendency to look at a 'national cause' through the local is perhaps inevitable in a place like Río Gallegos, which has a long history of connection to the Malvinas (e.g. Graham-Yooll, 2007; Pierini and Beecher, 2011). Once again, there is space for different interpretations, political agendas and emphases when presenting the history of Santa Cruz province alongside that of the Malvinas.

The majority of teachers focused on the conflict in 1982, which was directly experienced by communities living in Río Gallegos, possibly because it was relatively easy to access objects, newspapers and the testimonies of people who lived in the city at this time. It was not unusual for adults and ex-combatants to visit schools to talk to students about their experiences during the war or for students to visit the Malvinas war museum in the city. Indeed, some staff at the provincial educational authority for Santa Cruz were developing an online resource for use in classrooms entitled '74 days' (the duration of the Malvinas War) which explored how the war was experienced in the province. This social-memory project looked to present the oral histories and photographs of civilians, journalists, the military and others through an interactive webpage that also included suggested activities for teachers. Although this represented an attempt to think about the war in ways which were not exclusively militaristic, the focus here was still on the war of 1982, an event which inevitably emphasises division and antagonism between the Argentine mainland and the Islands. In contrast, several teachers preferred to place attention on connections that characterised relations between the continent and the territories before 1982:

> The population of Santa Cruz is a product of the expansion of livestock activities of farms located in the Malvinas. So, we can't avoid the historical relationship that the Malvinas had, not only as an important geo-political or strategic point for the British Empire at some moment in history. [...] Rather, in our case we try to see the relationship the Malvinas had with the territory of Santa Cruz under British domination because it's going to be a fundamental part of how Santa Cruz was populated. [...] So we work with a concept called the autarkic region that is to do with the development of livestock and sheep activity in this region of Santa Cruz, Tierra del Fuego, Malvinas and the south of Chile. So, we look at it as one territory (History teacher, state secondary school, Río Gallegos, 5 March 2013).

This teacher identified the importance of students understanding the historical context and power relations that marked connections between the south of the continent and the Malvinas in the nineteenth and early 20th centuries. While there was co-operation and trade at this historical juncture, he made a point in his teaching of highlighting the ways in which these were dominated by British imperial and business interests in the region. Thus, there were variations in how local framings of the Malvinas were transmitted to students in secondary school classrooms in Río Gallegos. Some teachers and educational officials chose to examine the war of 1982 and its impact on Río Gallegos and Santa Cruz, while others considered some of the human and commercial links that existed prior to these more recent events. These histories of connection, co-operation, migration as well as asymmetric geo-political relations appeared to offer the opportunity to explore more peaceful exchanges in relation to the Malvinas, especially when compared with those associated with the conflict in 1982.

Conclusion

The Malvinas question continued to be *the* principal foreign policy issue for the government of Cristina Fernández de Kirchner, evidenced by the creation of a dedicated Malvinas secretary in Argentina's *Cancillería* in early 2014. Reference to the quantity and production quality of educational resources for Argentine classrooms in recent years tells a similar story about how the issue is being prioritised at the national level. There appears to be an imperative to keep on reminding Argentine children and young people of the 'incomplete' nature of their national territory (Escudé, 1987) and the traumas the nation (and its young conscripts) suffered as a result of the war in 1982. The textbooks, DVDs, webpages and posters for use in institutional spaces are useful resources and representations, but analysed alone tell us little about how schools and their teaching staff (and, for that matter, children and young people) are engaging with them (vom Hau, 2009). The insights of teachers in Río Gallegos presented in this chapter both reflect and resist some of the initiatives being promoted by the national government in relation to the teaching of the Malvinas in secondary schools. They show how the Malvinas are being interpreted and sometimes re-worked according to local histories, something which the Ministry of Education has actively encouraged. Here, the Malvinas, and typically the war in 1982, are (re)produced as a national issue/cause which can be remembered in and through local spaces. While Río Gallegos and its neighbouring provinces have a unique and intimate history of connection to the Malvinas, this ability to frame the Malvinas through a local lens is not exclusive to this southern region. For instance, communities in the northern provinces of Argentina were profoundly scarred by the loss of conscripts in the war and one might assume that these local histories would be equally prominent in schools in Corrientes and Chaco (Guber, 2001). Of course, further research in different provinces of Argentina would enable firmer conclusions to be drawn about the national-local nexus in relation to classroom discourses about the Malvinas. This could include, as in the case of the next stage of the Río Gallegos research project discussed here, working with young people themselves to understand more about how they learn about, receive and (re)interpret such national and local narratives.

We have suggested through the interview extracts that the teaching of the Malvinas issue was ultimately determined by the institution and teaching staff responsible for its delivery. Thus, some teachers (and not all, as we have stressed) in Río Gallegos opposed or ignored what they understood to be the dominant discourse promoted by the nation through its suggested classroom activities. For these individuals there was a nationalistic undertone to how the Malvinas were presented which over-emphasised the war of 1982, leaving little room for more 'critical' and 'contextualised' readings of history in relation to the sovereignty dispute. These teachers turned to colonial and local histories, as well as eras when relations between the Islands were characterised by co-operation and peaceful co-existence (albeit relations set in the broader context of colonial politico-economic dynamics) as an alternative to emphasising conflict and difference. Others decided to analyse the respective sovereignty arguments, including the perspective of the Falkland Islanders, something that is never acknowledged in 'official' educational resources. These are, then, attempts to think about Argentina's relations with the Malvinas in different ways which do not simply reproduce the national discourse. They draw on perspectives which need not renounce the sovereignty claims of any side, yet instead might encourage a more complex and nuanced discussion of the historical and contemporary events that characterise the Malvinas dispute.

References

Barbería, E. (1995) *Los dueños de la tierra* (Río Gallegos: UNPA).

Benwell, M.C. (2014) 'From the banal to the blatant: expressions of nationalism in secondary schools in Argentina and the Falkland Islands', *Geoforum*, 52: 51–60.

Benwell, M.C. and K. Dodds (2011) 'Argentine territorial nationalism revisited: the Malvinas/Falklands dispute and geographies of everyday nationalism', *Political Geography*, 30: 441–9.

Bhattacharya, N. (2009) 'Teaching history in schools: the politics of textbooks in India', *History Workshop Journal*, 67: 99–110.

Billig, M. (1995) *Banal Nationalism* (London: Sage).

Constitución de la Nación Argentina (1994), available at: http://www.constitution.org/cons/argentin.htm (accessed 18 Aug. 2018)

Coronato, F. (2011) 'The Falkland Islands Company's aborted project of sheep ranching in Patagonia', *Falkland Islands Journal*, 9: 39.

Dodds, K. and M. C. Benwell (2010) 'More unfinished business: the Falklands/Malvinas, maritime claims and the spectre of oil in the South Atlantic', *Environment and Planning D: Society and Space*, 28: 571–80.

Edensor, T. (2002) *National Identity, Popular Culture and Everyday Life* (Oxford: Berg).

Escudé, C. (1987) *Patología del nacionalismo: el caso argentino* (Buenos Aires: Instituto Torcuato Di Tella).

— (1988) 'Argentine territorial nationalism', *Journal of Latin American Studies*, 20: 139–65.

Flachsland, C., M. C. Adamoli and F. Lorenz (2010) *Pensar Malvinas: una selección de fuentes documentales, testimoniales, ficcionales y fotográficas para trabajar en el aula*, 2nd edn (Buenos Aires : Ministerio de Educación de la Nación).

Graham-Yooll, A. (2007) *La colonia olvidada: tres siglos de habla inglesa en la Argentina* (Buenos Aires: Emecé Editores).

Guber, R. (2001) *¿Por qué Malvinas?* (Buenos Aires: Fondo de Cultura Económica).

Hau, M. vom (2009) 'Unpacking the school: textbooks, teachers, and the construction of nationhood in Mexico, Argentina, and Peru', *Latin American Research Review*, 44: 127–54.

Iglesias, F. A. (2012) *La cuestión Malvinas: crítica del nacionalismo argentino* (Buenos Aires: Aguilar).

Lagmanovich, D. (2005) 'Visiones de escritores de lengua inglesa de Faulkner a Theroux', *Spéculo. Revista de Estudios Literarios*, 31, available at: http://pendientedemigracion.ucm.es/info/especulo/numero31/patagon.html (accessed 18 Aug. 2018).

Minsterio de Educación de la Nación Argentina (2012) *Malvinas: educación y memoria. Material para trabajar en las aulas sobre historia, memoria y soberanía de las Islas Malvinas, Georgias del Sur, Sandwich del Sur y los espacios marítimos circundantes (Escuelas Secundarias)*.

Palermo, V. (2007) *Sal en las heridas. Las Malvinas en la cultura argentina contemporánea* (Buenos Aires: Editorial Sudamericana)

— (2012) 'Falklands/Malvinas: in search of common ground', *Political Insight*, 3: 18–19.

Pierini, M. and P.G. Beecher (2011) *Cien años del club británico de Río Gallegos: los británicos en Santa Cruz* (Río Gallegos: Club Británico de Río Gallegos).

— (2012) 'Malvinas y Santa Cruz: una relación histórica quebrada por una guerra', *Malvinas en la Universidad: concurso de ensayos* (Buenos Aires: Ministerio de Educación de la Nación), pp. 37–63.

Pinkerton, A. and M. C. Benwell (2014) 'Rethinking popular geopolitics in the Falklands/Malvinas sovereignty dispute: creative diplomacy and citizen statecraft', *Political Geography*, 38: 12–22.

Pykett, J. (2009) 'Making citizens in the classroom: an urban geography of citizenship education', *Urban Studies*, 46: 803–23.

Ram, H. (2000) 'The immemorial Iranian nation? School textbooks and historical memory in post-revolutionary Iran', *Nations and Nationalism*, 6: 67–90.

10. Chronicle of a referendum foretold: what next for the Malvinas–Falklands?*

Cara Levey and Daniel Ozarow

The announcement of the result of the March 2013 referendum on whether the Falklands–Malvinas should remain a British overseas territory came as no surprise in either Britain or Argentina, or on the South Atlantic islands themselves. Indeed, perhaps the biggest shock of all was the news that three inhabitants actually voted against remaining under British rule (Benedictus, 2013). As bewildered Kelpers in the close-knit island community speculated on where the voices of dissent had come from, in the aftermath of the referendum we consider what has really changed and offer insight into what will happen next. In particular, we argue that it is in both British and Argentine self-interest to change their stances in order to resolve the issue.

The elephant in the room

Before considering the significance of its outcome, it is worth mentioning that historically and, in particular, since 1982, media and populace alike, to the contingent stances of the respective political leaders at specific junctures, often rather disingenuously attribute the re-emergence and heightening of the territorial dispute to the respective political leaders in power at the time. Most notably with Margaret Thatcher and the third military *junta* led by General Galtieri in 1982 and more recently with the somewhat frosty relations between Cristina Fernández de Kirchner and David Cameron at the time of the referendum. In both cases, one might be forgiven for thinking that political elites pulled the issue out of the hat at critical moments in order to distract an easily led populace from the beleaguered economy, low popularity or highly mobilised resistance they faced at home.

---

* An early version of this chapter was originally published as an op-ed for Al Jazeera in the days following the 2013 referendum. It has subsequently been updated significantly to account for developments that have taken place since then. The authors would like to thank Uriel Erlich for his comments on the draft of this chapter.

C. Levey and D. Ozarow, 'Chronicle of a referendum foretold: what next for the Malvinas–Falklands?', in G. Mira and F. Pedrosa (eds.), *Revisiting the Falklands–Malvinas Question: Transnational and Interdisciplinary Perspectives* (London: University of London Press, 2020), pp. 185–97. License: CC-BY-NC-ND 4.0.

Yet, although the issue undoubtedly serves as a convenient political football and lends itself to political point-scoring, it is worth noting that Argentine claims to the 'Malvinas' have never been far from the public arena (albeit somewhat more muted at times), both before and since the conflict. Indeed, intermittent secret discussions took place over sovereignty between the Argentine and British governments during the 1950s and right up until the war of 1982. A WikiLeaks cable found that the dictator Juan Carlos Onganía (1966–70) considered retaking them in 1966[1] and, more crucially, Argentina's Foreign Ministry documents reportedly reveal that the British secretly offered former president Juan Perón (1946–55 and 1973–4) shared control of the Islands on 11 June 1974, with a carefully considered proposal and concrete plans for making it a reality. The plan only failed to materialise because Perón died three weeks later, otherwise the course of history would have been quite different (Jastreblansky, 2012).

Perhaps most controversially, and barely featuring in British collective memory, Sir Lawrence Freedman, professor of War Studies at King's College London recounts how Margaret Thatcher's government offered to hand over sovereignty of the Islands at a clandestine meeting with a senior member of the Argentine military *junta* in June 1980, less than two years before the conflict in the South Atlantic and, unlike in 1974, to a dictatorship rather than a democratically elected government (Freedman, 2005, p. 698). In *The Official History of the Falklands Campaign,* Freedman explains how the Foreign Office devised a plan to cede sovereignty to Argentina with a leaseback agreement to Britain for 99 years. This was agreed at a secret meeting between Foreign Secretary, Nicholas Ridley and his opposite number, Comodoro Cavandoli in Switzerland. Given that Britain had already enjoyed a cosy relationship with the ruling dictatorship, having sold Lynx helicopters and naval missiles (which were later used against the British forces in 1982) to the regime, the deal was a masterstroke from a business perspective as it would lay the ground for further multi-million pound arms sales for as long as the *Junta* remained in power. The deal was only scuppered when Ridley visited the Islands in November 1980 in an effort to persuade the Islanders to agree. When Conservative and Labour MPs got wind of the proposal, they objected, as much as anything to its lack of transparency, and it was soon shelved.

Meanwhile, two-time President Carlos Menem (1989–99) – the first Argentine head of state to visit Britain since the conflict in 1982 – may have outwardly promoted more cordial and economic relations between the two nations, but one cannot forget how an amendment to the Argentine Constitution in 1994 [First Temporary Provision] that remains in place today, stipulated that the government can only seek the recovery of the Islands

---

1   *Urgente 24*, 2010.

peacefully (in accordance with international law), and also must respect the Islanders' existing way of life:

> The Argentine Nation ratifies its legitimate and non-prescribing sovereignty over the Malvinas, Georgias del Sur and Sandwich del Sur Islands and over the corresponding maritime and insular zones, as they are an integral part of the National territory. The recovery of said territories and the full exercise of sovereignty, respectful of the way of life of their inhabitants and according to the principles of international law, are a permanent and unrelinquished goal of the Argentine people.[2]

To this end then, the 1990s represented a period of 'rapprochement', defined as such by Argentina's then Vice-Foreign Minister Andrés Cisneros, as much towards the Islanders as towards the British government. This policy centred around the prioritising of the need for cooperation in (among other things), the areas of hydrocarbon extraction, fishing and flights – which in turn required a stable political climate without the threat of military conflict. In other words, this desire for advances in these areas by Argentina's government supplanted the pushing of the sovereignty question on its political agenda, despite the fact that the legal claim persisted. Indeed, the idea that the Malvinas should be Argentine was avoided during diplomatic exchanges at the time precisely in order to further such advances. Effectively its policy was one in which they aimed for discussions around sovereignty to take place at the *end* of the road towards improving practical understandings, not at the beginning (Erlich, 2015, p. 123).

Although the constitutional clause precludes any possibility of violent conflict, it sought to reassert and legally embed a claim that would not simply dissipate with military defeat. Moreover, although British–Argentine diplomatic relations have fluctuated between moments of tension and affability during the 37 years since the end of the 1982 conflict, a resolution – one that might provide closure to the issue – remains elusive.

The following point of departure came with the election of Néstor Kirchner in 2003, at which point the fulcrum of the change in the Argentine government's foreign policy centred on its position with respect to the Malvinas. The new diagnosis was that, during the 1990s, President Menem's policy that focused on cooperation on a range of issues to initiate a path that, in time, would lead to a new discussion around sovereignty, had failed. This was attributable to a number of unilateral acts of British policy, which as Erlich claims, 'showed them that the United Kingdom did not wish to conform to the spirit of the cooperation agreements'. Therefore, instead, from the inception of *kirchnerismo*, the axis of the relationship with Britain should centre on the sovereignty disagreement taking the dispute itself as a point of departure and with a series of more agitational tactics employed (Erlich, 2015, pp. 163–4).

---

2 Constitution of the Argentine Nation, 1994.

This explicit reassertion of sovereignty translated into the diplomatic arena was manifest from the very first meeting that Néstor had with then British Prime Minister Tony Blair, just weeks after his inauguration as president. At this meeting, which marked a watershed moment, Kirchner reaffirmed to his opposite number that the United Kingdom should re-establish a dialogue over the Falklands–Malvinas question, even if the resulting friction caused practical cooperation over the areas named earlier to be suspended. Thus, the origins of Cristina Fernández de Kirchner's rather boisterous attempts to expose, in public arenas later on, the British government's anachronistic attitude to the Malvinas can be traced back to the approach that was formulated under her husband's presidency. This occurred in 2003.

A pointless referendum?

With all this in mind, and given the apparent stalemate, where does that leave things in the wake of the referendum? Arguably, the result has not told us anything that we did not already know. What it has revealed is the need for negotiation and the fact that self-determination is not the only issue at stake here. However, the referendum has served political interests for all parties involved: for the British it has 'proved' that the Falklanders are 'British'; and for the Argentines (who rejected the outcome) that the British are settlers and illegitimate heirs to the territory.

The UN refused to recognise the referendum and hope for a resolution was not aided by its ambiguous and contradictory position in relation to the dispute. Article 1 (paragraph 2) of its Charter of the United Nations enshrines the right to 'self-determination for all people'. This stance, the British and Falklands governments claim, was confirmed once and for all by the referendum. The Argentines meanwhile claim that article 2 (paragraph 4) includes 'the inviolability of the territory of the State', and that the Falklands form part of its national territorial integrity. The clearest position held by the UN is, perhaps, resolution 2065 (passed in 1965), which invites the Argentine and British governments to proceed with negotiations 'with a view to finding a peaceful solution', something that the British government has refused to do since 1982. Indeed, the Assembly has not considered the 'Falkland Islands (Malvinas) Question' nor adopted any resolution on the question since 1988 when resolution 43/25 reiterated its appeal for the dispute to be resolved through negotiations between the two governments. The case currently sits with the UN Decolonisation Committee.

The problem is that the referendum is not a process into which all parties entered equally, nor did it reveal whether the Islanders wish to keep the status quo as a precursor to full autonomy or to seeking independence from Britain. To add to the ambiguity, the most recent census on the Islands in 2013 suggests that only a third of the Islanders identify as British.³ Had a different question been asked in the 2013 referendum, there might well have been a different outcome. In this sense, the referendum feels like a missed opportunity to engage in a profound and meaningful debate. Yet in spite of the seemingly polarised stances of their respective governments, the reality is that there is much more common ground on which to build than meets the eye.

For a start, whereas Britain highlights the self-determination of the Falkland Islanders as the defining issue and focuses on their 'British' identity and way of life, Argentina has already promised to respect these entirely, as stated in its aforementioned constitutional clause. Argentina's concern is instead one of territorial integrity and sovereignty over the land (and surrounding sea). Such declarations make it even more absurd that the two parties cannot sit around the negotiating table and talk about cooperation.

The emergence of alternative legal interpretations makes prompt dialogue essential

Another consequence of attention once again being drawn to the Falklands dispute in the months leading up to the referendum was that it led several researchers to forensically examine the plethora of pacts and agreements signed by the various imperial powers as part of the decolonisation process in the 1800s. Of course, a number of diverse conclusions were reached about the legality of control of the Islands. Generally these were less favourable for Argentina than previously assumed, but far more serious for Britain. Britain's claim to the Falklands has always relied not on prior discovery (which occurred before the first British flag was planted on the Islands), but on a small settlement established in 1766 (and abandoned in 1774). When Britain recognised Argentine independence in 1825, it did so without any claim to the Falklands, which were then under an Argentine governor living there. This fact casts doubt over the historic foundation of the legality of the claim, which only became live after the (illegal) 1833 invasion, when the Islands reverted to British rule.

An alternative interpretation that does not sit well with either side can be found in Juan Ackermann y Alfredo Villegas' 2013 book, which claimed that Uruguay is in fact the only legitimate legal owner, due to its 1841 pact with the Spanish crown, according to which the latter ceded authority over the Islands (Ackerman and Villegas, 2013). The book also provides evidence that both the British governments and Argentine senate subsequently recognised the pact. While the Uruguayan government is yet to lay official claim to the Falklands–Malvinas, this may change if the oil deposits under the sea surrounding the Islands ever become fully refinable and lucrative. Britain and Argentina should

---

3   *The Guardian*, 2013, https://www.theguardian.com/uk/2012/sep/13/falkland-islands-census-british-identity.

seek to reach an agreement now while the fate of the Islands is still within their control.

Singing from the same hymn sheet

The respective governments' shared visions (yet differing perspectives), combined with the convoluted history of the ownership of the islands, demonstrate the need for dialogue. With this in mind, let us consider what happened in the days, weeks and months after the referendum in both Britain and Argentina, and what might be required of each side in order to break the deadlock.

In the aftermath of the referendum vote, Argentina continued its policy of diplomacy through building alliances in the global south in order to to pressure Britain to return to negotiations, coupled with occasional episodes of publicly embarrassing the British government (such as the attempt by former president Cristina Fernández to hand British prime minister David Cameron a letter marked 'UN Malvinas' at the 2012 G20 Summit). It was reported that the Argentine government also wanted to persuade the UN Decolonization Committee potentially to force a UN General Assembly vote, which would pressure the British government into coming to the negotiating table. Given that a year after the vote, a ministerial declaration of the 130 nations of the G77 plus China called upon Britain and Argentina to resume dialogue following a manoeuvre by the latter to make this so in June 2014 (MercoPress, 2014). This declaration gives a strong indicator of how the Assembly might have voted. Indeed, it was arguably only because Argentina was being held to ransom by US vulture funds that the Falklands–Malvinas dispute was not brought before the UN General Assembly.[4] Instead, Argentina was heavily distracted, as President Cristina Kirchner sought to focus her UN Assembly business on proposing new basic principles on sovereign debt-restructuring processes that were eventually approved in 2015.

While this may have been brinkmanship, such is the potency of the Malvinas issue and its centrality in Argentina's national identity, that Argentina's government and entire political class would in fact benefit from having the sovereignty question left perpetually unresolved. Indeed *La Cuestión de las Islas Malvinas* remains one of only three obligatory subjects that schoolchildren must learn under the National Education Law. Symbols of Argentina's sovereignty claim are omnipresent in street-names, on school buildings, commemorated in town squares, are a popular choice of tattoo, a regular theme of street demonstrations and a fixture in the school curriculum. If the Falklands were ever 'returned' to Argentina, it would no doubt bring enormous short-term

---

4   These vulture funds were NML and Aurelius Capital, and between 2013 and 2015 they sued the government and threatened to ignite a debt default on the scale of 2001 over debts they claimed they were owed on prior speculative bond purchases.

popularity for the government in power at the time. Nevertheless, the evidence suggests that Argentines are becoming increasingly cynical about their claim to the Malvinas, especially young people. Some 45% of the Argentine population have little or no interest in the Malvinas, with 18 to 29 year-olds being the most indifferent of all age groups.[5] Although the recognisable outline of the Islands and accompanying rallying cry remain omnipresent, just how long the claim will remain potent and carry political sway, remains to be seen. With this in mind, the Argentine government is effectively facing a race against time to reach a negotiated compromise agreement.

Curiously, while the claim to sovereignty proved a source of distraction from domestic political problems for both Galtieri's *Junta* and Margaret Thatcher's Conservative government in 1982, the Falklands–Malvinas issue has never become one that possesses electoral potency in either country. Indeed, in Argentina the Malvinas claim is instead arguably a 'policy of the state' that transcends party affiliation. This position is illustrated by former president Macri's (2015–19) perceived 'weak' position vis-à-vis reasserting Argentina's sovereignty claim. Yet although his popularity was damaged by several years of austerity and corruption allegations against his government, the same cannot be said of his return to 1990s-style rapprochement in relation to the Islands. His political opponents struggled to convince the population that he genuinely wanted to forfeit Argentina's historical demand for control of the disputed territory that dates back to 1833. Further, the Malvinas question barely featured in Alberto Fernandez' successful presidential election campaign in late 2019. In other words, the issue seems to be one less of electoral significance and more one that is so embedded in the national imaginary for much of the population that to play politics with it domestically is largely symbolic. Meanwhile in the United Kingdom, while the 1982 war is commemorated annually, it barely features in daily political discourse, much less at election time.

However, in terms of how winning over the Islanders might be achieved, Argentina needs seriously to reappraise its perceived hostile approach, because its reference to them as an 'implanted' population, as well as its refusal to negotiate with them face-to-face, is not winning them any allies in the South Atlantic. The Argentine government has repeatedly stated that it is 'committed to respecting the identity and way of life of the inhabitants of the Malvinas, as we do with the 250,000 British descendants living in mainland Argentina' in spite of the fact that the 'territory belongs to Argentina' (Castro, 2013). Yet they need to work on building fraternal relations with the Islanders themselves, or at the very least to adopt a less bellicose discourse towards them. It is naïve of any government to think they can lay claim to an inhabited territory without considering relations with existing residents. This argument has been put

---

5 'Varied views towards the Falkland Islands dispute', University of Liverpool Press Release, 7 March 2012, available at: https://news.liverpool.ac.uk/2012/03/07/varied-views-towards-the-falkland-islands-dispute/ (accessed 27 April 2020).

forward by a number of Argentine scholars and intellectuals, such as Osvaldo Bayer, who argued that Argentina needs to offer grants for university study in Argentina and organise cultural events to encourage trust-building exchanges between the Islanders and Argentine citizens (Bayer, 2012). Small gestures like these are surely necessary before any meaningful negotiations can take place. In the battle for the hearts and minds of the Falkland Islanders, the British, for now, hold all the cards.

The British government's position has not changed substantially. The successive Conservative administrations that have been in power since 2010 make negotiation with the Argentines very unlikely, arguably in part because of post-1982 party leaderships not wanting to renege on Margaret Thatcher's 'victory', or the memory of the fallen armed forces personnel. The referendum result served to reinforce its view that the Falkland Islanders have now decided their own fate. Appearing to respect their wishes certainly disguises the government's rabid enthusiasm for exploiting the hydrocarbons that lie under the seabed. However, like Argentina's stance, Britain's position is looking increasingly unsustainable in the face of mounting global opposition. Not even the United States, its closest global ally, was willing to support Britain's claim (Foster, 2014).

Like the Argentines, the British also need to realise that negotiation is crucial and that the issue will not dissipate, regardless of which president is in power in their southern relation. The government should reflect on the absurdity of clinging onto such a colonial outpost in the 21st century and the reality that it merely serves to buttress a false sense of national pride, years after the sun set on the Empire. Unlike in the 1980s, there is now significant Latin American unity and some form of coherent consensus over the Malvinas question as well as a revival of anti-imperialist discourse that made up part of the pink tide (the election of leftist governments throughout the region). For example, in 2011 the members of Mercosur, the organisation for South American regional cooperation, agreed to close their ports to ships flying the Falklands–Malvinas flag and in 2015, the 18 nations of the Union of South American Nations (UNASUR) repeated its call for Britain to return to dialogue, with the presidency (albeit Venezuelan) of the same organisation condemning British military exercises in the seas surrounding the Islands in a statement that was strongly supportive of Argentina's 2016 sovereignty claim (UNASUR, 2016). Given the post-Brexit scenario, in which Britain's trading and investment relationship may well come under significant strain (the EU accounts for £236bn or 43% of all the UK's exports of goods and services and £318bn or 54% of all imports (ONS, 2018)), developing stronger commercial ties with the region looks vital. Key to the new diplomatic charm offensive will be a softer tone on the Falklands, as the military presence of an imperialist power in Latin American waters continues to prove a source of irritation not just in Argentina, but also from Havana all the way down to Santiago de Chile.

Ironically, Britain's stubborn refusal to adopt a more flexible approach on the sovereignty question may be entirely self-defeating in terms of both the national self-interest and the Islands' economy. This is because being able to exploit the recently discovered Islands' hydrocarbon deposits on a significant scale would depend on access to the Argentine mainland, a condition that Argentina can use as leverage to encourage talks (Milne, 2013). There are surely few stronger incentives for Britain to return to dialogue than that.

Finally, amid the ongoing tension, it is worth briefly speculating on the prospects of a re-run of the conflict of 1982. This scenario seems somewhat unlikely. Britain's various ill-fated military invasions and occupations in the Middle East, such as of Iraq (2003–11) and Afghanistan (2002–14), mean that overseas wars are increasingly difficult to justify to a sceptical public. Furthermore, British defence spending was slashed following the 2010 Budget review, making another war impossible to afford. Crucially, in 2016 the Royal Navy withdrew from the South Atlantic after 34 years and currently has no aircraft carriers (Axe, 2016). While two new carriers will be deployed from 2021, neither are planned to have a semi-permanent presence in the South Atlantic, so an aerial battle (key to the victory in 1982) appears unlikely. On the Argentine side, army numbers have been drastically reduced since the 1980s; its defence budget has also been exhausted in army pensions; and it is untrained to fight wars against an external enemy. Military solutions, both in terms of possible invasions and defences of the Islands are completely implausible.

The current scenario: temporary détente or decisive breakthrough?

The referendum result itself may not have revealed any hidden or unknown truths, but it showed that dialogue is sorely needed because positions on both sides remain untenable. It also set in motion many of the above events that have seen a softening not only of rhetoric on both sides, but also of genuine bilateral negotiations on a range of questions relating to the Islands and the wellbeing of the Islanders. However, the red line for the British government has been that negotiation of mutual issues does not extend to sovereignty.

Certainly, the abrupt political change marked by the election of Mauricio Macri in late 2015 had a significant impact. In its enthusiasm to deliver on its election pledge to 'return to the world', to attract foreign investment as a key tenet of its neoliberal economic programme and establish closer ties with the world's leading powers in order to enhance its legitimacy internationally (of which Britain has become a prime target), the Cambiemos government led by Macri faced accusations that it has in fact sacrificed Argentina's claim to sovereignty at the altar of investment opportunities and profit. For instance, the 2016 agreement signed between Argentina's foreign minister Susana Malcorra and the UK's secretary of state for the Americas, Sir Alan Duncan, proved highly controversial. While on the one hand, Buenos Aires and London agreed to establish a direct flight between the Falklands and Argentina, explore the possibility of joint hydrocarbon exploration in the South Atlantic and speed up the DNA identification process for unknown fallen soldiers in the 1982 war, many politicians, journalists and civil society groups have been fiercely critical of a series of subsequent actions by the Argentine state.

First, Malcorra's claim that 'the Malvinas is no longer the main issue' for the British–Argentine relationship and also a clause in the agreement that stipulated that appropriate measures would be taken 'to remove all obstacles limiting the economic growth and sustainable development of the Falkland Islands, including in trade, fishing, shipping and hydrocarbons', prompted indignation. Not only was this statement interpreted as capitulation to British demands to refrain from any future attempt to assert economic pressure in support of its sovereignty claim, but also the latter was not mentioned in the text at all (Anon, 2016). Second, President Macri did not raise the sovereignty question in any of the meetings that he conducted with the then British prime minister Theresa May. Third, at the time of writing the Argentine ambassador in London, Carlos Sersale, enraged many by doing the unthinkable, and allegedly recognising British authority over the Malvinas by referring to members of the Falkland Islands' government as the Islands' 'top authorities' in a tweet in December 2018. In an unprecedented act, Argentina's congress has summoned him to appear before it to explain his actions (Anon, 2018).

There has been an increase in diplomatic activity between the two countries since 2018. In May 2018 Boris Johnson (later Theresa May's successor as prime minister) became the first British foreign secretary since 1993 to visit Argentina, and numerous senior Argentine government ministers including Chief of Cabinet Marcos Peña, Trade Secretary Miguel Braun, Argentine Central Bank President, Guido Sandleris and Buenos Aires City Governor Horacio Rodrigo Larreta and others have all travelled to London to meet British government officials in an effort to strengthen commercial and political ties. A £1 billion export trade initiative was signed to support British–Argentine trade.[6] However, for all the rapprochement, only interrupted by the UN Decolonization Committee's June 2017 Draft Resolution calling once again upon the two nations to resume talks over the dispute,[7] the retreat from diplomatic pressure on Britain by Argentina has left its north Atlantic nemesis feeling emboldened in its insistence that the 2013 referendum result has resolved the sovereignty question once and for all. The parallels with the Peronist government's policy during the 1990s and that of *Cambiemos* since 2016 are striking; the latter's strategy was overtly to forego the sovereignty question in favour of political

---

6   British Embassy, Buenos Aires, 2017.
7   United Nations, 2017.

manoeuvring (even though the legal route persists) so as to advance economic cooperation.

The reality is that the dispute remains wide open. It will possibly reignite at a diplomatic level following the victory of President Alberto Fernandez' Peronist government in October 2019 (especially if, as anticipated, it is strongly National–Popular at the level of discourse). And while the wounds of 1982 are still too raw for an outright handover of possession of the Islands to be palatable to the British public, softening inter-generational public opinion as the collective memories fade may make a solution like a Hong Kong style long-term lease back agreement a real possibility at some point in the next decade. One thing is certain, a lasting solution will only be found through negotiation. The 2013 referendum may have done more to facilitate such a possibility than it did to end it.

References

Anonymous (2016) 'Polémica por el acuerdo firmado con Reino Unido por las Islas', 18 Sept., available at https://www.perfil.com/noticias/politica/polemica-por-el-acuerdo-firmado-con-reino-unido-por-malvinas.phtml (accessed 29 Dec. 2018).

Anonymous (2018) 'Enraged Congress demands answers over ambassador's Malvinas tweet', *Buenos Aires Times*, 19 Dec., available at https://www.batimes.com.ar/news/argentina/enraged-congress-demands-answers-over-ambassadors-malvinas-tweet.phtml (accessed 29 Dec. 2018).

Ackerman, J. and A.M. Villegas Oromi (2013) *Las Malvinas ¿son Uruguayas?* (Botella al Mar Ediciones).

Axe, D. (2016) 'What the U.S. should learn from Britain's dying navy', *Reuters*, 10 Aug, available at https://www.reuters.com/article/us-uk-military-navy-commentary/commentary-what-the-u-s-should-learn-from-britains-dying-navy-idUSKCN10L1AD (accessed June 2020).

Bayer, O. (2012) 'Malvinas latinoamericanas', *Página/12*, 3 March, available at http://www.pagina12.com.ar/diario/contratapa/13-188819-2012-03-03.html (accessed 18 Aug. 2018).

Benwell, M.C. (2014) 'From the banal to the blatant: expressions of nationalism in secondary schools in Argentina and the Falkland Islands', *Geoforum*, 52: 51–60.

Benedictus, L. (2013) 'Who were the three Falkland Islanders who voted no?', *The Guardian*, 12 March, available at http://www.guardian.co.uk/uk/shortcuts/2013/mar/12/falkland-islanders-who-voted-no?INTCMP=SRCH (accessed 18 Aug. 2018).

British Embassy, Buenos Aires (2017) 'UK Minister of State for Trade and Investment announces £1 billion export credit support for trade with Argentina', available at https://www.gov.uk/government/news/uk-minister-of-state-for-trade-and-investment-announces-1-billion-export-credit-support-for-trade-with-argentina (accessed 29 Dec. 2018).

Castro, A. (2013) 'The Falklands: a vote with no purpose', *The Guardian*, 11 March, available at http://www.guardian.co.uk/commentisfree/2013/mar/11/falklands-vote-no-purpose-referendum-malvinas (accessed 18 Aug. 2018).

'Constitution of the Argentine Nation', 22 Aug. 1994, archived from the original on 4 June 2011, available at https://web.archive.org/web/20110604215413/http://www.senado.gov.ar/web/interes/constitucion/english.php (accessed 8 Jan. 2019).

Erlich, U. (2015) *Malvinas: soberanía y vida cotidiana* (Buenos Aires: Eduvim).

Foster, P. (2014) 'Britain is "disappointed"' with America over Falkland Islands, finds Commons report', *The Telegraph*, 3 Apr. 2014, available at https://www.telegraph.co.uk/news/worldnews/northamerica/usa/10740605/Britain-is-disappointed-with-America-over-Falkland-Islands-finds-Commons-report.html (accessed 29 Dec. 2018).

Freedman, L. (2005) *The Official History of the Falklands Campaign Vol II* (Routledge).

Jastreblansky, M. (2012) 'La propuesta secreta de los ingleses a Perón por las Malvinas', *La Nación*, 29 March, available at http://www.lanacion.com.ar/1455991-la-propuesta-secreta-de-los-ingleses-a-peron-por-las-malvinas 4 (accessed 18 Aug. 2018).

Milne, S. (2013) 'This isn't self-determination. It's a Ruritanian colonial relic', *The Guardian*, 12 March, available at http://www.guardian.co.uk/commentisfree/2013/mar/12/falklands-vote-ruritanian-colonial-relic?INTCMP=SRCH (accessed 18 Aug. 2018).

Office of National Statistics (2018) 'Who does the UK trade with?', available at https://www.ons.gov.uk/businessindustryandtrade/internationaltrade/articles/whodoestheuktradewith/2017-02-21 (accessed 29 Dec. 2018).

UNASUR (2016) 'Statement Pro Tempore Presidency of UNASUR about military exercises of the British government in Malvinas Islands', 15 Oct., Caracas, available at https://www.unasursg.org/en/node/984 (accessed 12 Jan. 2019).

United Nations (2017) Press Release GA/COL/3314 'Special Committee on Decolonization approves draft resolution calling for Argentina, United Kingdom to resume talks over Falkland Islands (Malvinas) dispute', 23

June, available at https://www.un.org/press/en/2017/gacol3314.doc.htm (accessed 29 Dec 2018).

Urgente 24 (2010), available at http://www.urgente24.com/622-wikileaks-en-diciembre-de-1966-ongania-ya-sonaba-con-malvinas (accessed 18 Aug. 2018).

11. The limits of negotiation

Andrew Graham-Yooll

For a few people in Argentina, and some further afield, the G20 conference on 30 November 2018, seemed to hint at a door opening when Theresa May, British prime minister, arrived for a rushed photo opportunity with a collection of world leaders in Buenos Aires. There was little time for anything more, and back home, Brexit beckoned. Soon afterwards, on 10 December, came the news that Argentina and Britain would co-chair the UN's Equal Rights Coalition to monitor and counter gender discrimination. Previous to both events, in November 2018, when the Humanitarian Project Plan signed by Argentina and Britain in 2016, reported that 105 bodies of Argentine soldiers killed in 1982 and buried at Darwin Cemetery had so far been identified out of a total of 114. The remains of 105 people now had names and families and ceased to be known only as 'soldier known unto God'. It was positive and welcome news, although Argentine officials had provided scant help.

The Malvinas–Falkland Islands (the UN denomination agreed in the mid 1960s), belong to Argentina, or should belong to Argentina. Historically and geographically, that assertion seems reasonable.

In any case, that is the cliché imposed on Argentines as from elementary school eight or nine decades ago. The truth is that we do not know how to find a solution of any kind beyond the cliché. Even so, it is worth noting that, recently in Argentina, there are from time to time different voices expressing greater moderation without the imposition of political passion. They are quieter, more reasoned voices, counselling against the shallowness and stridency of national populism. This new discourse, seen in articles, some interviews and in the paragraphs of some books, can vary, upholding different arguments; and in each case, there is the need for a specific focus on a wider horizon in tune with the times.

There must be a solution, of course, in the long run; one that will be constructive for two different societies and that might even put behind us the short-termism that we have suffered, and which is our Argentine style. Such a solution will require learning a new form of diplomatic negotiation, in diplomatic circumstances.

A. Graham-Yooll, 'The limits of negotiation', in G. Mira and F. Pedrosa (eds.), *Revisiting the Falklands–Malvinas Question: Transnational and Interdisciplinary Perspectives* (London: University of London Press, 2020), pp. 199–207. License: CC-BY-NC-ND 4.0.

For the present case, it will be interesting to take the 30th anniversary in 2012 of the South Atlantic conflict, which produced a substantial volume of articles and media commentary of all kinds. Some of the views showed new elements; others were simply repetitious and brought little novelty. One example, too-often forgotten, is the case of 17 intellectuals who tried to publicise a document that recommended taking into account the different factors in the dispute over the Islands. Equally interesting was the reaction produced by the text from that group of 17 intellectuals and journalists, including writer Beatriz Sarlo, philosopher Santiago Kovadloff and journalist Jorge Lanata, among others, in the last week of February 2012. The date chosen was a little over a month before the anniversary of the Argentine landing at Port Stanley/Puerto Argentino three decades previously. Those signing advocated the need for a more relaxed approach to the Islands and their inhabitants and included the argument that the Islanders' rights should be respected. The statement, which had been hinted at in two columns by Lanata who also suggested the need for scholarships and exchanges, sparked a wave of threats and insults which were out of all proportion to what had been written. The stridency of the objections grew to a point where the signatories were unable to find a venue from which to make their opinions public. One site was made available, but the owners of two or three other venues refused, arguing that they feared reprisals. Finally, the manifesto was not made public because the date chosen for publication coincided with the tragedy at the Once railway terminal of the Sarmiento Line in Buenos Aires on 23 February 2012, when 52 commuters were killed.[1] Besides that terrible incident which was later found to be the product in part of existing corruption, the refusal of possible venues for launching and debating a moderate statement was clear evidence that there was public fear in Argentina. We lived in a fearful society, with a varied list of causes for fear. It should not be denied. And if there was fear of hearing an opinion different from that of a government that claimed to represent the majority, could a society or a country be seen as reliable when government and population deny the existence of fear and play down the evidence? This is just one of several circumstances regarded as minor. But the fact is that wide-ranging negotiation is complicated if there is the presence of fear in that society. Fear can be a poor counsellor (even if in some specific circumstances it can be admitted as an acceptable argument).

Another small contribution to a new form of argument was an article by the historian Luis Alberto Romero, who asked if Argentina really wanted the Islands, given that they constitute such a useful distraction from situations which happen accidentally or from sensitive decisions taken at the centre of power (*La Nación*, 1 April 2012). And on 21 March 2012, the same newspaper published an article by the author and journalist Claudio Negrete, who asked himself whether we (Argentines) deserved to own the Islands with so much else

---

1 The tragedy drew little concern from President Cristina Fernández de Kirchner's government.

to be sorted out on the mainland. On 26 March, a former cabinet minister and former senator for the Radical Party, lawyer and historian Rodolfo Terragno, issued a little-noted circular encouraging the idea that new forms of negotiation with Britain should be sought. To be regretted is the fact that politicians from government and opposition parties did not use the anniversary to try to offer fresh ideas for possible ways forward, a few of them being still trapped in the attitudes that in a previous generation led to the support of the landing ordered by General Leopoldo Fortunato Galtieri in 1982.

Mention of Galtieri is played down, very much down, nowadays, and the role of the badly armed and badly dressed soldiers is enhanced at every anniversary. But if history should ever be pushed to make people think that Galtieri was a leader with a wild ambition to do something great for his country, it will be important that 'history' should remind us that he was a murderer, a cheat, an incompetent leader and, of lesser consequence, a drunk.

The above events, which now feel like the distant past, draw attention to the repetitious nature of the claims and counter-claims. The fact is that there has been no firm move by a country (Argentina) that believes itself to be in search of a solution of substance, even if it is one having to bear the political weight of a defeated army – a painful experience to live with. Still, in contemporary terms and with many 'newer' palliatives available in modern diplomacy, Argentina has not been able to look for fresh ways of negotiating, or genuine diplomatic approaches that might allow facilitate change.

Even more regrettable in the political classes is that they were, perhaps still are, the country's spokespeople and representatives who collectively do not look reliable. What is worse, they ensure that the whole of Argentine society fails to appear trustworthy to the world. In fact, the political community's behaviour allows the conclusion that we are very good company individually but a disaster as a society. The absence of the political or diplomatic ability to offer renewed and moderate opinion leads us into a series of dead ends. On a personal basis, we are quick to demand respect for our rights (in this case the territorial claim) but in no hurry to show equal respect for those of others (note the diplomatic contortions and low respect for the Islanders). The anarchic-need-for-talks front we offer, to be repetitive, is confusing and does not make us reliable.

One of the keys to the argument is how to contemplate the Malvinas–Falklands as a subject in the context of a normal relationship with the United Kingdom. We were taught that the Islands are Argentine. Physically they are not, even if it can be argued that they are sitting on the continental platform. We believe they should be part of the national territory, but for now they belong to the Islanders and the penguins. Based on those leading facts, claim and possession, we should be able to contemplate all the other elements that hamper us in moving on to good dialogue and negotiation. Anything else will mean we cannot be taken seriously.

The favourable vote at the United Nations General Assembly each year is a mere nod at Argentina. No more: a great number of diplomatic missions installed in New York will continue to vote for Buenos Aires as many times as needed in exchange for some other concession or arrangement (these issues can be expensive, although they are of only minor significance in domestic elections) in the hope that friendly nations will rise up as bastions against colonialism. But even that will mean little. This brings to mind action in Venezuela in 1982, when it was announced that there would be a lights-out protest in solidarity with Argentina. It was all the Venezuelans were prepared to grant a regime about which their government, at that time led by President Carlos Andrés Pérez, had been severely critical on more than one occasion.

It is not reasonable at this point to think that the Malvinas–Falklands issue can be broken up into little packets of topics which we would like to discuss (history, territorial rights, Islander rights, weekly flights, fishery rights, etc.) and another set containing the less attractive matters (combat, the veterans, the dead, Argentina's international image, disorderly street demonstrations or individual statements, sometimes encouraged by government quarters, etc.). There have been some promising events, such as in the aforementioned identification of dead soldiers, some cooperation on fisheries, and connecting flights, etc. But the eventual transfer of government of the Malvinas–Falklands, the negotiated run-up to a shared administration for an effective transition or change of administration, the drafting of a constitution for a territory different from the other 23 Argentine provinces and which might consider preferential treatment for a variety of reasons, must incorporate all these matters, big and small. The war in 1982 delayed any possibility of a transfer or change for a generation – and we are going for a second generation – and imposed a failure to move on from the policies of door-slamming and vituperation that could well see a third generation come and go.

It would be advisable not to play down the fact that the two most important steps towards the eventual possibility of a solution between Buenos Aires and London were taken at the United Nations. First, both sides submitted to the recommendations of the Decolonisation Committee (the Labour government in Britain in the 1960s saw it as a good idea, if difficult to apply without offending part of the electorate). Second, talks were held more recently by the late ambassador Lucio García del Solar (1922–2010) towards the resumption of diplomatic relations.[2]

Thus it is that within another generation or a little more, we might hope to see one positive action with a long-term view, one with a thought to the years ahead and not just to the immediate months: the resolution (2065) secured during the government of Dr Arturo Illia at the United Nations in 1965. This

---

2   The first talks were held during the three-year government of Arturo U. Illia (1900–83) and the second during the government of Carlos Menem (1989–99), two governments that, for one reason or another, Argentina does not want to remember nowadays.

resolution imposed on both sides the need to negotiate an arrangement that might put an end to the colonial status of the Islands (which from then on had to be identified formally as the Malvinas–Falklands). Argentina went ahead with plans to improve the landing strip in the Islands; the British Hospital in Buenos Aires made available 'beds for Islanders' in case of emergencies; and the former Argentine domestic gas utility company, Gas del Estado, introduced a supply system.[3] The postal system, via mainland Argentina, was improved. That resolution, reached by a government to which, in Argentina, little value or notice is given, was the accord which has been much quoted by one and all five decades later but which in essence, was rubbished by a military expedition staged nearly four decades ago.

Seen at a distance, the ploy by foreign minister Guido Di Tella (1931–2001) – whom, again, repetitiously and emphatically few wish to remember – of sending Islanders Christmas presents in the early nineties in the form of VHS cassettes of the Pingu character created by the BBC and, some time later a consignment of woolly bears (paid for out of Guido Di Tella's own pocket), may now seem a decision (or a form of gaining access) far more enlightened than what followed a decade later. That involved asking or ordering local political representatives to search for adjectives with which to rubbish the government of David Cameron and his successors as 'piratical and colonialist'. This latter seemed childish, while the toy ploy had elements of charm.

In Argentina we had a government that announced, on 1 March 2012, in an address aimed more at the cheering crowds than the diplomatic process, that there would be three flights a week to the Islands from the mainland. But months and years passed and no flight took off. This came from a president whose husband, in a statement also aimed at the crowd, told the British to 'fly off'. That was when new ways to be taken seriously should have been found. The lessons of diplomatic failure are varied and abundant, but it must be clear now, in 2020, that nothing done before this date will be of much use.

The age before failure is now distant. My father, who farmed in Río Negro, and others of his generation further south, remembered the 'thirties when farmers in small craft (and good weather) crossed the water between the Santa Cruz mainland and the Islands to visit family and friends.

Argentina has tested theoretical ways of blockading the Islands. Little real effect arises from such thinking. That may be because there are people in the corridors of power who know well that boycotts lead to no more than bad tempers and remonstration. If the flag of the *Falkland Islands* cannot enter Mercosur ports, does it mean much? The suggested boycott of imports of British products is also theoretical. The TamLan (Chilean/Brazilian) flights are always under official scrutiny. Cruise ships at times do not reach Antarctica because they cannot take on provisions in Ushuaia, Tierra del Fuego. None of

---

3   This was a well-intentioned move, if not perfectly implemented.

this will force Whitehall to negotiate. London will be portrayed as the victim of a belligerent nation which, in 1982, went to war and is now a nuisance.

Politics and diplomacy in both Britain and Argentina will have to put aside short–term action and concentrate on the medium term. This should take place within a generation, the next preferably, and no more time should be wasted on vacuous statements or accusations which achieve nothing. Self-determination has to secure international acceptance or be put aside. In this sense, Argentina's diplomatic body has to convince the world that self-determination is not a sovereign solution. The British Nationality (Falkland Islands) Act of 1982 was a parliamentary reform in an emergency which did not substantially change the nationality and residence act of 1981. Now (and since then) the Islanders are part of Great Britain, with passports almost identical to those of any British citizen or subject. But if that is the case, the Islanders cannot be the arbiters in a conflict between their own country and Argentina.

And in the reckoning, Argentines cannot cheat themselves into arguing that opinion surveys are real indicators of voters' intention. In 2012, one of those opinion surveys, commissioned by the conservative *Daily Telegraph*, showed that many Britons see the Malvinas as an Argentine territory. In the circumstances, this is an attractive fantasy that decides nothing. Neither did it influence the then prime minister David Cameron, who knew that the Conservative vote would not back the survey results, mainly because the British voter would be of the opinion that abandoning the Islanders in the present circumstances would be an act of treason. The survey in fact informed us that the British voter cares little for the Islands or to whom they belong, and that Argentina should use that fact seriously to seek negotiations from other angles. For Argentines, there is a need to appear confident, reliable and to be trusted.

Argentina (2003–15) was ruled by a family regime which considered it was reasonable to pursue negotiation by means of threats and harsh language. It is not clear how that language could be used to negotiate any form of treaty. For example, the same regime as that led by Néstor Kirchner cancelled landing rights on the continent for flights to the Islands. That policy has not changed, even with the weekly flights suggested by President Cristina Fernández de Kirchner. More helpful might have been the implementation of a moderate, convincing tone aimed at establishing the genuinely desired and useful frequency of flights. It is not reasonable to assume that weekly flights could be established when at the same time a head of state was planning to visit London for a summit meeting at which she might have ticked off the prime minister of the host country. Of course, this could be applauded back home, but beyond the immediate effect of the stunt, not much would be secured on the Malvinas.

The debate in Argentina over the Malvinas–Falklands, where the discourse on all sides begins (as in the case of this article) with the affirmation that the Islands should belong to Argentina, could improve if a few minor circumstances were taken into account.

First, the dispute over the Islands should not be seen as an issue that could be overcome in a single term of government. This was in evidence during the government (1989–99) of Carlos Menem. It is best to start thinking in terms of a more distant future, which is what international politics advises. Sturdy trees are planted for the benefit of our grandchildren, without thinking that we could be sitting in their shade by the end of the summer vacation.

Second, the Islanders have to be convinced that we could be good, or at least amiable neighbours, and that we could be good citizens beyond the fact of being bad invaders, offensive and authoritarian. Even if we have decided that we do not like the 'Kelpers' (a name the Islanders dislike because it refers to an alga, healthy in terms of nutrition, but not one anybody would want to be named after, given that it is a weed), the Islanders are there, a few with an ancestry running back through three or four generations, and many would remain even if Britain were to transfer administration to Argentina. And the rights and wishes of those people will have to be taken into account, just as we claim to respect any community on Argentine soil.

Third, there is a need to be selective with texts that can be quoted or are to be used for reference; there are too many and they are too repetitive. However, an example of what should be avoided is described by the author and journalist Carlos Gabetta (former editor of the Argentine edition of *Le Monde Diplomatique*). In an article first published in Argentina in the newspaper *Perfil* (10 March 2012),[4] Gabetta remembers signing a statement with well-known writers such as Julio Cortázar (1914–84) and Osvaldo Soriano (1943–97), among others. The writers said that, a) the Malvinas belonged to Argentina, b) this fact is acknowledged throughout the world, c) the military dictatorship had staged an invasion because of issues in domestic politics, d) British action and US support appeared to have been planned well ahead and e) Argentina ran the risk of seeing its rights postponed.

The full statement is reduced to telegraphic length here but is, even now, valid in part. The materialisation of rights has been postponed. However, the fact of this being stated in a 'communiqué' – with a number of similar partisan statements – had the strange effect of turning readers who were opponents of the regime into patriotic defenders of the national cause (after June 1982 it was hard to find any defenders of the cause), and assured the Parisian signatories a catalogue of threats. Argentines abroad reflected their fellow nationals at home: any person who disagreed was a traitor. And the threats were not isolated. It was common practice throughout the country and could not be ignored. Trying to be indifferent to these far-off incidents makes us less reliable. Where Gabetta and colleagues may have failed is on the fourth point. There is no evidence to date that shows the United Kingdom wanted or needed the Islands in March 1982, before the landing.

4   Originally printed in *Le Monde*, May 1982.

What did exist after 2 April, if not before – and Argentina's officials did not want to see it – was the agreement of support between Ronald Reagan, president of the USA, and Prime Minister Margaret Thatcher, allegedly based in part on the US leader's admiration for his British counterpart's style of government. A historical 'special relationship' existed between the two countries too. At that time, there was little care about the risk of the UK turning its back on the European Community: Thatcher wanted the trade that Europe, and later the Soviet Union, could build with Britain. For such a purpose (trade) Thatcher wanted an efficient and modern nation without the weight of old colonies, even if her political discourse often referred to the imperial progress of old. Patriotism on the right is always superior to that on the left, and the pragmatism of the right allows it to ignore often the patriotic side of a political equation if circumstances so require. In 1981, Thatcher had reduced the Islanders' status as British subjects. That was part of the new nationality law. Also, we can believe or reject the reports in the months just before the conflict that, in 1982, spokesmen for the Foreign Office in London or other sources had approached Argentina's ambassador to Britain, Carlos Ortiz de Rozas, right up to the last moment, asking for or offering an arrangement concerning the Islands. There are those who believe no such offers existed, or that if contact was made, it was simply a form of distraction and delay or even a hoax. The messages did exist on paper, but could have been forged, hence the mention of offers of shared administration might have been nonsense. However, years later, Ambassador Ortiz de Rozas went on record as saying that had there been no war the Islands would have been governed by Argentina within a short time.

However, a more recent envoy at the Argentine embassy in London, Ambassador Federico Mirré, wrote a series of articles in the newspaper *Perfil* at the time of the 30th anniversary tracing the history of the Argentine claim and playing down the war. It does not seem reasonable to invoke 200 years of history and claims if in more recent times guns were fired in anger. There is the enormous political weight of men killed in combat, of the wounded and of the fighting itself (even if in Argentina the veterans have often been treated with indifference because the wider public could not stand the shame of defeat).

Turning history on its head and asking 'what if' – a line that Argentine political analyst Rosendo Fraga likes taking – what if the plan attributed to general Galtieri and admiral Jorge Isaac Anaya to land, raise a flag, salute and withdraw, with full naval support in open sea, had worked? It would have been a remarkable strike: it would have shown the world how easy it was to seize claimed territory; it would have shown great military and political cunning; and would have given credit to Galtieri and friends. Perhaps for the future benefit of Argentina, the plan did not happen and the venture failed. When the landing took place, every Argentine general ran to share Galtieri's Black Label scotch and share in the game, while it seemed to be successful.

And when the Malvinas–Falklands become Argentine, what will happen? Will the package tours rush in on three flights a week? Will the estate agents and developers see wealth overnight and ruin nature's beauty, just because the Islands 'are ours'? That too, can be seen as a minor issue, but it carries weight in international negotiations at a time of greater concern for the environment. Argentina will have to bear in mind that such issues are important to a large part of the European electorate. The fear of neglect and damage does influence decisions. For a start, negotiators have to look no further than the disgusting urban coastline on the Atlantic coast of southern Buenos Aires province. It is not unreasonable that everything said here be dismissed on the agenda of a foreign ministry that has failed at diplomacy because it is felt that international politics only deals in major issues. It is no longer that way in many parts of the world, and should not be in this particular case. Of course, there are claims that go back 180 years or more. They would also have to include the attempt by Buenos Aires governor Juan Manuel de Rosas to exchange administration of the Islands for the outstanding debt to Barings in 1837, and the many speeches at the United Nations general assembly. But we cannot forget that there was a war; and the dead, the heroes, the veterans from both countries cannot simply be pushed aside. The Malvinas dispute needs a new form of negotiation.

12. It breaks two to tangle: constructing and deconstructing bridges

Bernard McGuirk

Ever-unfinished business

Books can be the blocks of bridge-building. As for the mortar and the steel, the design and the engineering, metaphors might not suffice. As a result of *Falklands–Malvinas: An Unfinished Business*, which was published on 2 April 2007 and launched on the 25th anniversary of the conflict in the South Atlantic, I have been invited consistently to reach beyond the role of commentator on the literary and cultural reactions to and consequences of that sad war to assume a role not unfamiliar in the climes of my ostensible expertise in the Castilian- and Portuguese-speaking countries of Europe and Latin America. Quite commonly there it is expected that an author or speaker on however esoteric a topic might step beyond an announced remit and express opinions thence to be (mis)quoted in press and sound media, whether out of respect, local interest or, it must be said, for manipulative political purposes. Yet *caveat emptor* can work both ways. For I have often gained, be it in knowledge, from weighing differing views and opinions, via introductions to other specialists from a variety of disciplines and perspectives, or through privileged access to informed sectors on both sides of the Atlantic, more than I have lost through calculated or accidental misrepresentation. At the time of researching for and writing the book, I had little idea that I was pioneering an approach to 'unfinished business', the terms of a subtitle that have grown ever-more relevant to Anglo-Argentine and other relations in the intervening decade.

The arrival at the London Embassy of the Argentine Republic in early 2012 of Ambassador Alicia Castro, after a nearly four-year hiatus, inspired a notable dimension of dialogue and influence in the area and perspective from which I have written in my capacity as president of the then International Consortium for the Study of Post-Conflict Reconstruction and Reconciliation (ICSP-CRR), since 2015 the International Consortium for the Study of Post-Conflict Societies (ICSP-CS). It is my purpose here to meditate somewhat less, and

---

B. McGuirk, 'It breaks two to tangle: constructing and deconstructing bridges', in G. Mira and F. Pedrosa (eds.), *Revisiting the Falklands–Malvinas Question: Transnational and Interdisciplinary Perspectives* (London: University of London Press, 2020), pp. 209–49. License: CC-BY-NC-ND 4.0.

predictably, on pertinent developments in the political and diplomatic relations between Argentina and the United Kingdom, but rather more on intellectual and cultural issues and challenges in a rapidly changing climate of international communications strategies and cross-disciplinary discourses and debates. In the aftermath of the November 2015 elections that brought to power the coalition, led by Mauricio Macri, called *Cambiemos* [*Let's Change*] and the first non-Peronist government for twelve years, the very term 'reconciliation' has been thrown further into, and will no doubt be used pragmatically or dubiously in, a different light. But one instance of the shifting discourses that will challenge, if not invalidate, some of my reflections, pursued as they were initially at a juncture of resonant transition from the presidency of Cristina Fernández de Kirchner, is the very word 'reconciliation', which already and predictably had been re-appropriated:

> Another possible area of confrontation is the future of human rights trials dating back to the murderous 1976–83 military dictatorship. While Kirchnerist supporters say justice must be done, many middle- and upper-class Macri supporters want the trials to end. They prefer to speak of 'reconciliation', a catchword for amnesty, now that hundreds of former officers have been convicted – many of so advanced an age that about 300 are estimated to have died so far in jail, either serving their sentences or pending trial. 'No more revenge' was the headline in the conservative daily *La Nación* in an editorial on Monday, calling for the prosecution of military officers to be stopped. 'One day after the citizenship voted for a new government, the hunger for revenge must be buried forever,' the article read. Macri has yet to make his position clear on this emotive issue. In his victory speech [on] Sunday night, he spoke out against 'vengeance' and 'the settling of accounts'. In his first press conference [on] Monday morning, however, he stressed the need for a more independent judiciary and continued investigations of human rights offenders and corruption cases (Watts and Goñi, 23 November 2015).

To such issues I shall return in a now necessary updating of a no less unfinished, unfinishing, coda.

The neat, and often conveniently separate, corridors of power and non-power wherein and whereby entities such as political parties, governments, embassies, the military, the judiciary or other legal authorities conduct their respective affairs have been paced and populated, perforce though not consistently, by specialists astute enough to look and consult beyond their discrete and ordered realms. Today, such professionals must also be not least attentive to unalleviated media power and the ever-less-controllable internet and its unmanageable social media off-shoots, whether within or, increasingly, beyond the rule and reach of laws national and international.

Alert, it may be presumed, to the plurality of interests, points of view, approaches and expertise across a broad range of disciplines and specialists, Ambassador Castro soon made her mark not only in the time-honoured manner of testing the waters of diplomacy but also by dipping the toe into the often-unfathomed currents of academe and its tributaries. As author of *Falklands–Malvinas: An Unfinished Business*, I found myself not only invited to meet with academics, journalists, trade unionists as well as politicians and diplomats with a long-standing interest in and commitment to the affairs, history, politics, literature and culture of Argentina but also, reciprocally, hosting the ambassador at one of the annual colloquia of the International Consortium. Here, participants could observe from the outset, was a listening as well as an articulate presence, more than able to explain and defend her own and her government's stance. At the ICSP-CRR colloquium *Anglo-Argentine Relations 1982–2012* in May 2012, ex-military veterans from both Argentina and the United Kingdom, international lawyers, media specialists, historians, cultural critics and psychiatrists from the fields of post-traumatic stress disorder (PTSD) and trauma treatment spent several days together in the spirit of looking beyond respected differences towards necessary and inevitable pressures for reconciliation and negotiation. The 2012 colloquium, far from being the first coming together of Argentine and British colleagues, in the company of, variously, specialist professionals from Norway and Denmark, France, Spain, Italy, Portugal, the USA, Canada, Australia, Brazil, Chile and Uruguay, was a successor to the momentous meeting of November 2006 when, for the first time, ex-combatant veterans from both sides and representatives of universities and research institutions worldwide had met in what was to culminate in *Hors de Combat: The Falklands–Malvinas Conflict Twenty-Five Years On* (2007) and in a second, extended, edition *Hors de Combat The Falklands–Malvinas Conflict in Retrospect* (2009), jointly edited by Commander (ret.) Diego García Quiroga and Major (ret.) Mike Seear. On a yearly basis ever since, the International Consortium has sponsored the participation of its members in international colloquia throughout the United Kingdom or elsewhere, for example in Amsterdam, Bologna, Madrid, Lisbon, Coimbra, Paris, Lyon, Lille, Rio de Janeiro, Santiago de Chile, Buenos Aires, Córdoba, addressing various aspects of post-conflict studies with particular reference to the period since the 1982 South Atlantic conflict.

Under the auspices of Ambassador Castro and her colleagues at the London embassy, what had been previously the sometimes isolated activities of academic-led initiatives regularly involved open, frank and healthily uncensored encounters whereby opinions were exchanged, debated and measured to the benefit of all interests, vested or otherwise, at the very heart of Argentine representation. Uniquely, the enterprise of the embassy extended also to an overture whereby I was invited, in March 2013, to visit the Instituto del Servicio Exterior de la Nación of the Ministerio de Relaciones Exteriores y Culto de la República Argentina and to conduct in Buenos Aires a day school for the 2012 and 2013 intakes of graduate trainee diplomats. The visit to ISEN, following indispensable orientation offered by embassy specialist advisors, was supplemented by consultations involving Ambassador Juan Valle Raleigh, Professors Franco Castiglioni and Diego Lawler and Counsellor Javier Binaghi with a six-strong ICSP-CRR deputation of academics, veterans and a BBC journalist in what was to be but a first step in such international exchanges. The ISEN experience was replicated in March 2015 by day schools conducted by the historian of the Spanish Civil War and the contemporary legacies of the Franco regime, including the controversies over current exhumations and the work of Judge Baltasar Garzón, Dr Gareth Stockey, Director of the ICSP-CS, and myself, for the 2014 and 2015 intakes of trainee diplomats. In the United Kingdom, a similar initiative took the form of an invitation for me to address, in May 2015, in the House of Lords, members of the South Atlantic Council, a body including academics, former diplomats, parliamentarians, and others with expertise in legal, commercial and business matters. These and other overtures, including invitations to the Copenhagen meeting of the NORDEFCO (Nordic Defence Cooperation) Veteran Conference in April 2014 and the Maison de l'Amérique Latine and Argentine embassy in Paris in October 2014 and April 2015 to debate with the recently appointed Minister Daniel Filmus (as 'Secretario de Asuntos Relativos a las Islas Malvinas, Georgias del Sur y Sandwich del Sur') and internationally concerned parties on the legacies of the 1982 war, are prominent instances of urgent encounters and exchanges organised mutually and via the good graces of a diplomacy imaginative enough to delve into the niceties and complexities not always or easily evinced in the often cliché-ridden media reporting of relations between Argentina and Britain. Alas, there remain stubborn if unexpected pockets of resistance to any reading, let alone analysis, of the past and the status quo, even when no hint of threat to respectively entrenched, albeit thoroughly re-examined, positions is proffered. An egregious instance deserves airing, in the form of a communication received 48 hours after the following press release on a film-screening and a debate in the Argentine embassy in London on 4 November 2015:

> According to an official release from the Argentine embassy, the film, 'Enlightened by Fire' was preceded by a brief introduction from Edgardo Esteban, a Malvinas veteran author of the book 'Enlightened by Fire: confessions of a soldier who fought in the Malvinas'. Directed by Tristán Bauer and based on Edgardo Esteban's book, the film offers a profound reflection on the bravery of the Argentine soldiers and the sacrifices they made, whilst also denouncing the human rights violations that they suffered during the South Atlantic conflict at the hands of their officers. In a groundbreaking event, the film was screened besides a group of British veterans to film makers, students and members of the public from both communities. Following the film, a panel of academics from Cambridge University and the University of London shared their thoughts. The panel was chaired by Professor Bernard McGuirk, head of Nottingham

University's International Consortium for the Study of Post-Conflict Societies. Members of the large audience also participated, and expressed how moved they were to witness this moment of union, fraternity and reconciliation. 'Former enemies, now brothers in arms', the British veterans observed, thanking the Embassy of Argentina for offering 'A unique opportunity to meet other veterans, helping to heal the wounds of the past. A great number of us have suffered as a result of the conflict, many sadly taking their own lives'. 'If those soldiers who faced each other on the battlefield are today able to shake hands, it is inconceivable that politicians are incapable of engaging in dialogue', Ambassador Castro pointed out.

Texts in contexts

Deserves? … Nay. Demands: for the understanding of the right to self-expression of all, and of any text … in context:

> Results of the referendum on the Political Status of the Falkland Islands

On Monday 11th March 2013, Keith Padgett, Chief Referendum Officer gave notice that the result of the referendum on the Political Status of the Falkland Islands are as follows:

> The number of ballot papers issued was 1,522
> The number of votes cast at the referendum was 1,518
> The total number of rejected ballot papers was 1
> The total number of votes validly cast at the referendum was 1,517
> The percentage of turnout at the referendum was 92%
> The number of 'Yes' votes cast was 1,513 (99.8%)
> The number of 'No' votes cast was 3 (0.2%)
> 1 vote was unaccounted for

(*falkadmin* in *press release*, 11 March 2013)

Sicut locutus est: 6 November 2015

> Professor

Fraternising with the enemy used to be a hanging offence – and Argentina is most definitely the enemy.

You are being used for political purposes –

That said, Nottingham University has a poor reputation when it comes to recognising the human rights of the Falkland Islanders.

Perhaps I may assist by ensuring at least that you are fully informed about the history – which does not support Argentina's spurious claims in any way.

> Sad to see the Veterans being used so shabbily.
> Roger Lorton

Ipse dixi: 9 November 2015

Dear Mr Lorton

Thank you for contacting me. Your views have been noted and I am happy to invite you to express them at any forthcoming event of the International Consortium for the Study of Post-Conflict Societies at which related issues will be discussed. As for veterans, I prefer not to speak or write on their behalf but to ensure that they have a forum in which their voices may be heard. This then is a further such opportunity.

Best wishes
Bernard McGuirk

Et seq: 9 November

Dear Prof McGuirk

Thank you for responding, particularly as I see that you have had a busy week at the Argentine Embassy; first the veterans and then with Argentina's master propagandist Daniel Filmus. It is fortunate that the future of the Falklands now so clearly lies in the hands of the Islanders themselves and does not fall to you or your friends. Fortunate that self-determination is now the only factor recognised by the UN. Fortunate that Argentina's spurious claim is now irrelevant. As for your offer, I am rarely in the UK these days but would be happy to attend one of your events if my presence coincides. The Islands host a post-conflict society – perhaps you have studied them? In any event my views are well known – even to Daniel Filmus.

Regards
Roger Lorton

Having been the principal agent of friendship with Edgardo Esteban, and the mover behind the attendance of fellow-commando ex-combatants at the Embassy event, David 'Charlie' Brown, Regional Co-ordinator (North) of SAMA (South Atlantic Medal Association), duly received and curtly responded to the copy of the message and correspondence:

Arma virumque…: Mon, 9 Nov 2015

Hi Bernard

I have E Mailed him back, waiting for a response to him calling me a traitor as well.

To be continued? Meanwhile; … *cano*

Et canam: I record and shall record again that my role has been and will continue to be the bringing together not of '[my] friends' but, for example, of British and other specialists not only on the perennially urgent issue for veteran ex-combatants of the conflict in 1982 and its legacies but also on the shifting preoccupations of Argentine society of the last forty years. Thus, the film maker Stuart Urban (*An Ungentlemanly Act* (1992)), Jeremy McTeague (former Platoon Commander, D Company, 1st Batallion, 7th Duke of Edinburgh's Own Gurkha Rifles), Tessa Morrison (University of London), reflecting on the deleteriously gendered discourses of a *machismo* both military and civilian, and Niall Geraghty (then of the University of Cambridge), addressing the structural underpinnings of the ethical and moral issues arising from the state's treatment of PTSD victims, joined me at the said event. None mentioned either sovereignty or self-determination. They were not 'used for political purposes'.

Wherein lies the difference in the various open and closed stances taken? Let but a few examples stand for the kind of attitudes that, albeit with difficulty, will have to be recognised, confronted and overcome; for *plus ça a chang*é. Mike Seear, Operations and Training Officer seconded to the 1st Battalion, 7th Duke of Edinburgh's Own Gurkha Rifles and who served with them throughout the war, author of *With the Gurkhas in the Falklands: A War Journal* (2003), in his book, *Return to Tumbledown: The Falklands–Malvinas War Revisited* (2012), reports tellingly, in respect of *Falklands–Malvinas: an Unfinished Business*, as follows:

> Published on 2 April 2007, the book's rear jacket carried my enthusiastic endorsement, 'I do believe that this is one of the most remarkable books I have ever read on the War. [...[It is a blockbuster and a remarkable piece of literature. Every veteran should read it'. *Clarín*, Argentina's largest daily newspaper, was more precise in its praise and described the work as 'imposing' and 'the most complete and all-encompassing study of the impact of the War in the South Atlantic on the Argentine, British and world-wide cultural production, including narrative prose, poetry, theatre, cinema, graphic humour and television'. However, it did not appeal to the library management in the Falkland Islands capital of Stanley. They refused to hold a copy because its title contained the taboo name 'Malvinas' and their local myopic view that the 'business *was* finished' stubbornly contradicted Bernard's realism.

Of his most recent visit to the Islands, Seear continues:

> Business was good for the POD Gift Shop. I had a few more copies of my book to give him, and also some of *Hors de Combat: The Falklands–Malvinas Conflict Twenty-Five Years On*. 'Would you be interested in selling it?' I asked [the owner] hopefully. [He] took the book and looked seriously at the front cover for five seconds. He shook his head. 'Sorry, but I can't', he replied. 'If I sold that book in my shop with the name 'Malvinas' in the title, then people would object'. My writing therefore suffered the same fate as Bernard's in Stanley. It also impressed me as to the extent this vulnerable community's post-conflict culture was still affected by the war. Disappointed, I said goodbye and hurried along [...] The Capstan Gift Shop (or any other bookshop in Stanley) also does not hold copies of *Return to Tumbledown: The Falklands–Malvinas War Revisited*. I was tipped off about this by [a friend] a few months ago. The reason is probably the same: 'Malvinas' is in the sub-title! (Seear, 2012, p. 37).

The *de facto* censorship called fear – fear of words, of hyphens, of bridge building – prompts the question: can entrenched positions change? The news of the appointment in the Islands to the post of the government's public relations media manager of Krysteen Ormond was strikingly relevant. She could be expected to carry out her duties with a high degree of professionalism, yet with a singular advantage. As an ICSP-CRR member, at the 2012 colloquium and subsequently, as the author of an original and impressively objective study of the sometimes surprising reactions of the Islanders to the respective occupation and re-occupation of their place and space between April and June 1982, she was able to meet, exchange views or share a platform with Ambassador Castro and her colleagues. Informed knowledge and mutual respect, deriving from such encounters as those inspired by the International Consortium, must be the keynote of any and all successful representation and negotiation. By the same token, it cannot be sufficient, intellectually, let alone politically, for such as an Argentine foreign secretary (Héctor Timerman) visiting the United Kingdom with the expressed intention of pursuing negotiations over 'Las Malvinas' to strike poses of the variety that there is no such thing as a Falkland Islander in the same breath as refusing to meet with a deputation on the grounds that the so-called non-existent party was present.

On goals and own goals

Whenever populism conspicuously rises to 'nod home', in football parlance, one might as well draw on the love-hate discourses of soccer fans since it is long established that the English admire Argentine football and footballers, never more so than now when the Premier League benefits from imported talents and the unprecedented effects of having the all-time lowest percentage of home-grown players available to represent the national team. *Sic transit* the uncontrollable economy of neoliberal open-market thinking: but to the diminishing power and influence of publically reluctant whilst privately compliant sovereignties one must return in respect of current Anglo-Argentine relations and the need to penetrate intrusive posturing in order to confront *realpolitik*. Thus, and reinforcing the challenge to any and all sovereign governments attempting to control events that can suddenly undermine the best efforts of politicians, diplomats and others in respect of reconstruction, communication and negotiation, two recent cases spring to mind. In retrospect, after the BBC's eventual sacking of Jeremy Clarkson for the insulting of and physical attack on a producer colleague, it might be too easy to forget or underestimate the offence and hurt caused by *Top Gear*'s prank in Patagonia. Most attention revolved around the intentionality or otherwise of the H982FKL number plate: to be or not to be *1982 Falklands* … that is the question. Whether 'tis (ig)nobler in behind to suffer the open boot of mud slings and the arrows of outrageous (mis)fortune – a pair, one white, one yellow, of registration plates bearing (baring?) BE11 END? read by some as a second Clarkson cock-up enhanced by the *Daily Mirror*'s prolonged treatment on 8 October 2014: 'We know bellend doesn't mean the end of the bell and is a word used instead to describe the head of the penis which is often employed as an insult in England'. Was I stretching the point too far to detect and opine on an obscene reference to the END of the BEl grano? Fanciful; an absurdly semiotic over-reading ... with one 'l' of a *différance* (it must be all that over-exposure to the world of post-structuralist French letters, they will have thought).

Anything goes when it comes to populist mud-slinging, whether it be the *Sun*'s sensationalist coverage on 4 May 2012 of what the Buenos Aires media described as a high-impact publicity stunt which showed Argentine hockey captain Fernando Zylberberg in different captions running past iconic Falklands–Malvinas landmarks and ended with the slogan: 'To compete on English soil, training on Argentine soil' (the video went viral); or the *Daily Mail*'s question on 20 November 2014, 'Haven't you got anything more urgent to deal with?', as, scornfully, it reported: 'Argentina has passed a new law stating that all public transport and stations must display the inflammatory words: "The Falklands are Argentina's"'. Instances abound, but an underlying problem here is the irreconcilability – a form of the cliché 'Lost in Translation' – of national discourses (and I emphasise national as distinct from linguistic: the use of *castellano* rather than *español* in Argentina is an early lesson for the first-time visitor).

Overarching considerations

A sad alternative to constructive approaches to the business of imbalance in international affairs is to claim as un-negotiable a given position amidst the clamour and in the knowledge that important obtruding factors continue to be raised, bruited, exaggerated – or ignored. One lamentably unresolved issue has arisen as much from ignorance as from obduracy on both sides: the plight of veteran ex-combatants, many suffering from PTSD. Whether as principal investigator of the European Union-funded project A Lesson for Europe: Memory, Trauma and Reconciliation in Chile and Argentina (2014–17) or from discussions and debates in many an ICSP-CRR forum with members of the South Atlantic Medal Association 82, Combat Stress, Ex-Services Mental Welfare Society, meetings with ex-combatants from both the UK and Argentina, with Dr Eduardo Gerding, Medical Coordinator of the Malvinas War Veterans, and Esteban Vilgré La Madrid, Director General of the Centro de Salud 'Veteranos de Malvinas', I have encountered broad agreement and indignation over the neglect of those who have never recovered from the trauma of the ten-and-a-half-week war, not least in respect of the high incidence of suicides.

In encounters with numerous agencies and individuals such as Lars Weisaeth MD, world authority on the psycho-traumatology and psycho-social support aspects of war and major civil disasters, Cliff Caswell, former editor of the British Army's *Soldier* magazine with its circulation of 90,000, and invitations to debate with Edgardo Esteban, a Malvinas veteran and author of the book and screenplay of Tristan Bauer's *Iluminados por el fuego*, controversial enough to have incurred the wrath of certain Argentine military precisely because it deals with, for many of them, the taboo reality of 'trastorno por estrés postraumático' (TEPT) and the effects of depression and suicide on families and loved ones in an imposed post-conflict *omertà* culture of 'Don't talk about it', I have become ever more aware of the still-unfathomed depths of the unfinished business of my initial concern. In Argentina, in radio and television interviews including a recent broadcast with Malvinas veteran and radio journalist Darío Squeff ('el Turco'), or in discussions with Nora Hochbaum, Director of the Buenos Aires Parque de la Memoria, and a harrowing visit to the Córdoba Museo de la Memoria with ex-detainee Elena Pacheco Quiroga, who had sat through the *juicios* of such as Luciano Benjamín Menéndez ('la Hiena' of 'I'd do it all again' notoriety), one signal fact stands out. The keynote has ever been and is the urgent demand for the lifting of impunity for the torturers and murderers of a criminal regime and compensation for the victims of tortures suffered at the hands of their own military, not least in the light of President Cristina Kirchner's final congressional address on March 2015, which reiterated public support for the veterans and their appeal to the Court of Latin American States. *De eso no se habla* is a metaphysics of absence that, because of present vociferations, is, however, slowly being erased.

And deconstructing? ... post-

A future – however unpredictable – is gleaned each and every time, for example, the refuting or lampooning of an untenable stance, a xenophobic posture, a populist claim, occurs. It is on such a note that I 'un-finish'; for there cannot be an end-note. Of the many slants and topics that I have been invited to take up with regard to Anglo-Argentine relations, it has habitually been the gently tongue-in-cheek projection of political cartoons – also the subject of my forthcoming book *It Breaks Two to Tangle: Political Cartoons of the Falklands–Malvinas War* – that has brought smiles of (mutual) recognition on either side of the Atlantic. I thus revisit the selection deployed in October 2014 at the Maison d'Amérique Latine at the invitation of María del Carmen Squeff, Ambassador of the Argentine Republic to France.

Cartographies 1989 – annus mirabilis? Imaginary islands or 'unas islas demasiado famosas'?

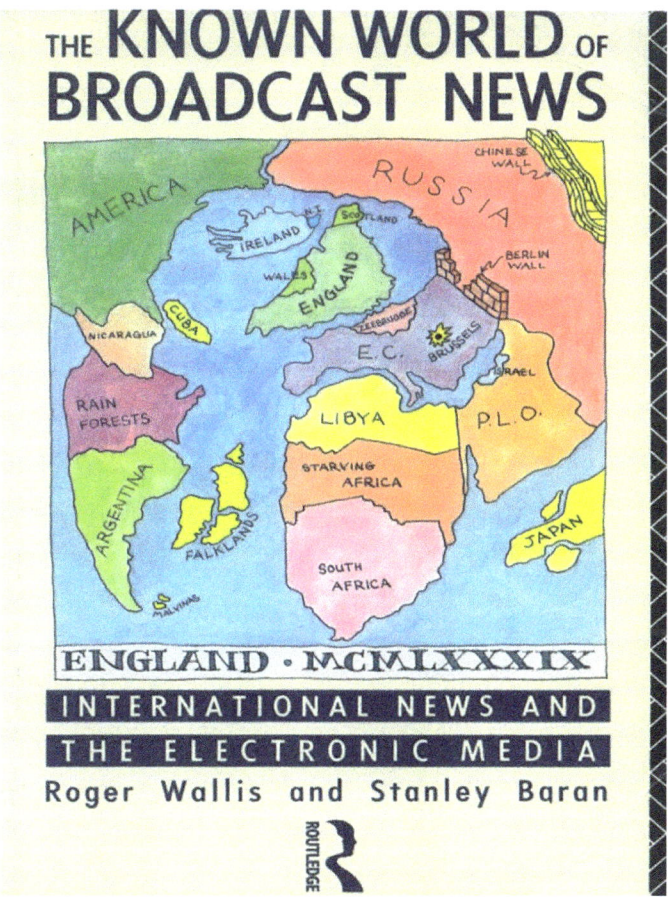

Figure 12.1. © Wallis and Baron 1989.

In the United Kingdom rhetoric, official or parodic, had produced, before the decade of the war was out, a re-mapping of *The Known World of Broadcast News* (Fig. 12.1). In the cover illustration of Roger Wallis and Stanley Baran's 1989 analysis of the media representation of the political and cultural imaginary of the 1980s, the hilarious cartography of British neo-*Weltanschauung* reflected many a spacious conviction. Anglo-centric and nostalgic post-colonial consciousness of newsworthiness situated the power-blocks and the debris of ideological walls breached or still-to-be-stormed. Amidst the perceived threats of the inherited prejudices of an all-too unknown world – Brussels ever at the

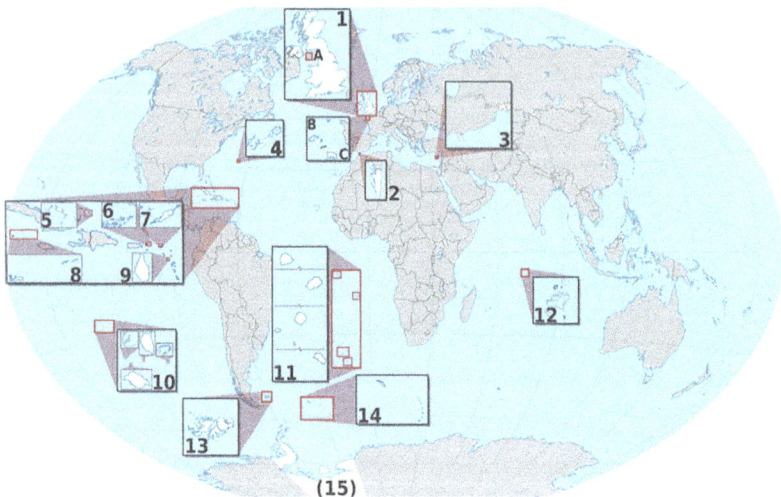

Figure 12.2. United Kingdom overseas and crown dependencies, administrative divisions. © *widespread open map scheme.*

explosive epicentre of potential loss of sovereignty – were the floating islands of real and virtual danger. The 'Malvinas' remained in their proper place; the 'Falklands' had been invented only to be displaced; to occupy a notional space and preponderant role in the Atlantic-laden imagination of a nation still struggling with its reality as a post-imperial power. There where Empire was will figment be; epigraph to last-gasp colonialism.

A cartography including the South Atlantic with its UK crown dependencies highlights the prescience of what might have been easily dismissed at the time as mere caricature in the depiction of the virtual floating islands of international news and electronic media analysis by Wallis and Baran (Fig. 12.1). What has shifted in the interim is a form of riposte, a move onto the strategic real, not the imaginary, qua the perception – like it or not – of now solidarity-driven South (even Latin) American and West (even South) African nations voicing aspirations to a demilitarised South Atlantic upon which their coastlines, their borders and their political interests touch. The point is too easily masked by such slanging matches as that prompted by the visit to London and the Canning House presentation in April 2015 by Argentine minister Daniel Filmus, his condemning of the UK's decision to increase its military presence in the area and his outlining of the criminal lawsuit against oil companies he claimed to be illegally operating in the Malvinas and warning of the environmental risks implied; to which UK foreign secretary Philip Hammond responded by accusing Argentina of an outrageous piece of bullying in starting legal action against companies drilling for oil and gas near the Falkland Islands. Similarly obfuscating had been the immediately preceding (pre-election) tit-for-tat summoning of respective ambassadors to account for their nations' stances in a Cold War style of heated demonstrations of indignation and counter-reaction. The underlying tensions cannot simply be indulged as if the period since the 1982 conflict had not changed the stakes and the relative uncontrollability of supra-sovereign interests. However, before updating the insights and impact of more recent political cartooning of UK and Argentine stances and war dances, it is instructive to recall ever-urgent shared or comparable preoccupations amidst a seemingly frozen scenario of conflicting interests.

Aporia ... a robot and the clones.

Figure 12.3. © *Steve Bell 1982 first published in* The Guardian.

What, for instance, of the treatment, on both sides, in the post-official conflict era, of ex-combatants? By way of illustration of the theme of the veteran as a political embarrassment, I recall one of Steve Bell's most celebrated, and controversial, early cartoons depicting the London Victory Parade of 12 October 1982 (Fig. 12.3).

The march-past of the navy, army and Special Air Service (SAS) and the salute from the Union Jack-bedecked rostrum of Margaret Thatcher and her entourage of husband Denis, defence secretary John Nott and a Blimpish retired officer (with incongruously 'Latin-length' moustache) are the staple ingredients of Bell's lampoon. The killer touch comes in the last panel when, after the parading clones of a steel-jawed, neck-bepearled Thatcher herself, and of her then and since notorious hard-line cabinet ministers of (un-) employment and (3Rs) education, respectively, Norman Tebbit (shouldered bicycle pump with limp connector in place of cocked rifle) and Rhodes Boyson (nail-pierced educator's cane erect and at the ready) have trooped by, an uninvited and unexpected ambulance with bandaged driver and passenger joins the procession. The reaction of the PM is to cover with her left hand the gaze of the diminutive onlooker immediately to her right and, with her right hand, her own unblinking stare. Her trio of acolyte grandees follow suit. '¿Qué pasa?' [What's going on?], the uninvited Argentine might have asked. Lawrence Freedman's account, in the 'Thanksgiving' chapter of his *Official History of the Falklands Campaign*, of the background to the victory parade in October 1982 offers the outsider looking in a clue: 'A small pacifist demonstration made little impact: more upset was caused by an initial reluctance to allow wounded servicemen in their wheelchairs to have a prominent position' (Freedman 2005, p. 664).

What was 'going on', whether for semiotically inclined Argentine analysts or exo[ce]tically cross-channel post-structuralist French neighbours, and, simply, in the common parlance much-vaunted by pragmatically empiricist Brits, is as explicable now as it was then clear. The little attendant – the omnipresent infernal machine of state – is a configuration of humanoid camera and gun: 'The *Panopticon* of Bentham is the architectural figure of this composition. We know the principle on which it was based. [...] All that was needed, then, is to place a supervisor in a central tower. [...] Visibility is a trap' (Foucault, 1977, p. 200). Bell had introduced Margaret and Denis to 'Robot' but recently, on a 'Far Eastern jaunt'. Impressed, she had had it imported, her 'Think Tank' tasked to come up with the year's 'catchphrase' for the 1982 Conservative Party conference. It spewed out two possibilities: 'either "Crawl, you scum" or "Next Stop, Oblivion"'. The prime minister had opted for the latter. Potential, however, in the crossing of the prime minister's hands – blinding and self-blinding simultaneously – was an erasure of both the all-seeing panopticon and (wilfully) of its self-benighted supervisor; Bell's prolepsis to post-Foucauldian critiques of the device's effectiveness. More alarming, however, is the less embryonic prefiguration in the (herself ever-under-surveillance) orchestrator's double-armed gesture of a malformed swastika, a sign to be read in consonance with the accompanying iconography of cloned, look-alike, storm-troopers, unapologetically visible as they march past, in contrast with the facially invisible but powerfully influential SAS.

Shifting attention across the Atlantic to the Argentine military dictatorship's self-entrapment in emergency powers and the supposed need and efficacy of placing 'a supervisor in a central tower', during the 'process of national reorganization' period of 1976 to 1982, we might judge that, *pace* Michel Foucault, and supplementarily, '[in]visibility is a trap':

Facially, indeed, brazenly visible and more than powerfully influential in turning its nation's military apparatus on its own perceived 'enemy within' was the Argentine dictatorship of the *proceso* years. To cartoon the however recognisable perpetrators of state-authorised crime, however, was not a luxury left to victims, *morituri* …

Penguin plaza

Figure 12.4. © *Montag* Humor *1982.*

Amidst the apparently unyielding post-conflict plethora of political, drumbeating, commemorative, nostalgic or vituperative re-evocations of the conflict in the South Atlantic in 1982, to revisit the imaginative representations of war has continued to foster an understanding of other predicaments, other needs and different cultures. Thus, for example, a British social imaginary suffused for more than two decades with the penguins and politicians of Steve Bell's cartoons in *The Guardian* both sought and found its Argentine counterpart in the exterminated bravery of the censored and eventually shut-down satirical review *Humor*. In bringing to the fore caricatural depictions of and in conflict, to adopt an international comparative approach to cartoonists who later, and elsewhere, whether in the Gulf War, the Iraq or Afghanistan conflicts, analysts have begun, at least, to come to terms with a 'radically foreign' self-in-other/other-in-self, so that we, too, confronting Jacques Derrida's *animots*, are tempted 'to envisage the existence of "living creatures" whose plurality cannot be assembled within the single figure of an animality that is simply opposed to humanity' (Derrida, 2002, p. 409). The pages of *Humor*, in the immediate post-conflict phase of mid-to-late 1982, abounded with released animo(t)sity. The demons of a repressed national psyche, however, as was soon to become clear, often bore an uncanny resemblance to those of the adversary. From the many striking cartoon representations of the Argentine magazine's take on the recently ended conflict and on a continuing struggle with the still-sullied mind-cast of a far-from-finished dirty war, the cartoonist Montag's transmogrification of a populace's plight is chosen because of its adjacency to what was to become, in the UK and in *The Guardian* newspaper, Steve Bell's foundational configuration of his more than a quarter-of-a-century critique of Thatcherism and its aftermath, 'The Penguin' and his matelot matey 'Kipling'. As contemporary Argentina has been obliged to demand international recognition of the unending pain of the citizen-victims long ago evoked by the cartoonist and to come to terms with a 'radically foreign' self-in-other/other-in-self, we, too, and currently, *d'après* Derrida, are re-invited to assess the 'figure of an animality that is simply opposed to humanity'.

Montag's mock epigraph to his cartoon 'Viva la vida' [Long live life] reads: '"Las penas son de nosotros, los pingüinos son ajenos" (Cantito folklórico japonés)' ['The pains are our own, the penguins someone else's' (little Japanese folksong)] (Fig. 12.4). It lays the path for a distancing effect that, to the uninformed observer, might do little to contextualise, let alone explain, the ostensible disparity between the depiction of the military figure, a hardly disguised and ever-perplexed head of state, *à la* General Leopoldo Galtieri, ensconced in the Casa Rosada, initially disturbed, irritated and eventually uncomprehending in the face of the mass protest of an identifiably caricatured Plaza de Mayo. The banners and placards glimpsed through the window of the presidential office carry the familiar demands of a nation's urgent need for survival, for legality and for a future freed from the fear of the disappearances either of loved ones or, even, of the selves of an abject body politic. What the dictator sees, however, when he can be bothered to look, is a population transfigured ... for his is an exclusively Malvinas-coloured perspective on the relationship between government diktat and civil society. The dye, the dying and the many dead were cast by Montag's imaginative vision of what is seen and yet not seen of the body politic, whether by yet another in a long line of self-blinding military presidents or by an on-guard common soldier blithely off-guard (perhaps because of over-familiarity) to the repression on which he turns his back but, at the same time, serves to enforce, reinforce and perpetuate. Without a blush himself, he vacuously underpins the governmentality of the Casa Rosada.

The cartoonist drew on a classic trope of delay: seen from inside the presidential palace, the windows frame and disclose 'QUE'; then 'QUEREMO', 'DESAPAREC' and 'NO HA DERECH' ... less than prevaricating, more than provocative. The reader-viewer, proleptically more knowing than the superannuated misreader of the signs and sighs of a stutteringly anguished nation, namely *el Señor Presidente*, invests in decoding the metonymic populace's ever-attenuated and too-often strangled cry. So persuaded is the dictator that the *vox populi* can be controlled and redirected by the slogan of the nation's collective obsession that 'Las Malvinas son argentinas' [The Malvinas are Argentina's] that he overlooks its inevitable inversion. For, in Montag's 'Viva la vida' [Long live life] and in the transmogrified *animot* imaginary, 'las argentinas son las Malvinas' – the 'Madres de la Plaza de Mayo' [The mothers of the Plaza de Mayo], *en masse*, demand and achieve the completion of their plea, the full articulation of their and the nation's sovereign right to self-expression and freedom of speech: 'Queremos vivir', 'Futuros a desaparecer', 'No hay derecho' [We want to live; Disappearing futures; You've no right]. *Specters of* Ma---s? Or *The State of the* [Argentine] *Debt, the Work of Mourning*, though hardly, as yet, for Argentina's mothers and grandmothers, *The New International*.

For the penguin *animot* remains the abject oppressed; the nation is as yet protected, albeit preposterously, by the anachronistic man-at-arms of a haughty, oblivious, uncaring military against the overdue fall of the abject oppressor. In the state of siege of 1982, Montag's depiction juxtaposed, brutally, a gender-marked confrontation of pregnant female protest and sterile male power. Clustered around the statue of a spear-holding warrior-maiden figure – 'Liberty leading the penguins' – the *animots* mothers-to-be, mothers nursing, or mothers bereft, beaks tight shut, conducted with improvised banners and placards their silent vigil *cum* demonstration. The solid edifice of bureaucratic institutionalism that sheltered the military dictator can be the better understood in the light of what Claire Johnston has defined as that dangerous iconography that 'places man as inside history and therefore changing and woman as outside of it and eternal' (Johnston, 2000, p. 23). Montag's cartoon, however, inverted and subverted such a staged relationship by having the radical change engendered by female animosity towards the unchanging sovereign power of Argentine fascism outed as a uniform male preserve. Thus, both in the Plaza de Mayo and throughout the nation, 'the time is out of joint' in the rotten den marked 'state'. *Pace* Johnston and her otherwise reasonable claim regarding 'man as inside history and therefore changing', many an Argentine male has had cause to resent the ostensibly eternal role of falling outside the official history of the Guerra de Malvinas and into the pit of neglect and despair. Little doubt can there be that

Cristina Kirchner's final congressional address was tapping in to that legacy of a shared victim status of resentment on the part of both women and men, veterans all, at the unchanging script of a history to be re-written. Being re-written, however, embrionically, against the grain of still power-driven forces resistant to ... change.

Plus ça change

Figure 12.5. Anonymously distributed poster, March 2003.

Too late? Take your partners, please, for the next (war) dance? But wait... *ipsa dixit*: 'There is no such thing as society; there are only men and women and their families' (Margaret Thatcher, 31 October 1987). No meeting half-way?

The risk-taking response of the poster detects the chimera, the *un*reality effect of the easy passing of the spurious mantle of power; for so long as the silent image performs the farce – the *fabula* – of national delusion. The two shall not be one in the marriage of convenience made in hellish coupling; the third term – *Il n'y a pas de hors-texte* – is neither one nor the other. It is, inseparably in the genre of the cartoon, both *animage* and *animot*. If it is thus that the world moves on – *sic*(k) *transit gloria* (im)*mundi* – what chance does a present-day Argentina have of engaging the attention and interest of the UK government and public when subsequent further war engagements ever preoccupy the British voters ... for better or worse, for richer or poorer, in *sic* – ness or in wealth? It may well prove forever difficult, if not impossible, for 'the British Establishment' to 'piss on victory' (Jenkins, 2003, pp. 35–6), especially after so many ostensible or perceived defeats since 1982, by no means limited to the poster's reference to Tony Blair's intentions with regard to Iraq (Fig. 12.5).

Requiescat ... (in pace?)

Figure 12.6. © *Austin 2003; first published in* The Guardian.

A British populace justifiably alert to tragic consequences of adventurisms, the fatalities of which were mourned never more publically than in Royal Wootton Bassett (granted royal patronage in March 2011 in recognition of its role in the early 21st-century military funeral repatriations which passed through the town), might hardly have paused to meditate on the unusual intervention of a government ministry in the statistics of supposed post-Falklands, directly related suicides. The assertion made by the South Atlantic Medal Association, representing veterans, that the number of suicides almost certainly exceeded the conflict toll of the 255 UK personnel who died in action, placing the blame primarily on a lack of care for those suffering post-traumatic stress disorder, is not borne out by statistics, according to a ministry of defence study from 2013. Whilst the MoD said that every suicide was a tragedy and urged veterans of any conflict needing support to seek help, it found 95 deaths were recorded as suicides or open verdicts. Disagreements over numbers – or dates – are undoubtedly inevitable yet rarely more capable of capturing the imagination than a single telling perception:

Whilst Argentines constantly stress the suffering of the nation's citizens at the murderous hands of a criminal regime up to 1982, and whilst there may never be a fixed toll regarding the estimated thirty thousand *desaparecidos* of the period of *el proceso*, the 'Galtieri' factor retains a fixed image in the UK national imaginary, possibly one unlikely to undergo change (*à la* Hitler, *à la* Franco) (Fig. 12.6). Even at the level of popular culture, the British admiration for an Argentine national hero may, alas, be tainted with an epitaph of monumentally stone-like fixity: 'Maradona' *qua* 'great genius and … cheat'. Yet, more encouragingly, Argentine insistence on 'Nunca más' and the harrowingly moving experience, for any and all, of visiting, for instance, the River Plate-side Parque de la Memoria, of reading the names and the often shockingly young ages of the dead inscribed on the seemingly interminable memorial walls, stress the emergence of a newly educated generation of 'Never again' … Who, in the UK, might have anticipated that the 'no', 'never' and 'not an inch' man, Protestant extremist of the 1960s and of the ensuing so-called 'troubles', Ian Paisley, as Northern Ireland's First Minister, would end up leading a power-sharing executive at the Stormont parliament in Belfast, 40 years on, sitting down with Gerry Adams – his former bitter enemy, the leader of militant republicanism – as the Democratic Unionist Party and Sinn Fein decided to work together in a power-sharing executive, going on to enjoy such a cosy relationship with his deputy first minister, Sinn Féin's Martin McGuinness, that they became known as the 'Chuckle Brothers'. As the BBC news reported to a disbelieving world, the seemingly impossible had happened; yet unlikely bed-mates can find each other across borders, seas … and oceans.

Apocalypse Now … and again
Pinochet takes Thatcher for a ride … or for cucumber sandwiches?

Figure 12.7. © Steve Bell 2006; first published in *The Guardian*.

Even after the British public – habitually blithe in respect of affairs trans-Atlantic – had had explained or spelled out the Bell-cartoon reference to the Spanish judge Baltazar Garzón's role in having the former Chilean dictator, Augusto Pinochet, detained, albeit temporarily, in London, with the attendant if unintended consequence of a traditional English afternoon-tea hospitality, it is still pertinent to ask whether and how many of them were or are prepared to address or confront Margaret Thatcher's support for and attitude towards a mass murderer (Fig. 12.7). 'Shy' apologists to this day will still elect to 'remind' the enquirer of the role of extreme-left *guerrilleros* in the 1960s and 1970s in the 'creation' of the criminal military right ... as if it did not *a priori* exist. Distorted causalism, hardly disinterested, from fellow-travelling apologists? 'He was a dictator, yes, but at least he was ours', parroted the former diplomat.

Things appeared to be getting better by 2012 when the UK's then ambassador to Chile, Jon Benjamin, was obliged to apologise for a Twitter teasing of Argentina over its defeat in the Falklands war: '¿Cuáles son las islas que te quitaron a quien por ser qué cosa?' [Which islands did they take off whom and for being what?], in a most un-diplomatic echo of a Chilean football taunt: 'Argentines, faggots, you lost the Malvinas because you are idiots' [Argentinos, maricones. ¡Les quitaron las Malvinas por huevones!]. The self-styled 'Hammers fan, Londoner at heart, Jewish atheist', bombarded by threats of violence and anti-Semitic responses, deleted his offending tweet and apologised, saying it had been a private tweet and that he had 'great affection for my Argentine friends and respect for their team'. 'The Argentine sports daily *Olé* said that was no excuse. The Foreign Office said: 'Our ambassador to Chile appears to have inadvertently caused some controversy in a tweet. He has deleted it'. Benjamin was tweeting as usual on Tuesday, but on safer ground: re-tweeting the Foreign Secretary William Hague' (*The Guardian*, 16 October 2012).

Foreign Office sensitivity may be relied upon ... but to foreign secretaries, their prime minister and the cabinet – Her Majesty permitting – in fine we shall return. Meanwhile, the perennial role of soccer in the popular imaginary and in populist manipulation has since been turned to different effect ... with a gender twist. A visit today to the museum of memory that was the headquarters of the former Escuela de Mecánica de la Armada and notorious site of imprisonment, torture, murder and disappearance bears witness to a strategy adopted by the Abuelas [Grandmothers] de la Plaza de Mayo, notably expressed in that section of ESMA devoted to their recent engagement with modern science and, in particular, the resonance and revelations of DNA and related advances:

In recruiting such internationally recognised, and youthful, profiles as that of Lionel Messi, bearer of national aspirations, hopes and, here, the slogan 'RESOLVÉ TU IDENTIDAD' AHORA', they refer to the lost children sequestered from disappeared or murdered mothers and clandestinely adopted

Figure 12.8. © *Fútbol Rebelde*, June 2014.

by sometimes witting, sometimes unwitting, members or associates of the discredited criminal military. Thereby they render potentially illegitimate a whole generation of their fellow citizens in order to regain and restore a legitimacy for a nation, a state, a besmirched sovereignty in need of their more-penetrating-even-than-surgical intervention.

'Resolve' ... 'identity' ... 'now'? 'you/r'? Already, in response to the notion that the State could 'disappear' victims but not their genes, caveats have been raised to the effect that recourse to would-be solutions via DNA 'evidence' will have to take into account how many identified victims did not, do not, or will not want to know and might say (culturally) 'No'. 'I am not yours'. Are we to be further locked into dualist thinking, feeling? I think (therefore) I am to move away – now – from the notion of being and not being the other one and to suggest that here, indubitably, is an entrenched Cartesian binary: you and me; the self and the other. Momentarily, I want to mind-sweep aside – implausible task – one of the weighty legacies of our western (post-)conflictive thinking and to broach the Spinozarian alternative, namely the concept of becoming. And when I act thus I am (again) thinking, particularly, of the near-contemporary philosopher Emmanuel Lévinas. For Lévinas was saying – amongst many poetic insights – something very political, namely, that the self is in the other and the other is in the self. 'You'/ 'I' can see why and how this proposition is a calmative subverting of confrontational Greco-Roman (*donc* – post-Hegel – transatlantic) binaries. The insight helps us also to address the oft-bruited notion that victimisation denies agency and, consequently, the possibility that, as a therapeutic response to victimisation denying agency, we might even concede that 'recovery is impossible'. Yet what of healing? I would further suggest that *reconstitution* rather than *recovery* is what might be developed in the post-traumatic phase; and it is the Lévinasian and the

Spinozarian notions of *becoming* that allow us thus to operate. Because, if I obliterate you, I have obliterated me; if, indeed, 'self' is in 'other' and 'other' is in 'self'.

Alison Landsberg, in 2004, coined the term 'prosthetic memory' to describe the way mass cultural technologies of memory enable individuals to experience, as if they were memories, events through which they themselves did not live. Whereas the prosthetic operates *after* the body (politic) has been operated on, my proposed shift from damaged or incomplete, still-to-be-completed, being is not supplement but complement. Complemented by the becoming procedure of the graft – itself not on but of a reconstituted self which coincides with a former other 'memory' – post-memory promises that '*il n'y a pas de hors-corps*' … For I wish to consider winning and losing, as I proceed. What is a winner, what is a loser? In a Spinozarian world, the winner is in the loser and the loser is in the winner, in the process of becoming a reconstituted alternative identity thereafter. Not in the 'post-' conceived of only chronologically, but in the *space* of the 'post-'. Time is in space and space is in time in such a conceptualisation as I have outlined it, deriving not from a different but from a parallel philosophical tradition (that is, not in difference; ever in *différance*). Of course, I am speaking about constructs, about 'meaning effects'; and I have already made the point that the burden of our sovereignties, of our responsibilities, of our citizenships propels us always to remember that the 'post-', as well as the past, are in the present. Here is what we can do about it, responsibly. Take up the challenge: to express and distribute memories – on such vehicles as might come to hand or to mind – as effects of meaning but, politically, too, as meanings turned to effect. Contemplate, even concede, that recovery is impossible in the post-traumatic phase; yet the talking cure may go on, never completing; ever reconstituting. 'You'/'I' … 'I'/ 'You'.

And you, do you know who you are? Again, '*Ecce animot*'? – 'assuming the title of an auto [biological] animal, in the form of a risky […] [chemical] response to the question "But me, who am I?"'… *pace* Jacques (à *suivre*).

Les animots

> *Animal*: I was tempted … to forge another word in the singular, at the same time close but radically foreign, a chimerical word that sounded as though it contravened the laws of the French language, *l'animot* … *Ecce animot* … We have to envisage the existence of 'living creatures' whose plurality cannot be assembled within the single figure of an animality that is simply opposed to humanity … *Ecce animot* … assuming the title of an autobiographical animal, in the form of a risky, fabulous, or chimerical response to the question 'But me, who am I?' (Derrida, 2002, p. 409; p. 416).

It might now be the moment to apply instrumentally, in focussed targeting, Derrida's prior and broader interrogation to a familiar rivalry, with its attendant insults and expletives, to which the cartoon genre draws attention; evoked again by Steve Bell but with calculated echo of the philosopher's reminder of the perhaps insurmountable difficulty of coming to terms with a 'radically foreign' self-in-other/other-in-self. Playing up, and on, a stereotyping and the puncturing of it that has been his iconography since his first cartoons appeared in *The Guardian* in the early phase of the South Atlantic conflict in 1982, Bell has latterly depicted his Union of Jack penguins as overfed (not noticeably oversexed despite their expletive-deleted 'fucking' chant) but assertively over there (*pace* the British civilians and their originally WWII cliché re United States troops stationed in Blighty).

Animo(t)sities. 'Stop the drilling, penguin bastardos!'

Figure 12.9. © Steve Bell 2010; first published in The Guardian.

In *Animal Farm* fashion, to assert one's power by mere reiteration requires the subjection of an abject 'other', here as ever the plumage-and-power stripped albatross of Southern Cone climes. What at once conjures up a military cadence call at the same time draws on the classic double meaning of the word 'drilling'. Hardly necessary for the exegete to explain the overt references to militarisation; so up pops a rare bird – uninvited, unwelcome, defeated intruder – to remind the cartoon's reader-viewer of the (pre-)occupying protected interests of not 'unas islas demasiado famosas', *à la* Jorge Luis Borges, but resources, fisheries, minerals, hydrocarbons, tourism ('penguins, ah!') … oil.

Coda… decoder; and Scotland's long-prior to the 2014 referendum cry: 'It's oor oil'

Re-arrange the following into a well-known phrase or saying

shell

                          exon

                                                mobil

                  jet

q8

                          gulf

           bp

                                           total

        Amoco

Cherchez Saddam…

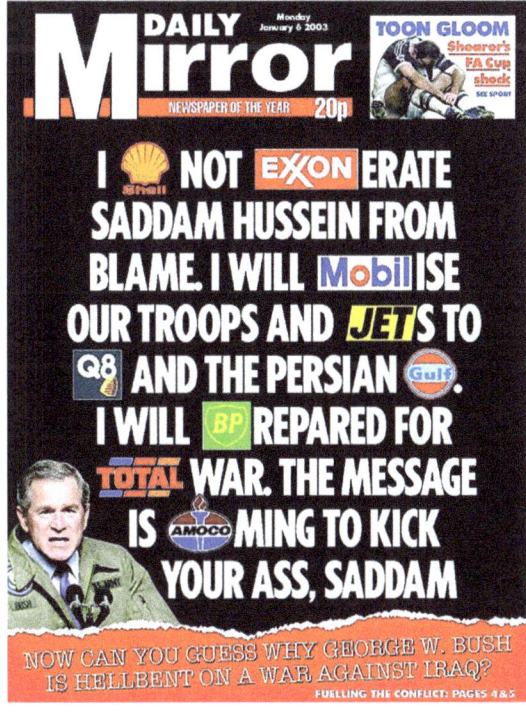

Figure 12.10. The Daily Mirror, 6 January 2003.

Update: *Sky News*, April 2015
> Daniel Filmus, Buenos Aires' Minister for the Malvinas, as it [*sic*] refers to the British Overseas Territory, threatened legal moves over the drilling earlier this month and is reported to have confirmed today that Argentinian judicial authorities will take on the case. Three British firms, Premier Oil, Rockhopper Exploration and Falkland Oil & Gas, are reported to be among the five firms targeted by the action. Philip Hammond [since William Hague's demotion in July 2014, Secretary of State for Foreign and Commonwealth Affairs] criticised Argentina's stance. Mr Hammond told Sky News: 'It is an outrageous piece of bullying and threatening against the Falkland Islanders' perfect right to develop their own economic resources and Argentina needs to stop this kind of behaviour and start acting like a responsible member of the International community'.

Gulf? Of Mexico? Ummm. BP? A drilling catastrophe… Ring a Bell? If so, then re-arrange the following into another well-known phrase or saying:

Which
      transnational insurance company
                              will cover
the risk of a Gulf-style spill
      off the coast
                              of the country
the emergency services of which
      would have to be called upon?
Get real.

Note to the reader:

The task has been rendered the easier as the first steps of the re-ordering have been taken.

Caveat emptor:

Subsequent intelligence (London markets consulted): 'Not a problem. Insurance premiums will rocket … and multinational financing will ride roughshod over national (sovereign?) stances. It's an economic risk worth taking'. Take over … and Argentina over a barrel? Which empty barrels make most sound? Falkland Sound … Sound investment?

Such presumptuousness cannot operate in a void; for in the echo chamber of transatlantic stridencies Argentine ears are pricked, Argentine voices, such as that of Carlos Escudé, cast into play, increasingly, less belligerent if still challenging ripostes:

> Curiously, such systematic underestimating of Argentine power has led us, out of frustration, to suppose that we have no power at all. One of the scant areas of foreign policies in which we do have effective power,

manifesting itself as the power of veto, is that of investments in the maritime floor of the south Atlantic. This power stems from the fact that for a capitalist to venture the anchoring of hundreds of millions of dollars at the bottom of the sea, the operational risk must be minimised. The natural risks of all sea-bed investments are inherently high. If to this is added the political risk of an unsuitably disposed Argentina there will be no investments. Thus we have the power to avoid the extraction of hydrocarbons from the south Atlantic. Although not even remotely do we have the power to re-conquer the Islands, multi-million investments in the ocean bed can be destroyed in a moment of madness, and no investor is going to put in its money if such a risk has not been minimised. Naturally, the Argentine veto must not be used obstructively and destructively, therefore blocking investments, but in a manner ensuring for all concerned a significant participation in the operations, including the levying of taxes on companies in charge of exploring in any part of the territorial seas of the Malvinas Islands […] the proposed solution [is] to share equitably the resources of the ocean, only then apply fiercely our power of veto, in order to render impossible, high-risk maritime investments (Escudé, 2015, pp. 49–51, my translation).

Cherchez … la femme. Entente?

Figure 12.11.

The Queen greeted ministers shortly after 10am and became the first monarch to attend a cabinet meeting in more than 200 years. The monarch, wearing a royal blue wool dress and a sapphire and diamond broach, sat beside the Prime Minister and William Hague, the Foreign Secretary, for the weekly discussion of Government business.

Mr Cameron congratulated her on her 'fantastic' Diamond Jubilee year and said the last monarch to visit the Cabinet was believed to have been George III in 1781 (Rowena Mason, *The Daily Telegraph*, 18 Dec 2012).

One ... is not amused

Figure 12.12. © Jeremy Selwyn Evening Standard PA.

['Queen Elizabeth Land']

Figure 12.13.

> In a further gift, the Foreign Office declared that a tract of frozen land about twice the size of the UK in Antarctica was to be named after her as Queen Elizabeth Land. The land in the British Antarctic Territory had been previously unnamed. The prime minister's spokesman was unable to say whether it had any flowers, fauna or people. She otherwise remained silent apart from wishing the rest of the cabinet a merry Christmas on her departure (*The Guardian*, 18 December 2012).

... cordiale?

Figure 12.14. © Steve Bell 2012.

Cordiality one does not do; stony-faced dignity amidst Cabinet Bullingdon-boys' riotous guffaws and arriviste pleb giggles of obsequious tie-touchers, hair-smoothers, knee-jerkers *inter alia* ... all in a day's (or sixty years') 'work'. Job done; public engagement; Cabinet assuaged.

Entente? Contente? The transition from photo opportunism self-control to caricatured grimace reflects what, in private, the British populace readily spots (diamonds are forever). Bondage to the slavery of duty above all as Her Majesty saves face amidst that mixture of respect and domestic pride, self-containment and smug insularity, of those with much to gain, politically, from the celebrating of her Commonwealth and post-Empire reign. 'There Are Powers At Work' [rictus] '... Of Which We Know Nothing' echoes the revelations made at the inquest into the death of Princess Diana by Paul Burrell who 'had joined the Royal Household at Buckingham Palace in 1976 and served the Queen for ten years as her personal footman [...] Mr Burrell said he did not ask the Queen what she meant when she told him "to be careful" at the infamous "dark forces" meeting, the inquest heard' (The *Daily Mail*, 15 January 2008). In dangerous waters, Ship of State QE2 is all-too-aware of supra-sovereign powers and the need to be careful of uncontrollable transnational politico-economic interests. Britannia waives the rules no more? Shhh ... Keep it in the family. One is not to be embarrassed. One is not to be used. Understood?

At times, the press is at a loss to decide how to differentiate between the uncontrollable and the calculated political manoeuvre or, alas, gaffe. What could be wrong with the renaming of a piece of Antarctica as 'Queen Elizabeth Land', a gift to go with sixty decorative place mats as Prime Minister Cameron congratulated her on her 'fantastic' Diamond Jubilee year? Entirely innocent and perhaps, even, appreciated: as many a true-Brit would recognise: or would 'one'?

Would 'one', indeed?

Figure 12.15. © Steve Bell; first published in The Guardian, 19 December 2012.

Misunderstood … Misunderstandings give rise to jokes; jokes quickly turn into insults. 'UP YOURS ARGENTINA' besmirches the Union Jack in front of which the monarch is *faux pas* marooned; the twelve fat penguins (born of the Thatchery) look on in dumb obedience … unaware, or in 98.8% approval, of the re-evocation of the *Sun*'s notorious out-of-Europe headline 'UP YOURS DELORS' from 1 November 1990. The sun *ever* sets on the British Empire … as Her Majesty knows best.

Lèse majesté … Slips of the tongue are inevitable; diplomats learn – or are taught – to avoid them. Their role is to cover up for their governments, for their prime ministers or presidents and, *in extremis*, for their foreign secretaries; whether, proleptically, at *The Guardian*'s Steve Bell end-of-the-telescope view of William Hague's champagne-bottle de-launching, or at the *finis terrae* of the trademark Zimmer-frame stumbling of an Argentine career politician:

A number two?

Figure 12.16. Héctor Timerman © The Guardian, 5 February 2013

Please police me, oh yeah ... Tonight the Super [Blooper] lights are gonna find me, feeling like a number [two] (*pace* Abba ... A blah blah). Timerman-zimmerman, zimmerman-Timerman ... Either ... neither? 'Let's call the whole thing off.' The same old songs, whether in London or Buenos Aires: 'Miró fijo al periodista de la BBC Mundo, en Londres, y se embaló: "Dentro del fin del colonialismo *va a estar el fin del colonialismo en las Islas Británicas* ... eh, en las Islas Malvinas, y la Argentina va a recuperar los 5.000 kilómetros cuadrados de mar y tierra que hoy ... eh, que le han sido arrebatadas en 1833"' [He looked the BBC World reporter in London straight in the face and blurted out: 'Within the ending of colonialism *will be the ending of colonialism in the British Isles* ... er, in the Malvinas Islands, and Argentina is going to recover the 5,000 square kilometres of land and sea that today ... er, that were snatched from it in 1833'] (Mayol, 2013).

His 'K gag' removed whilst playing away from home, a Héctor(ing) foreign minister, momentarily left to represent Argentine affairs in one capital, no doubt had to face the music, and the challenge, in the other, on his return to within clawing distance of Cristina. The gaffe, however, was blown: '"I'll be the judge, I'll be the jury", said the cunning old Fury'...

'I meant "there's a nice knock-down argument for you!"'

Figure 12.17.

> 'I don't think it will take another 20 years. I think that the world is going through a process of understanding more and more that this is a colonial issue, an issue of colonialism' (Héctor Timerman, *The Guardian*, 5 February 2013).

Looking Glass ... or Wonderland? Alas. When would *he* be through? Twenty days, 20 weeks, 20 months ... '"*There's glory for you*!" "I don't know what *you* mean by '*glory*'", [Cristina] said'. Glory? Sick transit.

Imagine...

Figure 12.18. Anonymous.

> It's easy if you try...
> Nothing to kill or die for...
> Imagine no possessions
> I wonder if you can...
> You, you may say
> I'm a dreamer, but I'm not the only one.   © John Lennon 1971

Coda ...

When, at an early juncture, I was asked by Alicia Castro whether I wished to join a pro-negotiation grouping, she understood at once and accepted without demur my response: namely, that the academic freedom without affiliation which I and others have enjoyed because it must be taken for granted was the very status that would allow me to continue to bring together individuals and views of the most plural, varied and often unexpected, at all levels, and without shifting my critical stance. These undertakings have been achieved in the most cordial and respectful frame of thinking, speaking and, above all, listening. In a future when multi-national enterprises will often compete with the very national governments upon which they albeit decreasingly also depend, not least, for instance, in the exploitation of energy and mineral resources, novel and imaginative approaches will be seen, in hindsight, to have anticipated the powerful discourses of threatening eras, approaches concomitant with, I stress, and therefore the less controllable by, the ever-challenging international communications strategies mentioned at the outset. The term 'post-' by no means suggests that conflicts are over and done with; on the contrary, it is lessons learned and deepened that will aid, though never guarantee, the courageous conjoining of the discourses of reconstruction and reconstitution through effective and inevitable negotiations of both mind and will. Consider the following texts:

> There is a growing body of opinion that nation-states are declining. Nationalism, or so it is said, is no longer a major force: globalization is the order of the day. But a reminder is necessary. Nationhood is still being reproduced: it can still call for ultimate sacrifices; and, daily, its symbols and assumptions are flagged (Billig, 1995, p. 9).

> We can pronounce not a single destructive proposition which has not already had to slip into the form, the logic, and the implicit postulations of precisely what it seeks to contest (Derrida, 1978, p. 280).

> *The Sun* has claimed that the UK Defence Ministry will request more troops to be sent to the disputed Malvinas Islands, due to an alleged threat of an Argentine invasion bankrolled by Russia. Using the title 'We've gotcha backs' – a clear reference to the infamous 'Gotcha' headline which announced the deadly sinking of the *General Belgrano* cruiser during the 1982 Malvinas War […] Defence Secretary Michael Fallon will 'tell MPs that he is ordering a significant increase to the South Atlantic islands' garrison'. The front page cites an 'increased invasion threat

from Argentina' […] 'Unstable Argentina is said to be rearming 33 years after the Falklands [Malvinas] war, helped by Russia's Vladimir Putin', the tabloid claims. The […] head of the Russian parliament's foreign affairs committee, Alexei Pushkov, referred to the Malvinas conflict in response to UK criticism over the Crimea affair. 'Attention London: Crimea has far more reason to be in Russia than the Falklands have to be part of Great Britain' (*Buenos Aires Herald*, 23 March 2015).

'… and that shows that there are three hundred and sixty-four days when you get un-birthday presents.' 'Certainly', said Alice. 'And only one for birthday presents, you know, there's glory for you!' 'I don't know what you mean by "glory"', Alice said. Humpty Dumpty smiled contemptuously. 'Of course you don't – till I tell you. I meant "there's a nice knock-down argument for you!"' 'But "glory" doesn't mean "a nice knock-down argument"', Alice objected. 'When I use a word', Humpty Dumpty said in a rather a scornful tone, 'it means just what I choose it to mean – neither more nor less'. 'The question is', said Alice, 'whether you can make words mean different things'. 'The question is', said Humpty Dumpty, 'which is to be master – that's all' (Carroll, 1871, p. 134).

Dialogue (open)? Negotiating regime change in 2015

Figure 12.19. © MercoPress, Friday 27 November 2015.

Cameron and Macri agree to 'strengthen relations'" and 'to pursue a path of open dialogue'.

Britain's David Cameron and Argentina's president-elect Mauricio Macri agreed to 'strengthen relations' and 'to pursue a path of open dialogue' between their countries after a phone call Thursday, Downing Street said. 'Acknowledging differences, both leaders agreed the need to pursue a path of open dialogue and work towards a stronger partnership', said the release. Cameron's office said the PM had called Macri to congratulate him, and also pledged support for Argentina's economic reform program (*MercoPress*, South Atlantic News Agency, Friday 27 November 2015).

... dialogue (closed)

Monologue (and markets) open: Davos, 21 January 2016. 'Absolutely clear…'

Figure 12.20. © Reuters, 21 January 2016

LONDON (Reuters) – Old foes Britain and Argentina said on Thursday there was an opportunity to open a new chapter in diplomatic relations after a meeting between British Prime Minister David Cameron and newly elected Argentine President Mauricio Macri. […] Finally on the Falklands the Prime Minister was clear that our position remained the same and that the recent referendum was absolutely clear on the Islanders' wish to remain British […] 'And to British people I would say, there is the prospect of the best of both worlds'.

Ipse dixit David, pre-Brexit …

Stop press: 'Blooper' pooper … a fouler howler

'The finest statesman Britain ever produced'. *Ipse scribit* Boris, post-Brexit, latter-day Goliath:

Figure 12.21. © BBC.

Author of *The Churchill Factor: How One Man Made History,* Boris Johnson was, until 9 July 2018, Foreign Secretary, charged to represent United Kingdom affairs in one capital, Buenos Aires, no doubt *not* to 'face the music', but perhaps to challenge Cameron's successor, in the other, London, his former mayoral domain, on his return to within 'at-heel' distance of Teresa May. Whose heel? *His* gaffe never blown, for '*He*'ll be the judge, *He*'ll be the jury…', ever Boorishly, 'the cake and eat it', 'best of both worlds' envoy, in the lens, again, of Steve Bell:

Figure 12.22. © Steve Bell.

Hell-bent on evoking many a 'cunning old Fury', *inter alia*, Winston, he yet 'doth [not] bestride the narrow world/Like a colossus' for, 'under his huge legs' walk not 'petty men' but just one mere 'underling', his erstwhile rival as would-be Prime Minister, Michael Gove, bespectacled, shat upon and semi-crushed, painted out of the dog-eat-dog political scenario not by canned Dulux but by uncanny Bolux-spieler Boris, already with trans-Atlantic ambitions in a post-Brexit free-trading, free-wheeling and free-loading adventurism:

Figure 12.23. © Steve Bell first published in The Guardian, 1 July 2016 and 15 July 2016

So why not include Argentina?

Figure 12.24.© Télam, 20 May 2018

No less 'blooperista' than a Héctor Timerman, the proleptic counterpart of a (dis)United Kingdom's own foreign secretary, Boorish, the notoriously unpoliceable clanger-dropper, was soon to appear – the Argentine but not the international press excluded, no doubt in order to avoid the posing of awkward questions – on the red carpet of previously 'alien' territory, hosted by Macri ministers Jorge Faurie, Oscar Aguad and Patricia Bullrich. The first such British incumbent was there to pay respect to the Argentine fallen of 1982. Ostensibly; though, ever alert to the implications of this, as of any, G-20 gathering, that of 20–21 May 2018, Steve Bell's take on, and advice to, Boris put a different face on matters. In the diplomatic domain of *De eso no se habla/That is not spoken about*, it took the cartoonist little time to find a cultural parallel closer to home:

Figure 12.25. © Steve Bell; first published in The Guardian, 7 June 2017.

Just two days before the G-20 summit, a transatlantic noise that could no longer be muzzled had been borne, in the same newspaper, by the simple headline 'Argentina forced to seek IMF aid over fears for economy' (*The Guardian*, 18 May 2018).

At the time of writing and no less alert to the ever 'unfinished business' of Falkland-Malvinas affairs, and though the then UK Foreign Secretary had other matters on his mind, one noted that what emerged from under the thatch – when it comes to international negotiations – remained, on 6 July 2018, substantially unchanged and predictably fecal; in his own words, those in disagreement with him are 'polishing turds'. It might still break two to tangle but all the more so if the surface is that slippery.

Post-scriptum: 10 October 2020

Icy contempt… and now one is amused. Recalling, dare it be said, the 2012 gift to Her Majesty proffered by the then-smiling Cameron cabinet of a newly named 'tract of frozen land about twice the size of the UK in Antarctica […] named after her as Queen Elizabeth Land' (supra) – and of Steve Bell's instant lampooning of the vapid gesture – a further slippery surface of signification has been more recently projected:

Figure 12.26. © The Economist *from CLCS; COPLA; Flanders Marine Institute 10 Oct. 2020.*

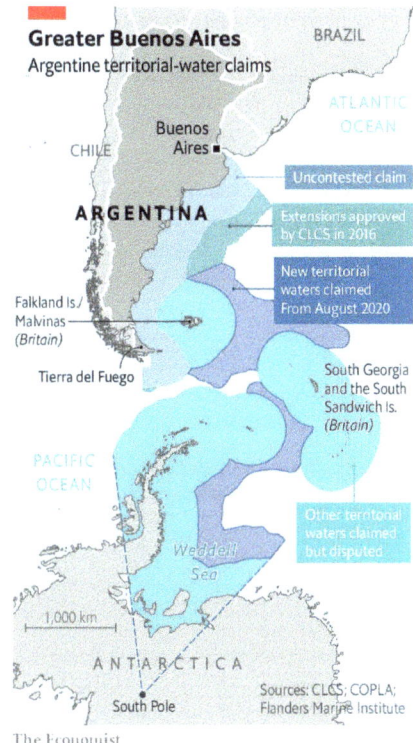

The Isle of Wight has got nothing on this; Guile of the White…? Last word then to – hardly a bastion of revolutionary British political thinking – *The Economist*?

ARGENTINA'S PRESIDENT, Alberto Fernández, has plenty to worry about: a soaring covid-19 caseload and a depressed economy. So it must have been delightful for the government to change the subject on September 21st by issuing a map showing that the country's territory is nearly double its former size. It illustrates the effect of a law Mr Fernández signed in August, which expands Argentina by 1.7m square km (650,000 square miles), an area three times the size of metropolitan France. Argentina now bestrides South America and Antarctica, from the Tropic of Capricorn to the South Pole. Its territory includes some of the world's richest fishing grounds and possibly oil and gas. The Falkland Islands, which Argentines call the Malvinas, lie within it.

'Lie…'? Whatever will Roger Lorton Esquire have to say about this one? Will it be deemed just another ploy of 'Argentina's master propagandist Daniel Filmus'? *Qui vivra verra* … (translation available on request, post-Brexit, for those 'rarely in the UK these days'):

> This is not entirely based on fantasy. In 2016 the UN's Commission on the Limits of the Continental Shelf (CLCS) issued a ruling, based on the UN Convention on the Law of the Sea, that fixes the edge of the vast shelf that juts out from Argentina's coast. There the seabed is shallow enough – less than 2,500 metres deep – to count as an extension of Argentina's mainland. The effect of the ruling is to extend Argentina's territorial waters beyond the normal 200 nautical miles (370km). The new official map shows South Georgia and the South Sandwich islands (also British), as part of Argentina, too, and adds areas that had it not claimed in law before. The British are mainly interested in the water's riches, Argentina's government thinks. That explains the 'stubbornness of British colonialism', suggested Daniel Filmus, the government's secretary for the Malvinas, Antarctica and South Atlantic. The map asserts Argentine sovereignty over the Antarctic peninsula, an ice-cream cone poking into the Weddell sea, which is also claimed by Chile and Britain. In fact, the UN commission avoided taking a position 'in a case where a land or maritime dispute exists'. The areas it awarded Argentina are a fraction of the country's claim.
>
> Argentina does not plan to try to reconquer the islands, but it does hope to use its interpretation of the commission's ruling to press Britain to negotiate. 'The UN is saying that the Malvinas is a matter of dispute', contends an adviser to the president. 'The British always try to say there is no dispute over the islands'. Argentina's foreign ministry put out a video calling for 'dialogue' under UN auspices. Britain is unlikely to agree.
>
> Argentine oceanographers are now in demand from other countries.[1]

Il n'y a pas de dernier mot … Whence, again, *Falklands-Malvinas: an Unfinished Business*.

---

1 This article appeared in the *The Americas* section of the print edition under the headline 'Alberto of the Antarctic' (*The Economist*, online edition, 10 October 2020).

References

Billig, M. (1995) *Banal Nationalism* (London: Sage).

Carroll, L. (1871) *Through the Looking-Glass and what Alice Found There* (London: Macmillan).

Derrida, J. (1978) *Writing and Difference*, trans. by A. Bass (London: Routledge & Kegan Paul).

— (2002) 'The Animal That I Am (More to Follow)', trans. by D. Wills, *Critical Enquiry*, 28 (2): 369–418.

Escudé, C. (2015) 'Cuestionando lo incuestionable: hacia un intercambio negociado de tierras por recursos marítimos', *Agenda Internacional: Visión desde el Sur*, 32: 44–52.

Foucault, M. (1977) *Discipline and Punish: The Birth of the Prison*, trans. by A. Sheridan (New York: Pantheon).

Freedman, L. (2005) *The Official History of the Falklands Campaign* (London: Routledge).

García Quiroga, D. and M. Seear (2007) *Hors de Combat: The Falklands–Malvinas Conflict Twenty-Five Years On* (2007); 2nd (extended) edition (2009) *Hors de Combat: The Falklands–Malvinas Conflict in Retrospect* (Nottingham: Critical, Cultural and Communications Press).

Landsberg, A. (2004) *Prosthetic Memory* (New York: Columbia University Press).

Mayol, F. (2013) 'Los papelones de Timerman. Sus bloopers en Londres y en el polémico acuerdo con Irán. Las Malvinas "británicas", su rol en la dictadura y los retos de Cristina', *Política* (12 February).

McGuirk, B. (2007) *Falklands–Malvinas: An Unfinished Business* (Seattle: New Ventures).

Seear, M. (2012) *Return to Tumbledown: The Falklands–Malvinas War Revisited* (Nottingham: Critical, Cultural and Communications Press).

Watts, J. and U. Goñi (2015) 'Mauricio Macri has won Argentina's presidency – but his work has just begun', *Buenos Aires Herald* (23 November), p. 2.

Information resources on the Falklands–Malvinas conflict

Christine Anderson and María R. Osuna Alarcón

The aim of the present chapter is to make public knowledge all the existing documents about the Falklands–Malvinas War preserved in the institutions of all involved governments and in other institutions with contemporary sources. In order to carry out this task we follow the well-known protocol of the University of Chicago's *Sources for History* (2010).

The Falklands–Malvinas War remains an open conflict. The press in both countries recently published the heated debate that emerged during the negotiations between Theresa May and Mauricio Macri (*The Guardian*, 2016 and *La Nación*, 2016) as well as their different demands: for instance, an increase in commercial flights to the Islands, which would represent good news for their inhabitants. It would seem that as long as the debate, heated as it seems, remains circumscribed within the diplomatic arena, it will benefit the inhabitants of the Islands; and that theirs will be the decision about the Falkland–Malvinas future. We consider that in this task it would be of great benefit to have access to the historical sources about the Islands' recent past. We would like to point out that the present chapter remains an open document which is still subject to permanent review and that further sources will be added as they become available.

C. Anderson and M.R. Osuna Alarcón, 'Information resources on the Falkland–Malvinas conflict', in G. Mira and F. Pedrosa (eds.), *Revisiting the Falklands–Malvinas Question: Transnational and Interdisciplinary Perspectives* (London: University of London Press, 2020), pp. 251–67. License: CC-BY-NC-ND 4.0.

Index of Resources:

1. Institutional Archives

   1.1 Argentina

   1.2 United Kingdom

2. Institutional repositories, libraries and museums with specialised collections on the subject

   2.1 Argentina

   2.2 United Kingdom

3. International Organisations Repositories

4. Media, 'raw resources', audio, images and videos

   4.1 Argentina

   4.2 United Kingdom

Introduction

After more than thirty years, the Falklands–Malvinas War remains a polemical conflict, generating intense disputes between the governments of the involved countries. While a large number of the documents listed here have been traced from the two countries directly involved, it is true that the war affected other interests. Inhabitants of the Islands have been left out of the debate. The sources presented here are organised using the protocol proposed by the University of Chicago (*Chicago Manual of Style*, 2010, pp. 1–2). This work has been undertaken with the idea of collaboration and service and to facilitate general public access to the sources. We have focused on primary sources and therefore left out fiction and art in general 'created at the time an historical event occurred' (*Chicago Manual of Style*, 2010, pp. 1–2) and focused on those direct primary sources that the University of Chicago calls 'raw material' (*Chicago Manual of Style*, 2010, pp. 1–2).

On 2 April 1982, under the chairmanship of Lt. facto. Gral. Leopoldo F. Galtieri, Argentine troops landed on the Falkland-Malvinas Islands in an attempt to recover this part of the territory that had been held by Britain since 1833. It was an attempt to win popular support by the military government, increasingly discredited by the consequences of economic policy and complaints of human rights violations. Large sectors of the Argentine population reacted favourably to the recovery of the Islands with demonstrations across the country. The support was, however, differently nuanced: those who considered the 'Malvinas' an anti-imperialist cause; those who openly supported the actions of the armed forces; and those who sympathised with the young fighters. 'The Malvinas are Argentine, the missing too', said the Mothers of the Plaza de Mayo.

Press information during the war, as during the entire dictatorship, was subject to strict control. Added to this, the triumphalist tone that drove the military government, which controlled the media, ensured people were unaware of actual developments. Thus when the surrender came on 14 June 1982, Argentine bewilderment and then indignation were very deep and contributed to the final discrediting of the military. The war left 649 Argentine soldiers dead and over a thousand injured in the Islands and has to-date caused the suicide of hundreds of former fighters returning to the continent. The young soldiers who survived were instructed to maintain absolute silence about the events of the war. Even today, many demand, appearing as plaintiffs in court, that the abuse and torture of soldiers at the hands of their superiors should be investigated. There are at least one hundred complaints filed in various courts for humiliation, torture and even the murder of a soldier and the death of another by starvation.

The Falklands–Malvinas War (also known as the Falklands Conflict/ Falklands Crisis/Guerra de las Malvinas/Guerra del Atlántico Sur) lasted for 74 days, between 2 April and 14 June 1982. It cost the lives of 255 British military personnel and three Falkland-Malvinas Islanders and left 777 British wounded. Official documents and files are now being made available. On the British side, it was reported in December 2012 that the British government had so far released over 3,500 official documents from 1982 related to the Falklands War. These papers were released under the 30-year rule, which states that official documents must be declassified after 30 years, that is, unless the information contained within those papers could put Britain's national security at risk. Examples of the documents released include testimonials by then British prime minister, Margaret Thatcher, given behind closed doors to the Falkland-Malvinas Islands Review Committee in October 1982; and material from *The Franks Report* (also known as the Falkland Islands Review). *The Franks Report* (1981–3), was a government report produced by the Franks Committee in 1983. It reported on decisions taken by the British government in the run-up to the landing of Argentine troops on the Falkland-Malvinas Islands in 1982:

> The Falklands War of 1982 was one of the defining events of recent British history, a sudden and almost revolutionary shock to the national psyche which transformed the domestic political scene, and much else besides.

There are thousands upon thousands of secret documents on the war, as one might expect, and their release on 28 December 2012 marks the beginning of analysis rather than its conclusion. We will return to them many times on this site, but here is the first bite, an upload of all of MT's 1982 files on the topic, filmed by us in preview at the National Archives in Kew.

Much more will follow, from the archives of the Foreign Office and Ministry of Defence especially (*The Franks Report*, 1983).

On the Argentine side, speaking on the 33rd anniversary of the start of the conflict on 2 April 2015, President Cristina Fernández de Kirchner of Argentina ordered the declassification of all secret documents on the Falklands–Malvinas War with Britain, giving the Argentine defence ministry 30 days to make all files on the conflict public (Argentina. Ministerio de Defensa. Archivos Abiertos).

Lieutenant Benjamín Rattenbach had chaired a commission looking into the failings of the war from an Argentine perspective. The resulting Rattenbach Report, written in December 1982, was declassified on 22 March 2012.

A documentary on the Rattenbach Report was produced by Canal Encuentro (2 April 2012) and includes exclusive material on the declassification of the report, as well as the testimonies of Defence Minister Arturo Puricelli, Rattenbach's son Augusto, veterans Ernesto Alonso and Rodolfo Carrizo, US Ambassador Jorge Arguello and others.

1. Institutional archives

1.1 Argentina

Casa Rosada. Archivo oral de las memorias de Malvinas
'The project consists in the construction of a biographical archive of oral history about the South Atlantic conflict known as the Falklands–Malvinas War. The purpose is to let the protagonists tell their own history through their voices, allowing their families and future generations a first-hand account of the combatants' life experiences':
http://www.casarosada.gob.ar/pdf/archivo%20oral%20de%20las%20malvinas.pdf.

Ministerio de Defensa
Website for the Argentine Ministry of Defence Malvinas Archive. It provides access to the *Informe Rattenbach*, to the *Veteranos de Guerra de Malvinas* and to *legislation* on the conflict:
http://www.mindef.gov.ar/malvinas.php.

Servicio Histórico del Ejército (SHE)
Archives: The Archive contains documents produced by the Argentine army that are considered of historical value, instruments of description, guides and publications. The inventory is relatively shallow.
Institutional History: Its origins date back to the creation of the Registro Marcial on 20 August 1813. In its more contemporary form, it dates back to 1884, when the División III 'Historia' del Estado Mayor Permanente was formed. Throughout the 20th century it experienced different changes in its name and organisation, successively becoming División VII – Historia del Estado Mayor General del Ejército (1924); División Histórica y Geográfica del Ejército (1959); Dirección de Estudios Históricos (1961). At first it was under the administration of the war ministry (Secretaría de Guerra); and then the army commander-in-chief (Comando en Jefe del Ejército); and, finally, the army historical service (Servicio Histórico del Ejército) in 1983. In 2000, it became part of the recently created Directive for Army Historical Affairs (Dirección de Asuntos Históricos del Ejército).

Cultural and geographical context: the SHE is located in San Telmo quarter, Buenos Aires. The building belonged to the former Casa de Moneda (The National Mint) and was declared 'national patrimony'. It shares the building with the Archivo General del Ejército, the Comisión Evaluadora del Ejército, the Instituto de Estudios Históricos del Ejército and the Jardín de Infantes del Ministerio de Defensa.
Address: Defensa 628 / 630 PB. Ciudad CABA. Buenos Aires
Url: https://www.argentina.gob.ar/buscar/malvinas

Departamento de Estudios Históricos Navales y Archivo Histórico de la Armada Argentina: Departamento de Estudios Históricos Navales de la Armada Argentina (1 January 1961–today).

Since its origins as the División Historia Naval (1957) the archive has contributed to the cultural development of the country through continuous research into and revelation of Argentina's naval and maritime history and a specialised library on naval subjects. It keeps and preserves historical objects and documents. The Departamento de Estudios Navales rests in la Casa Amarilla (a replica of Admiral Guillermo Brown), built in the neighbourhood of de La Boca in the Autonomous City of Buenos Aires.

Ministerio de Defensa. Archivos Abiertos. Malvinas

'Through the decree 503/15, the President of the Nation de-classified all documentation linked to the Armed Conflict of the South Atlantic from the Archivos de las Fuerzas Armadas (the Armed Forces Archive) and instructed the Ministry of Defence to make all documents and registers publicly accessible within thirty days. The following link gives you access to the necessary information about the requirements of each branch of the Historical Archives for consultation of the de-classified documents, as well as downloading the full indexes of all available documents and other descriptive tools of the Archives. It is recommended to read carefully the Consultation Conditions for Documents of the Armed Conflict of the South Atlantic.'

https://www.argentina.gob.ar/malvinas-1

Archive Norms and Regulations:

http://www.mindef.gov.ar/archivosAbiertos/downloads/malvinas/ejercito/descripcion_institucional.pdf.

Ministerio de Relaciones Exteriores y Culto. Secretaría de Asuntos Relativos a las Islas Malvinas, Georgias del Sur, Sandwich del Sur y los Espacios Marítimos Circundantes

http://eespa.mrecic.gov.ar/es/content/la-cuesti%C3%B3n-de-las-islas-malvinas-0

La cuestión de las Islas Malvinas

www.mrecic.gov.ar/es/la-cuestion-de-las-islas-malvinas.

Comunicados de Prensa sobre La Cuestión de las Islas Malvinas www.mrecic.gov.ar/es/la-cuestion-de-las-islas-malvinas.

Documentos. Naciones Unidas y Foros internacionales

https://cancilleria.gob.ar/es/politica-exterior/cuestion-malvinas

Ministerio de Educación

https://www.educ.ar/sitios/educar/seccion/?ir=archivo_historico

INFORMATION RESOURCES 257

Designación de un comandante para las Malvinas en 1829
https://archive.org/details/
Caviglia2015MalvinasSMJVolIIBallenerosLoberosMisionerosSXVIIIXIX/
page/n2

Archivo General de la Nación de la República Argentina
Mission: 'To gather, preserve and keep for public consultation all the written, photographic, filmed, video and sound-recorded material of interest to the country as a testimonial for its past, present and identity, independently of the origins of the material, official records, donations or purchases. To track public documentation in general, its preservation and destiny in permanent collaboration with the Nation's Institutions' (author's translation).
It keeps historical documents such as:
- Decreto de creación de la Comandancia Civil y Militar, Buenos Aires, 10 de junio de 1829 (A.G.N. Fondo Luis Vernet, Sala VII 2-3-3t)
- Proclama de Luis Vernet en el momento de tomar posesión de su cargo, Puerto de la Soledad, 30 de agosto de 1829 (A.G.N. Fondo Luis Vernet Sala VII 2-4-6)

https://www.mininterior.gov.ar/agn/funciones.php.

1.2 United Kingdom

AIM25 Archives in London and the M25 Area
http://www.aim25.ac.uk/index.stm
Examples of repositories containing archival material on the Falklands–Malvinas included within AIM25.

King's College London Archives (King's College London Department of War Studies Records)
http://www.kcl.ac.uk/library/collections/archivespec/index.aspx.

Liddell Hart Centre for Military Archives, King's College London
http://www.kcl.ac.uk/library/collections/archivespec/collections/lhcma.aspx
Address: King's College London Archives, S3.02 Strand Building, Strand, London WC2R 2LS
Tel. +44 (0)20 7848 2015
Fax : +44 (0)20 7848 2760
Email: archives@kcl.ac.uk.

National Maritime Museum
http://www.rmg.co.uk
The National Maritime Museum's Archive catalogue:
http://collections.rmg.co.uk/archive.html#!asearch

Address: The Caird Library, National Maritime Museum, Greenwich, London SE10 9NF
Tel: +44 (0)20 8312 6516
Email: library@rmg.co.uk.

The **Institute of Commonwealth Studies**
Archives and Special Collections at Senate House Library include material relating to the Falklands Islands conflict in 1982, official statements, press releases, press cuttings, and printed books.

The **Institute of Latin American Studies**
Archives at Senate House Library include a donation of Falkland-Malvinas Islands press cuttings, consisting of newspaper cuttings and whole issues of newspapers relating to the Falkland-Malvinas Islands conflict. These are dated between 1978 and 1985 and include a set of cuttings relating to the impact on British libraries of the war.

Archon – The National Archives
www.nationalarchives.gov.uk/archon/
This is a portal to an electronic directory of repositories holding manuscript sources for British history and web-based information on archival resources. To find an archive in the UK and beyond:
http://discovery.nationalarchives.gov.uk/find-an-archive.

Chatham House: The Royal Institute of International Affairs
http://www.chathamhouse.org/about/library/archive-and-catalogue
Address: The Royal Institute of International Affairs, Chatham House 10 St James's Square, London SW1Y 4LE
Tel: +44 (0)20 7957 5700
Fax: +44 (0)20 7957 5710
Email: contact@chathamhouse.org.

Commonwealth Parliamentary Association
https://www.parliament.uk/cpauk

Commonwealth Secretariat
http://thecommonwealth.org/library-and-archives
Address: Commonwealth Secretariat, Marlborough House, Pall Mall, London SW1Y 5HX
All visits by the public must be arranged in advance by appointment.
Tel: +44 (0)20 7747 6164
Email: library@commonwealth.int.

Imperial War Museums
http://www.iwm.org.uk
http://www.iwm.org.uk/visits/iwm-london
Address: Imperial War Museum London, Lambeth Road, London SE1 6HZ
Tel: +44 (0)20 7416 5000
Email: contact@iwm.org.uk.

The National Archives (UK)
http://www.nationalarchives.gov.uk
'Discovery', the catalogue of The National Archives, holds (as of April 2015) more than 32,000,000 descriptions of records held by The National Archives and more than 2,500 archives across the country. Over nine million records are available for download.
To search Discovery: http://discovery.nationalarchives.gov.uk/
Results will include: material held within The National Archives, material within The National Archives that is available for download only and material held within other archives.

National Maritime Museum
http://www.rmg.co.uk
The Caird Library, National Maritime Museum, Romney Road, Greenwich, London SE10 9NF
Library / general enquiries: tel: +44 (0)20 8312 6516
Email: library@rmg.co.uk
Manuscripts, charts, atlases: email manuscripts@rmg.co.uk.

Royal Geographical Society (with the Institute of British Geographers (IBG)).
http://www.rgs.org
Address: 1 Kensington Gore, London, SW7 2AR
Tel: +44 (0)20 7591 3000
Fax: +44 (0)20 7591 3001
Email: enquiries@rgs.org.

UK Parliament website
http://www.parliament.uk
A range of reports, research publications, briefings, statements etc. are available to download.

2. Institutional repositories, libraries and museums with specialised collections on the subject

Oral sources, biographical sources, university collections, non-profit institutions and foundations, collections, etc.

2.1 Argentina

Biblioteca Nacional Mariano Moreno de la República Argentina
Address: (Calle) Agüero 2502. CP C1425EID Ciudad Autónoma de Buenos Aires consultas@bn.gov.ar
http://www.bn.gov.ar

Memoria abierta. Selección de revistas de la época
Address: Av. Libertador 8151, (C1429BNB) CABA
Email: memoria@memoriaabierta.org.ar
http://www.memoriaabierta.org.ar/materiales/serper_malvinas.php

Red de Archivos orales de la Argentina contemporánea
The Network of Oral Archives of Contemporary Argentina (Red de Archivos Orales, RAO) is an inter-university project aimed at the generation and publishing of the testimony of the protagonists in Argentina's recent history. The research groups that constitute the RAO constantly conduct interviews that become part of the diverse collections of the repository and give researchers, teachers and students access to such sources. Currently it contains over two hundred testimonies.
http://www.archivooral.org/busqueda_palabra.php

Museo Malvinas e Islas del Atlántico Sur
Created in June 2014 by the Argentine government in Buenos Aires. The museum depends on the Ministry of Education, Culture, Science and Technology. Through Decree 809/2014, published in the Official Gazette of the Argentine Republic on June 6, 2014, one of its principal objectives is to disseminate, communicate, exhibit and raise awareness among all the inhabitants of the nation about the Argentine sovereignty over the Malvinas Islands and the South Atlantic Islands, particularly the South Georgia and the South Sandwich Islands. The Museum opened in February 2015 under the Ministry of Culture of the Argentine government. The building is on three levels and has differently themed rooms, including audio-visual displays with support of technology and tactile LCD, historical objects, literary texts, images, paintings, letters and historical documents, ambient sound, photographs, maps and plans.
Address: Av. del Libertador 8151, Ciudad de Buenos Aires
Tel.: +54 (011) 5280-0750

Email: contacto@museomalvinas.gob.ar
Web: http://www.museomalvinas.gob.ar

Museo de la Memoria. Archivo Oral de veteranos de la Guerra de Malvinas del sur de Santa Fe
"The oral archive of the Malvinas War is a record of the testimonies of veterans about their experience of participating in the South Atlantic Conflict in 1982, which includes aspects of their own life before and after the event. This task is framed in general way in the presidential decree 1245/2015, of creation of the National Oral File of Malvinas and is a task proposed and organised by the Area of Veterans of War of the UGL IX of the Pami, the Center of ex-Soldiers Fighters in Malvinas de Rosario and the Rosario Memorial Museum". http://www.museodelamemoria.gob.ar/page/noticias/id/2146/title/Archivo-Oral-de-veteranos-de-la-Guerra-de-Malvinas-del-sur-de-Santa-Fe

Portal de datos del Sistema Nacional de Repositorios Digitales (SNRD)
Under the aegis of the Ministry of Science, Technology and Innovation (Ministerio de Ciencia, Tecnología e Innovación Productiva; Mincyt) its aim is to publish and divulge the nation's academic and scientific production. http://cosechador.siu.edu.ar/bdu3/Search/Results?lookfor=malvinas&type=AllFields

2.2 United Kingdom

Birmingham: Birmingham University Library
http://www.birmingham.ac.uk/libraries/search.aspx
Address: Main Library, University of Birmingham, Edgbaston, Birmingham B15 2TT
Tel: +44 (0)121 414 5828
Email: library@bham.ac.uk.

British Film Institute
http://www.bfi.org.uk

BFI National Archive Enquiries
http://www.bfi.org.uk/bfi-national-archive-enquiry

BFI Reuben Library
http://www.bfi.org.uk/education-research/bfi-reuben-library
Address: BFI Southbank, Belvedere Road, South Bank, London SE1 8XT
Enquiries: http://www.bfi.org.uk/form/contact-bfi-library.

The British Library
http://www.bl.uk

Address: 96 Euston Road, London NW1 2DB
Switchboard: +44 (0)330 333 1144   Customer Services: +44 (0)1937 546060
Email: Customer-Services@bl.uk
Falkland Islands Collections:
http://www.bl.uk/reshelp/findhelpregion/europe/uk/falklandislands/
The **British Library Sound Archive**
http://www.bl.uk/soundarchive
This has a number of recordings relating to the Falklands War of 1982, including Margaret Thatcher's speech to the House of Commons on the Argentine invasion: http://www.bl.uk/onlinegallery/onlineex/voiceshist/thatcher/.

Humanities Reference Service and Sound & Vision Reference Service
Tel: +44 (0)20 7412 7831
BL telephone and email contacts list: http://www.bl.uk/aboutus/contact/list-of-contacts/.

British Library of Political and Economic Science (LSE)
http://www.lse.ac.uk/library/home.aspx
BLPES Library, 10 Portugal Street, London WC2A 2HD
Tel: +44 (0)20 7955 7229
Email: library.enquiries@lse.ac.uk.

Consortium of Online Public Access Catalogues (COPAC)
COPAC is a free, online, merged library catalogue which enables researchers and information professionals to search the catalogues of approximately ninety libraries at once. These libraries include the UK national libraries, many university libraries and specialist libraries such as the Wellcome Trust and the National Art Library at the V&A. COPAC lists materials in all different formats: e.g. books, journals, conference proceedings, theses, electronic resources, music and multi-media materials such as DVDs. You can also find rare and unique materials such as early manuscripts and archive materials. You can use COPAC as a resource discovery tool to search for resources not available in your local public or institutional library. Librarians and researchers often use COPAC to check bibliographic information.
http://copac.ac.uk

The London Library
http://www.londonlibrary.co.uk
Address: The London Library, 14 St James's Square, London SW1Y 4LG
Main switchboard: +44 (0) 20 7930 7705
Email: reception@londonlibrary.co.uk
enquiries@londonlibrary.co.uk
Book enquiries: +44 (0)20 7766 4745/4747.

M25 Consortium
http://www.m25lib.ac.uk
Search25 helps you discover library resources across London and the South East; providing one-stop access to the library catalogues of nearly sixty world-renowned institutions and specialist collections within the M25 Consortium of Academic Libraries. You can also see where the libraries are and find out how to visit them:
http://www.search25.ac.uk

Senate House Library
http://senatehouselibrary.ac.uk
Senate House, Malet Street, London WC1E 7HU
Tel: +44 (0)20 7862 8500 (general enquiries) or
Tel: +44 (0)20 7862 8456 (subject librarian)
Email: senatehouselibrary@london.ac.uk.

Southampton: University of Southampton
https://www.southampton.ac.uk/library/
Address: University Library, University of Southampton, Highfield, Southampton SO17 1BJ
Tel.: +44 (0)23 8059 2180 (general enquiries)
Email: libenqs@soton.ac.uk (general enquiries)
Archives & Special Collections:
Tel: +44 (0)23 8059 2721
Email: archives@soton.ac.uk.

University College London
http://www.ucl.ac.uk/library/
Address: Main Library, Wilkins Building, Gower Street, London WC1E 6BT
Tel: +44 (0)20 7679 7792
Enquiries: library@ucl.ac.uk

3. *International Organisations Repositories*

Comité Internacional de la Cruz Roja. CICR. Conflicto de las islas Falkland-Malvinas: la acción del CICR en favor de los prisioneros de guerra = **International Committee of the Red Cross. ICRC.** Conflict of the Falkland Islands-Malvinas: the ICRC action in favour of the prisoners of war https://www.icrc.org/en/resource-centre/result?t=falkland+malvinas

Naciones Unidas. Sistema de Documentos Oficiales (ODS). United Nations. Official Document System (ODS). Searching=Búsqueda: Falkland–Malvinas: 11,135 Documents for Falkland-Malvinas search.
Resolución 502 del Consejo de Seguridad de las Naciones Unidas de 1982.

http://www.un.org/es/comun/docs/?symbol=S/RES/502%20(1982)
Resolución 505 del Consejo de Seguridad de las Naciones Unidas
http://www.un.org/es/comun/docs/?symbol=S/RES/505%20(1982).

Global Security Organisations
'The Argentine Seizure of The Malvinas [Falkland] Islands: History and Diplomacy'. American report from 1987 by Richard D. Chenette, Lieutenant Commander, United States Navy, laying out the history and background of the disputed claims. http://www.globalsecurity.org/military/library/report/1987/CRD.htm.

4. Media, 'raw resources', images and videos

RadioTapes.com. Coverage of the Falklands–Malvinas War (1982).
http://radiotapes.com/specialpostings.html#Falklands.

4.1 Argentina

Canal encuentro. Gobierno Argentino.
Programación especial a 33 años de la Guerra de Malvinas.
http://www.encuentro.gob.ar/sitios/encuentro/Noticias/getDetalle?rec_id=125767

La Nación. Search Engine: results 1–10 of 15,779 with the following keywords Malvinas + Between 17 February 1995 and 21 September 2016. The search engine does not go further back in time. Filter options include author, places, topics etc. (accessed September 2016).
http://buscar.lanacion.com.ar/malvinas/date-19950217,20160921/sort-old.

Clarín. Search Engine: approximately 132,000 results. Filter options include web page, images and dates (accessed September 2016).
http://www.clarin.com/buscador/?q=malvinas

4.2 United Kingdom

BBC. On this day. 1982: Argentina invades Falklands http://news.bbc.co.uk/onthisday/hi/dates/stories/april/2/newsid_2520000/2520879.stm.

The Guardian: **Falkland Islands**
https://www.theguardian.com/uk/falklands
About 533 results for Falkland Islands from today (19 August 2018) to 1982 with two news items from 1833: from *The Guardian* archive: 'Observer: Buenos Aires protests the British occupation of the Falklands. South American republics appeal against British "act of aggression"' (Sunday 8 December 1833, 15.07 GMT)

https://www.theguardian.com/theguardian/2012/dec/08/falkland-islands-british-occupation-1833.

Finally, we would like to point out that the preservation, accessibility and dissemination of the Falklands–Malvinas Conflict Documents is a task under construction.

The will for transparency of the governments that guard the documentary collections, expressed sometimes in a theoretical way in the national legislations, must be fulfilled and be effective, allowing this accessibility to the citizens. Efforts have been made by both parties, by the professionals responsible for the archives and official documents, for opening, preserving and making them accessible.

The Minister of Education of Argentina, Arberto Sileoni (2009–15), during his period in the ministry, was involved in the preservation and dissemination of historical sources in general and sources from Malvinas especially. He created the Museum Malvinas e Islas del Atlántico Sur, and inspired documentation of compiled sources for the History of Malvinas (Flachsland, C., Adamoli, M.C., Farias, M. 2014). The current government, through the different departments, perseveres, giving continuity to these projects which are being developed in the Malvinas Museum and other institutions.

In the United Kingdom we can mention the creation of the National Archives Repositories with the digitalisation and accessibility of the documents that are preserved there, 'We collect and secure the future of the government record, from Shakespeare's will to tweets from Downing Street, to preserve them for generations to come, making it as accessible and available as possible'. (The National Archives, 2018).

The creation of Heritage Repositories, (Osuna and Rodríguez, 2018) has proven to be the most effective tool to make this accessibility of documents possible. The digitisation programmes are a fine investment for the best preservation and accessibility of the official collections. The preservation and dissemination of the documentary collections should be protected, conserved and disseminated to all administrative levels seeking the digital integration of the collections, now possible thanks to the OAI-PMH protocols. The documentary collections are also protected by several international programs such as Unesco Memory of the World which is truly inspiring: "Building peace in the minds of men and women" (Unesco, 1992–present).

References

Argentina Ministerio de Defensa. Archivos Abiertos. Malvinas – Colección Temática, available at: https://www.argentina.gob.ar/defensa/archivos-abiertos/instituciones-de-archivo/direccion-de-estudios-historicos-de-la-fuerza-aerea/historia-institucional-dehfaa.

The Chicago Manual of Style: The Essential Guide for Writers, Editors, and Publishers (2010), 16th edn (Chicago: University of Chicago Press), available at http://www.mtroyal.ca/library/files/citation/historydocumentation.pdf (accessed 19 Aug. 2018).

The Falkland Islands Review Committee (1981–3) *The Franks Report Files*, The National Archives, Kew, reference: CAB 292, available at http://discovery.nationalarchives.gov.uk/details/record?catid=69947&catln=3.

Flachsland, C., Adamoli, M.C. and M. Farias (2014) *Pensar Malvinas: una selección de fuentes documentales, testimoniales, ficcionales y fotográficas para trabajar en el aula* (3rd edn., Buenos Aires: Ministerio de Educación de la Nación), available at http://educacionymemoria.educ.ar/secundaria/wp-content/uploads/2011/01/pensar_malvinas.pdf.

Informe Rattenbach (1982) *Resolución de la Junta Militar y acta de constitución de la Comisión de Análisis y Evaluación de las responsabilidades en el conflicto del Atlántico Sur* (Cescem Corrientes), available at http://www.cescem.org.ar/informe_rattenbach/parte1_01.html.

Informe Rattenbach Documental (2012) Canal Encuentro, available at https://www.youtube.com/watch?v=WnEHb4nauoA

Margaret Thatcher Foundation (2012) *Margaret Thatcher's files on the Falklands*, available at http://www.margaretthatcher.org/archive/falklands-PREM19.asp (accessed 19 Aug. 2018).

La Nación (2016) 'Malvinas: la cronología de la polémica tras el acuerdo del Gobierno con Gran Bretaña. Las idas y vueltas comenzaron hace once días, con la firma de una declaración que mencionaba el aumento de los vuelos desde el continente y acuerdos para la explotación de petróleo', *La Nación* (21 Sept.), available at http://www.lanacion.com.ar/1939919-malvinas-la-cronologia-de-polemica-tras-el-acuerdo-del-gobierno-con-gran-bretana (accessed 19 Aug. 2018).

The National Archives (1979) *The Cabinet Papers. Margaret Thatcher 1979*, available at http://www.nationalarchives.gov.uk/cabinetpapers/cabinet-gov/margaret-thatcher-1979.htm.

OAI-PMH, Open Archives Initiative Protocol for Metadata Harvesting, available at https://www.openarchives.org.

Osuna Alarcón, M.R. and M.P. Rodríguez Hernández (2018) 'Los Repositorios Patrimoniales, normas e interoperabilidad para definir un modelo', in E. Simeão, A. Cuevas-Cerveró, R. Botelho and J.A. Gómez-Hernández (eds.), *Competencias en Información y Políticas para Educación Superior. Universidad Complutense* (Madrid: Facultad de Ciencias de la Documentación), vol. 1, pp. 47–71, available at: https://eprints.ucm.es/59952/25/volumen1.pdf.

Unesco (1992–) *Memory of the World. Program*, available at: https://en.unesco.org/programme/mow.

Wintour, P. and U. Goñi (2016) 'Theresa May calls on Argentina to lift Falklands oil exploration restrictions. UK prime minister's letter to Argentina's president also calls for more flights to the disputed South Atlantic islands', *The Guardian* (10 Aug.), available at https://www.theguardian.com/uk-news/2016/aug/10/may-calls-on-argentina-to-lift-falklands-oil-exploration-restrictions (accessed Sept. 2016).

Index

Abba, 239
Abós, Álvaro, 69
Abuelas, 229
abuse, 16, 19, 35 fn.5, 37, 39, 46, 55, 87 fn.25, 120, 142, 150, 159, 162, 164, 253
accomplice, 141, 157
Ackermann, Juan, 189
Adams, Gerry, 228
Adellach, Alberto, 65, 72
Adorno, Theodor, 34, 50
Aerolíneas Argentinas, 8
Afghanistan, 76, 103, 130, 193, 224
Agamben, Giorgio, 32, 39, 50
Agretti, Dacio, 112, 119
Aguad, Oscar, 246
Alfonsín, Raúl, 9–11, 24
Alertondo, Eduardo, 20
Alonso, Luis, 57, 254
Altamirano, Carlos, 15
Amado, Ana 148, 159
Amati, Mirta, 163, 165, 169, 170
Anaya, Isaac, 53, 206
Andrés Pérez, Carlos, 87–8, 202
Animal Farm, 232
animots, 224–5, 231
archipelago, xiii, 13, 17, 57 fn.8, 58, 60, 63, 64, 177
archive, x, 32, 75 fn.1, 141, 147, 152, 252–66
Arendt, Hannah, 31, 32, 34, 50
Argentine Navy, 75 108
argentinidad, 27, 53
Argentinity, 2–4, 6, 14, 20, 23

Arias, Lola, 21
army, 3, 5, 15, 26, 68, 100, 105, 167, 193, 201, 221, 255
Astiz, Alfredo, 63, 70
Austin, 227
Avellano, Suzanne, 98, 110

Baran, Stanley, 219–20
Barcelona, 56–8, 59, 60, 62, 63, 66, 68, 70
Bases para la reconstrucción nacional, 156
Baudrillard, Jean, 42
Bauer, Tristan, 43, 143, 212, 218
Beagle Channel, 8, 9 fn.6, 10, 28, 29
Beck, Ulrich, 16
Belaunde Terry, Fernando, 76
Belgrano, 30, 65, 67, 115, 117, 147, 149, 165–7, 241
Bell, Steve, 221–4, 228, 229, 232, 234, 237–8, 244–6, 247
Benjamin, Jon, 229
Benjamin, Walter, 32, 33, 50
Benjamín Menéndez, Luciano ('la Hiena'), 218
Billig, Michael, 166, 167, 170, 180, 183, 241, 249
Binaghi, Javier, 212
bio-power, 31–49
Black Label, 206
Blair, Tony, 188, 226
Blaustein, David, 67, 102, 107
Blejmar, Jordana, 148, 159
blooper, 239, 244, 246

Bolaño, Roberto, 35–6 fn. 4, 5, 39 fn.10
Bolivia, 15, 103, 104
Borges, Jorge Luis, 15, 22, 133, 232
Borrat, Héctor, 62–3
Boym, Svetlana, 122
Boyson, Rhodes, 222
Brandt, Willy, 86–90, 93, 94
Brexit, 192, 199, 244–5, 248
British, xiv, xvii, 6–7, 8, 10, 16, 17, 20, 22, 25, 37, 56, 57, 60, 62 fn.17, 63, 65–6, 71, 75–6, 79, 81–93, 97, 104, 115–16, 130, 134, 136, 137, 142, 155, 175, 178, 179, 180, 181, 185–99, 203–6, 211, 212, 213, 214, 215, 219, 223, 226–7, 228, 229, 232, 234, 236, 237, 238, 239, 244, 246, 247, 248, 253, 258, 262, 264
Brown, David 'Charlie', 214
Bruschtein, Luis, 54 fn.2
Buenos Aires Herald, 8, 242, 249
Bullrich, Patricia, 246
Burrell, Paul, 237
Bush, George W., 127

Callaghan, James, 79, 80
Calveiro, Pilar, 33–5, 37, 40, 41, 42, 44, 49, 153, 159
Cambiemos, 193, 194, 210
Cameron, David, 185, 190, 203, 204, 235, 237, 243, 244, 247
Canning House, 220
Cardoso, Julio, xvii, 20 fn.21, 141, 144, 146, 147–50, 151–2, 154–6, 158–9
Cardozo, José, 84
Carlsson, Bernt, 79 fn.3, 80 fn.5–7, 82–4, 90–1 fn. 33–9, 93 fn. 45–8
Carri, Albertina, 144–9, 153–4
Carroll, Lewis, 242

Carter, Jimmy, 76, 88, 94, 96, 101, 103
cartography, 219, 220
Casa Rosada, xvii, 161, 173, 224, 225, 255
Casabé, Daniel, vii, 21, 111, 115, 120, 128, 132
Caso-Rosendi, Carlos, 41, 42, 43 fn.14, 45, 48 fn.20, 49 fn.21
Castañeda, Carlos, 48
Castiglioni, Franco, 212
Castro, Alicia, 196, 209, 211, 213, 240
Castro, Fidel, 86, 191
Cataluña, 53, 60, 61
catharsis, 39
Catholics, 5, 6, 158
Cavandoli, Carlos, 186
Centro de Salud 'Veteranos de Malvinas', 217
Céspedes, Marcelo, 144
Chile, viii, x, 8–10, 28, 33–4, 35 fn.4, 38, 39 fn.10, 79, 91 fn.38, 100, 101, 103, 104, 106, 129, 130, 135, 176, 181, 192, 203, 211, 217, 229, 248
China, 70, 190
Chumbita, Hugo, 55, 60 fn.12, 66, 69
Churchill, Winston, 7, 244
Ciencias morales, xvii, 161, 165–6, 167, 169–70
cinema, 20, 113, 128–30, 141–59, 215
Cisneros, Andrés, 187
citizenship, 2, 17 fn.14, 34, 151–2, 169, 210
civil society, 1–3, 9, 21, 34, 39, 53–4, 63, 141–59, 162–5, 169–70, 194, 224
civilians, 3, 16, 98, 101, 105, 141, 142, 153, 177, 181, 215, 232
Clarín, 215, 264

Clarkson, Jeremy, 216–17
Cold War, 28, 76–7, 80, 87, 101, 103, 104
combat stress, 217
commemoration, ix, 11, 17, 38, 97, 113, 144, 164, 166, 168, 170, 190, 191, 223
communism, 5, 6, 8, 58, 77, 84, 85, 94, 100, 101, 103, 104
compensation, 92–3, 142, 218
concentration camp, 32–5, 37, 38, 40, 41–2, 44, 46, 49, 116
Cóndor II programme, 10
Conte, Augusto, 67
Conversación con Antonio, 148
Córdoba, 131, 211, 218
Cortázar, Julio, 205
Costa Méndez, Nicanor, 86
coup, 5–7, 9, 23, 35 fn.4, 55, 64, 80, 100, 103, 162
crown dependencies, 220
cruise ships, 203
Cuba, 8, 66, 70, 80, 84

Daily Mail, 217, 237
Daily Mirror, 217, 233
Daily Telegraph, viii, 204, 235
Darwin, 119, 120, 135, 136, 143, 156, 199
Darwin, Charles, 115, 122, 123, 136
Daversa, Fabiana, 19
De eso no se habla, 218, 246
defeat, xvi, 3, 9–10, 22–4, 37, 45, 63, 69, 76, 93, 97, 102, 104–7, 116, 142–4, 152, 154, 159, 162, 164, 187, 201, 206, 226, 229, 232
de Man, Paul, 33
De la Rúa, Fernando, 11
Deleuze, Gilles, 32, 124
Delors, Jacques, 238
demalvinisation, 10

demilitarisation, 10, 220
democracy, xvi, 5, 6, 20, 24, 26, 34, 37, 45, 55, 57, 60 fn.13, 62, 69, 71, 77–9, 84, 86, 92, 94, 97–110, 115, 141, 142, 144, 150–1, 157, 162, 163–5
Denti, Jorge, 20
Department of Mineral Resources, 132
Derrida, Jacques, 33, 224, 231–2, 241
desert, 4, 124, 127
desmalvinización, 142, 151
Diamond Jubilee, 235
dictatorship, viii, xv Di Tella xvi, xvii, 9, 11, 12, 21, 22, 24, 25, 26, 31–50, 54–9, 61–6, 68, 70–2, 77–9, 83, 85, 88–9, 97, 100–2, 104–7, 115, 127, 141–6, 151–4, 157, 159, 161, 163–4, 165, 169, 173, 178, 186, 205, 210, 222, 253
différance, 217, 231
diplomacy, xviii, 13, 190, 201, 204, 207, 211, 212, 264
Di Tella, Guido, 203
disappearance, 1, 35, 37–9, 41, 64, 66, 70, 153, 224, 229
disappeared, 14, 51, 54, 58, 64 fn.21, 67, 70 fn.27, 115–16, 141, 144–6, 148, 150, 153, 158, 229
disillusionment, 141, 154
documentary, xi, xvi, xvii, 20, 105 fn.7, 111, 112–59, 254, 265
Dominican Republic, 76, 94, 103
Donghi, Halperín, 4, 6
Dorrego, Manuel, 22
Drake, Paul, 100–2
Duhalde, Eduardo, 11
Duncan, Alan, 193
Dunwoody, Gwyneth, 83

Eckhardt, Marcelo, 19
Economist, 247–8
education, xvii, 3–4, 11, 24, 158, 161–2, 165–70, 173–83, 190, 221, 265
El país de la guerra, 164, 167, 170, 171
El Salvador, 80, 87, 103
Empire, 181, 192, 220, 237–8
Enriori, Carlos, 112, 119
entente cordiale, xviii
Erlich, Uriel, 185, 187
Escudé, Carlos, 173–5, 182, 232, 235
Estaqueamiento, 46, 150
Esteban, Edgardo, 38 fn.9, 41–9, 143, 212, 214, 218
ethics, 32–7, 39, 42–3, 68
Evita, 70
ex-combatants, xi, 24, 39, 41, 46, 112–14, 117–20, 129–31, 143, 145, 151, 180, 181, 211, 214, 217, 221
Ex-Services Mental Welfare Society, 217
exile, viii, xv, 8, 14–15, 22, 53–72, 86
external debt, 37, 98, 104

Falkland Islanders, xvii, 15, 17–18, 21, 25, 26, 88, 93, 136, 183, 186–9, 191–3, 200–6, 213–16, 234, 244, 253
Falklander, 188
Falklands–Malvinas: An Unfinished Business, xviii, 109, 209, 211, 215, 248
Fanjul, Ángel, 57
Faurie, Jorge, 246
Fernández, Alberto, 248
Fernández Engler, Rodrigo, 21

film, vii, xvi–xvii, 20–1, 24, 43, 111–25, 127–39, 141–59, 212, 254, 257
Filmus, Daniel, 212, 214, 220, 234, 248
fisheries, 202, 232
flâneur, 112
flights, 8, 129, 131, 187, 194, 202–4, 207, 251
Flores, Rafael, 55, 58, 63–4, 73, 88
Fogwill, Rodolfo, 19, 35 fn.3, 44
Foix, Lluís, 56
football, 4, 86, 216, 229
Foreign Office, 63, 186, 206, 229, 236, 254
Foucault, Michel, 32, 222
Fraga, Rosendo, 206
Freedman, Lawrence, 102 fn.4, 108, 186, 222
Fresán, Rodrigo, 19, 45, 116
Frondizi, Arturo, 7, 23
fundamentalism, 5–6, 81, 151

Galtieri, Leopoldo Fortunato, viii, xvi–xvii, 21, 53, 59, 63, 65–6, 69, 71, 83, 89, 92, 152, 161, 185, 191, 201, 206, 224
Gamerro, Carlos, 19, 28, 44, 115, 116
García, Charly, 43
García Costa, Víctor, 79–80, 89 fn.30
García del Solar, Lucio, 202
García Fanlo, 2–5, 27
García Lorca, Federico, 49
García Quiroga, Diego, 45, 51, 211
Garzón, Baltasar, 212, 229
gaucho, 4, 130, 136
Georgias del Sur, 62 fn.19, 64, 187, 212, 256
Geraghty, Niall, 215
Gerding, Eduardo, 217

Germany, 6, 91 fn.38, 102, 104
Gibraltar, 85
Gieco, León, 143
Godoy, Carlos, 19
Goligorsky, Eduardo, 55, 59, 65–7, 68, 70–2, 73
Gondwana, xiii, 132
González, Felipe, 80, 94
González, Horacio, 63
Gove, Michael, 245
Greece, 77, 102, 104
Grenada, 76
Grimson, Alejandro, 163, 165, 169
Guber, Rosana, 2, 3, 13, 15–16, 27, 53, 142, 162–3, 182
Guebel, Daniel, 19
Guardian, viii, 108, 109, 189 fn.3, 195, 196, 221, 223–4, 227, 228, 229, 232, 236, 238, 239, 245, 246, 251, 264, 267
Guarini, Carmen, 144
Guerra, Lalo, 128
guilt, 48, 141, 157
Gurkha, 45, 215
Guyana, 76

Habegger, Andrés, 144, 146–7
Habermas, Jürgen, 32
Hague, William, 229, 234, 235, 238
Haig, Alexander, 68 fn.26, 76
Hammond, Philip, 220, 234
Hayward, Ron, 83–4
Hegel, Georg Wilhelm Friedrich, 230
Held, David, 16
Hermo, Leonardo, 128
Hernández, José, 155–6
heroic deed, 12, 20, 24–5, 37, 116, 152
HIJOS, el alma en dos, 144, 145
Historias cotidianas, 144, 146–7
historiography, viii, xiv, 5, 12
Hochbaum, Nora, 218

homeland, 2, 7, 23, 26, 65, 66, 67, 70, 118, 121–2, 150, 179, 180
Hong Kong, 195
Hors de Combat: The Falklands– Malvinas Conflict, 108, 211, 215, 249
House of Lords, 212
human rights, 9, 11, 14, 16, 19, 21, 26, 37, 39, 53–72, 78–9, 83, 101, 103, 141–2, 146, 150, 159, 161, 162, 173, 178, 210, 212, 213, 253
Humanitarian Project Plan, 199
humiliation, 23, 46, 253
Humor, 162 fn.3, 223, 224
humour, 15, 40–5, 48, 49, 119, 215

iconoclasm, xviii
identity, xvii, 1–26, 37, 39, 44, 45, 48, 54, 56, 58, 121, 129, 147, 149, 161–70, 174, 189, 190, 191, 230, 231, 257
ideology, 4, 101, 141, 154
Iglesias, Fernando, 2, 3, 16, 28, 174, 175
Illia, Arturo, 7, 202
Iluminados por el fuego, 20, 38 fn.9, 40, 43, 45–6, 48, 50, 120, 143, 154, 218
immigrants, 3–4
imperial, 8, 12, 13, 14, 38, 56, 57, 58, 60–3, 65, 70, 85 fn.20–1, 89, 101, 137, 141, 155, 156–7, 158, 181, 189, 192, 206, 220, 253
independence, 3–4, 62 fn.17, 163–4, 165, 168, 188–9
Iran, 76, 103, 184
Iraq, 25, 33, 130, 193, 224, 226
Irazusta, Julio, 6
Irazusta, Rodolfo, 6
irridentists, 71
ISEN, 211–12

Islas imaginadas, xi, 29, 46 fn.17, 111, 115
Isle of Wight, 247
Israel, Alejandro, 128, 134

Jamaica, 76, 82 fn.11
Jaramillo, Ana, 155–5
John Paul II, Pope, 9, 77, 103
Johnson, Boris, 194, 244
Johnston, Claire, 225
Jospin, Lionel, 88
journalism, viii, 12, 66, 71, 116, 135, 168, 200, 205, 218
junta, 9, 53, 54, 57, 59, 60–3, 67, 68–9, 71, 83–4, 92 fn.45, 93, 105–6, 161, 162, 163 fn.4, 168–9, 185, 186, 191, 266
just cause, 18, 23, 38, 60, 61, 62, 65, 68, 87 fn.25, 116, 120, 142, 157, 173, 205
Justicialist Party, 106–7

Kamín, Bebe, 20, 142
Kant, Immanuel, 34, 51
Kelper, 17, 19, 25, 45, 81, 114, 138–9, 185, 205
Kipling, 224
Kirchner, Cristina Fernández, 12, 17, 141, 157, 173, 174, 182, 185, 188, 190, 200, 204, 210, 218, 226, 254
Kirchner, Néstor, 11, 18, 25, 141, 157, 173, 174, 187, 188, 204
Kitson, Alex, 88
Knight, Alan, 100, 101 fn.3
Kodama, Kaori, 163, 165, 169
Kohan, Martín, xvii, 19, 116, 145, 161, 163–70
Kovadloff, Santiago, 17 fn.13, 200
Kusch, Rodolfo, 156

La historia oficial, 28, 153
La Opinión Austral, 176

La Nación, 200, 210, 251, 264
Labour Party, 79–83, 84, 85, 89–93
Lami Dozo, Basilio, 53
Landsberg, Alison, 231
Latin America, xvi, 8, 13, 38, 58, 68–71, 75–96, 97–110, 143, 156, 192, 209, 218, 258
laughter, xv, 31–49
La Vanguardia, 56, 70
Lawler, Diego, 212
legitimacy, xv, 1, 11, 19, 33, 38, 45, 59–60, 62, 64, 68, 72, 178, 187, 189, 193, 230
Le Monde Diplomatique, 205
Le Monde, 56, 57
Lennon, John, 240
Levi, Primo, 31, 33, 36, 41, 51
Lévinas, Emmanuel, 31
liberalism, 5–6, 100–1, 104
Locke, John, 1
Locos de la bandera, 141, 144–51
London Victory Parade, 221–2
Lorenz, Federico, 13–14, 19, 24, 44, 67, 97 fn.1, 102 fn.4, 106, 109, 146, 150, 153, 157, 162–4
Lorton, Roger, 213–14, 248
Los chicos de la guerra, 20, 39, 142–3, 154
Los rubios, 144–54
Luna, Oscar, 152–3

Macri, Mauricio, 193–4, 210, 243–4, 246, 251
Madres de Plaza de Mayo, 64, 66, 70, 146, 225
Madrid, 55, 58, 60–2, 64, 65 fn.23, 68, 72, 79, 211
Maison de l'Amérique Latine, 212, 218,
Malcorra, Susana, 193–4
Malvinas, una visión alternativa [an alternative vision], 17, 154

Malvinas: Viajes del bicentenário, 141, 152, 155–9
Manichean, 34, 71, 151
manifesto, 17, 145, 200
Maniglia, Eduardo Aníbal Rómulo, 168
Martella, Luis Carlos, 120
Martín Fierro, 4, 155
Márquez, José Luis, 21
Marxism, 57–8, 79, 100, 103
May Revolution 1810, 168–9
May, Theresa, 194, 199, 251, 267
McGuinness, Martin, 228
McTeague, Jeremy, 215
memory, vii, viii, ix, x, xvi, 9, 12, 14, 33–4, 39, 46, 49, 55, 78, 97–8, 113–21, 123, 128–9, 139, 142–5, 147–51, 153, 155, 159–60, 161, 166, 173, 175, 177–8, 181, 186, 191–2, 195, 217–18, 228–9, 231, 255, 260–1, 265, 267
Menem, Carlos, 10–11, 25, 97 fn.1, 107, 109, 186, 187, 202 fn.2, 205
Mercosur, 192, 203
Messi, Lionel, 229
Messianic, 6
Mexico, 54, 55, 56 fn.6, 57, 61, 234
middle classes, 5–6, 210
Mikardo, Ian, 79–80
militarism, 2, 5
military dictatorship, xv, xvi, 2, 5, 6, 8–15, 22–4, 33–4, 37–9, 40–1, 49, 53, 57–63, 64–5, 68, 70, 77, 81 fn.8, 83–4, 86, 89, 92 fn.42, 97, 98, 104–7, 122, 130, 141, 144, 151, 157, 159, 161–7, 169–70, 173, 178, 205, 210, 222, 252–3
military service, 3–4, 67, 167
Mirré, Federico, 206
Mitre, Bartolomé, 165

Molina, María Elena, 13, 18
Montag, 223, 224–5
Montoneros, 8, 44–5
Morrison, Tessa, 215
Mount Pleasant, 130
Museo de la Memoria, Córdoba, 218
myth, xiv, 23, 59, 122

Naifleish, Jaime, 55, 71 fn.71
Narrar a San Martín, 164, 171
narrative, xvi, 1, 3, 11–12, 13, 14, 16–17, 19–24, 26, 33, 40, 42, 43, 45, 49, 101, 111–13, 114, 115–17, 118, 120, 122, 154, 161–2, 164, 165, 175, 182, 215
national security doctrine, 8
nationalism, xvii, 2, 6–8, 10, 16, 24, 38, 39, 84, 94, 116, 122, 123, 131, 134–5, 137, 142, 144, 152, 154, 156–9, 166, 169, 170–1, 173–83, 241
Nazi, 34, 44, 70, 89
negotiation, 7, 17, 60, 76, 83, 85 fn.19, 91, 93, 105–6, 190, 192, 193, 195, 199–207, 211, 216, 241, 247, 251
Negrete, Claudio, 200
Nicaragua, 76, 80, 85, 87, 94, 103
Niebieskikwiat, Natasha, 10, 16–17, 29
Niedergang, Marcel, 56, 73
Nott, John, 221
Nuclear Non-Proliferation Treaty, 10,
Nüremberg, 68, 70
objectivity, xiv, 111, 216

O'Donnell, Guillermo Philippe, 99
O'Donnell, Pacho, 155
Official History of the Falklands Campaign, 186, 222
Olivera, Javier, 20

omertà, 218
Onganía, Juan Carlos, 186
Operativo Cóndor, 8, 10, 23
Oppenheimer, Joshua, 129
Ormond, Krysteen, 216
Ortiz de Rozas, Carlos, 206

Pacheco Quiroga, Elena, 218
package tours, 207
Padgett, Keith, 213
Páez, Roberto, 61
Paisley, Ian, 228
Palacios, Alfredo, 6
Palavecino, Ramón Orlando, 120
Palermo, Vicente, 15, 17 fn.13, 24, 97 fn.1, 102 fn.4, 142, 144, 152–3, 156, 162, 173–4, 175
Panagea, xiii
Panama, 76, 176
panopticon, 222
Papá Iván, 144, 146–7
Paraguay, 3, 103
Parque de la Memoria, 218, 228
Parra, Carlos, 79
Patagonia, xiii, xvii, 175–6, 216
patriotism, xvii, 4, 18, 21, 24, 53, 58, 87 fn.25, 116–17, 143, 144, 146, 150–1, 157–8, 161–70, 205–6
Peña Gómez, José F., 79, 82
penguins, 49, 114, 122, 131, 201, 223–5, 232, 238
Pereira, Miguel, 20, 154
Pérez, Carlos Andrés, 82 fn.11, 87–8
Pérez, Miguel, 20
Pérez de Cuéllar, Javier, 76

Perfil, 205–6
Peris Blanes, Jaume, 32–4
Perlonger, Néstor, 14

Perón, Juan Domingo, 6–7

Peronism, 2, 6, 7–11, 22, 25, 58, 59–60, 62 fn.20, 64, 66, 68, 70, 194–5, 200
Peru, 76, 86 fn.24, 103, 129
Pestanha, Francisco, 155–6
Pingu, 203
Pinochet, Augusto, 33, 38, 39 fn.10, 228–9
Plaza de Mayo, xvi, 57 fn.8, 64, 66, 69, 70 fn.27, 146, 152, 154, 224, 225, 229, 253
plebiscite, 6
populism, 1, 100, 141–59, 199, 216–17, 218, 229
Portugal, 77, 90, 102, 104, 211
positivism, 4, 5
Posse, Abel, 55, 70–1
post-conflict, xviii, 9–19, 24, 33, 105, 209, 211, 212, 214, 215, 218, 223–4, 230–1, 241
post-dictatorship, 141–2, 143, 146, 151, 152, 153–4, 159, 161–2, 164–5
press, 176, 209–10, 212–13, 237, 243, 244, 246, 251, 253, 258
Princess Diana, 237
Prividera, Nicolás, 144, 146, 153, 154
Pron, Patricio, 19, 29
Propaganda, 63
PSOE (Spanish Socialist Workers' Party), 80, 85, 88–9
PTSD (post-traumatic stress disorder); TEPT in Spanish (trastorno por estrés postraumático), 211, 215, 217, 218
Puenzo, Luis, 153

Queen Elizabeth II, 7, 235, 236–7, 247
Quesada, Ernesto, 5
Quieto, Lucila, 148, 160

Quiroga, Facundo, 22

Radical Civic Union, 9
Radical party, 24, 79, 106, 201
Raleigh, Juan Valle, 211
Rattenbach Report, 106, 204, 254, 255, 266
Ratto, Patricia, 19
Reagan, Ronald, 68, 76–7, 90 fn.36, 94, 103, 104, 107, 206
Reale, Victoria, 20
realpolitik, 216
referendum, xvii, 10, 185–95, 213, 233, 244
regime, viii, xvii, 7, 8, 9, 10–11, 37, 57, 63, 68–9, 70, 72, 78, 97–9, 101, 104–5, 107, 115, 122, 130, 141–2, 144, 146, 151, 152–3, 154, 157, 159, 161–3, 165, 168–9, 186, 202, 204, 205, 212, 218, 243
repression, viii, 8, 9, 12, 14, 21, 24, 34, 37–8, 54, 57 fn.8, 60, 70 fn.27, 78, 85 fn.22, 104, 106, 157, 225
republicanism, 24, 163, 228
Resolution 502, 75–6, 81
Resolution 2065, 7, 80, 188, 202
resources, 2, 11–12, 16, 25, 122, 132, 173–5, 177–83, 232, 234–5, 241, 251–67
Return to Tumbledown, 215
revisionism, 1, 5–6, 14, 17, 20, 141, 155–6, 157
Reyes Mate, Manuel, 34, 36, 51
Ridley, Nicholas, 186
Río Gallegos, xvii, 129, 145, 173–84
River Plate, 228
Roca-Runciman Agreement, 22–3
Rock, David, 98
Rodríguez, Luis, 59,

Romero, Luis Alberto, 3–7, 9–11, 17 fn.13, 21, 81, 97 fn.1, 151, 162, 163–4, 200
Roqué, María Inés, 144, 146–7
Rosas, Juan Manuel de, 5, 22, 207
Rouquié, Alain, 162, 164, 168 fn.5
Royal Navy, 59, 115, 193
Rozitchner, León, 15, 55, 62, 67 fn.25, 68, 102 fn.4

Saint Helena, 136
Saldías, Adolfo, 5
Sandwich del Sur, 62 fn.19, 184, 212, 248, 256, 260
Santa Cruz, xvii, 129, 173–84, 203
Sarlo, Beatriz, 15, 17 fn.13, 33–4, 78, 145, 200
Sarmiento, Domingo F., 3, 127–8, 132, 200
SAS (Special Air Service), 221, 222
Savater, Fernando, 56
Scalabrini Ortiz, Raúl, 156
Schama, Simon, 129
Schmidt, Carl, 1
Schmidt, Helmut, 86
Schmitter, Phillipe C., 77–8, 99, 100
Schmucler, Héctor, 54 fn.2
Sebreli, Juan José, 15, 17 fn.13
Second World War, 6, 104, 137
Seear, Mike, 211, 215, 249
Semprún, Jorge, 33, 36, 41–2, 43, 49
Sileoni, Alberto, 175, 177–8, 265
Sloterdijk, Peter, 32, 34, 36 fn.6, 51
social democrats, xv, 75, 78, 79, 81, 82, 84, 86–7, 91–3, 103
Socialist International (SI), xv, 75, 79–82, 83–4, 88, 90–2 fn.36–8; 42–4, 102
Soldier magazine, 218

solidarity, 20, 36–7, 40, 42, 46, 48, 55, 82–4, 87 fn.25, 150, 153, 202, 220
Soriano, Osvaldo, 205
Sources for History, xviii, 251
South Atlantic Medal Association, 214, 217, 227
South Georgia, 53, 62 fn.19, 63–4, 83, 248, 260
Southern Cone, 33–4, 105, 232
sovereignty, 7–8, 10, 12, 13–14, 17–18, 22, 33, 38 fn.8, 45, 53, 59–69, 71, 80–1, 84, 85 fn.19, 87 fn. 25–6, 89, 91–2, 97, 102, 115, 127, 132, 139, 142, 143, 146, 149, 158, 175–6, 178–80, 182–3, 186–94, 215, 220, 230, 248, 260
Spain, 6, 54, 55, 56 fn.6, 57, 77, 85, 168, 211
Spinoza, Baruch, 230–1
Stagnaro, Bruno, 20
Stamadianos, Jorge, 19
Stanley, 112, 119, 123–4, 130–4, 136–8, 200, 215,
Stewart, Celia, 131, 138
Stockey, Gareth, 212
Stoltenberg, Thorvald, 89–90
Squeff, Darío ('el Turco'), 218
Squeff, María del Carmen, 218
subalternity, 38–9, 46
subversive, 8, 34, 63
suicide, 40–1, 217–18, 227, 253
surrender, 8, 10, 24, 44, 45, 91, 120, 253
survivors, 38–9, 41–2, 115
Sweden, 54, 57, 60
Syria, 33

Taylor, Diana, 163, 168
Tebbit, Norman, 221
TEPT (see PTSD)
Terragno, Rodolfo, 201

terrorism, 14, 16, 25, 34, 54, 60, 65, 72, 78, 130
Tesaire, Alberto, 7
testimony, xv, 33, 35, 43, 44 fn.15, 57 fn.8, 135, 145
Thatcher, Denis, 221–2
Thatcher, Margaret, xvi, 27, 81, 85 fn.18 & 22, 103, 104, 115, 185, 191, 192, 206, 221, 224, 226, 228–9, 253, 262, 266
The Exact Shape of the Islands, xvi, 21, 111, 112, 114–21, 128
The Franks Report, 253–4, 266
Tierra del Fuego, 176, 181, 203
Timerman, Héctor, 216, 238–9, 246
Tlatelolco Treaty, 10
Todorov, Tzvetan, xv, 32–4, 37, 40, 41, 42–3, 48–9
Top Gear, 216
Torrijos, Omar, 76
torture, 35, 38–9, 41, 44, 46, 64, 70, 142–3, 150, 218, 229, 253
tourism, 131, 132, 232
trade unions, 2, 78, 85, 211
transition, xvi, xvii, 10, 13, 20, 24, 77, 97–110, 135, 202, 210
trauma, 33, 41, 48, 78, 92 fn.45, 112, 123, 131, 175, 182, 211, 217–18, 227, 230–1

United Kingdom, xiii, xv–xviii, 5 fn.4, 7, 9–10, 17 fn.14, 103, 187–8, 191, 201, 205, 210–12, 216, 219–20, 224, 226–9, 236, 241–2, 244, 246, 252, 257, 258–9, 261, 262,264, 265
United Nations, 7, 23, 62 fn.17, 75, 188, 202, 207, 263
United States, 6, 8, 10, 23, 25, 100–2, 103, 127, 192, 232, 264
Urban, Stuart, 215
Uriburu, José, 5
Urioste, Federico , 20

Uruguay, 75, 84, 103, 104, 189, 211
Ushuaia, 203
USSR, 70, 94, 101
usurpation, xv, 7, 23, 61, 89

Valdés, Hernán, 33, 52
Verbitsky, Horacio, 38, 102 fn.4
veterans, xv, xvi, 11, 13, 45, 157, 202, 206, 207, 211–15, 217–18, 221, 226–7, 254, 255, 261
Vezzetti, Hugo, 17 fn.13, 159
victim, xvi, 12–15, 21, 33, 35, 38, 39, 41, 47, 54, 57, 58, 60, 66, 70, 78, 83, 115, 141, 142, 146, 150, 153, 156, 215, 218, 223, 224, 226, 230
victimiser, 35, 42
Vietnam War, 8
Vieytes, Raúl, 19
Vilgré La Madrid, Esteban, 217
Villegas, Alfredo, 189
violence, 7–9, 19 fn.17, 31, 32–7, 38, 39, 40, 41, 42, 44, 48, 49, 50, 53, 55, 62 fn.17, 64–5, 67, 71, 78, 92 fn.45, 141, 142, 143, 145, 151, 157, 159, 229
Voyage of the Beagle, 123, 125
Vuelta de Obligado, 22, 157

Wallis, Roger, 219, 220
War of the Triple Alliance, 167
warrah wolf, 123, 136
Weisaeth, Lars, 218
With the Gurkhas in the Falklands, 215
Whitehead, Laurence, 78, 99
Wonderland, 239
World Cup, 24, 86

Yrigoyen, Hipólito, 5–6
Yssel, Rob, 133

Zimmer frame, 238
Zylberberg, Fernando, 217

Recent and forthcoming titles from the Institute of Latin American Studies:

Rethinking Past and Present: Essays in memory of Alistair Hennessy (2018)
edited by Antoni Kapcia

Shaping Migration between Europe and Latin America: New Approaches and Challenges (2018)
edited by Ana Margheritis

Brazil: Essays on History and Politics (2018)
Leslie Bethell

Creative Spaces: Urban Culture and Marginality in Latin America (2019)
edited by Niall H.D. Geraghty and Adriana Laura Massidda

Cultures of Anti-Racism in Latin America and the Caribbean (2019)
edited by Peter Wade, James Scorer and Ignacio Aguiló

A Nicaraguan Exceptionalism? Debating the Legacy of the Sandinista Revolution (2020)
edited by Hilary Francis

Memory, Migration and (De)Colonisation in the Caribbean and Beyond (2020)
edited by Jack Webb, Roderick Westmaas, Maria del Pilar Kaladeen and Robert Tantam

Cultural Worlds of the Jesuits in Colonial Latin America (2020)
edited by Linda A. Newson

Supervivencia indígena en la Nicaragua colonial (2021)
by Linda A. Newson

New World Objects of Knowledge: A Cabinet of Curiosities (2021)
edited by Mark Thurner and Juan Pimentel

www.ingramcontent.com/pod-product-compliance
Ingram Content Group UK Ltd.
Pitfield, Milton Keynes, MK11 3LW, UK
UKHW061834210426
5322IPUK00026B/670